1. This
2. A

Jilly Cooper comes from Yorkshire although she was born in Essex and educated at Godolphin School in Salisbury. She originally worked as a journalist on provincial newspapers before lapsing and going into publishing. She graduated back to journalism through the pages of the *Sunday Times* and for thirteen and a half years her column was one of the most widely read features in the paper. During 1982 she moved to Gloucestershire and began writing a column for the *Mail on Sunday*. Recently she has devoted her time to writing books.

Jilly Cooper is the author of many non-fiction books, including *Class* and *The Common Years*; the best selling novels, *Riders* and *Rivals*, a book of short stories and two anthologies. She has published, in addition, several children's books. She makes frequent appearances on television – including 'What's My Line?' – and has done numerous radio broadcasts.

# JILLY COOPER

## Angels Rush In

The Best of Her Satire
and Humour

Methuen · Mandarin

ANGELS RUSH IN

First published in Great Britain 1990 by Methuen London Ltd
Reprinted 1990 (twice)
Paperback edition published 1990 by Mandarin Paperbacks
Michelin House, 81 Fulham Road, London SW3 6RB
Reprinted 1990 (twice)

Mandarin is an imprint of the Octopus Publishing Group

A CIP catalogue record for this title
is available from the British Library
ISBN 0 7493 0604 1

*How to Stay Married* first published 1969 by Methuen & Co Ltd
*How to Survive from Nine to Five* first published 1970 by Methuen & Co Ltd
*Men and Super Men* first published 1972 by Eyre Methuen Ltd
*Women and Super Women* first published 1974 by Eyre Methuen Ltd
*Class* first published 1979 by Eyre Methuen Ltd
*Intelligent and Loyal* first published 1981 by Eyre Methuen Ltd
*The Common Years* first published 1984 by Methuen London Ltd
*How to Survive Christmas* first published 1986 by Methuen London Ltd
*Turn Right at the Spotted Dog* first published 1987 by Methuen London Ltd

The lines of poetry on page 241 are from 'The Garden', taken from Ezra Pound's *Collected Shorter Poems*, quoted by kind permission of Faber & Faber Ltd. The lines on page 119 are from John Betjeman's 'Slough', quoted by kind permission of John Murray Ltd.

Printed in England by Clays Ltd, St Ives plc

# CONTENTS

Drawings from *How to Stay Married, How to Survive from Nine to Five, Men and Super Men, Women and Super Women, Class* and *How to Survive Christmas* by Timothy Jaques

Drawings from *The Common Years* by Paul Cox

Photographs from *Intelligent and Loyal* taken by Graham Wood

To *Sophie Irvin* with love,
because of the largeness of her heart.

# INTRODUCTION

*Angels Rush In* is an anthology taken from nine of the books I have written
for Methuen over the last twenty years. Re-reading them – particularly
those I wrote in the late sixties and early seventies – gives me a very strange
feeling. Did I really say and think things like that? Was I really that smug
and sure of myself? How arch some of the phrases sound, how cack-handed
some of the others. How laboured the puns, how sanctimonious the
attitudes. How embarrassing that I freely used expressions and words
which I later discovered when I wrote a book about the English class
system, were irredeemably genteel. And then suddenly my mood switches
from shame to deep gloom, as I stumble on a comment or some anecdote
from the past which makes me scream with laughter or even occasionally
marvel at my own perception, and I promptly wonder why I can't write
with that clout and fearless irreverence today.

I suppose it is the difference between youth and middle age. When I
started writing, I couldn't take in the fact that I was addressing four million
readers in *The Sunday Times*, and many thousands more in my books.
Unaware of my audience, I realise I was mostly writing to sort myself out,
and work out old grievances – rather like a small boy swinging a brick
round on the end of a piece of rope, not minding whose ankles I hit. As I
grew older, I hope I became gentler and kinder, but probably like an old
dog I attacked my targets with fewer teeth.

One must, however, remain true to one's prejudices, and although in
some cases these books seem to have been written by a different person,
that doesn't give me the excuse to alter them or recant what I said.

On 17 June 1982, for example, in *The Common Years*, I wrote, 'The
Falklands War is over. Lefties and Liberals are finding it very difficult to
curb elation and emergent jingoism. Nor do the media make any attempt at
impartiality. I heard a man on Capital Radio today saying, "I'm sure we're
all absolutely – I mean I'm sure Mrs Thatcher's absolutely delighted that
we've taken Port Stanley." I think it's wonderful. Hurray for Maggie,

she should call an election now. How disgustingly right-wing I've become.'

Today those sentiments make me blush a little, but I suspect an awful lot of people of all parties felt as euphoric then as I did. The one merit perhaps, if you 'rush in' as I do, is that you tend to see things at the time like they were.

Which brings me to the title – *Angels Rush In*. I hope it is not too conceited. It originated from a kind review of my book *Class*, by John Mortimer, in which he complained how lily-livered the sociologists were in their attitude towards the class system and that, 'Angels like Mrs Cooper rushed in where academics feared to tread.'

I had admired John Mortimer for ever and, when I read the review, didn't flap down from heaven for at least forty-eight hours.

The aim of this collection is to cheer people up. Even today, having published thirty-five books altogether – all too fast, all to placate the bank manager, I still feel a joy and amazement and a deep sense of privilege and gratitude that publishers were willing to publish them.

I would like to thank my friend, editor, and prince of publishers, Geoffrey Strachan (ably assisted by Louise Moore and Jenny Rhys), for helping me choose the extracts included. I should like also to thank my family for so cheerfully providing so much of the copy, and my four dogs, the late Maidstone, Fortnum and Mabel and the still joyously extant Barbara, for their comfort, inspiration and merry companionship.

*Gloucestershire 1990*

# PART ONE

---

# Some People

# HOW TO STAY MARRIED

It all began in 1968, when my husband Leo left Hamish Hamilton to start his own publishing business, and I left Collins to adopt a baby. Shortly afterwards at a dinner party I met Godfrey Smith, the enchantingly jocund and ebullient editor of *The Sunday Times* colour supplement. As he was planning an issue on women, I expounded at length on the traumas of being a young wife, which included making love all night, getting up at dawn to race to the office, followed by those shopping scurrying lunch hours, then rushing home weighed down by carrier bags from the office at 5.30 pm to clean and cook one's husband's dinner, then making love all night before crawling off to the office, until after six months one collapsed from exhaustion.

Godfrey Smith invited me to translate this invective into a piece which appeared in the *Sunday Times* colour magazine in February. As a miraculous result I was offered a *Sunday Times* column the next week, and Michael Turner, a director of Methuen, still my publishers today, asked me to write a book called *How to Stay Married*.

I was so ecstatic at the prospect of becoming a real author, I didn't fully appreciate the hubristic nature of the title of the book. Today, 22 years later, I have been married for 28 years, and as marriages collapse around me, and all marriages are under siege, I feel the book should be re-titled: *How to Stay Married as Long as Possible*.

Also, because the book was produced amid the chaos of looking after a small baby and my husband, and trying to turn our Fulham house into a home, as well as writing a weekly *Sunday Times* column, my sorely neglected husband complained that it should be retitled *How to Get a Divorce*.

Nothing can describe the joy however of holding an early copy of one's first book in one's arms. On the front of the dust jacket of *How to Stay Married*, Leo and I stand back to back. He smoulders Byronically and has jet black hair. I have dyed blond hair and to match my roots am wearing a

3

black dress which was so short that when I once wore it in Bond Street an ancient American clapped his hands over his eyes, saying 'Oh my God, can they go any higher?'

My husband, however, forgave me for the neglect, and when I went North to promote the book, returning exhausted in the small hours, I found he had put all our son's teddy bears, one on each step, up the stairs to welcome me home. These are the things that help a marriage to last.

In many ways *How to Stay Married* is a period piece. It was written before the advent of Women's Liberation when wives automatically did all the cooking and housework and looked after the children, even if they had a full-time job. It is full of advice about avoiding rows by always having a clean shirt ready for your husband in the morning, and not forgetting to pass on his telephone messages, and that as long as you please a man in bed he won't worry about the mountain of dust underneath.

The extracts we have chosen deal mainly with adjustment in the early days, and how to diffuse rows. But even 22 years later, I still think that kindness, humour and a merry heart are the secret of a good marriage.

# How to Stay Married

## HERE COMES THE BRIDE

*The Wedding*

This is blast off – the day you (or rather your mother) have been waiting for all your life. It'll pass in a dream and afterwards you won't remember a thing about it. It helps, however, if you both turn up. Dope yourself with tranquillizers by all means, but watch the champagne later: drugs mixed with drink often put you out like a light. And don't forget to take the price tags off your new shoes, they'll show when you kneel down in church.

*Brides:* don't be disappointed if you don't look your best, far more likely you'll be scarlet in the face and piggy-eyed from lack of sleep.

*Bride not looking her best*

*Bridegrooms:* remember to look round and smile as your bride comes up the aisle. She'll be too busy coping with her bouquet and veil to notice, but it will impress those armies of guests lined up on either side of the church.

*Groom smiling
at bride*

Coming down the aisle's more tricky – you never know where to look, that radiant smile can easily set into a rictus grin, and there's bound to be one guest you know too well, whose eye you want to avoid (like Tallulah Bankhead's remark about one couple coming down the aisle: 'I've had them both and they were lousy!').

If you look solemn, people will think you're having second thoughts. Best policy is to settle for a cool smirk with your eyes on the door of the church.

Be careful what hymns you choose. People like a good bellow at a wedding, so don't choose anything obscure. Equally, be careful of hymns with double meanings like, 'Jesu – the very thought of thee', which will make everyone giggle and spoil the dignity and repose of the occasion.

### The Reception

First there's the line up, and you'll get so tired of shaking hands, trying to remember faces and gushing like an oil well, you'll begin to have a real sympathy for the Royal Family.

Don't worry when you circulate among the guests afterwards if none of them will speak to you. They'll all feel you're far too important to waste time talking to them, and you'll wander round like a couple of wraiths.

If you must make speeches, keep them short. Thank everyone in sight, and tell one stunning joke to convince your in-laws you do have a sense of humour after all. Never let the best man either speak or read the telegrams.

Don't flirt with exes. One girl I know, whose husband spent the reception playing 'do you remember' with an old girlfriend, refused to go on the honeymoon.

6

Try not to get drunk – you may feel like it – but it will cause recriminations later.

# THE HONEYMOON

Originally, the honeymoon was intended for husbands to initiate their innocent young brides into the delights and mysteries of sex. Today, when most couples have slept together anyway and are already bankrupted by the cost of setting up house, the whole thing seems a bit of a farce and a needless expense. You probably both need a holiday, however.

When you arrive at your destination, you're likely to feel a sense of anticlimax. You're exhausted and suffering from post-champagne depression (a real killer). For months you've been coping with squabbles with the caterers, bridesmaids' tantrums over their head-dresses, parcels arriving every day, the hall littered with packing straw, writer's cramp from answering letters, traumas with the dressmakers – every moment's been occupied, you're wound up like a clock, and suddenly it's all over and you've nothing to do for a fortnight except each other.

For the wife in particular, everything's suddenly new and unfamiliar, her spongebag and flannel, new pigskin luggage, a whole trousseau of new clothes, dazzling white underwear instead of the usual dirty grey – even her name is new.

The thing to remember is that your wife/husband is probably as nervous and in need of reassurance as you are, like the wild beast surprised in the jungle who's always supposed to be more frightened than oneself.

*Saboteurs*
The first thing to do on arrival at your honeymoon hotel is to search the bedroom for signs of sabotage. Jokey wedding guests may well have instructed the hotel staff to make you an apple pie bed, or wire up the springs of the bed to the hotel fire alarm.

One couple I know reached their hotel to be confronted by the manager waving a telegram from one such joker saying: 'My wife has just run off with my best friend, I believe they are booked into your hotel under the assumed name of Mr and Mrs So and So. Could you refuse to let them have the booked room until I arrive.' Whether you're heading for the Bahamas or Billericay, the best way to scotch honeymoon saboteurs is not to be coy about your destination. Simply tell everyone you're staying at the Grand and then book rooms at the Majestic.

7

Then there's the problem of getting used to living together. Here again the wife in particular will be worried about keeping up appearances. Before marriage she's relied on mud packs and rollers and skinfood at night, but now her husband's going to be with her every moment of the day, and the mystery's going to be ruined. When's she going to find time to shave her legs? And she's always told her husband she's a natural blonde, and suddenly he's going to find the home-bleacher in her suitcase.

She'll soon get used to it all, just as she'll get used to sitting on the loo and gossiping to her husband while he's having a bath, or to wandering around with nothing on instead of discreetly changing in the bathroom.

If she's ashamed of her small breasts and mottled thighs, he's probably equally self-conscious about his narrow shoulders and hairless chest.

*If she's ashamed . . .*

*First thing in the morning*

If you're worried you look like a road accident in the mornings, sleep with the curtains drawn, and if you're scared your mouth will taste like a parrot's cage when he bends over to kiss you, pretend you're going to the loo, and nip out and clean your teeth.

DON'T PANIC if you get bored, or have a row, or feel claustrophobic or homesick. These are all part of growing-together pains. They won't establish a behaviour pattern for the next fifty years.

A vital honeymoon ploy is to go somewhere where there is plenty to do. It's not sacrilege to go to the cinema or watch a soccer match or even look up friends in the district. Take lots of books and sleeping pills.

DON'T PANIC if you get on each other's nerves. My mother, who's been happily married to my father for almost fifty years, nearly left him on honeymoon because he got a line of doggerel on his mind and repeated it over and over again as they motored through the cornfields of France.

We drove round Norfolk on our honeymoon and I nearly sent my husband insane by exclaiming: 'How lovely', every time we passed a village church.

## Sex

I'm not going into the intricacies of sexual initiation – there are numerous books on the subject – I would just plead for both parties to be patient, tolerant, appreciative and understanding. Temporary frigidity and impotence are not infrequent occurrences on honeymoon, and not to be taken too seriously.

Take things slowly, you've probably got a lifetime in front of you – all that matters at this stage is to get across strong that you love each other, and you're not sorry you are married.

DON'T WORRY if, unlike the girl in *The Carpetbaggers* who wanted to see nothing but ceilings on her honeymoon, you don't feel like leaping on each other all the time. As I've already pointed out, you're probably exhausted and in no condition for a sexual marathon.

Do take a red towel if you're a virgin, or likely to have the Curse. It saves embarrassment over the sheets.

Even if you've been sleeping together for ages beforehand, and sex was stunning, don't worry if it goes off for a bit, or feel convinced that it can

*Eases tensions*

only work in a clandestine setting. You haven't been married before, and may just be having initial panic because the stable door is well and truly bolted.

One friend told me he was woken up in the middle of most nights of his honeymoon by his wife staggering groggily out of bed, groping for her clothes and muttering she must get home before her parents woke up.

It's a good idea to borrow someone's cottage in the country for a honeymoon. It's cheaper than an hotel, and you won't be worried by the imagined chortlings of chambermaids and hallporters, and you can cook if you get bored.

Don't worry if he/she doesn't gaze into your eyes all the time and quote poetry. Most people don't know enough poetry to last more than a quarter of an hour. A certain amount of alcohol is an excellent idea – it eases tension, breaks down inhibitions. Take the case of the girl in our office who on her arrival with her new husband at the hotel was presented with a bottle of champagne.

'It was wonderful,' she told us. 'We shared a glass each night and made the bottle last the whole fortnight.'

### Wedding presents

Get your thank-you letters written before the wedding. Once the pre-wedding momentum has been lost, you'll never get down to them.

Don't beef too much about the presents your partner's family or friends have given you, even if they are ghastly. No one likes to be reminded that they are related to, or acquainted with, people of execrable taste. Try and keep a list of who gave you what, so you can bring those cake forks out of hiding when Aunt Agatha comes to tea, and you won't, as we did, give a particularly hideous vase back to the woman who gave it to us, when later she got married.

# 'IF THERE'S ONE THING I CAN'T STAND . . .'

### Changing people

You shouldn't go into marriage expecting to change people. Once a bumbler always a bumbler, once a rake always a rake (a gay eye isn't likely to be doused by marriage). Once a slut – although she may make heroic and semi-successful attempts to improve – always a slut. When we were first married, my husband used to dream of the day I stopped working in an office, like the Three Sisters yearning for Moscow: 'The house will be tidy,

we shall make love every morning, and at last I shall be given breakfast.'

Well, I left the office, and chaos reigned very much as usual. It's a case of
plus ça change, I'm afraid.

Your only hope is that by making people happier and more secure they
may realise the potential inside them and develop into brilliant businessmen, marvellous lovers, superb cooks, or alas, even bores. And remember,
the wife who nags her husband on to making a fortune won't see nearly so
much of him. He'll be in the office from morn until night. She can't have it
both ways.

### Differing tastes

Certain things are bound to grate. He may have a passion for flying ducks
and Peter Scott and she may go a bundle on coloured plastic bulrushes and
a chiming doorbell.

The wife may also use certain expressions like 'Pleased to meet you',
which irritate her husband to death; or he may say 'What a generous
portion' every time she puts his food in front of him.

Now is the time to strike. If you say you can't stand something in the first
flush of love, your partner probably won't mind and will do something
about it. If, after ten years, you suddenly tell your husband it drives you
mad every time he says 'Sit ye down' when guests arrive, he'll be deeply
offended, and ask you why you didn't complain before.

### Irritating habits

Everyone has some irritating habits – the only thing to do when your
partner draws your attention to them is to swallow your pride and be
grateful, because they may well have been irritating everyone else as
well.

I have given up smoking and eating apples in bed, or cooking in my fur
coat, and I try not to drench the butter dish with marmalade. My husband
no longer spends a quarter of an hour each morning clearing the frog out of
his throat, and if he still picks his nose, he does it behind a newspaper.

There are bound to be areas in your marriage where you are dia-
metrically opposed. Compromise is the only answer. I'm cold blooded, my
husband is hot blooded. I sleep with six blankets, he sleeps half out of the
bed.

I like arriving late for parties so I can make an entrance, he likes arriving
on the dot because he hates missing valuable drinking time. I can't count

the number of quiet cigarettes we've had in the car, waiting for a decent time to arrive.

Don't worry too much that habits which irritate you now will get more and more on your nerves. My tame psychiatrist again told me: 'Those quirks in one's marriage partner which annoy one in early days often become in later years the most lovable traits.'

# ROWS

My husband and I quarrel very seldom except when we've had too much to drink. We both loathe rows and hate being shouted at. I was very worried when I first married because I read that quarrelling was one of the most common methods of relieving tensions in marriage, and was confronted with the awful possibility that our marriage had no proper tensions.

It is very hard to generalise about rows. Some of the happiest married people I know have the most blazing rows, and then make it up very quickly – like MPs who argue heatedly in the House all night, and then meet on terms of utter amicability in the bar five minutes later.

However much a row clears the air, one is bound during its course to say something vicious and hurtful, which may well be absorbed and brooded upon later. Try therefore to cut rowing down to the minimum. It will upset children when they come along, and if you row in public, it's boring and embarrassing for other people, and you won't get asked out any more.

We found the occasions when rows were most likely to break out were:

*Friday night* – both partners are tired at the end of the week.

*Going away for weekends* – one person is always ready and anxious to avoid the rush-hour, the other is frantically packing all the wrong things, so the first five miles of the journey will be punctuated with cries of 'Oh God' and U-turns against the ever-increasing traffic to collect something forgotten.

*Weddings* – the vicar's pep-talk in church on Christian behaviour in marriage always sets us off on the wrong foot. Then afterwards we'll be suffering from post-champagne gloom and wondering if we're as happy as the couple who've just got married.

*Television* – husband always wants to watch boxing, and the wife the play.

*Desks* – the tidy one will be irritated because the untidy one is always rifling the desk, and pinching all the stamps and envelopes.

*Clothes* – men not having a clean shirt or clean underpants to wear in the morning.

*Space in the bedroom* – the wife will appropriate five and three quarters out of six of the drawers and three out of four of the coat hangers, and leave her clothes all over the only chair.

### Minor irritations all likely to cause rows

The wife should avoid using her husband's razor on her legs and not washing it out, or cleaning the bath with his flannel, or using a chisel as a screwdriver, or pinching the husband's sweaters. There are also the eighteen odd socks in her husband's top drawer, the rings of lipstick on his best handkerchief, running out of toothpaste, loo paper, soap. Forgetting to turn out lights, fires, the oven. Forgetting to give her husband his letters or telephone messages.

### Making up

Never be too proud to apologise, but do it properly; none of that 'I've said I'm sorry, haven't I?', followed by a stream of abuse.

Don't worry about letting the sun go down on your wrath – it's no good worrying a row to its logical conclusion when you're both tired and then lying awake the rest of the night. Take a sleeping pill, get a good night's sleep and you'll probably have forgotten you ever had a row by morning.

Try not to harbour grudges, never send someone to Coventry.

*Poor Tibbles*

A sense of humour is all-important for ending rows. My husband once in mid-row put both feet into one leg of his underpants and fell over. I went into peals of laughter and the row was at an end.

Once when I was threatening to leave him he looked reproachfully at the cat, and said: 'But we can't let poor Tibbles be the victim of a broken home.'

# A NOTE ON FEMININE PROBLEMS

*Black glooms*
Suffered particularly by wives in the first six months after marriage, they usually stem from exhaustion, feeling totally unable to cope, and reaction after the wedding. They are extremely tedious for the husband, but nothing really to worry about unless they linger on longer than a week. Nothing will be achieved by telling her sharply to snap out of it – patience, a lot of loving and encouragement are the only answer.

*The curse*
Should be re-named the blessing. Every row two weeks before it arrives, and a week after it's finished, can be blamed on it.

*Anniversaries*
Husbands are notorious for forgetting birthdays and anniversaries. Don't expect a heart-shaped box of chocolates on Valentine's Day, but avoid a row over anniversaries by saying loudly about three days before: 'What shall we do on my birthday/our anniversary on *Friday*, darling?'

# CONCLUSION

I am fully aware of the inadequacies of this book. Some aspects of marriage are covered very scantily and some not at all, and because I was writing about staying married, I have dwelt more on the pitfalls than on the very considerable joys of marriage.

'For everyone, and particularly for women and children,' Cecil King wrote recently, 'the essential basis for security and happiness is a loving home.'

Marriage is not a battlefield, it is a partnership, and married people should be partners not rivals. And although it is important to be a reliable wage earner, a splendid cook, a good manager, and magnificent in bed, the most priceless gift one married person can give to another is a merry and a loving heart.

# HOW TO SURVIVE FROM NINE TO FIVE

*How to Survive from Nine to Five*, from which the following extracts are taken, was written in 1970, only 18 months after I stopped working in an office – so the horrors were still fresh in my mind. Having left a job as a cub reporter which I adored when I was 21, I was then sacked from 22 jobs. They included being a puppy fat model, an account executive for the pig industry and the Tory party at the same time, a P.R.O., copy writer, publisher's reader, information officer, demonstrator of candelabra, and very temporary typist. I therefore felt I had a wide non-working knowledge of most levels of the office caste system.

This book is based on the shared experience of myself and my husband who has also worked in several publishing firms. Beneath its iconoclastic exterior it has serious undertones. I have always felt that if you seek latterday Hitlers or Caligulas you need go no further than the office round the corner where you will find petty tyrants bullying their unfortunate staff into states of inefficiency, screwing up their self respect so badly they feel incapable of getting another job.

I was the one that got away, but I still, 20 years later, think of all those millions of people battling their way into ghastly jobs every morning.

# How to Survive from Nine to Five

## THE NEWCOMER

*The first day*

The first day at any office is absolute hell. When I'm king I shall make it law that everyone starts a new job on Friday instead of Monday. Monday morning, in particular, couldn't be a worse time. All the incumbents are feeling anti-establishment, ill tempered and are desperately trying to catch up on all those very urgent things that didn't seem to matter a damn on Friday.

Monday morning is also No Man's Land, a limbo between home and the office. The staff have been isolated from each other for two days over the weekend, and have lost any corporate enthusiasm, which will only emerge about Thursday. By Friday it will be joined by excitement about the coming weekend and they will feel in a good enough mood to give newcomers the welcome they deserve.

As it is, you arrive about 8.30, sick with nerves, to find the building locked or deserted except for the odd cleaner morosely pushing a squeegee over the floor. You then kick your heels in Reception until a few 'sekketries' (as they describe themselves) arrive from the country lugging pigskin suitcases and the pick of Daddy's herbaceous border (which will either be arranged in jam jars, or block the basins of the Ladies for the rest of the week).

About eleven o'clock, Miss Hitler from Personnel will bustle up and cause a rumpus because you've forgotten your P.45 and your insurance cards. She will then direct you to your office. If you are an executive you will either find an in-tray groaning with bucks other people have passed, or even worse, a completely bare desk with empty drawers and an empty filing cabinet, and you'll sit gazing at a huge sheet of virgin blotting paper, wondering what to write with all those sharpened pencils.

It's also possible that there's no job and you've just been brought in to swell the shadow Managing Director's faction in office politics. The sekketry promised you has decided to work for someone else (a blessing because you've no work for her anyway) and the rest of the department are wearing black ties and flying the Office Crone at half mast in mourning for your predecessor, whom they consider was unfairly ousted.

Occasionally people will shuffle into your office and say: 'Oh, you're the new chap,' and shuffle out again. Endeavour to appear busy. One man I know brought in at a very senior level wrote a novel during his first three months. Thinking he was writing reports, everyone was deeply impressed. Ask for progress reports for the last year (this will throw them, because they probably don't have any), or files, or the minutes of recent meetings. Then you can fill in your time, shuffling papers back and forth, frowning and nodding gravely. Soft pedal the hatchet approach: 'I'm a new chap, just getting my sea legs, perhaps you can help me,' will work wonders.

If you join as a sekketry you will probably be fobbed off with a desk with uneven legs, and an old battleship of a typewriter which everyone else has rejected and which tabulates automatically every time you press the A key.

*An old battleship of a typewriter*

Suddenly a choleric, fire-breathing old man will rush out of a nearby office, shout at you and rush back again. Alas, that is the cosy pink-faced, sherry-bestowing old gentleman who seemed such a darling when he interviewed you last month. Bosses are invariably April when they woo, December when they wed. He wants you to take dictation.

Nearby sekketries will not speak to you except to tell you what a snake he is, and that everyone's leaving the firm because he's so vile to work for. You daren't interrupt their Monday morning panic with questions, so you will automatically have to re-type all your letters tomorrow because you didn't know about the lilac flimsy for the Art Department, or not putting a full stop after the date.

Remember to bring in two large shopping baskets to smuggle out all the botched-up letters you have to throw away. Miss Hitler from Personnel will not be amused by those brimming waste-paper baskets of scrumpled paper.

You will sit crossing your legs wondering how much longer you can hold out because no one has told you the firm shares a loo with Golberg's Imported Goatskins on the next floor.

At twelve-fifteen someone looks at her watch and says with obvious relief, 'I should go to lunch now,' then they can all discuss you.

Not knowing where to go, you will be deceived by the peeling paint and gloomy exterior of a little place on the corner which will turn out to be French and cost you at least a fiver.

Then there's the ghastly prospect when you get back to the office dead on 1.15 of how you're going to survive until 5. Although the work is piling up, you're terrified to type because you do it so slowly compared with the rest of the sekketries, whose hands are moving over the keys with the speed and dexterity of concert pianists. By tea time you're so grateful to some whiskery old boot for offering you a Lincoln cream that you strike up a friendship you'll never be able to shake off.

There are, however, advantages in being a newcomer. Everyone expects you to be inoperative for the first six months anyway, and you can blame every mistake you make on your predecessor.

On my father's first day at Fords, he was sent down to the foundry to report to the chief metallurgist. When he arrived one man seemed to be giving all the orders, so he turned to a nearby workman and asked if this man was the metallurgist.

'No Buddy,' came the reply, 'I think he's a Russian.'

## THE HIERARCHY

*Give people enough rope, and they'll hang you.*
If you are to survive from nine to five, you must understand that nothing is more rigid than the office caste system, which is based on the premise that subordinates, unless kept ruthlessly in their place, will cheek you when you try to pull rank on them.

It is therefore unwise to risk being seen more than once in the company of a high-ranking member of the firm; people will suspect sexual commitment or political intrigue.

Nor is it done for women executives to go to lunch with the sekketries unless it's a birthday treat. Also, remember that if one of your old mates is promoted over you, your relationship will never be the same again. In no time he'll be goose-stepping all over you – power élite swagger and all.

Members of the staff, however, are always trying to wriggle their way up the hierarchy, typists calling themselves sekketries, sekketries calling themselves personal assistants, senior sekketries signing themselves Sekketry to the Deputy Managing Director whenever the Managing Director goes on holiday.

There will also be ridiculous wrangling over whether you are high enough up the ladder to rate a teaspoon or a bone china tea set with roses on it. In some firms they even have a special directors' lavatory, the only difference being that they have two kinds of loo paper – hard and very hard. If a woman were promoted to the board, it would be interesting to see if she would be expected to use it.

Your actual hierarchy will most probably consist of:

The Office Junior who knows nothing and does everything.

The Sekketry who knows everything and does nothing.

The Office Deb who knows everybody, my dear, and does nothing.

The pink and white Etonian trainee who knows the Office Deb.

The Personal Assistant who knows nothing and does nothing.

The Executive who interferes and prevents everyone from doing anything.

The Deputy Head of Department who panics.

The Head of the Department who signs letters, writes his report and doesn't give a damn because he's retiring at the end of the year.

The Managing Director, who can't read anyway.

Let us now look more closely at a few members of the hierarchy.

### The boss
*Work hard and you will be rewarded by the promotion of your superiors.*
Some bosses are good, some are not. Try very hard to give yours some responsibility. Bosses with nothing to do will always poke their noses into your affairs.

Here are some typical bosses:

*The bully*
He can't leave his staff alone and bullies them into a state of jibbering inefficiency because it makes him feel superior. Stress is transmitted down the hierarchy until even the messenger boys are on tranquillizers. Like the circumlocution office, the bully is always beforehand in the art of seeing how not to do things. Stand up to him, or leave immediately before mental paralysis sets in.

*The man on the make*
He certainly won't want to make you, you're not important enough. He'll be far too busy sucking up to senior sekketries and the Managing Director's wife. He will take credit if anything goes right, but you will carry the can if anything goes wrong.

A favourite expression will be: 'I'm going to give you a free hand with this one' (but he'll keep a free foot to boot you out if you make a hash of it). Or 'You're going to have rather fun with this', before he hands you 20 pages of figures to type.

*The dreaming boffin*
You'll spend your time sewing on buttons, collecting brief cases from the lost property office and rushing in with the fire extinguisher when he sets his wastepaper basket on fire. When he dictates he will probably eat his biscuits, then your biscuit, then drink his tea, then your tea. He will carry his washing round in his brief case, and suddenly pull out his underpants by mistake and say: 'Would you possibly mind typing this for me?'

*The aristocrat*
Work for him and you've got a cushy number. He will wear tweeds on Thursday for going to the country and he will not return until Tuesday morning. He will also be inoperative during the summer months, going to Ascot and Henley etc. Your time will be spent answering invitations, ordering caviar from Fortnums, and finding out how to address Duchesses and Earls on envelopes.

Moving down the hierarchy we come to:

*The executive*
*Avoid thought, it inevitably clouds the issue.*
The executive has nothing to do except decide what is to be done, tell someone to do it, listen to reasons why they shouldn't do it, or why it should

be done differently, and think up a crushing and conclusive reply. A week later he will follow up to see the thing has been done, discover it has not been done, ask why it hasn't been done, and listen to excuses from the person who didn't do it.

He will then wait another week before making further investigations, and avoid the temptation to wonder why he didn't do it himself in the first place. It would have taken him five minutes, instead it has taken a fortnight to find out that someone has taken at least a week to do it wrong. He then sits back and decides it's good for subordinates to learn by their own mistakes.

## Deadwood
*Nothing ventured, nothing lose.*

A step further down the hierarchy you will find the men the bosses hang their coats on – poor old dodderers in their late fifties, their false teeth rattling with nerves. Loss of pension hangs over their heads like a sword of Damocles. Knowing that they won't get another job if they're fired, they refuse to stick their necks out.

Weighed down by megaworries, the Dodderer will be convinced that people who couldn't even plot their way to the loo are conspiring against him. Shut doors will drive him into a frenzy, and every time he hears a typist whispering, even if it's only asking her next door neighbour if she can borrow a tampax, he's convinced she's whispering about him.

*Home-made fishpaste
sandwiches*

At lunchtime, he takes a packet of home-made fishpaste sandwiches out of a shabby brief case. Occasionally at weekends, he gets drunk on Guinness. He often develops crushes on ugly typists.

Beneath this trembling exterior, however, lies a knight of the festering grievance, who can generate quite a force of discontent around the office. Avoid antagonising him. He sneaks like wildfire.

## Piggies

Piggies exist in most firms. They are sly, insensitive, unimaginative and always eating, particularly toffees, which they suck noisily and never offer to anyone else. Piggies never rise to the top of the tree, but they never get ulcers. They irritate subordinates and superiors equally, but are never fired because they are moderately efficient. Never work for a Piggy. Once you are directly below one in the hierarchy you will never rise to the top of the tree either.

## The personnel department

Usually manned by a mini-bitch, who goes round measuring skirt lengths and calling sekketries by their surnames. Often she'll crouch for hours in the loo waiting to catch staff in indiscreet gossip.

Personnel are supposed to help you to hire people, but most of their day is spent forcing the squarest pegs into round holes. Whenever a new sekketry is required, they produce two identically grey, ugly, characterless girls to choose from.

Personnel departments are always having pointless economy drives. Even executives have to waste a ridiculous amount of time cajoling another biro out of them. In one office I remember the Personnel director hanging two rolls of lavatory paper, Bronco and Andrex, out of a top storey window to see which was the longer.

In another, the four members of the Personnel department decided to go to Ireland together for the weekend on a special outing but insisted on flying on separate planes like the Royal Family, as the loss to the firm would have been so immeasurable if they had all been killed off in one go.

## The Office Crone

She usually runs the typing pool. As soon as she arrives she puts on her mauve office cardigan to stop her 'good' clothes getting dirty. All her energies are channelled into bullying the typing pool like galley-slaves, and satisfying her insatiable appetite for new office equipment: dictaphones, electric typewriters, roller towels and Imperial Leather in the Ladies.

Much of her day will be spent foraging inside her transparent cream-coloured blouse to haul up a bra strap, eating biscuits, and surreptitiously plucking out her beard with a bulldog clip. She will be driven to a frenzy

*The Office Crone*

by two things: lateness even if it's only thirty seconds, and mislaying her fingerette, which is a rubber thimble covered in spikes and looks like some weird Indian erotic device, but is actually used for turning pages quickly.

Sucking up is the only way to woo her. Hold her wool for her, ask her advice on beauty problems, give her the odd bar of Turkish Delight as a present.

One of her arch enemies will be:

### The office deb
Miss Nitwit-Thompson, a decorative quarter-wit who comes wrapped in cashmere and scotch mist on the end of a long yellow Labrador. She is working for a pittance 'because the job sounded so interesting', and is always having time off to go to mid-week weddings. She takes long weekends, and invariably rings Mummy on Friday and asks her to 'stop the train'.

Originally employed for her style and 'lovely speaking voice' which would impress clients and Americans on the telephone, she is usually hogging the telephone making personal calls to Jeremy, Caroline or Fiona to discuss last night's ball.

Another of the Office Crone's sworn enemies is:

*Miss Nitwit-Thompson*

### The little home-breaker

The office sex kitten, who has a lived-in look about her and is far more preoccupied with outgoing males than outgoing mail. The only filing she does is to file her nails, and the only use she makes of the office pencil sharpener is to sharpen her eye-pencil and her claws. She is not to be dismissed, however, for she usually knows a lot of high-level secrets, leaked by chief executives in moments of passion. She is also quite capable of hooking the Managing Director, and suddenly becoming the Boss's wife.

### The little home-maker

Who puts sticky buds in jam jars on her boss's desk, and is always whisking round with a feather duster and percolating coffee. She will spend more time indulging her 'office beautiful' pretensions than actually typing. When asked what she does at parties she will call herself a Personal Assistant.

### The undiplomatic bag

The senior sekketry who will guard her boss with such ferocity that she's quite likely to keep important clients and the Managing Director away from him until everyone forgets his existence. She will, however, be an excellent chucker-out if undesirables manage to insinuate themselves into his office.

Finally, we come to:

*The typing pool*

Generally called Maureen or Eileen. Their function in life seems to be to slop tea and type back letters that don't always make sense. If any of their carbons reach the files they will be spotted with rubbing-out smudges like a Dalmatian. Brainwashed by the system, they generally go to the loo in triplicate.

The Average Typists' Day, however, will go something like this:

9.10 Arrives generating bustle, hidden behind huge tinted spectacles, and muttering about de-railed carriages on the line. Disappears to the loo to tart up.

9.30 Removes typewriter cover, discusses what 'he' did and said last night, what television they saw, speculates on boss's mood, reads own and other typists' horoscopes in the morning papers.

10.00 Coffee break. Eats cheese roll.

10.15 Takes spare pair of shoes out of plastic bag in bottom drawer of desk. Changes into them.

10.30 Takes dictation.

10.45 Returns from dictation. Grumbles for thirty minutes about the horrible mood the boss is in.

11.15 Called to window by fellow typist to ogle comely man who is walking down the street. Snags tights on central heating, fills in hole with brown pencil.

11.40 Goes to loo to tart up.

12.00 Gone to dinner.

1.15 Returns with carrier bags, discusses dinner, eats yoghurt and Mars Bar.

2.30 Boss comes back from lunch in better mood.

2.31 Goes to the loo to re-do face.

2.45 Tries to read shorthand back, holds book upside down.

3.00 Starts grumbling about non-arrival of tea.

3.15 Tea arrives, eats home-made cake out of paper bag, reads own and other typists' horoscopes in evening paper.

3.20 Types lethargically.

3.30 Slips out, ostensibly to the chemist's, so no one can ask why she's going.

4.00 Returns ostentatiously waving a Boots paper bag, which is actually full of make-up and tights.

4.10 Starts muttering about catching post, tidies ferociously for five minutes. Assembles one letter in large leather folder and gets it signed by boss.

4.30 Grabs floral plastic bag and joins queue for the loo for a good wash to get 'all the ink off my hands'.

4.45 Tears out of the office, muttering 'must try and catch the early train tonight'.

4.50 Building deserted.

*The office boy*

Office boys – the avant garde of the company – live in the postroom. In my day, they all used to smoke pot, strum guitars, and grow their hair halfway down their backs. Now they're all punk rockers. Invariably they get into trouble because the photographic machine decides to break down when they are photostating some writhing nude, or the roneo machine gives up the ghost when they are running off 500 copies of an obscene poem.

*The office boy*

As an office boy you'll be paid a rotten salary, but you can make a bit on the side, taking buses whenever you have to deliver anything and charging up for a taxi.

The office boy's prime function is to give his superiors racing tips, keep them posted on what's top of the hit parade, and to rise eventually to Managing Director, so people can say: 'I remember him when he was only an office boy.'

When you get to the top, remember to sack all the people who knew you as an office boy. They won't take you seriously, and will instil lack of respect into their colleagues.

One office boy I know left a firm, made his packet and came back ten years later as a client. Not realising he had left, the Managing Director met him in the passage, handed him a parcel and asked him to take it to the post office.

*People who knew you
as an office boy*

*The gripevine*
*'Our recording machine is broken – this is a person speaking.'*
Always chat up the switchboard girls, they wield enormous power. If
you get across them they can 'forget' to take messages, keep you hanging
about for hours waiting for a line, cut you off, and, worst of all, tip off Miss
Hitler from Personnel that you've been making too many private calls – one
of the most heinous of office crimes. They are also the hub of the gripevine
and extremely valuable as a source of gossip. I also think that every
member of the staff – particularly the men – should spend a day on the
switchboard to see what pressures the telephonists are subjected to. I
arrived at a temporary job once, and was asked if I could man the
switchboard. No switchboard was ever more rapidly unmanned: all those
horrible flaps signifying incoming calls came down at the same time, and
the discs indicating that someone wanted a line started flickering as well.
Flap, flap, flicker, flicker, they went all morning, until I was reduced to a
state of nervous collapse. 'Just putting you through,' I would say hopefully,
cutting off the sales manager's deal-clinching call to Australia for the
seventh time.

On the receiving end there are those terrible occasions when the switchboard closes down and your lover, who's been soaking in some drinking
club all afternoon, suddenly decides to ring you up and gets straight
through to the Managing Director, who has to walk down three flights of
stairs to find you.

Or those awful personal calls that come through when a meeting is being
held in your office, and you hold the telephone very close to your ear so no
one else in the room can hear the flood of invective.

Every so often there is a purge on private calls which no one takes any
notice of. In one office a circle of paper was stuck on every telephone
saying: 'Please be brief. No private calls allowed.' Some iconoclast
promptly whipped it off and stuck it on the door of the Gents.

# EXTRA-MURAL ACTIVITIES

A lot of your working day will be spent out of the office:

*The lunch hour*
*Never drink black coffee at lunch; it will keep you awake in the afternoon.*
Euphemistically called the lunch hour, this interval in the day's in-
activities runs from twelve to three-thirty. This is the Piggies' High Noon

when, snorting with delight, they pour out of their offices like their Gadarene forbears into the café opposite where they eat three courses of soup, shepherd's pie and chips, and treacle pudding followed by white coffee, after which they waddle back to their office to eat biscuits all afternoon.

The sekketries will reach peak activity during the lunch hour, when they hare round doing their shopping, getting clothes out of the dry cleaners and having their hair done. They also squeeze in three-quarters of an hour to have lunch, sitting in each other's laps in steamy coffee bars, fat girls eating salads, thin girls eating spaghetti, their dissection of last night's escapade only interrupted by the hiss of the espresso machine.

Invariably just as they're getting down to a good bitch about the office, they feel a heavy hand on their shoulder; it will be Miss Hitler from Personnel asking if she can join them.

Office Crones seldom go to lunch, but spend their hour brewing tomato soup in the basement (or, because they're on a diet, sourly nibbling at cottage cheese and a piece of celery), adding another two rows to their green open-work jersey, and waiting to tear latecomers limb from limb.

Then, of course, there's the office canteen, with its menu improperly typed by one of the sekketries.

> Clean Soup
> Boiled button
> Stewed rears and naked egg custard.

Unless you want fat meat or the boniest piece of the fish, it's essential to waste a great deal of time chatting up the woman who runs the canteen. (She's the only woman in whom the Piggies display any interest.)

Meanwhile the directors are roughing it at the Ritz.

If you are to get on as an executive, you must realise that in order to do business with anyone, you must down two large pink gins, a three-course lunch with a good bottle of claret, and two double brandies, not forgetting cigars, at every stage of the deal.

How well I remember those nightmarish business lunches when I was a very junior Public Relations executive, entertaining lady journalists and wondering desperately when would be the right moment to tell them about the product I was supposed to be trying to flog.

Usually I funked it until the coffee stage, then said timidly, 'Well-er about these fascinating rubber gloves.' And the lady journalist would

*A heavy hand on
their shoulder*

glance at her watch, mutter about a deadline, leap to her feet, thanking me profusely for a divine lunch, and disappear double quick out of the restaurant . . .

It always seems a slight anomaly that managements expect their executives to spend at least a tenner a day on lunch, then only issue the rest of the staff with 15p luncheon vouchers. I suppose this ensures wakefulness in the afternoon. No one could sleep on a 15p lunch.

A friendly grocer will usually exchange your vouchers for groceries. I used to buy cigarettes with mine.

*Lunge hour*

The lunch hour is invariably followed by the lunge hour. This is the period of rocketing libidos and octopus hands, when bosses and executives return from lunch swollen with insolence and wine, and make passes at their sekketries and any pretty girls who seem to be around.

*Sex in the office*
*Dear Sir Stroke Madam*

Offices vary: some are like monasteries, and the only thing you're likely to get raped by is the spacebar on the long-carriage typewriter. Others out-thrum *Peyton Place*. As an ex-colleague said: 'You have to knock on people's office doors before you go in, not out of courtesy, just to give them time to get their trousers up.'

There's certainly nothing like the odd pass to lighten the tedium of office life, nor the odd crush on your boss to make you look forward to Monday morning instead of dreading it.

You'll find too that the Personnel Lady and Judy O'Grady are nymphos under the skin. As soon as a new Adonis joins the firm, the Office Crones start dunking themselves in Devon Violets, the typing pool turn their skirts up to groin level with the office stapler, and even the senior sekketries treat themselves to a home perm and set the directors' floor throbbing with middle-aged desire.

In my experience, sex in the office is catching like the measles. Once one director discovers another director is knocking off his sekketry he starts wondering why he shouldn't have a bit on the side as well, and lust is transmitted down the hierarchy. When you consider that a boss spends more of his waking life with his sekketry than with his wife, it's hardly surprising that accidents happen.

Another contributing factor is that most women are attracted by power, and absolute power attracts absolutely. Thus the most grey, sexless men take on a lustre when they assume the mantle of Managing Director or head of the department. All women want to play Egeria, but on the other hand

*The most grey,
sexless men*

they are seldom drawn to subordinates. I don't think Lady Chatterley's Office Boy is a viable proposition.

I think there should be lots of pretty girls in the office too. It cheers the men up if they can wolf-whistle while they work.

Some people are very clever at concealing the fact that they are having an affaire with someone in the office. One woman executive I'd always thought was a pillar of respectability told me long after I'd left the firm that she'd been to bed with three members of the board in the same day: one first thing in the morning (he'd been spending the night with her), the second she took home to lunch, and the third had her for supper.

Usually, however, the couple having a walk-out congratulate themselves on being terribly discreet, carefully leaving the office at different times, meeting half-a-mile down the road and ostentatiously not speaking to each other when they meet in the passage. When in fact the forked tongues have been wagging for weeks and the whole of the building has been watching the affaire develop with passionate interest.

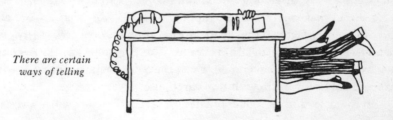

*There are certain ways of telling*

There are certain ways, too, of telling if your boss is having an affaire with someone:

If he starts getting in when the dew is still on the filing cabinets, and you're knocked sideways by the smell of *Brut for Men*.

If he keeps getting calls on the internal telephone and makes ambiguous remarks into it: 'We must play this one very close to the chest, we'd better thrash the whole problem of production out over lunch. How about Overton's at 1 o'clock?'

If he comes back after a three-hour lunch ostensibly with a client, and immediately sends you out for sandwiches, or yawns his head off and spends the afternoon loudly rustling papers to disguise the fact that his stomach is rumbling.

If he and Miss Nitwit-Thompson both disappear individually but at the same time to buy the evening paper, stay away for an hour and return having forgotten to buy it.

If he and Miss Nitwit-Thompson both ring in to say they're ill with gastro-enteritis.

If he's having an affaire with someone outside the office, he'll get lots of handwritten letters marked Private and Confidential which he'll rush off to the loo to read.

*Office politics*
*The trouble with this sinking ship is that all the rats are staying.*
Apart from making and evading passes, eighty per cent of your time in any office will be spent in the area of competition: playing the power game and jockeying for position. Executives will go round after dark emptying your wastepaper basket and piecing your confidential memos together. Every time you go down the passage you'll be subjected to a party political broadcast on behalf of the Accounts Department.

Feuding goes on between person and person, and between departments, who will all try to shift blame onto each other. The Publicity Department, for example, will drive other departments into a frenzy of rage, merely because they make more noise and appear to do less work than anyone else, and consider the fact that they work late occasionally on a press party gives them the excuse to swan in late every day. The Personnel and the Accounts Departments fight with everyone. Even the Sales Department will be in a state of constant warfare with the warehouse.

As a young executive, sooner or later one of the directors will ask you out

*Lunch at a five-star restaurant*

to lunch at a five-star restaurant. When you get to the swirling brandy stage he will start rhubarbing about getting the dead man's hand off the wheel, and then offer you a junior ministry in his Shadow Cabinet.

Don't commit yourself to joining his faction, just say you absolutely see his point. And don't let him see you going out with his rival director to another five-star lunch the next day.

Your real office Machiavelli, however, will place his own men in key positions throughout the firm and then set up:

*The palace revolution*
A palace revolution will be heralded by the following signs:

Various top brass will start getting in unusually early in the morning and stand about in the corridors whispering. Directors who are known to loathe each other start going out to lunch together. Strange files are suddenly sent for, urgent calls are made to the firm's accountants or solicitors from directors who normally don't deal with them. A publicity handout is run off in conditions of great secrecy and circulated to the press, who are told to treat the matter in confidence and not to release the news until they get the OK from the Deputy Managing Director's sekketry. The Deputy Managing Director having set the whole thing up, flies to Hamburg to see a client and waits to see what happens.

If the Managing Director is overthrown by the rest of the Board, the Deputy Managing Director will fly back and take over. If not he will deny all knowledge of the conspiracy.

The Piggies will take absolutely no notice and go to lunch.

# SOCIAL OCCASIONS

*The office outing*
Whether it's *Tulip Time in Spalding, Lincs.*, *A Charity Walk to Gravesend* or *A Night out in London's Theatreland*, this beastly romp is loathed both by the people who go on it, and by the people who organise it. It's a hangover from feudal forelock-tugging times, when the Lords of the Manor used to give charity banquets for the poor. It should be abolished and the money spent on extra bonuses.

*The leaving party*
In some offices, there's a permanent round of parties after work. Either you're celebrating landing a big contract, or cheering each other up for

losing it, or saying good-bye to someone, or wishing them happy birthday, or celebrating the fact that their cat's just had kittens.

Leaving parties are occasions when sex rears its ugly head, for while you are saying good-bye to dear old Fothers from Production who's been with the firm for forty years, you will probably drink enough to say a big hello to Miss Twink from the typing pool, whose knickers are bursting into flames at the thought of you.

Hardly a day passes either without some office junior coming round waving a manilla envelope collecting for someone's birthday or leaving present – executives will be considered very mean if they give less than 50p, and directors must give at least £1. Later in the day you will have to add your name at an acute angle to a myriad others on a leaving card. It is interesting to note how much more talent and imagination manifests itself in leaving cards than in any other project produced by the art or copy departments; it is the one example of work that is not fettered by red tape or mucked about by senior members of the hierarchy.

### The Christmas Party

Finally there's the Office Christmas Party – subtly different from the Office Dance, because no wives or husbands or lovers are invited to inhibit the fun.

This is a typical office party:

It's Christmas Eve in the workhouse. The typing pool has been transformed into a fairy grotto. The typists are red-faced from the hairdresser's and blowing up balloons – they have been making furtive trips to the Ladies all afternoon to see if their dresses have hung out properly. Excitement seethes. This is the night when supertax husbands are hooked. In other parts of the building the higher echelons anticipate the evening with trepidation and veiled lust. The building already reverberates with revelry. The Art Department, having declared UDI, held their party before midday and are still going strong.

At 4.55, when it's too late to rush out and get her something, the Office Crone makes everyone feel a louse by handing out gaily wrapped presents. At 5.00 everyone stops typing in mid-word and thunders down to the Ladies which soon resembles the changing room at Way In. The office junior has used hair lacquer under her arms instead of deodorant and is walking round like a penguin.

The party begins with everyone standing under the fluorescent lighting wondering what to say next – strange, considering they find no difficulty during working hours. Miss Nitwit-Thompson, who has been putting her Christmas cards through the franking machine all afternoon and telephoning her friends to say what a bore the party is going to be, has not bothered to change out of her grey jersey dress. She will be leaving after five minutes to catch a train home to Daddy.

In an attempt to please everyone, the £80 collected for drink has been spent on one bottle of everything from Brown Ale to Babycham. The caretaker who is manning the bar has assembled a strange collection of glasses: flower vases, toothmugs, bakelite cups. The Office Wolf is busy lacing the typists' orange juice with vodka.

Neatly displayed in out-trays is food cooked by members of the staff; curling sandwiches, flaccid cheese straws with baker's droop, and an aggressive-looking Christmas cake covered in festive robins baked by the Office Crone. The Piggies have already got their heads down in the trough.

Conversation is still laboured, but the arrival of the Production department, who've been boozing all day on free liquor, helps to jolly things along. Soon, members of the Board drift down from Olympus, genial from a succession of long Christmas lunches.

The Receptionist, who is not famed for the strength of her knicker elastic, is making a very alive set at the handsome Director of Public Relations. Miss Nitwit-Thompson discovers she's met the Managing Director's son at a number of dinner parties. Soon they are nose to nose.

People are relaxing. Someone puts on a record and two typists dance together. One of the young men on the make is overheard boasting about his expenses by the Financial Director and loses his chance of promotion. The office cat has wriggled out of his green Xmas bow and is thoughtfully licking fishpaste out of the sandwiches.

Faces are reddening, backs are being slapped, people are passing round packets of fifty cigarettes. The Managing Director needs little encouragement to get up and say what a big happy family they all are.

The Office Junior swells with pride at the thought that she and about 400 other people are entirely responsible for the firm's turnover. The caretaker takes the opportunity to rinse some glasses in the fire bucket.

A packer arrives from the warehouse with shiny blue suit and horny hands, and claims a dance with one of the senior sekketries, who bends over backwards to avoid his four-ale breath. The Receptionist and the Director of Public Relations are having private relations behind the filing cabinet.

The Managing Director's wife, who has come to collect her husband, has taken a piece of Christmas cake in deference to the typing pool. She didn't realise the robins were made of plaster, and is now desperately trying to spit out a beak.

*Claims a dance with a senior sekketry*

Lust is rising in the vast jacked-up bosom of Miss Hitler from Personnel, and she is jostling the newest trainee towards the mistletoe. The Office Boy has hiccups and is trying to roll cheese and chutney sandwiches into an electric typewriter.

'God bless you all, Merry Christmas,' cries the departing Managing Director.

Now he's gone the fun is unconfined. There is a general unfastening of chastity belts. The Sales Director is playing bears round the furniture, the Office Wolf keeps turning off the lights. Squeaks and scuffles break out in nearby offices. The oldest member of the staff is telling anyone who will listen how the firm grew from a tiny two-room business to the 'great concern we are today'. The Director of Public Relations is in the Gents desperately scrubbing lipstick from his shirt front.

The drink has run out. Miss Nitwit-Thompson, who is now quite giggly, is being taken to Annabels by the Managing Director's son. She'll be lucky if she gets home to Daddy before Boxing Day.

Reluctant to end the evening, people are making plans to meet in pubs or the backs of cars. Others are saying 'Merry Christmas', exchanging beery kisses and taking uncertain steps towards the nearest bus stop.

The caretaker, who has appropriated several bottles of drink, shakes his head over the pair of rose-pink pants in the Gents. Under a pile of forgotten coats and umbrellas lies a doll's tea set and a mournful-looking turkey. As he locks up, a telephone rings unaccountably in one of the lifts.

*Lust is rising*

# MEN AND SUPER MEN

*Men and Super Men* was written in 1972, when the Women's Movement was in its infancy in England and stinging the opposite sex with all the painful potency of young nettles. Reading *How to Stay Married* again and appreciating how much more than men, women were expected to do, one must admit that the reforms of the feminists were long overdue, and we all have reason to be grateful to them. What repelled was their stridency and virulence. Each day through my letter box thundered furious tomes: 'The Feminine Mystique', 'Women on Women', 'Women under Women', until, fed up, I decided to write a book in men's defence before the species disappeared altogether.

I found, however, as I progressed, how deep the antagonism between the sexes really is, and that, while I loved a few individual supermen very dearly, men as a sex drove me up the wall. I resented the fact that I couldn't live without them, that they hurt me emotionally, that I hated yet secretly enjoyed being bullied by them, that when they bother, they cook far better than women, that they generally prefer the company of their own sex and that only when they are too old to have a bat on the side, do they start looking for a bit on the side instead.

# Men and Super Men

Men, according to legend, want only one thing, are deceivers ever, are not interested in gossip, like a cosy armful, need two eggs, and seldom wash behind their ears.

They come in all shapes and sizes except for their organs, which according to all the sex books, are exactly the same size when erect and similarly capable of giving pleasure.

This is a book about men – at work and play, in bed and out of bed, in sickness and in stealth. It is also about Superman. Superman is a cross between Charles Atlas and Einstein. He keeps his figure by lifting dumb-blondes above his head before breakfast, and is sent to stud like Nijinsky at the age of twenty-one. The real hero of the book, however, is an individual called Sexual Norm.

Sexual Norm lives in the suburbs. He is married to a wife called Honor whom he has 2.8 times a week. Honor is sometimes satisfied. Norm thinks continually about other girls, but never does anything about them unless it is handed to him on a plate. He is riddled with guilt afterwards. He is doggy, pink faced, with sticking-out ears, nudging eyes, a road-up neck and a fixed avid grin. He blushes easily, laughs loudly, sweats profusely at the back of his neck, and wears dandruff blazers.

He always has a bath in the morning – just in case – and although he has never dared enter a strip club, if a girl makes him promise not to look he usually does. He is inclined to get out of hand at office parties. His lifelong ambition is to meet a nymphomaniac.

*The services*
*'I'm bi-sexual – I like Sailors and Soldiers.'*
Soldiers have yelping laughs and very short hair, tend to have very shiny buttons on their blazers, and never talk about women in the mess. They have broad shoulders and narrow outlooks. They are straightforward and uncomplicated. Occasionally they pounce on the wives of junior officers,

but the passes they are most interested in are forty-eight-hour ones. They wear mental battle dress in bed, and fatigues afterwards.

Soldiers tend to be overridden by their wives. Behind most famous soldiers you will find a very powerful dragon who has rammed her husband up the army list as a gunner might force the charge into the breech.

Sailors are always away or having it away. They have far-seeing blue eyes, and there are very few of them left now. Although they have a wife in every port, and two in Cape Town because they stop there twice, nice girls are supposed to love them. Twenty years ago they were considered very glamorous, now they are all trying to get out of the Service and failing to make it in Industry.

Sailors are always rabbiting on about their fine tradition, which as Churchill claimed consisted of nothing but Rum, Sodomy and the Lash.

There is absolutely nothing I can think of to say about Airmen at all.

## Scientists

Scientists have the shortest hair and the thickest spectacles. They wear white coats, talk in whispers, and have never read a book. When they meet a pretty girl they turn pink like litmus paper and have difficulty raising a retort stand. They are all described as brilliant to compensate for being on the non-smart side of the two cultures, and tend to be left wing.

They have a curiously cold analytical approach to women, and are too busy making explosions to have much fire in their bellies.

They are the first target for Rats' Lib.

## Stockbrokers

Stockbrokers play squash all the time – they squash themselves against women all the way to the City on the Tube, then play squash in the evening to keep their weight down. Later in the evening they play bridge, or go to cocktail parties and shout at girls with flicked up hair and bare foreheads. During the day they make up filthy stories and think about Bulls and Bears.

At weekends they make desperate attempts to be trendy, tripping off to the launderette in sweaters, paisley scarves flowing through a brass ring, their trousers held up under a spreading stomach by a stockbroker belt.

There are very few pretty girls working in the City, which is one of the places to go to if you want to hook a man.

*Television (See Fairies)*

Men in television brush their hair forwards, and wear white polo-necked sweaters, suede jackets, name-tag bracelets, and deaf aids. They spend their time gossiping – the television centre in Wood Lane is built in a circle to enable the gossip to travel more quickly – and in back-biting – you can recognise a television man once he takes his clothes off because his shoulders are covered in stab marks.

*Farmers*

Farmers have red faces, purple raw hands and straw in their turnups. They wear long jackets, frequently suffer from calf love, and wear gumboots to keep the sheep steady. They get up very early in the morning and assist in the sexual couplings of animals. In summer they get bitten by insects, and summon milkmaids and landgirls to come and see their itchings. Their houses smell of pigs.

'*But I* have *taken them off, darling.*'

Gentlemen farmers spend their time drinking at lunchtime, butchering wildlife, riding in point-to-points and swapping wives. At hunt balls, one glass of champagne turns them as scarlet as their coats, and soon every cordoned-off fourposter is heaving with occupants.

# STAGES OF MAN

*Now leaving the professions we move on to some of the stages of man.*

### Fiancés

Fiancés are out of date and not getting it. If pressed they will say: 'My fiancée and I have slept together all night in the same bed, but we haven't actually slept together.' Fiancées never give their fiancés their all – only about seven-eighths.

*'Oh for heaven's sake, Harriet . . .'*

Fiancés have soft curly hair, pink faces from permanently blushing at their predicament, starry eyes, and a mosaic of scarlet lipstick on their downy cheeks from having been embraced by so many new aunts-in-law.

They also manage to appear vacant and engaged at the same time by having a far away abstracted expression on their faces. People naturally assume they are dreaming of the moment when they and their betrothed will be one flesh; actually they are completely shell-shocked by all the talk about soft furnishing and wedding-present lists.

Caught off guard, they have a trapped expression.

As one fiancé said, just before his wedding: 'I feel as though I'm going into hospital for a major operation and all the anaesthetists are on strike.'

On their desks they have photographs of their fiancées given them by their fiancées, looking mistily soppy in pearls.

*Bachelors*

Bachelors begin at thirty-six. Up till this age they are regarded as single men. Most of them are very tidy, smell of mothballs, and have an obsessional old maid's fix about one of their ashtrays being moved an inch to the right. Because they are not married, or living with a woman, they don't feel the need to bath very often. Occasionally they have a shower after cricket and pinch their married friends' towels. They can be recognised by their white underpants. (Married men have pale blue or pink-streaked underpants, because one of their wife's scarves has run in the washing machine.)

Bachelors dread Christmas because they've got so many god-children to remember, and have a very high threshold of boredom through enduring so many grisly evenings with awful girls thrust on them by their married friends.

By way of revenge, they spend a great deal of time sponging off their married friends, turning up for lunch on Sunday and not leaving until the Epilogue, and knocking their disgusting pipes out on the carpet so that they get a chance to look up the wife's skirt when she bends over to sweep up the mess.

They also get wildly irritated by their friends' children, cast venomous glances at a two-year-old, and say: 'Isn't it time he went to prep school?'

A married man often rings up his bachelor friend and after a lot of

'So *pleased to beat you* . . .'

humming and hawing asks if he can borrow the flat to 'change in' that afternoon. When the bachelor gets home in the evening, he often finds various bits of female underclothing, and his bed has been far more tidily made than he left it that morning.

Married friends are also inclined to turn up with whisky bottles, having been locked out by their wives, and spend all night berating the matrimonial state.

It is hardly surprising that although a lot of bachelors would like to get married, they cannot bring themselves to take the plunge – like bathing on Christmas Day.

### Married men
*Let's Play Monogamy.*

Younger married men often have their trousers done up with a nappy pin, and black rings under their eyes, not from making love all night but from teething babies. Wedding rings are worn by men who marry foreign girls or who think other people might think they were not attractive enough to get anyone.

# ACTION

### The Date
Sexual Norm usually takes girls to his pub on the first date, because it's cheap, because his friends will be impressed if they see him with a girl, because there's someone else to talk to if he runs out of conversation. And he knows where the Gents is.

### The Pass
Sexual Norm by this time will be treading out the ground for the pass. We all know the tell-tale signs: the slowing down of a car on a lonely road, the hand edging along the back seat, the manoeuvring into an empty office in the lunch hour, the sidling up on the faded rose-patterned sofa accompanied by a murmur of: 'Are your flat mates really out?'

The girl if she fancies the man is wondering how much and how soon she can give in without feeling cheap.

Norm has been known to pounce from the arm of a girl's chair, and be rudely deposited on the floor when she leaps to her feet.

A lot of men reluctant to face a rebuff, make verbal passes.

'Can I come up for coffee?'

'Does your husband ever go away?'

'When are you next going up to London?' (This to a country wife.)

'I thought next time we lunched it might be fun if we had a leg of chicken and white wine at my flat.'

'The grass really isn't wet, you know.'

'Our bodies do talk the same language, don't they?' (This one usually on the dance floor.)

Or the more direct but less subtle approach: 'I fantastically want to fuck you.'

Sexual Norm, who realises the importance of being a good sexual conversationalist, sometimes says: 'Would you mind awfully if I kissed you, Jennifer?' and then lunges even if she says no.

It must be difficult being a man. If you pounce too soon everyone calls you a wolf, if you hold off too long everyone calls you a queer. If you make a pass of Khyber-like proportions at a girl who fancies you, she'll say you're wonderfully passionate, if you do exactly the same to a girl who doesn't, she'll complain you're mauling her.

# BED

*'Sex isn't the best thing in the world, or the worst thing in the world, but there's nothing else quite like it.'*

W. C. FIELDS

## Location

Once a man knows a girl's interested, where does he take her? It's all right if both of them have got a flat – but if they haven't there's all the hassle of packing a suitcase to spend a few hours at a hotel, or borrowing a friend's flat to 'change in', or waiting till nightfall to do it in the back of a car, or for summer to do it in the long grass.

Some women with marvellous figures like to be undressed before they leap into bed. And for this reason boys ought to take a course in undoing bras at prep-school. But with most people it's a race to get undressed and into bed before the other person has time to see their stretch marks or spindly calves.

Adulterers look in the cupboard or under the bed. Superman takes the telephone off the hook. He also has a fire extinguisher on the wall in case the girl bursts into flames.

Once in bed both parties breathe deeply and say 'A-a-a-ah' several times.

51

*'But Angus, I always thought one* never *wore anything underneath . . .'*

This is usually construed as ecstasy, but is in reality because of the coldness of the sheets and other people's hands.

People always try harder with new people. Sexual Norm will spend the next ten minutes worrying whether he's giving the girl enough sexual foreplay or fiveplay, and then grimly thinking about cricket or football to keep his mind off sex. He occasionally says *'Howzat'.*

The girl, remembering what the sex books told her about not lying back and being passive, will be frenziedly stroking Norm's neck, tickling his toes, kissing his navel, and putting on such a display of acrobatics that he has to try and think even harder about cricket or football.

Finally with the words 'there are no frigid women, only incompetent men' ringing in his ears, Norm starts threshing away like a sewing machine that's got out of hand.

*The bland leading the bland*
Then come the lies.

The man, crossing his fingers, will say: 'I don't do this very often, you know.'

The girl, crossing her legs, will say: 'Neither do I.'
He: 'I've only been to bed with, er, five women in my life.'
She (uncrossing her legs): 'This is the first affaire I've had since I've been married.'

He: 'I wouldn't dream of going to bed with a girl I didn't feel deeply about.'
(Feeling deeply under her dress.)

Several asterisks later he will say: 'That was wonderful, darling. Was it
wonderful for you, darling?'

### Norman's sexual conquest

Being susceptible, Norm falls in love about three times a year. At present
he is hooked on a well stacked typist in the office called Dental Floss.

His wife Honor can always detect the signs. She hears Norm yelling for
clean underpants in the morning. She then watches him putting deodorant
between his toes, cutting himself shaving because his hand is shaking with
excitement, shrieking with agony when his new French aftershave gets
into the cuts, leaving a snowfall of talcum powder on the bathroom floor,
and cutting his toe nails surreptitiously into the waste-paper basket instead
of in bed as usual.

He then polishes his shoes, changes his mind five times about what tie
he's going to wear, picks the only rose in the garden for his buttonhole,
spends hours combing his hair over his bald patch, and can be seen slipping
a toothbrush into his briefcase. Sometimes he cleans his teeth.

Honor notices he has also taken to carrying cigarettes and a lighter
although he doesn't smoke, and spending a lot of evenings at regimental
dinners or out with the boys and returning completely sober. When she
rides in the car she finds her seat belt has been let out to accommodate a
vast bust.

# ORGIES

### Orgies

*Two-way mirror on the wall, who is the barest of us all?*

Very few people will admit they've been to an orgy, and those who do say
they only watched and it was very boring.

'No central heating, and not enough to drink,' said a male friend of mine.
'And lots of bank managers in their underpants talking about cars. It was
rather like having a bath with one's Nanny. Not much fun and nowhere to
look.'

This is a far cry from one's fantasies of pulsating wall-to-wall couples,
people in sheets drinking wine out of goat-skins, girls coming out of pies
and crushing black grapes with very white teeth, and sophisticates with
jaded parrots watching through two-way mirrors.

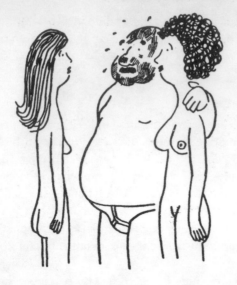

*'Er, yes, yes, Miss Weldon, the matter of your overdraft will be quite all right . . .'*

I'd be a dead loss at an orgy, for I'd be convinced everyone in the room was looking at my awful feet. In order to participate I'd have to drink myself silly, and as soon as I drink myself silly I feel sick and am a write-off sexually.

But I'm fascinated by the ethics of orgies. Do men come up to girls they want to couple with, tap them on the shoulder, and say shall we lie this one out? And to get everyone going, do they say: last man in works the gramophone? And do they have Ladies Excuse Mes? How awful too if no one asked you and you were a floor flower all evening.

If Superman goes to an orgy, of course, it's like the first day of the sales, with all the women trying to get at him. Sexual Norm however, although he is excited about loving dangerously, is worried about his wallet and the size of his member, and is still in his Y-fronts.

Dental Floss, who is looking skittish in Woolworths pearls, exhorts him to strip.

'You've got nothing to hide,' she says.

'That's what I'm afraid of,' says Norm.

Norm looks across at his wife Honor, who is still wearing her roll-on and talking about deepfreezes to another housewife. Norm decides he's really much better doing it with Honor. He wishes he was completely hairy up to his waist like a satyr, then it wouldn't show if he took his underpants off. It must have been easy for satyrs in the old days. He wishes he could go home.

Next day however he will regale his friends in the pub with a torrid account of the mountains of heaving flesh, adding: 'I really didn't know where to put myself.'

*'Come again?'*

# WOMEN AND SUPER WOMEN

Having written *Men and Super Men* I felt I must redress the balance two years later by writing *Women and Super Women*. Today I would probably be clobbered under the sex discrimination act. The book was serialised in the *Daily Mirror* because it made the then editor laugh. The female readers absolutely loathed the extracts printed, and sent me sacks of hate mail for mobbing up their sex.

Truly intended to amuse, in retrospect I suppose *Women and Super Women* is incredibly iconoclastic, but was supposed to be an antidote to all those appallingly earnest ladies, who never stopped grumbling about unpaid domestic servitude and male chauvinist piggery, and even banished boy children and male dogs from female communes.

In the following extracts we have included some female types and some female sexual adventures. Throughout the early seventies I established a reputation for being a sex-obsessed writer. In fairness, I think this was partly because I was writing at the height of permissive society, when the mini had given way to see-through shirts and topless dresses, and you could hardly go to a party as a couple without being accosted and asked to come upstairs by another couple. Multiple orgasms were *de rigueur* and Mary Whitehouse was carted off to hospital with writer's cramp.

# Women and Super Women

## THE AGES OF WOMEN

*Schoolgirls*

Schoolgirls write endless letters to schoolboys scented with Goya's Great Expectations, which progress from Dear to My Very Dear to Darling Darling Darling as the term passes. Status is entirely dependent on how many Valentines they get. A lot of wishbones are wasted on Paul Newman.

During the school term schoolgirls smoke like chimneys but don't inhale, smuggle in pornography and spend a good deal of time asking more sexually experienced pupils: 'What's it like, what's it really like?'

During the holidays they lie on the floor, play pop music too loudly for their parents' liking, and keep transistors under the bedclothes so they can listen to Capital Radio all night. A lot of time is spent reading beauty advice books about not squeezing blackheads and drinking P.L.J. Occasionally they make out lists of every part of their body, and launch heroic campaigns to make each part more beautiful.

Schoolgirls are supposed to be filled to the brim with girlish glee, but are actually permanently in despair because there is no possibility of Paul Newman or anyone else who looks like him ever loving them back. Meanwhile Paul Newman and thousands of men who look like him are having fantasies about nubile schoolgirls.

*Teenagers*

Teenagers have spots, puppy fat, immortal longings, sleep all day, and worry about kissing properly, whether they're exchanging too much saliva or going on too long, or whether they should be stroking the back of their boyfriend's neck as they do in films. When they first progress to French kissing all they can think of is how disgusting the underneath of men's tongues feels.

All teenagers live in jeans with mottoes embroidered all over them, which are evidently a great icebreaker: you read each other's private parts and suddenly you're friends. To quote from one teenage magazine:

'He had *Beauty is Truth* down one side of his jeans and *Abandon all hope ye* on the crutch and the sort of smile that labelled him a very real person.'

They change at least three times a day, and spend three hours on their faces before coming downstairs, in the hope that one of their father's friends will chat them up, or a group of workmen will whistle at them in the street. They also stuff Kleenex into their bras, giggle a lot, spend all their money on *Movie Magazine*, *Jackie* and pop records, and wonder why they can't marry Paul Newman. After all, Juliet was married at fourteen, wasn't she? Permanently Spock-marked, they believe the world owes them a living, and stay in jobs only three weeks.

Other occupations are slamming doors, having wild parties when their parents are away, smashing crockery from pre-menstrual tension and pinching their mothers' clothes.

'She's got a man, and she's past it, what does she need with clothes anyway?'

*Flatsharers*

You tend to see them most on Fridays, again with suitcases clutched in their hot little hands, as they surge towards bus stops in South Kensington and Knightsbridge, on their way to offices where most of them work as rather imperfect typists.

On the bus they will shout across to one another about 'Dominic and Gideon and those two perfectly super medical students we met skiing.'

Their suitcases, which block the cubby-hole under the stairs, contain a week's dirty washing for Mummy and a smart little dress in case there's a drinks party, or a smart long dress in case there's a hunt ball. Most of the weekend will be spent sleeping off the rigours of the week: a week of jousting for men, gossiping with other girls, rowing because Samantha hasn't cleaned the frying pan, and eating scant suppers off big knees in front of hired television sets.

These are the Guardswomen of SW3. London is the battleground and men are the prizes. Here in bathrooms festooned with drying bras and tights that drip like some Chinese torture, they will soothe their battered minds and bodies in tepid water from some rusty boiler that would put Heath Robinson to shame.

Here they will sleep in a bedroom not unlike the dorm at school. They have come to London because they've been told that is where the action is – most of them are a little bewildered to find they aren't having a more madly gay time.

Girls who share flats seldom have much in common except a desire to find a mate. They probably came together in the first place because two of them went to the same school, or their mothers did, and a third or fourth were needed to pay the rent.

Fed on a diet of *Woman's Own* and Barbara Carthorse, much of their time is spent reading their horoscopes or wishing on the New Moon: 'Oh find me a husband, a Prince Charming to whisk me away from this Squalor to St James, Spanish Place.'

Men visiting the flat are seldom allowed in the bedroom, not out of modesty, but because they would be so appalled by the mess: clothes everywhere, spilt make-up, a week's supply of coffee cups gathering dust under the bed. And yet from this squalor, elegant and beautiful girls will regularly issue forth for the cocktail party round.

Then there are those fiendish flat dinner parties, when the candles burn down and the ill-assorted guests, a farmer, a male model and a stock-broker, are forced to make stilted conversation until a revolting dinner that wouldn't disgrace the Borgias is served up three hours late.

But there are good moments: setting off for the fray in a shared taxi, which smells like a summer garden from everyone's scent, or those manic sessions at two o'clock in the morning when you all come back a bit tight from different outings and shriek about your experiences, until the old boot in the flat below starts tapping on the ceiling.

And it's somewhere to live even if the rent is high and the landlady's a nosy old bag, and you can always find a new flat or new flat-mates. For the Guardswomen of Chelsea have one aim in life, they're looking for a husband as hard as the landlady is looking for the rent.

*Wives*
*Wilt! Thou hast this woman for thy wedded wife.*
When a man asks if he can bring his wife, you can be sure she's a beauty or a battleaxe, he's either proud of her or too scared to leave her behind.

Super Woman is perfection as a wife, her house is always spotless, her husband's shirts laundered at home, 'because the laundry do them so badly'. Although she does a full-time job, she is able to give intimate little dinners for her husband's business clients once or twice a week, type out his reports, watch his calorie intake, rev up in gold lamé every night in bed, yet be up to cook his breakfast, and hand him his briefcase and umbrella as he sets out for work. All her girl friends detest her.

'My husband only has eyes for me,' she says smugly. Eyes maybe; presumably the sensible fellow keeps his member for someone else.

Super Woman is always flirting with her husband in front of other people. It looks bad: as Oscar Wilde says, rather like washing one's clean linen in public.

### Bachelor girls

*'A woman with fair opportunities and without a positive hump may marry whom she likes.'* THACKERAY

People always assume that bachelors are single by choice and spinsters because nobody asked them. It never enters their heads that poor bachelors might have worn the knees of their trousers out proposing to girls who rejected them or that a girl might deliberately stay unmarried because she didn't want to spend the rest of her life filling a man's stomach with food and washing his dirty shirts.

Invariably bachelor girls are referred to by their families as Poor Norma or Poor Honor, and one can understand why they go home so seldom, when their parents' eyes are so full of questions they daren't ask.

If a girl gets married too young, everyone assumes she's pregnant, or the marriage will break up in a few weeks, or she's such a rabbit she can't wait until she's older for regular sex. Between twenty and twenty-six is quite acceptable for a girl to be still single; after that parents get a bit shelf-conscious and start saying defensively: 'Jennifer hasn't got time to think of marriage, she's got this very important job at the Ministry – absolutely J.B.'s right-hand man.'

In a few years' time they will be hinting that J.B.'s relationship with their daughter isn't quite so platonic.

'I know if J.B. weren't quite so devoted to his children he and Jennifer . . .'

Then J.B. leaves his wife and elopes with a guardsman, which blows that one sky high.

An awareness of their parents' desire to get them married and the sight of all their girl friends with husbands and children often panics single women in their late 20s or early 30s into disastrous marriages. This is a vital time not to lose one's cool. It seems unfair, though, that so many women get divorced and remarried a number of times; and some of us don't get a chance at all.

When women get married over thirty they seldom wear white – it somehow doesn't seem fitting to flaunt one's lack of experience.

*Mother-in-law*
*'Behind every successful man, there's an astonished mother-in-law.'*
RICHARD NIXON

Princess Anne's got married, so they've got to make do with you.

The great mistake with a future mother-in-law is to assume she must be lovely to have produced anyone as lovely as 'him'. You roll up starry-eyed to meet her, forgetting that for her you're just the end of a string of girl friends, and she doesn't like your pedal pushers and sequinned shirt worn to impress his teenage sister, and your hips (because he likes you thin) aren't childbearing enough.

'She'll be extravagant,' she's probably thinking. 'Will she cook and mend and watch his weight, will she be the sort who rushes back to work the moment she has a baby?'

One of the troubles after marriage is that mothers-in-law only meet daughters-in-law when one of them is absolutely dead with exhaustion. When the mother-in-law comes to stay, the daughter-in-law sweats her guts out bulling up the house, trying to prove to her mother-in-law that she's keeping her son in the style to which he's accustomed. Then the mother-in-law arrives two hours early to find the house in chaos, the joint not in the oven and the children in their pyjamas.

Equally, when one goes to stay with one's mother-in-law she's absolutely knackered cleaning out spare bedrooms and cooking for five days ahead.

'I've run out of animals,' said my mother-in-law despairingly, wondering what on earth to feed my husband's sister and her family on after they'd been staying a week.

Don't be misled by the fact your husband bitches about his family. That's his privilege, and he won't be amused if you do the same yourself.


*The change of life*
*They're changing lives at Buckingham Palace.*

Men are always supposed to be the nicer sex, because they get on so much better together than women do, but I think it's a miracle any women are on speaking terms at all, as fifty per cent of the time one of them will be suffering from pre-menstrual tension.

As my housekeeper says, God was in a cranky mood when he made women, what with the curse, childbirth pains, post-natal gloom, pre-menstrual tension, all sorts of gynaecological capers, and finally the change of life as a last act, and not all that well written at that.

How old is she? people ask. About thirty-seven, comes the answer, and everyone nods knowingly, and mutters, The Change.

*'Maurice – I think I've started the change.'*

Must be hell, all those hot flushes like geysers in New Zealand, drenched sheets and going red as a radish. It's not much compensation either, the way women's magazines are always rabbiting on about not having to take the pill any more, and the joys of mature sex, and the quiet serenity of the older woman.

The mother's change of life often coincides with her daughter's adolescence, but the daughter invariably gets blamed for being difficult.

Women going through the change of life often pretend their daughters are older than they are so people will gasp, and say: 'You couldn't possibly have a daughter that age. I thought you were sisters.'

### Old ladies

Old ladies live with other older ladies whom they bully shamelessly, not because they need a companion, but a sparring partner.

Rich old ladies drench themselves in lavender water, and at Christmas their relations subject them to arselick and old lace in the hope of inheriting some cash.

Poverty-stricken old ladies have a frightful time, sitting with only one bar of the fire on, and buying dog scraps from the butcher for a dog they don't possess. They do have some compensations, they can travel free on buses, and if they live alone in Camden Town they are entitled to a free budgerigar.

The real poverty in fact is in ourselves. For not looking after them better.

### Working wives

Usually filled to the brim with resentment, encouraged by their mothers, who keep saying 'You must get so tired, darling, and why doesn't Norm ask for a rise?'

*'Dog's got in
again, Mum.'*

If a man leaves his wife and goes off with another woman and his wife is not working, society blames her for becoming a cabbage and getting bogged down with domesticity. If she is working they blame her for neglecting her husband and not providing him with hot dinners.

## WOMEN AND THEIR PASTIMES

*Housework*
*The call of the running tidier.*
*The glory that is elbow grease.*
Few tasks are more like the tortures of Sissy-fuss than housework, the clean being made dirty, the dirty clean. Houseproud ladies spend their lives ferreting out fluff from under beds, sponging fingerprints off their husbands, and moving ashtrays half a degree nor-nor-west. They also have Jay cloths permanently at the ready. All they think about in the Spring is cleaning, and when you hear them having intense discussions about fast coloureds and delicate whites they're talking about their washing machines not about sex.

Nowhere does Parkinson's Law operate so efficiently as in the house: mechanical gadgets don't cut down the time spent, they just mean you wash sweaters after you've worn them once instead of scraping the food blob off with your fingernail, and that you feel honour bound to make mayonnaise in the mixer rather than getting it out of a bottle.

Most housewives, Women's Lib tell us, work an eighty-hour week, and therefore get slightly irritated when people say:

'What do you do?'

'I'm a housewife.'

'What do you *do* with yourself all day?'

Or when their husbands say smugly 'Oh my wife doesn't work.'

Their status is consequently sustained by a spotless kitchen and by raising housework to an art form.

*'Get off, Roger –*
*the sheets were*
*changed this morning.'*

The whole scene is fraught with problems. On the one hand you read magazine articles warning you that the battle against decay is a denial of life, and that marriages break up because wives are always flapping dusters. Or that children's lives are very short, and how glad you'll be you let the washing-up pile up that Wednesday and spent all day making doll's clothes.

On the other hand you have vague worries, as you trip over a child's bicycle in the hall or look at your toy and nappy strewn kitchen, about the Greek love of order and beauty, and how men loathe muddle, and that behind every really successful man is a clockwork wife.

I think women do all that sighing and ferocious tidying and banging about of pans at weekends to show their husbands how hard they work and because they're panic-stricken that the place won't be tidy enough when the char turns up on Monday morning.

*Sex*

*'To make love without feeling a particle is sad work and sad and serious did I find it.'*

*'Everything's getting on top of me these days except Henry.'*

Hot on the trail of gourmet cooking comes gourmet sex. Today people start getting hang-ups if they don't have sex beautifully served up three times a day with a piece of parsley on top.

Honor wakes up on Sunday and wearily ticks off all the things that have to be done:

(1) Norman
(2) The children's breakfast
(3) The ironing
(4) The dog's breakfast
(5) Sunday lunch
(6) Norman

It amazes me how couples with young children ever make love at all. Thank God for *Catweazle* or *Doctor Who*, which at least gives you a clear childfree half hour. It should be re-christened family screwing time.

Honor, worried about hers and Norm's sex life and making heroic attempts to improve it, has been reading a book called *How to Improve your Man in Bed*, which tells her she must practise removing Norman's clothes 'without clumsiness or hold-ups and preferably with one hand'. But who does she practise on?

She is also told to acquire some sexy underclothes. She buys a garter suspender belt which slides down over her bottom the moment she puts it on and makes her new black stockings wrinkle. Another suggestion is to treat Norm to a strip show. She removes her bra as they're going to bed, and waves it round like a football rattle. Norm asks her if she's been at the gin.

Norm is even more worried when Honor, again acting on the advice of *How to Improve your Man in Bed*, moves in the builders to knock down the bedroom wall so they can have a bathroom adjacent to the bedroom, and 'not lose any sexual heat running down long cold passages'. The builders are shortly followed by the painters to re-decorate the bedroom in more intimate sexy colours. The bill is staggering, and there are more bills for Honor's school-girl outfit from Daniel Neals, a new double bed, and a huge looking-glass for the ceiling. Norm always believes if you take care of the penis, the pounds will take care of themselves.

Other hints on lovemaking include:

'Tying each other up.' (Norman feels Honor bound and then goes off to the pub.) 'Throw his pyjamas in the dustbin.' Norm is livid, his pyjamas were new, black with red piping, and what's he going to walk round in now when his mother-in-law comes to stay?

'Never tell him Jim was better. Get all dolled up for an evening and tell

*'Right – Catweazle, Treasure Island, Dr Who and then Golden Shot and not a sound for the next two hours.'*

him you've forgotten your pants.' (Norm is horrified and tells Honor to go upstairs and put them on again.)

'Offer to fellate him at odd moments of the day.' (She'll get a clip over the ear if it's during 'Match of the Day'.)

'Make the most of morning erections, but eat apples first to sweeten the breath.' (Poor Norman is woken from deep sleep by frenzied fiddling and scrunching, and grumbles he prefers his alarm clock.)

Honor gives up, throws *How to Improve your Man in Bed* in the dustbin with one hand and goes back to the missionary position once a week.

In Victorian times, women were disapproved of if they enjoyed sex; today they feel guilty if they don't want it all the time. Sex is often the loveliest thing in the world, but people shouldn't feel guilty about having too much or too little. And feeling you ought is just as oppressive as feeling you oughtn't.

*The date*

*'Is it one of my well looking days, child? Am I in face?'* GOLDSMITH

At last One Night Stan rings. Sexual Norma, who has been biting her nails for weeks, drops her voice three octaves and says Hello. Stan asks her out, she says she might be able to squeeze him in, what about Monday, Tuesday, Wednesday, Thursday or Friday? After she puts the telephone back her voice reverts to normal and she shrieks: 'He's rung, he's rung.'

She then goes out and buys a completely new set of clothes, including a new pair of jeans and a bra to look as though she's not wearing a bra.

On the day of the date, she spends three hours at the hairdressers. When a mirror is held up so she can see the back of her head, she mutters gosh, yes, marvellous. When she gets home she brushes it all out.

She then spends another three hours getting ready, rouging her navel, washing her ears and spraying scent onto her pulse spots, including the back of her knees.

The doorbell goes. She doesn't feel quite the million dollars she had hoped. A maddening piece of hair keeps sticking out at right angles, mascara has got into her eyes, her jeans, in spite of a 24 hour crash diet, are making her walk two inches off the ground, and even with layers and layers of Erace, a large spot on her nose is shining through like a lighthouse.

'Where shall we eat?' says One Night Stan when he arrives.

Sexual Norma can't think of anywhere except Claridges or Jo Lyons.

The next four hours are spent sipping cocktails, which go straight to Norma's head and other parts of her anatomy, dining by candlelight, dancing in a discothèque blacker than great Agrippa's inkwell, and groping in a taxi on the way back to Norma's flat.

Norma, who is feeling sick through too much drink, wonders if she asks Stan up whether she'll ever get rid of him.

'Would you like a nightcap?' she says timidly.

'Never wear them,' says Stan, pushing his way resolutely into the flat.

They then express a mutual interest in gramophone records, and Norma plays a record which she likes because she knows it, but Stan doesn't like because he doesn't know it. One really shouldn't on the first date, says Norma to herself rushing into the bathroom, cleaning her teeth, drenching her bosom in 100 per cent proof, and putting an intellectual French novel by the bed instead of Barbara Carthorse.

Back in the drawing room, Stan puts his hand over Norma's, she puts her other hand over his, he puts his other hand over hers, Norma pulls out her bottom hand to put over his, and this goes on faster and faster until they are slapping each other's hands.

In the bedroom Stan starts to undress her, Norma complies – anything to get out of these crotch-murdering jeans.

Norma doesn't enjoy much of what follows; she tries to remember what *The Sensuous Woman* told her, but all she feels is her mother standing at the end of the bed waving an admonishing finger.

Afterwards she wonders how long she has to lie in simulated ecstasy before charging off to the loo.

When she returns One Night Stan is dressed and about to disappear into the night. For the first time that evening, Norma feels she'll mind very much if she doesn't see him again, and shouts after him, 'You will ring me, won't you?'

Of course, he doesn't. Norma's flatmates sympathise with her, but in private they are delighted. They know men. It's all champagne and fairy tales until they've had their all, then you can't see them for dust.

*Love*
*'I said to Heart, "how goes it?" Heart replied:*
*"Right as a Ribstone Pippin!" But it lied.'* HILAIRE BELLOC

From smug middle age, it is very easy to be a little patronising about the agonies of being in love. Often when waiting to hear whether something I've written is going to be accepted, I recapture all the ghastly twitchy uncertainty of a life ruled by the telephone. You know the sort of thing.

He said he'd ring in the morning and now it's five past one, perhaps he's cooling off. And three other men have rung and had their heads bitten off for not being him. And I've just had a cold bath in case I might not hear the telephone over the sound of the geyser. And just rung up the engineer for the third time to see if the telephone's working. Why the hell can't he telephone me so I can stop thinking about him?

Conversely, the moment you go off a man he's never off the bloody blower making a nuisance of himself.

Then there's the agonising rat race of getting men to marry you. As a girl friend of mine screamed at her boy friend the other day: 'You haven't even given me a ring that I can give back to you.' Or another girl I know who was walking her boy friend purposefully past a jeweller's window, when he paused suddenly and peered inside, his eyes lighting on a large and beautiful ring.

'I like that,' he said gazing into her eyes, 'don't you, darling? Do you think we can afford it?'

'Oh, yes, darling,' she said, trying to control her ecstasy.

He then went into the shop – and bought the ring for himself.

Then an affair breaks up, and one has to cope with one's friends in a state of uncontrollable misery.

'You'll get over it,' you say feebly as though the sodden lump on the sofa was about to undertake the Olympic high jump.

One girl I remember going on and on all evening about how miserable she was, like a rat in a trap: 'I love him,' I heard her saying dramatically to my husband, 'I love him *per se.*'

'Who the hell's Percy,' said my husband irritably, 'I thought you were in love with someone called Paul.'

*Adultery*
*One crowded hour of glorious wife is worth an age without a name.*
*'For my part, when all's said and done I'd still rather be cuckolded than*
*dead.'* VOLTAIRE

## *All work and no play makes Jack adulterous*

I'd prefer not to know, says the reasonable husband. I'll kill you if you look at another man, says the chauvinist pig. The cuckolds in between – the majority – simply don't believe it.

Helen of Troy – a well known adulteress – allowed her husband Menelaus to wine and dine Paris for nine days. Under Menelaus' nose, Paris wrote 'I love you' in wine on the table, seized Helen's cup and drank from the same part of it as she did, making sheep's eyes at her, and generally behaving in a very adolescent way. The moment Menelaus was out of the house, Helen pushed off with Paris, abandoning her nine-year-old daughter, who might have grown into competition later, but taking her baby son, several of the palace treasures, gold to the value of five talents and five of the serving maids. Last week, Honor's friend Diana went off with the dentist and the furniture. So times haven't changed.

Adulteresses of today always tell their husband they've been shopping in Knightsbridge when he comes home in the evening and enquires why they weren't in when he rang.

'I tried on lots of things,' they say airily, 'but I couldn't find anything that fitted.'

Adulteresses get home very late and flustered, and have to placate the *au pair* with bunches of flowers. *Au pairs* often have bedrooms like funeral parlours.

Adulteresses gaze at their lovers for hours in parked cars, find they can't book into hotels together unless they've got luggage, and out of opening hours spend a lot of time sitting in residence lounges drinking black coffee and saying No to trolleys of cakes. Even in Paris, hotels with three stars pretend to be puritanical to force the adulterer into booking a second room.

Honor is not very good at being unfaithful to Norm. One day she planned to leave the children with a friend, who suddenly found she couldn't take them. Honor then rang up her lover to cancel lunch and found he had booked a table in another name, and there were five Browns and four Smiths with booked tables.

When she arranges a home fixture, the window-cleaner keeps turning up and grinning at every window.

Women when they start an affair improve enormously in looks; their eyes shine, and their coat gleams as though they've just taken a course of Bob Martins.

'You should have seen her before I moved in,' says the lover complacently.

Adultery has become very fashionable these days. It's now called extra-marital sex, and is regarded as a form of therapy: she'll perk up if she has a stint in another man's bed. Jealousy is very out of fashion, but there are an awful lot of bitten nails about.

# PART TWO

# The Rich Man
# In His Castle
# The Poor Man
# At His Gate

# CLASS

I have a great affection for my book *Class*, simply because it got us out of a terrible hole. Started in 1976, it took three years to write. At the time, everyone kept insisting class barriers were breaking down and we were living in a classless society, and were so shocked that I should be trying to disprove this, you would have thought I'd embarked on a treatise on coprophilia.

I toiled on however, until in November 1978 the *Sunday Times* went on strike for a year, and Leo and I found we had run out of money. We hadn't got enough to buy our children Christmas presents, and for months on end lived on bread and jam, and – almost worst – couldn't afford to buy drink. We left one bank because they bounced my son's first term's school fees, and joined another who told us we must sell our beloved Putney house to realise some capital. Somehow we soldiered on. *Class* was written mostly in the potting shed at the bottom of the garden to fool creditors I wasn't in.

Then in August, two months before the book was due to be published, my then agent, George Greenfield, rang me up:

'Jilly darling, are you sitting down? The *Daily Mail* have offered £37,000 to serialise the book.'

I burst into tears of joy, our house and we were safe. The subsequent dazzling inventive serialisation by the *Daily Mail*, and frantic hard work by the Methuen sales reps, who rushed round the country with car boots crammed with copies of the book, kept *Class* on the best-seller list for twenty weeks.

We had a lovely sausage and mash party to launch the book, where everyone dressed as the class above or below the one they thought they belonged to. Dear Norman St John Stevas – now The Lord St John of Fawsley – turned up in a tiara. A lot of people were furious when the book came out and accused me of being horribly snobbish.

The Duke of Edinburgh even accosted me at a party, saying:

'Rubbish, the class system doesn't exist any more.'

'That's odd,' I said politely, 'because according to the census, which lists people's social class according to their occupation, your daughter, Princess Anne, as a three-day eventer, is the same class III (non-manual) as a game-keeper.'

'Rubbish,' thundered the Duke. 'Keepers are working-class.'

Today, however, the book reads almost as a period piece because in 1979, when it was published, everything changed. Mrs Thatcher became Prime Minister, and suddenly the English became obsessed with making money, buying their own houses, and rising socially. The Yuppie was born. My next tragi-comedy will probably be called *Mortgage d'Arthur*.

As a key to *Class*, I divided the classes into six different types ranging from Harry Stow-Crat, the aristocrat, to the working-class man, Mr Definitely-Disgusting.

Descriptions of them, their families and their behaviour patterns are found at the beginning of this extract. Also included are chapters on the various classes' attitudes to children, work, sex, houses, gardens, food and death. The book is not meant to be taken seriously. Its sole purpose was to entertain.

# Class

## DRAMATIS PERSONAE

The people you will meet in this book are:

HARRY STOW-CRAT, a member of the aristocracy
CAROLINE STOW-CRAT, his wife
GEORGIE STOW-CRAT, his son
FIONA STOW-CRAT, his daughter
and numerous other children, both regularly and irregulary conceived
SNIPE, a black Labrador

GIDEON UPWARD, a member of the upper middle classes
SAMANTHA UPWARD, his wife
ZACHARIAS UPWARD, his son
THALIA UPWARD, his daughter
COLONEL UPWARD, Gideon's father
MRS UPWARD, Gideon's mother

HOWARD WEYBRIDGE, a member of the middle middle classes
EILEEN WEYBRIDGE, his wife

BRYAN TEALE, a member of the lower middle classes
JEN TEALE, his wife
WAYNE TEALE, his son
CHRISTINE TEALE, his daughter

MR DEFINITELY-DISGUSTING, a member of the working classes
MRS DEFINITELY-DISGUSTING, his wife
DIVE DEFINITELY-DISGUSTING, his son
SHARON DEFINITELY-DISGUSTING, his daughter
and numerous other children

MR NOUVEAU-RICHARDS, a millionaire

MRS NOUVEAU-RICHARDS, his wife
JISON NOUVEAU-RICHARDS, his son
TRACEY-DIANE NOUVEAU-RICHARDS, his daughter

# THE CLASSES

*The aristocracy*
*All the world loves a titled person*

According to sociologists the aristocracy is such a tiny minority – about 0.2% of the population – as to be statistically negligible. The ones who do not work or who run their own estates are not even listed in the Census. They are like the scattering of herbs and garlic on top of a bowl of dripping, or more poetically, like water lilies that float, beautiful and, some would say, useless, on the surface of a pond. Being a lord, of course, doesn't make you an aristocrat. Only about half the nobility are aristocracy, the rest being life peers, and only about a third of the aristocracy are ennobled, the rest being families of younger sons, or country squires living in manor houses, some of whom have had money and influence for far longer and can trace their families much further back than many a Duke or Earl.

A good example of this is Mrs James, the aristocrat in Pamela Hansford Johnson's novel *The Unspeakable Skipton*. Mrs James had an air of undefinable authority and spoke in a direct and barking shorthand:

'Feel sorry for poor Alf Dorset, son's marrying some girl who sings on the wireless.' Unbound by convention, she made all her own rules, making a point of going everywhere out of season.

'That's why seasons are inevitably such a flop,' says one of the other characters, 'because if they're out of season they're wrong anyway, and if they're in season, Mrs James had buzzed off to Gozo or somewhere extraordinary.'

As so many of the aristocracy don't have titles they regard Burke's, which covers the landed gentry as well as the peerage, a far more important source book than Debrett's. One peer told his secretary she must get up-to-date copies of Burke's 'so you'll know all the people I'm talking about'. The point about the aristocracy is that they all know each other.

Traditionally, as will be shown in later chapters, the aristocracy didn't work for their living and, although many of them have jobs today, they find difficulty in applying the same dedication to their work as the middle classes.

They used, of course, to be terribly rich. At the turn of the century, if you were asked to stay at Woburn one chauffeur and a footman would take you as far as Hendon, where another chauffeur and a footman would be waiting to take you to Woburn. As a gentleman never travelled with his luggage, another two cars were needed to carry that. So it meant two chauffeurs and two footmen to get you and your luggage as far as Hendon, and two more chauffeurs and footmen to take you to Woburn – eight men to transport one guest for heaven knows how large a house party, down to the country. The Marquess of Hertford had a house in Wales he'd never been to, but where, every night, a huge dinner was cooked by a fleet of servants in case he did turn up.

The Westminsters today own 300 acres in Belgravia and Oxford Street, 12,000 acres around Eaton, 14,000 acres in North Wales, 1,000 acres in Kent, 400 acres in Shropshire, 800 acres in New South Wales, 1,000 acres in British Columbia, Hawaii and Australia. The present Duke inherited £16 million on his 21st birthday. Hardly the bread line.

Today, as a result of death duties and capital transfer tax, most aristocrats are desperately poor in comparison with their grandfathers and are reduced to renting off wings as apartments, selling paintings, turning their gardens into zoos and amusement parks, and letting the public see over their houses. Anyone who has experienced the nightmare of showing a handful of people over their house when they put it up for sale will understand the horror of having a million visitors a year peering into every nook and cranny.

Although they have considerable influence in the Tory party, the aristocracy no longer run the country as they did in the eighteenth and nineteenth centuries. But if their privileges have been eroded, their responsibilities remain the same: responsibilities to the tenants, to the community (the good aristocrat always has a strong sense of public duty) and to the house he lives in, often so beautiful as to be a national monument, but to the upkeep of which the nation pays no contribution.

One of the characteristics of the aristocrat is the extreme sentiment he feels towards his house and his inheritance. His wife is expected to feel the same. When the Marchioness of Tavistock recently expressed her boredom at running Woburn her father-in-law's sharp reaction was quoted in the *Daily Mail*:

'If you marry some guy with a title, you have a duty and a responsibility to carry on what his ancestors did in the past. She was perfectly aware of what she was getting into. Trouble is she's an only child.'

Because they believe in their inheritance, the upper classes set enormous store by keeping things in the family. They don't buy their houses like the middle classes, they inherit them. When the house gets too big for a grandfather and grandmother, they might move into a smaller house on the estate, to make way for their eldest son, but they leave all the furniture behind, as their ancestors have for generations. One definition of the middle classes is the sort of people who have to buy their own silver.

Because the aristocracy were so anxious to preserve their inheritance, they tended only to marry their own kind. The middle classes married for love. The upper classes married to preserve their rank. All twenty-six Dukes are, at present, related to one another. And as long as rank was protected, and money obtained in sufficient quantities to support that rank, infidelity after marriage was taken for granted, as Vita Sackville-West points out in her novel *The Edwardians*:

'A painter,' screamed the Duchess, 'what painter? Sylvia Roehampton's daughter to marry a painter? But of course she won't. You marry Tony Wexford, and we'll see what can be done about the painter afterwards.'

As they weren't expected to be faithful, unlike the middle classes they didn't feel guilty if they wandered, which explains the over-active libido of the aristocrat. He expected to exercise *droit de seigneur* over his tenants but he also saw himself as a Knight Errant like Don Quixote living in a world of romantic adventure. 'When your ancestors have been fighting battles and seducing women for thousands of years,' said one German nobleman, 'it's terribly difficult to settle down to one wife and an office job.'

As a result of all this infidelity a high proportion of the aristocracy is irregularly conceived, but, as they tend to sleep with each other, they're still pretty dotty with inbreeding. When my uncle was Lord Spencer's agent, my aunt said she met all the local aristocracy, many of them as mad as hatters. When they talked about one of their friends 'coming out', you never knew if they were doing the season, or being discharged from a loony bin.

Colossal self-confidence is perhaps the hallmark of the aristocrat. Like the chevalier he goes through life unafraid; he doesn't question his motives or feel guilty about his actions. When I went shooting in Northumberland last summer I noticed a beautiful blond young man in a red sweater at the next butt. Why didn't he have to wear green camouflage like the rest of us, I asked.

'Because he's a duke's son,' said my host. 'He can do what he likes.'

Not answerable to other people, the aristocrat is often unimaginative, spoilt, easily irritated and doesn't flinch from showing it. If he wants to eat his peas with his knife he does so.

'Dear Kate,' said Henry V, 'you and I cannot be confined within the weak list of a country's fashion; we are the makers of manners, Kate; and the liberty that follows our places stops the mouth of all find-faults.'

As the makers of manners, many of the aristocracy, while feeling they have a duty towards the community as Sheriffs and Lord-Lieutenants, are indifferent to public opinion.

'One doesn't care what the press say,' said the Marquess of Anglesey at a dinner party. 'One's friends know what one's like and that's all that matters.' The only thing he minded, he went on, was that the National Trust film on television had said he was very rich. The hostess then asked him if he'd like moussaka or cold turkey.

'I'd like both,' he said.

Not caring a stuff what people think also leads to a rich vein of eccentricity: the Marquess of Londonderry throwing soup at a fly that was irritating him in a restaurant, and Sir Anthony Eden's father hurling a barometer out of the window into the pouring rain, yelling, 'See for yourself, you bloody thing.'

Or there was the imperious peer who, when he missed a train, ordered the station-master to get him another one.

Professor Ross has said that above a certain level all U people are equal. With respect, I think few upper-class people would agree with him. The ancient aristocracy consider it very vulgar to have been founded after the Tudors, which puts most of our present Dukes beyond the pale. In fact, in the nineteenth century many of them were so worried about the comparative youthfulness of their families that they employed genealogists to try and trace their ancestry back to the Conqueror.

When Oliver Lyttelton was made Viscount Chandos, his wife Lady Moira, who was the daughter of the 10th Duke of Leeds, was furious at becoming Lady Chandos, and having ostensibly to drop rank. Oliver Lyttelton was evidently so thrilled to be ennobled that he went round putting coronets on everything, including books of matches. Brian Masters in his book *The Duke* tells a story of the Duchesses of Buccleuch and Westminster sidling through a door together in their determination not to cede precedence.

Between aristocrats and other classes there is certainly a barrier of rank. My mother and father used to live near Hampton Court Palace, where widows of distinguished men, some of them aristocrats, have apartments.

My mother met a peer's widow at a drinks party and they got on so well that my mother wrote to her next day asking her to dine. Back came a letter of acceptance but with a PS: 'I hope you don't mind my pointing out, Elaine dear, that the Palace should be the first to issue invitations.'

Brian Masters thinks this obsession with rank probably had something to do with boredom. Without a career, the aristocrat had to fill his days. He was not a great intellectual: Jane Austen's Sir Walter Elliot, whose reading consisted of his own entry in The Baronetage, is fairly near the mark. He

*Harry Stow-Crat,*
*Caroline and Snipe*

preferred more exciting entertainment, hence his addiction to blood sports and to gambling. I shall never forget watching an aristocrat and a television newsreader playing backgammon one evening. The newsreader's wife, who was ravishingly beautiful and bored with the lack of attention, suddenly came in with no clothes on and danced round and round them. Neither of them took any notice.

The aristocrat, when he wants to, has very good manners. The Scottish upper classes in particular have that shell-shocked look that probably comes from banging their heads on low beams leaping to their feet whenever a woman comes into the room. Aristocrats are also deeply male chauvinist, and although you get left-wing extremists like Lord Weymouth, who sends his children to a comprehensive school and has revolutionary ideas, on the whole they tend to be reactionary.

While writing this book I found that there were very much two strands in the character of the aristocrat: first the wild, delinquent, arrogant, capricious, rather more glamorous strand; and second the stuffy, 'county', public-spirited, but publicity-shy strand, epitomised by the old baronet whose family were described 'as old as the hills and infinitely more respectable'.

Or, as a small boy writing in my son's school magazine pointed out: 'Gentlemen are of two types: the nose-uppish and the secluded.'

In order to write this book I have dealt in archetypes. The aristocracy and upper classes are represented by The Hon HARRY STOW-CRAT. Son of the sixth Baron Egliston, educated at Eton, he served in the Coldstream Guards. He now runs his diminishing estate, selling the odd Van Dyck to make ends meet, but does more or less what he pleases. He lives in a large decaying house in the North Riding of Yorkshire and has a flat in Chelsea. He has a long-suffering wife, CAROLINE, who does a great deal for charity, an eldest son, GEORGIE, a daughter called FIONA, and several other children. He has numerous mistresses, but none to whom he is as devoted as to his black labrador, SNIPE. He has had many moments of frustration and boredom in his life, but never any of self-doubt.

*The middle classes*
*'Would you come round the world next year in the France with me? I got a letter from Gerry Wellesley on a cruise saying he'd never met middle-class people before, and they are quite different from us. Isn't he awful?'* NANCY MITFORD

The middle classes are in fact *quite* different – being riddled with self-doubt, which is hardly surprising after all the flak they've received over the years. The upper classes despised them for their preoccupation with money, and because they suspected it was middle-class malcontents rather than the rabble who had plotted and set alight the French Revolution. 'How beastly the bourgeois is,' mocked the working-class Lawrence, and in fact *épater le bourgeois* has always been a favourite sport of both high and low. Marx, of course, divided society into two classes – the splendid workers, and the wicked bourgeoisie who owned the means of production. Even members of their own class, like Hilaire Belloc, attack them:

> *The people in between*
> *Looked underdone and harassed,*
> *And out of place and mean,*
> *And horribly embarrassed.*

And they have even been blamed for the evils of the class system. It is the middle classes, wrote one sociologist, with their passion for order and reason, who have sought to impose a kind of stratification on what is in fact an eternally malleable and bubbling class system. Which is rubbish because, as we have already seen, the aristocracy is just as obsessed with rank.

Occasionally they have their defenders. 'I come from the middle classes,' said Neville Chamberlain, 'and I am proud of the ability, the shrewdness, the industry and providence, the thrift by which they are distinguished.'

In a way the middle classes seem to suffer as the middle child does. Everyone makes a huge fuss over the firstborn and everyone pets and coddles the baby (who, like the working classes, is shored up by the great feather bed of the welfare state), but the child in the middle gets the most opprobrium, is often left to fend for itself and is ganged up on by the other two. It is doubly significant that in the Civil War, the rabble joined up with the King against the Puritan middle classes. For if Marx was the champion of the working classes, Calvin was the prophet of the middle classes. They believed implicitly in the Puritan Ethic, in the cultivation of such virtues as diligence, frugality, propriety and fidelity. Work to keep sin at bay, feel guilty if you slack. Shame is a bourgeois notion.

Although there is a world of difference between the top of the middle classes and the bottom, between the great merchant banker and the small shopkeeper, they are united in their desire to get on, not just to survive.

*The Upwards*

Unlike the upper classes and the working classes they think careers are
important. They start little businesses, they work to pass exams after they
leave school, they believe in the law of the jungle and not the Welfare State.
If you get on in life, good luck to you.

For this reason they believed in the importance of education long before
the other classes. They believed in deferred satisfaction. They saved in
order to send their children to private schools, or to buy their own houses.
If the upper classes handed on estates to their children, the middle classes
handed on small businesses. To the working classes the most important
criterion of middle-class membership after money or income is owning a
small business or being self-employed.

At the moment they are under increasing pressure, as the working classes get richer and more powerful. One of the great divides between the middle and lower classes used to be that the former used his brain and the latter his hands. Today, however, the miner and the car worker with their free housing and free education have far more spending money than a newly qualified doctor or barrister, and certainly than a policeman or a major in the army. According to my ex-bank manager, the middle classes are having increasing difficulty making ends meet. In 1976, they rather than the working classes became the chief candidates for the pawnbroker, bringing in watches, wedding rings, golf clubs, and binoculars.

Although they don't 'know everyone' like the upper classes, the upper-middles and many of the middles, having been to boarding school, have a much wider circle of friends than the working classes. They are able to keep in touch with them by telephone, or by their ability to write letters. Many of them also have a spare room where friends can come and stay.

They therefore tend to entertain 'outsiders' much more than the working classes, and don't need to depend on their immediate neighbours for help or for their identity. They can afford to keep themselves to themselves. Aloofness, reserve and a certain self-righteousness are also middle-class qualities.

To illustrate the three main strands of the middle classes we again fall into archetypes, with GIDEON and SAMANTHA UPWARD as the upper-middle-class couple, HOWARD and EILEEN WEYBRIDGE as the middle-middles and BRYAN and JEN TEALE as the lower-middles.

### Gideon and Samantha upward – The Merrytocracy

The upper-middle classes are the most intelligent and highly educated of all the classes, and therefore the silliest and the most receptive to every new trend: radical chic, health foods, ethnic clothes, bra-lessness, gifted children, *cuisine minceur*. Gideon Upward gave his mother-in-law a garlic crusher for Christmas. The upper-middles tend to read the *Guardian* and are proud of their liberal and enlightened attitudes. They are also the most role-reversed of the classes: Gideon does a great deal of cooking and housework: Samantha longs to be a good mother and have an 'int'risting job' at the same time. To save petrol she rides round on a sit-up-and-beg bicycle, with wholemeal bread in the front basket and a bawling child in the back. Sometimes her long dirndl skirt catches in the pedals. She has a second in history and a fourth in life.

Gideon and Samantha both went to 'good' schools, Gideon probably to Winchester or to Sherborne. He might be an architect or work in the City. He wears a signet ring with a crest on the little finger of his left hand, in an attempt to proclaim near aristocratic status, just as the middle-middles wear an old school tie to show they've been to boarding school, the lower-middles give their house a name instead of a number to prove it isn't council and the working classes bring back plastic bulls from Majorca to show they've travelled.

Gideon and Samantha have two children called Zacharias and Thalia, who they might start off sending to a state school, and trying not to wince at the first 'pardon', but would be more likely to send to a private school. They love their English setter, Blucher, and feel frightfully guilty about loving it almost more than their children. Harry Stow-Crat would have no such scruples. Gideon plays tennis and rugger at a club, but he wouldn't use the club to make friends, and he and Samantha wouldn't go near the Country Club which, to them, reeks of suburbia. They prefer to entertain in their own house, which is large and Victorian, and being restored to its original state rather faster than they'd like. Samantha is into good works with a slightly self-interested motive: pollution, conservation, the PTA.

As they can't be the most upper class in the land, Samantha is determined that they shall be the most 'cultured'. She and Gideon go to the theatre, the ballet and the movies, as they rather self-consciously call the cinema, and try and read at least two books a week.

In the last fifteen years, the upper-middles have aimed at a standard of living they can't afford, taking on many of the pastimes of the upper classes. Gideon goes shooting quite often; they have two cars, which are falling to pieces, and for which they have to pay a fortune every time they take their MOT; they used to have a country cottage, holidays abroad, and a boat. Now they have two children at boarding school. Since the advent of the permissive society Gideon is playing at adultery like Harry Stow-Crat. As a result he spends a fortune on lunches, and another fortune on guilt presents for Samantha afterwards. They are both so worried about trying to make ends meet, they're drinking themselves absolutely silly – hence the sub-title 'The Merrytocracy'.

Virginia Woolf once wrote an unfinished novel about an upper-middle-class family called the Pargeters. 'Parget' is an English dialect word meaning to smooth over cracks in plastered surfaces: the Pargeters gloss over the deep sexual and emotional fissures of life. In the same way Samantha doesn't particularly like her mother-in-law, or several of her neighbours; but she tries to get on with them because she feels guilty about her dislike. In the same way she feels guilty about telling someone she employs that they are not doing the job properly. Caroline Stow-Crat would never have that problem. If she hired a gardener even for two hours, she wouldn't flaunt him as a status symbol, she'd keep quiet about him, because she feels it's more creative to do the garden herself.

She and Gideon call each other 'darling' rather than 'dear', and try to remember to say 'orf'. Gideon's parents, Colonel and Mrs Upward, living on a rapidly dwindling fixed income, are much more thrifty than Samantha and Gideon. As they're not drinking themselves silly, they don't smash everything and still have the same glasses and china as they did when they were married.

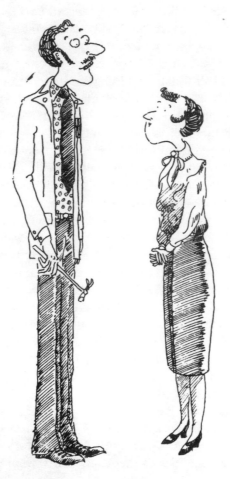

*Bryan and Jen Teale*

### Howard and Eileen Weybridge – the middle-middles

Howard Weybridge lives in Surrey or some smart dormitory town. He works as an accountant, stockbroker, surveyor or higher technician. He probably went to a minor public school or a grammar school. He never misses the nine o'clock news and says 'Cheerio'. He wears paisley scarves with scarf rings and has no bottoms to his spectacles. He calls his wife, Eileen, 'dear' and when you ask him how he is says, 'Very fit, thank you.' He is very straight and very patriotic, his haw-haw voice is a synthetic approximation to the uppers; he talks about 'Ham-shar'. His children join the young *Con*-servatives and the tennis club to meet people. He buys a modern house and ages it up. It has a big garden with a perfect lawn and lots of shrubs. He despises anyone who hasn't been to 'public school', and often goes into local government or politics for social advancement. He is a first-generation pony buyer, and would also use the Pony Club to meet the right sort of people. Eileen shops at Bentalls and thinks the upper-middles are terribly scruffy. They are both keen golfers and pull strings to get their road made private. Their favourite radio programmes are *Any Answers*, *These You Have Loved* and *Disgusted Tunbridge Wells*. They are much smugger than the upper-middles.

Howard Weybridge's father hasn't a bill in the world and is on the golf committee. He found bridge to be one of the most wonderful things in life; it's a very easy way of entertaining. He has a sneaking liking for Enoch Powell: 'We should have stopped the sambos coming here in the first place.'

### Bryan and Jen Teale – the lower-middles

The Teales are probably the most pushy, the most frugal and the most respectable of all the classes, because they are so anxious to escape from the working class. The successful ones iron out their accents and become middle like Mr Heath and Mrs Thatcher. The rest stay put as bank and insurance clerks, door-to-door salesmen, toast-masters, lower management, police sergeants and sergeant-majors. In the old days the lower-middles rose with the small business or the little shop, but the rise in rates, social security benefits and postage has scuppered all that.

The lower-middles never had any servants, but as they are obsessed with cleanliness, and like everything nice, they buy a small modern house and fill it with modern units which are easy to keep clean. Jen and Bryan have two children, Wayne and Christine, and a very clean car.

As Jen and Bryan didn't go to boarding school, didn't make friends outside the district, and don't mix with the street, they have very few

*The Weybridges*

friends and keep themselves to themselves. They tend to be very inner-directed, doing everything together, decorating the house, furnishing the car, and coaching and playing football with the children. Jen reads knitting patterns, *Woman's Own* and *Reader's Digest* condensed books. To avoid any working-class stigma she puts up defensive barriers – privet hedges, net curtains – talks in a 'refained' accent, raising her little finger when she drinks. Her aim is to be dainty and wear six pairs of knickers. She admires Mary Whitehouse enormously, disapproves of long hair and puts money in the Woolwich every week. She sees herself as the 'Woolwich girl'. The Teales don't entertain much, only Bryan's colleagues who might be useful, and occasionally Bryan's boss.

## The working classes

One of the great class divides has always been 'them' and 'us' which, as a result of the egalitarian, working-class-is-beautiful revolution of the 'sixties, and early 'seventies, has polarised into the Guilty and the Cross. On the one side are the middle and upper classes, feeling guilty and riddled with social concern, although they often earn far less money than the workers, and on the other are the working classes who, having been totally brain-washed by television and images of the good life, feel cross because they aren't getting a big enough slice of the cake.

In a time of economic prosperity everyone tends to do well. Wages rise; the middle classes can afford a new car, or central heating; the working-class man buys a fridge for the missus. Man's envy and rivalry is turned towards his neighbour – keeping up with the Joneses – rather than towards the classes above and below. But in times of economic stress, when people suddenly can't get the things they want and prices and the cost of living outstrip wages, they start turning their envy against other classes. Antagonism against a neighbour feathering his nest tends to be replaced by an awareness of class inequalities.

In a time of economic security, society therefore tends to look fairly cohesive, which is probably why in the early 'seventies a lot of people genuinely believed that class barriers had finally broken down; but, as the decade advanced, the working-class people who'd bought their own houses and were up to their necks in mortgage and hire-purchase payments suddenly found they couldn't keep up. Their expectations had been raised, and now their security was being threatened by the additional possibility of mass unemployment. This discontent, fanned by the militants, resulted in the rash of strikes in the winter of 1978/79.

Although the middle classes often think of the working-class man as earning huge sums on overtime, the rewards of his job in fact are much less. The manual worker seldom has job satisfaction or a proper pension; he doesn't have any fringe benefits such as a car, trips abroad, expense account lunches and longer holidays; he has to clock in and out and his earning span is much shorter. Once his physical strength goes, he can look forward to an old age of comparative poverty and deprivation. This all results in workers avoiding any kind of moral commitment to the management. 'We cheat the foreman,' is the attitude, 'he cheats the manager, and the manager cheats the customer.'

Richard Hoggart in *The Uses of Literacy* brilliantly summed up the workers' attitude to them:

'They are the people at the top, the highers up, the people who give you your dole, call you up, tell you to go to work, fine you, make you split up the family in the 'thirties (to avoid a reduction in the means test allowance) get yer in the end, aren't really to be trusted, talk posh, are all twisters really, never tell yer owt (e.g. about a relative in hospital) clap yer in the clink, will do y'down if they can, summons yer, are all in a click together, treat y'like muck.'

Because they dislike the management, the working classes don't like people saving their money or getting on through hard work. They put a premium on enjoying pleasure now, drinking their wages, for example, or blowing the whole lot on a new colour telly. The only legitimate way to make money is to win it. Hence the addiction to football pools, racing, bingo and the dogs.

Living from hand to mouth, they can't manage their money like the lower-middles. When the army started paying guardsmen by cheque recently, my bank manager said they got into the most frightful muddles. If he wrote and told one of them he was overdrawn by £30, he promptly received a cheque for that amount.

Traditionally working-class virtues are friendliness, co-operation, warmth, spontaneity, a ready sense of humour and neighbourliness. 'We're all in the same boat' is the attitude. That 'love', still the most common form of address, really means something. They have been defined as people who belong to the same Christmas Club, characteristically saving up not for something solid, like the deposit on a house, but for a good blow-out. They have a great capacity for enjoyment.

Because they didn't have cars or telephones and couldn't afford train fares, and the men tended to walk to work nearby, life centred around the street and neighbourhood. 'Everyone knew your business,' said one working-class man, so it was no good putting on airs because you earned more. The neighbours remembered you as a boy, knew your Aunt Lil, who was no better than she should be, and took you down a peg. The network acts as a constant check!

Girls seldom moved away from their mothers when they married; sons often came home for lunch every day, or lived at home, even after marriage. The working-class family is much closer and more possessive. They seldom invite friends into the house.

'I've never had a stranger (meaning non-family) in here since the day I moved in,' said one woman. 'I don't hold with that sort of thing.'

Being so dependent on the locality, the working classes are lost and desperately lonely if the council moves them to housing estates, or shuts them up in little boxes in some high-rise block. The men have also lost much of the satisfaction that came from the old skills and crafts. Many of these have been taken away from them and their traditional occupations replaced by machines. In the old days the husband gained respect as a working man in the community.

Women's Lib hasn't helped his self-respect much either. The working classes are the most reactionary of all the classes. (You only have to look at those Brylcreemed short back and sides, and wide trousers flapping like sails in the breeze at the TUC Conference.) But despite this, the working-class housewife now reads about Women's Lib in the paper and soon she's fretting to go back to work and make some extra cash, rather than act as a servant to the family and have her husband's dinner on the table at mid-day when he gets home. She starts questioning his authority and, having less autonomy at home, and never having had any at work, he feels even more insecure. Battering often starts if the woman is brighter than the man and the poorly educated husband sees his security threatened.

Leaving school at sixteen, he feels inadequate because he is inarticulate. He is thought of as being bloody-minded and lazy by the middle classes because he can't express himself and to snort 'Definitely, disgusting', in answer to any question put to him, is the only way he can show his disapproval.

The working classes divide themselves firmly into the Rough and the Respectable. The Rough get drunk fairly often, make a great deal of noise at night, often engage in prostitution, have public fights, neglect their children, swear in front of women and children, and don't give a stuff about anything – just like the upper classes, in fact. The Respectables chunter over such behaviour, and in Wales sing in Male Voice Choirs; they are pretty near the Tcales. They also look down on people on the dole, the criminal classes and the blacks, who they refer to as 'soap dodgers'.

### Mr and Mrs Definitely-Disgusting
Our archetypal working-class couple are Mr and Mrs DEFINITELY-DISGUSTING. They have two children, SHARON and DIVE, and live in a council house with walls so thin you can hear the budgie pecking its seed next door. Mr Definitely-Disgusting is your manual worker. He might be a miner in the North, a car worker in the Midlands, or a casual labourer in the South. He married young and lived for a while with his wife's parents. After a year or two he went back to going to the pub, football and

93

*The Definitely-Disgustings*

the dogs with the blokes. He detests his mother-in-law. But, despite his propensity to foul language, he is extremely modest, always undressing with his back to Mrs D-D and even peeing in a different way than the other classes, splaying out his fingers in a fan, so they conceal his member. He often does something slightly illegal, nicking a car or knocking off a telly. He is terrified of the police, who, being lower-middle and the class just above, reserve their special venom for him. Mrs Definitely-Disgusting wears her curlers and pinny to the local shop and spends a lot of the day with a cigarette hanging from her bottom lip gossiping and grumbling.

### Mr and Mrs Nouveau-Richards

The other couple you will meet are the NOUVEAU-RICHARDS, who are of working-class origin but have made a colossal amount of money.

*The Nouveau-Richards*

Boasting and ostentation are their salient characteristics. At coffee mornings Mrs Nouveau-Richards, who lives in lurex, asks anyone if they've got any idea 'whether gold plate will spoil in the dishwasher'. She has a huge house and lots of servants, who she bullies unmercifully. She is very rude to waiters and very pushy with her children, TRACEY-DIANE and JISON, who have several hours' after-school coaching every day. Mr Nouveau-Richards gets on the committee of every charity ball in London. The upper classes call him by his Christian name and appreciate his salty humour, but don't invite him to their houses. Jison goes to Stowe and Oxford and ends up a member of the Telly-stocracy, who are the real powers in the land – the people in communication who appear on television. They always talk about 'my show'.

95

# CHILDREN

*The kiddy is the dad of the guy*

At the beginning of the 'seventies the small-is-beautiful brigade mounted a campaign to bring down the birthrate. Family Planning Association supporters brandished condoms outside the House of Commons and at parties sidled up bossily to women who'd just had babies saying, 'Two's yer ration'. Middle-class lefties were rumoured to be concealing third babies in attics rather than display evidence of such social irresponsibility. Disapproving ads appeared in the cinemas showing defeated slatterns in curlers trailing herds of whining children along the street. 'Superdad or Scrounger?' demanded the *Daily Mirror* when a man on Social Security proudly produced his twenty-first child.

In the face of economic gloom, a rocketing dole queue and mothers wanting to get back to work, people probably thought twice about bringing more children into the world. Whatever the cause, the campaign worked. The birthrate in the United Kingdom dropped by 30 per cent. The working classes in particular, having discovered the pill, curbed production dramatically and at the last count were only producing 2.16 children per family, while the upper-middles were down to 1.7. Indeed, the higher you go up the social scale, the smaller the family, although the aristocracy tend to run unpatriotically riot, probably because, as Evelyn Waugh pointed out, 'Impotence and sodomy are socially OK, but birth control is flagrantly middle-class.' One can't imagine an aristocrat having a vasectomy.

With the working classes on the pill, the middle classes, particularly the wholemeal-bread brigade, started panicking about long term effects and switched to the coil or sterilisation. The respectable working class still favour the sheath, described by Mrs Definitely-Disgusting as 'my hubby always using something'.

*The birth*

If she has a job, which is unlikely, Caroline Stow-Crat gives it up the moment she discovers she's having a baby. The office is relieved too; they're fed up with the endless telephone calls, the Thursday to Tuesday weekends, and falling over the labrador every time they go to the filing cabinet. Samantha Upward tends to work until the last possible minute, ticking away like a time bomb and terrifying all the men in the office.

Our Queen was born by Caesarian, feet first. When Prince Charles was born the Duke of Edinburgh was playing squash. Today he would probably have been squashed into the maternity ward of St Mary's Paddington. The higher socio-economic classes now tend to favour epidural injections which make the whole thing less harrowing and allow the husband, albeit reluctantly, to be present at the birth. 'They do rather get in the way,' said my GP. 'It's best if they stand at the head of the bed to give their wife moral support, but they keep creeping down the bed to have a look.'

Despite working-class prudishness this trend will no doubt also creep down the social scale, since that sacred cow Esther Rantzen recently calved with husband Desmond Wilcox in attendance, beaming with besotted middle-aged joy afterwards. The labour wards will soon be as crowded out with nail-biting males as Twickenham during an England–Wales International.

When the wife of Super-dad-or-Scrounger produced their twenty-first child, four of the children were allowed to watch. Perhaps the television had broken down. 'It was very exciting,' said the eight-year-old afterwards.

The upper classes are not wild about new-born babies. Nancy Mitford once described one as a 'howling orange in a black wig'. But they are delighted to have their double-barrelled names carried on by male issue.

A few years ago *Harper's* published a brilliant piece on the 'Sloane Ranger', the girl who has a flat in Kensington and parents in the country, who lives in headscarves and went to a 'good' girls' boarding school. She epitomises the level at which the traditional upper-middles merge into the lower ranks of the upper classes. The Sloane Ranger husband is very chuffed whatever sex child he has. If it is a boy he goes to his club and writes two letters, one to 'my housemaster at Eton, and one to Mrs Ingham at Easton House'. Then he opens a bottle of champagne.

Harry Stow-Crat, who certainly wasn't present at the birth of any of his children, might ring up his mother or his old nanny, have a large whisky and soda, then go off and see his mistress.

Poor Gideon Upward is having a horrid time. He now knows exactly why it's called a 'confinement', that he's being conned rotten forking out for a private room, and it's not very *fine* the way Samantha who, disapproving of epidurals, insisted on natural childbirth and is now yelling her head off. Still he's delighted when little Zacharias appears. (Samantha went right through the Bible to find a name no one else had used.) It's so nice to have a boy first, so he can take little 0.7 to dances when they grow up. While Samantha is in hospital Gideon plans to have a crack at his secretary, but ever-thoughtful Samantha arranges for married friends to ask him out every night. Gideon gets drunk, partly out of frustration and partly at the prospect of his mother-in-law coming to stay next week, and makes sodden passes at the wives while their role-reversed husbands are doing the washing-up. The passes are tactfully forgotten about afterwards.

Mr Definitely-Disgusting finds it difficult to visit his wife in hospital because of shift work and National Health visiting hours. When he does, the conversations are usually monosyllabic and inhibited by groans from the labour ward next door.

Aristocrats often get married just before the birth to legitimise the child in case it's a boy. I attended one such wedding where the bride was actually in the last stages of labour. The hospital had thoughtfully provided an altar with a brass cross and two plastic orchids in a mauve vase. The bridegroom hadn't bothered to brush his hair but looked so impossibly handsome that the screaming queen of a hospital chaplain got thoroughly over-excited and spent so long holding his hand he almost forgot to join it to the bride's, who was manfully carrying on with:

'To have . . . (*groan*) . . . and to hold, from this . . . (*groan*).'

### The announcement

If you are very grand *The Times* reports the birth on the social pages free of charge. The rest of the upper classes put it in the birth column as briefly as possible:

'To Caroline, wife of Harry Stow-Crat – a son.'

Harry wouldn't have bothered, but Caroline thinks Mummy's friends would like to know. The Upwards' announcement would include the name of the baby (Zacharias Daniel) and a 'née Garland-Watson' to remind people of Samantha's up-market connections. Jen and Bryan Teale might include the name of the hospital and mention earlier children: 'a brother for Christine and Wayne.' Less smart but more reactionary members of the middle classes use the *Daily Telegraph*. The left-wing middles, conveniently combining parsimony with a flouting of convention, don't bother, which explains why the *Guardian* seldom has any birth announcements.

Mrs Definitely-Disgusting, who gets her children's names from the *TV Times*, tends to put the announcement of Sharon Esther, a sister for Dive Darren, in the local paper, with special thanks to the midwifery department at the hospital. It is a working-class characteristic to be touchingly grateful for any kind of hospital treatment, enjoying the rare treat of a rest and three free meals a day cooked by someone else.

Sometimes the Teales, who like a dainty word for everything, and the Definitely-Disgustings, who have difficulty in expressing themselves, will send out cards to friends and relations entitled 'Baby's Announcement' with a picture of a stork on the front. Inside they fill in:

'My name is Sharon Esther. I weigh 10 lbs. My happy Mum and Dad are . . .'

Receiving one of the these cards, Auntie might send off a nylon, quilted pram-set in canary yellow with the words 'A gift for baby from . . .' printed on the box. Other alternatives might be a fluffy, brushed-nylon stuffed rabbit or a teddy bear, referred to by the lower-middle classes and below as a cûddly (to rhyme with goodly) toy.

The upper classes, particularly the slightly retarded Sloane Ranger belt, have a tendency to add 'y' onto everything. In the twenties they did it with names: Bertie, Diney, Jakey, Piggy. Today they have 'choccy cake', 'pressies', 'cheesey things' which children like so much better, don't you agree, 'araby' which the private wards are getting awfully, and their 'gyny', whom they always fall in love with. The Queen's gynaecologist is called Mr Pinker, perhaps the colour he goes when he examines the royal person.

The upper classes don't mix socially with their doctors, but Caroline Stow-Crat makes an exception by asking her 'gyny' to her first dinner party after the birth. (Esther Rantzen did the same, so no doubt the entire working classes will start giving dinner parties in order to follow suit.) Fantasising about one's 'gyny' is the only thing that makes those agonising post-natal screwings possible. (Samantha Upward knows Gideon must not be denied sex longer than six weeks after the birth.) The crush on the 'gyny' usually lasts about six months.

On return from hospital the upper classes often get their old nanny out of mothballs to come and help with the baby. She usually leaves after a few days in high dudgeon because things are being done the wrong way. With the middle classes, Granny often forks out for a monthly nurse, or else the wife's mother comes to stay and husbands have to remember to put on a dressing gown when they go to the loo in the middle of the night. The working classes are often living with, or near, their parents anyway, or haven't got a spare room for anyone to stay in. The middle-class career mother, avid to get back to work, is praying that the new *au pair*, who isn't being very good about waking up in the night, is going to work out all right.

*Clothes*

*The wages of synthetic fibres is social death.*

The upper classes, as was pointed out in the Introduction, think Baby-Gros are common. Consequently, Caroline Stow-Crat prefers to dress babies of both sexes in long white dresses of wool or cotton. Which probably explains little Lord Fondle-Roy and the strong strain of sexual ambiguity about the aristocracy. 'Leggings and cardigans nubbly from being knitted by old Nannies,' say *Harper's*, are also all right; so is the matinee jacket, which always sounds like some moulting musquash cape worn by old ladies to afternoon performances of *The Mousetrap*. Anything nylon, polyester or made from any kind of synthetic fibre is definitely out.

Convenience, however, is a great leveller. Ironing long smocked dresses and washing eight Harrington squares and nappy liners a day was fine in the old days when there was nanny to do it. Today, when there aren't any servants and upper-class mothers often have to cook dinner for returning husbands, they may resort to Baby-Gros and disposable nappies when no one is looking, their babies only going into regulation white dresses for tea parties or when grandparents come to stay.

Zacharias Upward lives in Baby-Gros, in whatever colour *Vogue* is promoting for grown-ups. He only goes into pink and yellow nubbly cardigans knitted by Samantha's mother when the family go and stay with her.

The Nouveau-Richards, having denuded the Toddler's Layette at Harrods, have also acquired the biggest, shiniest Silver Cross Pram for Tracey-

*'Oh do stop being
so neurotic – you
look like a guttersnipe.'*

Diane. They have furnished it like their cars, with nodding Snoopies, hanging dolls, parasols and frilled canopies to keep off the sun. Tracey-Diane rises from a foam of nylon frills and lace like Venus from the waves. Mrs Nouveau-Richards and the *Daily Mirror* think the word 'pram' is common and refer to it as a 'baby carriage'.

Samantha Upward, conscious of how important it is for children to be brought up with animals, nevertheless invests in a cat net. She also knows how jealous husbands get with new babies around and is paying particular attention to Gideon. In many Stow-Crat houses the only member of the family who suffers from post-natal depression is Snipe the labrador. One monthly nurse said half her day in upper-class houses was spent boosting the morale of the dogs.

Breast-feeding is also coming back into fashion. In the old days the upper classes had their babies suckled by wet nurses, or fed from bottles at once. Jonathan Gathorne-Hardy, in *The Rise and Fall of the British Nanny*, quotes one nanny as saying her mistress was 'remarkable, in fact as far as breast-feeding goes was well nigh incredible'. It turned out she'd fed the baby for one month. Today, as a backlash against working mothers abandoning their babies to the bottle and rushing back to the office, Caroline Stow-Crat and certainly Samantha Upward are tending to breast-feed for several months.

Breast-feeding in public is indulged in by left-wing trendies, and surprisingly by Jen Teale who, probably thinking it's uninhibited upper-class behaviour, will even whip out a tit in the middle of a christening, sending uncles, grandfathers and male godparents fainting into the garden. Mrs Definitely-Disgusting feeds little Dive whenever he's hungry. One remembers Mum in *The Larkins* plugging little Oscar into her massive bosom in hotel lobbies, dining-rooms and on the beach. The left-wing middle-class mother also feeds her baby on demand, and it's been demanding ever since.

Old-fashioned nannies, who came from the working classes, tended to get their children on the pot and out of nappies very early – quite understandable as they had no washing machines or Napisan in those days. Geoffrey Gorer in his book *Exploring English Character*, suggests that the obsessive desire for privacy of the upper-class male is the result of being watched over on the pot:

'Immersed in clubs, behind ramparts of newspapers, silent in the corner of first-class carriages, at last he is free of Nanny.'

Caroline Stow-Crat talks about 'toilet-trining' with a cockney accent to excuse the word toilet.

It is very Jen Teale to use the word diapers. Caroline says 'nappies'.

Let us now digress slightly to nomenclature. While the upper classes say 'having a baby', Samantha Upward says 'pregnant', the lower-middle classes say 'expecting a baby' or 'starting a family'. The working-class mother, however, will say 'Three months after I had Dive, I fell for Sharon,' which doesn't mean that, due to post-natal gloom, she developed Lesbian tendencies, merely that she got pregnant again.

Upper and middle-class children call their parents 'Mummy' and 'Daddy', although the boy might call his father 'Dad' as he gets older, or refer to him as 'my father'. The lower-middles call them 'Mum' and 'Dad', and the working classes 'Moom' and 'Dud'. Socially aspiring lower-middles like Sandra in *The Liver Birds* also call their mother 'Mummy'. Trendy lefties and women who are reluctant to grow old, insist their children call them by their Christian names. Jen and Bryan Teale call each other 'Mummy' and 'Daddy', the working classes 'Mum' and 'Dad'.

A lot of confusion is caused by the word 'nanny'. To the upper and middle classes it means someone who looks after children for money, although Samantha Upward would prefer to call her 'my girl', or *'the au pair'*. To the working classes 'Nanny', 'Nana' or 'Nan' is one's grandmother who, as all the mothers are rushing back to work, probably also looks after the children – but is not paid for it. To the upper classes Nana means a large dog in *Peter Pan*.

The upper classes call their aunts 'Aunt Mary', the middle classes 'Auntie Mary'. Lower-middle and working-class children are forced to call any friend of their parents 'Auntie' or 'Uncle'. Two working-class expressions that seem to be creeping upwards are 'Baby needs changing', as though you were fed up with her already, and 'I've potted Sharon', as though she was a shiny red billiard ball. Confusion is also caused by the word 'putting down'. The upper classes 'put down' dogs, Jen Teale tends to 'put them to sleep' or 'send them to the Happy Hunting Ground'. The middle classes 'put down' children for schools, but when the working classes say 'I've put Sharon down', it means they've put her to bed. When they say, 'I mind children,' it doesn't mean that they dislike them but that they look after them.

The sociologist refers to the child as 'The Third Estate of the nuclear family'. The lower-middles and working classes call him a 'kiddy', the middle classes a 'kid'. The upper-middles and uppers talk about 'the children'. But upper-class people, trying to be democratic, have started to call them 'kids'. This unnerves Samantha Upward.

It is also an aristocratic trait to refer to members of one's family by name, assuming automatically that other people will know who one means. Caroline Stow-Crat would say,

'Harry's shooting. Can I bring Fiona and Georgie?'

She would also say the baby, rather than 'my baby', or 'Baby' or the American-influenced 'my little girl' which is very Jen Teale. Harry, on the other hand, if asking a friend how his son is getting on, might easily say: 'How's your boy?'

One of the first events in the baby's life is a trip to the clinic. On rainy days the place is deserted because the Mrs Definitely-Disgustings, who always dress up to wheel their prams to the clinic, don't like getting their best clothes wet. You can tell the middle-class mothers because they are much more scruffy and have smaller prams (to fit into the Volvo). When I visited a clinic in Putney there were naturally no upper-class mothers because they don't live south of the river and they never go to clinics. Several working-class mothers, in mini-skirts, leather coats and high-heeled shoes, with very done-up babies, were capping each other's crawling and teething stories. Two left-wing middle-class mothers with eager, unpainted faces, ragged hair and dirndl skirts were talking about an anti-aircraft noise meeting that night. Behind them a pretty Samantha Upward appeared to be carrying on a very enunciated conversation with another upper middle-class mum to which no one could help listening. Suddenly one realised that she was addressing a non-stop monologue to her own six-month-old baby, having obviously read somewhere that the more you talk to your baby, the sooner it talks back. The ratlet race had begun.

### The Christening

The next *big event* in a child's life is the Christening. The Queen was christened in a private chapel at Buckingham Palace at five weeks, baptised with water from the Jordan, and dressed in christening robes of cream Brussels lace, worn by every baby in the royal family since Queen Victoria's children.

The aristocracy tend to be christened in their own thirteenth-century churches, wearing slightly yellowing christening robes embroidered with the family crest. *The Times* will report it on the social page. A London christening takes place at the Guards Chapel or in the Crypt Chapel at the House of Commons, with lunch at Boodles afterwards.

Sloane Ranger christenings tend to have Earl Grey tea, not enough champagne and, if they're short of cash, the top layer of their wedding cake re-iced. Christening presents include silver mugs with at least four initials to take in the double barrels, and premium bonds, but not napkin rings or building society shares, which are very lower-middle class.

As the Merrytocracy are fast reaching a state when they can't open their mouths without a glass in their hand, christenings are tending to get later and later, with champagne, chicken drumsticks and leprous quiche at 5:30.

The suburbs and Jen and Bryan Teale tend to go in for multiple christenings with each couple looking beadily at everyone else's baby and thinking how much more 'well spoken' their own godparent is when she names this child. The vicar looks in at all the parties afterwards and has difficulty not shlurring his words at Evenshong.

The left-wing middles, combining parsimony with agnostic puritanism, don't have their kids christened.

Mr Definitely-Disgusting goes out mini-cabbing to pay for the party and a new costume for Mrs Definitely-Disgusting who makes all the food, which includes pork pie, apple pie with pastry leaves, sponge cakes and fruit punch. The godparents probably keep the local pub.

Social climbers choose famous or successful godparents who might advance their children's careers or improve their status. They've dropped all their childhood friends. Sloane Rangers' mothers advise them not to ask that awfully nice girl from next door in Fulham, because you probably won't see her again after you move to the country. Jean Cocteau once acted as a godparent, then promptly forgot about the child. Years later he met the father who reproached him for neglecting his duties. Mortified, Cocteau at once sent his godson a large teddy bear.

'Was he pleased?' he asked next time he met the father.

'Not awfully,' came the reply. 'He's a colonel now.'

The christening, like the wedding, is frequently an occasion when two different classes meet head-on. The baby's mother, for example, may be lower-middle and determined not to put a foot wrong, while the baby's father's family may be upper-middle and equally determined to patronise. Less smart relations are kept in the background or ruthlessly excluded. Examples of this can be found in Colin Bell's fascinating book, *Middle Class Families*, in which he devotes a chapter to describing three Welsh christenings.

The first involved a lower-middle-class couple, who asked a hundred guests to the church. Of these only six were manual workers and their wives. The baby's mother was awfully pleased that her cousin (the sole member of the family who'd been to a public school) had bothered to come. Only one manual worker and his wife, however, was asked back to the party at home after the service. The husband worked on the railways and they lived in a council house.

'But she's my auntie,' said the baby's mother, 'and they're the salt of the earth.' (An expression used by all classes to excuse those of lower station.) As a first grandchild, the baby was given a staggering £1000 by his grandparents and enough clothes to keep Dr Barnado's going for a year.

The second christening involved a slightly less smart family. The father was described as a 'geographically mobile plant superintendent', which actually meant he'd moved around the country in the course of his career, upping his salary each time. On this occasion their daily woman came to the church to keep the older children quiet, but was not invited back to the house for tea afterwards, even to help – a classic example of the *nouveau-riche* not knowing how to treat servants – and presumably because she was close enough to the family in class to be mistaken for a relation. In spite of this she sent the baby a coodly toy. Unsmart relations weren't asked, even though they lived nearby.

'Not because I'm a snob,' said the mother untruthfully, 'but he's a porter or something.'

In the final christening the parents were both bright children of working-class parents, who'd met at university and promptly moved to another part of the country, away from any embarrassing roots. The relations were mercifully too poor to come to the christening. Godparents were friends from work. The grandparents didn't send any presents, only vastly elaborate christening cards.

Another example of the clash between classes occurred at a recent middle-class christening I attended. One of the godfathers, a working-class actor who'd done very well for himself but had never been to a christening before, missed the church service and rolled up in time for tea, armed with a christening cake decorated with primrose yellow icing, the baby's name in mauve and a stork and a baby made out of a sugared almond with its features slipping. Alas, the baby's grandmother had also provided a large white christening cake complete with stork and slipping-featured sugared almond. The cakes were placed side by side – with Storky and Co gazing sourly at one another.

And while we're on the subject of cakes, Caroline Stow-Crat would never call marzipan 'almond paste'.

## *The ratlet race*

The christening over, the ratlet race starts in earnest. The battle is particularly vicious among the middle classes, where if you can't boast an 'int'risting' career, you justify your existence by rearing a little genius. This is another part of the backlash against women going out to work. Newspapers and women's magazines are constantly stressing the importance of the child being mentally stimulated during the first five years of its life. Journalists like Mary Kenny recant on women's lib principles and expound the joys of motherhood. This is very easy for lady journalists who can always write at home *and* see their babies when they want to. Middle-class society is teeming with women having nervous breakdowns because they feel so inadequate about only being a wife and mother.

*'Oh Gideon – do you think he's having his first breakdown?'*

At plonk-and-pâté-tasting-of-old-socks-parties beloved by the upper-middle classes, you can hear the battle raging. Samantha Upward who, in spite of having a degree, believes in staying at home to raise little Zacharias 'creatively', is talking to a career mum:

SAMANTHA (who knows one is never regarded as a cabbage if one's 'intrristed' in other people): How's the job?

CAREER MUM: Oh exhausting. I had to lunch George Best on Monday, look after Graham Greene all week, then we had a press party for Isherwood last night. (Fifteen-love to Career Mum).

SAMANTHA: And how's Damian?

CAREER MUM: All right, I think. How's the baby? (*Not being round much she doesn't even know Zacharias's name.*)

106

SAMANTHA: Oh he's just finished *Alice in Wonderland*. Simply couldn't put it down. I do recommend flash cards. And he can already beat Gideon at chess. We're a bit worried he's a Gifted Child, but you can't really tell at two. (Thirty-fifteen to Samantha.)

Harry Stow-Crat doesn't believe in wives working, or husbands for that matter. It would interfere with shooting and fishing.

The upper classes have nurseries upstairs. The upper-middles call them 'playrooms' and tend to have them downstairs so the children won't miss any cultural pearls dropped by their parents. In the kitchen a cork board groans with Zacharias's first drawings. Jen Teale, who is determined that little Wayne shall get on in life, has the nursery in the lounge with model soldiers on the mantelpiece and children's posters on the wall. The garden will be filled with Wendy huts and social climbing frames.

Dive Definitely-Disgusting has no room set aside for him and often sleeps in the same room, or even bed, as his brothers and sisters. The reason they go to bed so late is because Mrs Definitely-Disgusting has to ensure that one child is soundly asleep before she can put the next one to bed, and so on. The cot is often bought with Embassy coupons.

The upper classes send their children to bed at six-thirty so that they'll be out of the way before their father comes back from shooting or the city. The role-reversed upper-middles who believe that contact with the father is essential, tend to keep them up slightly later so they'll have half an hour with Daddy before going to sleep. Gideon Upward, knackered after a hard day, is corrected by little Zacharias every time he tries to skip a page of Paddington Bear and longs for a bit of upper-class peace downstairs with a large gin and tonic.

Sleeping alone, the middle-class child is often frightened of the dark, but his parents can afford to leave a light on all night outside his room.

The middle classes have always given a lot of parental authority to the father. The upper and working classes tend to leave discipline to the mother, nanny or grandmother. But, with shorter working hours and less shift work, the working-class father is tending to be at home more, take more interest in his children and no longer be ashamed to be seen pushing the pram.

'Vic takes baby up the park on the weekend, while I get the dinner on,' is a typical working-class remark.

Equally, as the upper classes get poorer and can't afford servants, the fathers are forced to pay more attention to the children.

'I used to shove the baby into his arms,' said one monthly nurse, 'and walk out of the room. He'd hold it like a rattlesnake; but by the time I left he was pushing the pram and changing nappies.' One upper-class husband, she said, refused to push the pram, but would walk behind his wife when she was pushing it, pushing her.

By the time the middle-class child is a year old, say the statisticians, he will be less likely to have a tantrum than the working-class child, will have had a much better diet and be off the bottle (as though he'd been on an alcoholic binge for the first twelve months). Harry Stow-Crat will have had a grille put in the back of the estate car to stop Georgie bothering Snipe. Georgie will have had his first party, which he won't remember, but which was a great show-off occasion for his nanny. Jen Teale's child will now be referred to as a 'toddler' or a 'tiny tot'. Samantha will be out on the culture beat hawking little Zacharias round museums and art galleries to stop herself becoming a cabbage. The Hayward Gallery won't allow prams inside but provides baby slings to help Mummy appreciate Dada.

### Children's clothes

Little Georgie Stow-Crat will be out of long dresses now and into romper suits with Peter Pan collars, or short trousers which he will wear until he's half-way through prep school. Occasionally in Hyde Park on cold days one sees the camp sight of little upper-class boys wearing tights under their shorts. He might occasionally be allowed to wear jeans like the middle classes, but never ones that fit, in case their tightness stops him carrying on the line. Upper-class little girls are smock-marked.

The middle classes dress their children like small adults in the hope that they'll grow brighter and more adult earlier. In the same way that the upper classes force boy babies into little dresses, the middle classes force little girls into jeans. Jen Teale's daughter, Christine, wears her dresses slightly too short, to display hen's bum knickers.

All little girls, in fact, are lower-middle by inclination. If allowed, they would always dress like Christine in peasant blouses with elasticated waists and sleeves, their hair in bunches, sticking out above the ears; or like Tracey-Diane Nouveau-Richards in earrings, with painted toenails, huge nylon bows in the hair, pink plastic butterfly slides and white slingback or even high-heeled shoes. The Teales and the Nouveau-Richards encourage such prissiness by saying, 'Always try to be a little lady,' or 'Isn't Tracey-Diane a little flirt?' Mrs Nouveau-Richards, who believes in getting her pound of flesh from the nanny, insists that all Tracey's clothes are 'hand' washed as she calls it. Mrs Definitely-Disgusting dresses her children in

*Tracey-Diane*
*Nouveau-Richards*
*in casual clothes*

brightly coloured polyester and acrylic – shocking pink, mauve, royal blue and turquoise being the most popular. They also wear very shiny T-shirts with 'Ars-nel' on them and mock suede coats with nylon fur collars. The upper classes only used to allow their children to wear anoraks on the ski slopes, but have now given in.

Hair is also a class indicator. Upper-class little boys have their curls brushed flat and cut in the shape of a pudding basin. The middle classes have their hair tapered like Cliff Richard. Upper-class little girls either wear their fringe on the eyebrows like Shetland ponies or drawn off their foreheads (pronounced 'forrids') with a small velvet bow at the side or the crown of the head. They sometimes wear Alice bands, but sewn and with proper velvet, not made out of stretch material. Jen Teale cuts Christine's fringe half-way down the forehead, so there is no danger she won't be able to see out. She cuts Wayne's hair short at the back so that half an inch or two of neck shows. The working classes no longer Brylcreem their kiddies' hair into tight curls – too much like the 'darkies' – but they do brush Baby's hair upwards like a Sioux Indian's.

Until recently it was much easier to tell a child's background from its clothes than its mother's. But since the entire nation's youth is now clad in spin-offs from whatever film is fashionable and since Mary Quant (who staged the great sixties revolution, making duchesses interchangeable with shop girls) has gone into children's clothes, all children will soon look alike.

### The régime

Upper-class mothers believe in fresh air and walks to feed the ducks in the afternoon. They're very park conscious. Ducks in Kensington Gardens ought to be members of Weight Watchers, so stuffed are they with bread (but never sliced, because the upper classes think it's common). Ducks that live near the Round Pond in Hampstead get whole-wheat crusts. As soon as Georgie Stow-Crat can walk he is put on a pony. From Monday to Friday upper-class London children have to make do with the rocking horse at Harrods.

Conventional upper-class children have cake, sandwiches and perhaps as a treat an ice at four o'clock, what the working classes describe as 'afternoon tea'. Middle-class children have high tea at about six consisting of baked beans, beef-burgers or fish fingers and yoghurt. The working classes tend to have the same, but if any of the food is cooked the meal is called 'a dinner': 'Karen has a dinner at lunchtime and a dinner in the evening.' The working classes might also say, 'I gave Baby juice and cereal at three.' The upper classes would specify 'orange juice', and 'cornflakes' or 'Weetabix'. The lower you get down the social scale the more likely people are to use convenience words, like 'teacher' for 'schoolmaster' or 'mistress'. The lower-working classes eat chip butties and sweets all day – they don't have meals.

Upper-class children tend to have other children over to tea at four as a social occasion. Middle-class children come over to play at any time. When the middle classes send their children to state schools the children ask their working-class schoolmates to tea, then feel hurt because they never get asked back. It never occurs to Zacharias Upward that Dive Definitely-Disgusting might feel ashamed of the smallness of his house and the fact that he doesn't have a bedroom to himself.

The working classes tend to cram their children with sweets, cheap placebos like 'Molteasers', 'Croonchy' and 'Cadbury's Fruit and Not'. Samantha Upward, having read about nutrition, tends to restrict Zacharias's sweet-eating, although career mums, conscious of being away too much, bombard their children with guilt presents every time they're late home. Little Zacharias, who is only allowed two sweets after lunch and is fed up with museums, wishes Samantha would get a part-time job, so he could get guilt presents too.

Upper-class children are taught nursery rhymes by their nannies and know them all by the time they're eighteen months, giving them a vocabulary of about 500 words. Traditionally a lot of nursery rhymes chronicle the activities of their forbears anyway. Little Jack Horner pulling out a plum, for instance, refers to the fat pickings culled by the Horner family during the dissolution of the monasteries.

Sharon Definitely-Disgusting only knows television jingles. In a recent quiz at a state school none of the eleven-year-olds could say what Little Miss Muffet sat on.

### Staying with granny

Working-class children, as has been said before, often live with or near their grandmother, so the working-class Nan is much the best with children because she's had the most practice. Georgie Stow-Crat's grandparents live in the country, have lots of room and servants to take the children off their hands. Zacharias Upward's grandparents live on their nerves and an ever-dwindling fixed income. They move into smaller and smaller houses but hang on to all the ornaments, which are double-parked on every piece of furniture, so that the place looks like an antique shop. All the china is moved up a shelf when the grandchildren come to stay, but eventually they break the place up because they're fed up with not being allowed to touch anything and with playing the same old brought-out game of bagatelle. A terrible family row develops because one ball-bearing disappears. Both daughters and daughters-in-law feel on trial all the time and the tension is transmitted to the children. If they're let out into the garden, footballs snap the regalia lilies. Mealtimes are a nightmare because the middle classes are obsessively hot on table manners.

'Why do all my grandchildren eat as though they're gardening?' is a typical upper-middle-class granny remark.

Children invariably let the side down by saying, 'Why can't we have baked beans in front of the telly like we do at home?'

Upper-middle-class grannies invariably had nannies to bring up their own children and cannot understand why their grandchildren should be so exhausting, or so much more badly behaved than their own children were. They forget that they only saw them when they were presented, newly washed, for an hour after tea.

Samantha Upward drives her mother-in-law crackers. Every time

Zacharias interrupts, she stops whatever adult conversation she is having to answer his question.

The middle classes tend to reason.

The working classes tend to clout.

The working classes have dummies. Middle-class children are more likely to suck their thumbs.

*Growing up*

Sexual modesty is also a good index of social class. The majority of the working classes never see their parents naked, which must be quite an achievement as they often sleep in the same room – rather like undressing on the beach.

Social Class 1 (which according to the Census, includes scientists, doctors and structural engineers) are much more likely to let their children see them with no clothes on. Pretty horrifying really, and enough to put one off sex for life, having a hairy scientist streaking round the house.

The upper-middles are less likely to worry about masturbation and more likely to tell their children the facts of life. They are aided in this by Althea, of Dinosaur Books fame, who has written a very explicit children's book about having a baby. Known locally as the 'rude' book, it is a great favourite to read aloud when Granny comes to stay.

To Jen Teale the word 'rude' means 'slightly smutty', to the upper class it means 'impertinent'. Similarly the uppers use 'cheeky' to mean impertinent whereas to Jen Teale it means a bit risque or near the knuckle.

The working classes are incapable of explaining anything so you get their children coming into the public library and saying,

'I want a book about life.'

'Whose life?' asks the librarian. 'Biographies are over there.'

'Facts of life, Miss.'

Georgie Stow-Crat doesn't need to be told about sex because he's seen plenty of farm animals copulating. As a result upper-class men often take their wives from behind.

My husband heard about sex for the first time when he was walking in a prep-school crocodile along the beach.

'I say, chaps,' said a boy called the Hon. James Stewart, 'I know how babies are made.'

Whereupon they all gathered round saying, 'Go on, Stewart, tell us.'

'The man lies on top of the woman,' said Stewart portentously, 'and is excused into her.'

The middle classes will start taking their children to the dentist almost before they've got teeth; the working classes tend only to go when their teeth ache. 'You can tell what class a person is the moment he opens his mouth,' said John Braine, 'by the state of his teeth.' That's why Sharon Definitely-Disgusting claps her hands over her mouth whenever she laughs.

The upper classes give their children 10p from the fairies when a tooth comes out. Inflation and indulgence have pushed the middle classes up to 50p. Among the upper-middle merrytocracy the fairies often get drunk and forget to put the money under the pillow and have to compensate with twice as much the next day. When the fair arrives each year, children have been known to tug teeth out with forceps for more money to spend on the fruit machines.

People are gradually realising that illiteracy in schools today is nothing to do with the teaching, but simply because children have been turned into a race of zombies by watching television. Soon the middle classes will start banning television altogether, and illicit watch-easys will be set up in darkened dives round the country.

Samantha Upward doesn't let Zacharias read comics or watch more than an hour's television a day. Upper-class children go into the kitchen and read the housekeeper's children's comics. Samantha reads out loud to Zacharias in a clear voice altering words she thinks are common and remembering to say 'orf'.

The Queen evidently read very early because in the evenings her mother used to read her books 'about animals and horses and they would recite gay poetry.' (Marlowe and Oscar Wilde perhaps.) Lower-class children can't read but they can write CFC and SHED and SOD and FUK in aerosol on bus shelters.

By the age of two little George Stow-Crat will be looking out on life with a clear blue gaze, frightened of no one, totally self-confident. He will also have a frightful accent from playing in the stable but no one is in the least bit worried. Working-class children always hold their noses in the country.

The middle-class child will already be shell-shocked with instructions. Don't tread in Doggie's duty; put your hand over your mouth when you cough; don't turn your fork over to eat peas; it's rude to whisper; it's rude to shout; talk in a low clear voice like Anna Ford or Mrs Thatcher. Class is beginning to creep in. Middle-class children twig that they can bully the char's children, but the char's children can't beat them up in return. They also know that there are certain children in the road their mother prefers them playing with to others. Samantha has great difficulty explaining to little Zacharias why he may sprinkle his pepper but not his salt.

I once heard my son regaling his friends:

'Mummy says "pardon" is a much worse word than "fuck".'

Jen Teale's child will be constantly pulled up for some real or imagined coarseness of speech or enunciation. It's so important to be 'well-spoken'.

Middle-class children put cherry stones on the side of their plate with their spoon and chant, 'Tinker, Tailor, Soldier, Sailor, Rich man, Poor man, Beggarman, Thief'. Upper-class children conceal the journey from mouth to plate with curled fist and say 'Army, Navy, Law, Divinity, Independent, Medicine, Trade'. The working classes only eat cherries out of tins of fruit salad with the stones already removed.

Children's parties are a sophisticated form of torture. The upper classes tend to give parties just for nannies and children, mid-week, and ending at six so as not to involve the husbands. No drink is offered to collecting parents.

Nanny Stow-Crat couldn't stop Fiona inviting Tracey Nouveau-Richards as they sit next to each other at nursery school, but Caroline says she's not having those ghastly parents in the house: 'They never know when to leave and once through the door, they might make a habit of dropping in.'

Samantha Upward, being very democratic, encourages Zacharias to invite all his little state school friends who run absolutely wild all over the newly planted perennials that were once going to make an herbaceous border. They refuse to play party games and drive the conjuror into hysterics by explaining in loud voices how every trick is done.

Mr Nouveau-Richards, who feels that only the best is good enough for my Tracey-Diane, employs Searcy's to do the catering, Dick Emery for the cabaret, gives each child a Tiger Tiger doll's house as a going-away present, and shows the première of *Star Wars II* after the interval. All the surrounding middle-class mums would like to refuse, but daren't because they'd get such flak from their children.

The upper-middle merrytocracy mix drink, nannies and mothers, thereby making the children's party a much more jolly occasion. Parties in Putney are rather like singles bars with separated fathers turning up to collect children and meeting pretty divorced mothers and getting nose to nose over the Soave and the hassle of bringing up children on one's own.

# WORK

*Oh let us love our occupations,*
*Bless the squire and his relations,*
*Live upon our daily rations,*
*And always know our proper stations.*

According to the sociologists the two most important factors affecting upward mobility are your job and your marriage. But this may be partly due to the fact that the Census, upon which most government and sociological statistics are based, judges a person's class entirely by the occupation of the head of the house in which they live. In all societies there is a division of labour and consequently a hierarchy of prestige, but such arbitrary distinctions as the Census makes lead to a gross over-simplification of the class system. Photographers, for example, are rated Class III which puts Patrick Lichfield, Anthony Armstrong-Jones and Christopher Thynne in the same social bracket as David Bailey and Terry Donovan. Brewers like the Guinnesses and the Cobbolds are even lower, in Class IV. Athletes all rate Class III which puts Princess Anne on a level with Kevin Keegan. While the Marquess of Anglesey, as a writer, is rated lower than all the dentists, chemists and opticians in Class 1. The deb, working as a waitress (Class IV) and having *nostalgie de la boue* fantasies about lorry drivers, is actually bettering herself because they're rated Class III. Peers of the realm don't get a rating at all, and if they don't work are lumped together with the disabled, undergraduates, ex-convicts and the chronically sick. Did Lady Chatterley, as the wife of a non-working baronet, enhance her social status when she embarked on an affair with a Class III gamekeeper?

Cabinet Ministers, MPs and diplomats are only graded Class II, which is logical. Once upon a time diplomats used to be Old Etonians with firsts, now they're parvenus like Peter Jay, and all the British embassies, according to a recent observer, ring with flat 'a's and regional accents. You also get a judge like Lord Denning, who would be rated Class I by the Census and upper class by the majority of the population because he's a peer, using such unpatrician expressions in an interview as having 'no help' in the house, 'a roast' for lunch on Sunday, and referring to his wife as 'Lady Denning'.

When you marry you automatically take on the class of your husband,

PERCENTAGE OF ECONOMICALLY ACTIVE AND RETIRED PEOPLE IN EACH SOCIAL CLASS IN
GREAT BRITAIN DEVISED FROM CENSUS, 1971

*SOCIAL CLASS I* – Professional – 4%

Accountants, chemists, university dons,
lawyers, vets, opticians, ornithologists,
scientists, vicars, engineers, architects,
dentists.

*SOCIAL CLASS II* – Intermediate occupations – 18%

Airline pilots, chiropodists, farmers,
members of parliament, schoolmasters,
police inspectors, artists, nurses, publi-
cans, journalists, sculptors, diplomats,
chicken sexers, actors, company directors.

*SOCIAL CLASS III* (N) – Skilled occupations – Non Manual – 21%

Sales reps, secretaries, shop girls, bank
clerks, photographers, restaurateurs, po-
licemen, cashiers, models, undertakers.

*SOCIAL CLASS III*(M) – Skilled occupations – Manual – 28%

Bus drivers, cooks, miners, guards in
trains, upholsterers, butchers, all athletes including horseback riders and foot-
ballers, plumbers, shoemakers, printers,
brewers.

*SOCIAL CLASS IV* – Partly skilled – 21%

Farm labourers, barmen, bus conduc-
tors, fishermen, postmen, telephonists,
milkmen, gardeners, hawkers, am-
bulance men, barmaids, brewers,
waiters and waitresses.

*SOCIAL CLASS V* – Unskilled – 8%

Office cleaners, porters, builders' labourers, messenger boys, lorry drivers'
mates, stevedores, window cleaners,
chimney sweeps, ticket collectors, char-
women.

which means that the day a duke's daughter (even if she's qualified as a Class I barrister) marries a chimney sweep she is promptly assessed with him as Class V.

What one does is certainly indicative of one's class. One thinks of solicitors as being middle-class and lorry drivers as working-class – but I know of a peer of ancient lineage whose daughter has been a long-distance lorry driver for the last five years. Again and again one is struck by the relativity of the whole situation. To the working class, barristers and solicitors seem not middle but upper class while to the aristocracy they are definitely middle class. A solicitor told me that lower-class women invariably put on a hat when they come to see him, and Michael Young, in *Family and Class in a London Suburb*, quotes a man from Woodford Green:

'We have a very dear friend who's a practising barrister, and it amazed us that people might want to know us because we knew him and called him by his Christian name.'

Similarly we had a lower-middle-class nanny who stopped going out with a solicitor because he made her feel socially inferior.

The other day I met a woman at a party who said her daughter had just got engaged to a dustman. Uncertain of her political affiliations, I was wondering whether to compose my features into a 'How Splendid!' or 'How Awful!' expression when she went on complacently, 'But it's quite all right. His father's a general.'

But of course a general who'd started his career in the cavalry would probably be of a very different class to one who had begun in the Royal Corps of Transport.

One poll conducted among the working classes showed that a footballer was regarded as the most prestigious career, followed by a chauffeur. My daily woman was grumbling one day that her daughter didn't speak to her any more since she'd married into the professional classes. What did her son-in-law do, I asked.

'Oh,' she said, 'he's an undertaker.'

One notices, too, that occupations that have a slightly ludicrous image acquire new, more euphemistic and therefore more Jen Teale titles: 'dental surgeon' instead of 'dentist'; 'rodent operative' for 'rat catcher'; 'public health inspector' for 'sanitary inspector'; and, worst of all, 'refuse collector' (presumably because they refuse to collect) for 'dustman'.

The position of the doctor is also ambiguous. The working classes think of him as upper-class. He has even usurped the lord as the most popular hero in romantic fiction. But a publisher I know was driving down the village street with a very grand old woman when he saw a man on the pavement waving to her.

'Some friend's trying to attract your attention,' he said.

'That's not a friend,' snorted the old lady. 'That's my doctor.'

I recently heard a very upper-class girl say she must go home to Lancashire because 'I've got to help Mummy with a horrors party for the doctor, the dentist, the solicitor and the agent.'

Medicine, except in the private sector, is fast dropping caste, along with teaching, nursing and the army, because they're all dependent on state pay, too ethical to go on strike, and getting broker and broker and more and more demoralised as the system breaks down.

Doctors, too, used to get invited to a lot of smartish parties, but now your GP won't come and see you any more, and you can't welcome him in a glamorous nightie in the privacy of your home, people tend not to know them socially. Certain doctors are also to blame for this loss of status. A friend who hadn't been to her doctor for over a year was greeted with the words, 'Not you again'.

The upper-class attitude to farmers is curious, too. Many aristocrats have land run by farm managers with whom they enjoy talking shop, and who they far prefer to businessmen or people in the professions who don't know their place – 'more genuine' is the phrase used. Harry Stow-Crat also has to suck up to neighbouring farmers in case he should want to hunt over their land. Upper-class young men often go and work on farms as apprentices, before going home to manage their own estates, and say 'How sooper the farm blokes are', although they don't drink in the same pubs as them. This preference of the upper classes for the working class because they are far enough away socially is exquisitely summed up by Jane Austen's Emma (who, I suppose, could be described as landed gentry):

'A young farmer, whether on horseback or on foot, is the very last sort of person to raise my curiosity. The Yeomanry are precisely the order of people with whom I feel I can have nothing to do. A degree or two lower and a creditable appearance might interest me, I might hope to be useful to their families in some way. But a farmer can need none of my help and is therefore in one sense above my notice, as in every other sense he is below it.'

Emma, believing her young friend Harriet to be the illegitimate daughter of a *gentleman*, firmly discourages her from marrying this particular young farmer as being far beneath her. When, however, Emma discovers

Harriet is only the daughter of a rich *tradesman*, she changes her mind and finds the farmer a perfectly suitable match.

Which brings us to the upper-class horror of trade. A gentleman didn't have to earn his living, as has been pointed out in chapter 4. 'The acceptance of high living and leisure,' wrote Evelyn Waugh in *Noblesse Oblige*, 'as part of the natural order, is a prerequisite of the aristocratic qualities and achievements. [The aristocrat] who goes into business and sticks to it and makes good, is soon indistinguishable from his neighbour in Sunningdale. You should have said, not that aristocrats can't make money in commerce, but that when they do they become middle-class.'

In fact, if one looks back at most of the great families one will find that they started off in trade. Many of them got rich lending money to both sides in the Wars of the Roses, and then bought land. But once one's pile was made, the life of leisure was espoused and one's origins rejected, which goes a long way to explain the parlous state of British industry today.

This horror of commerce is further expressed by John Betjeman:

> *Businessmen with awkward hips*
> *And dirty jokes upon their lips,*
> *And plump white fingers made to curl*
> *Round some anaemic city girl.*

Conversely the moment the businessman gets his foot on the ladder he'll start gathering round him upper-class trappings: going out hunting, buying boats, leasing a reach of a good salmon river and joining several smart clubs.

Firms like Plessey even employ upper-class ex-army types to organise shooting parties and get very grand people along to impress the customers, often with disastrous results. One adviser remembers a peer arriving drunk from shooting with President Giscard, and telling such filthy stories at dinner that the great industrialist invited to meet him left the table in high dudgeon and cancelled the order.

Trade seems less despised if one is flogging works of art, and somehow shipping or oil seem to be more respectable.

'Wouldn't it be heaven if Hamish got a job in Shell at £600 a year,' wrote Nancy Mitford in the thirties, and the Onassis and Niarchos families seem to have been totally accepted by the English and French aristocracy, if not by the Greeks, which is often the case. One's social deficiencies always seem more glaring to one's fellow-countrymen than they do abroad.

Onassis and Niarchos have been brilliantly described as 'parachutists', people who drop out of nowhere into a new class. The French have a splendid word, *rastaquouère*, to describe foreign nobility of dubious origin.

Social advancement is also dependent on access. Businessmen tend not to meet the upper classes. But members of the 'professions' – architects, doctors, dentists, estate agents, solicitors – encounter all classes, as do West End tailors, interior decorators, dressmakers and some journalists, while chauffeurs, nannies and masters at boarding schools have long-term access. All these people not only see the upper classes at close range and have ample opportunity to observe them and ape their manners, but also, if they have charm and a certain deference, often get taken up. When Michael Fish was invited to some frightfully smart house, the housekeeper was overheard saying to the butler:

'Things have come to a pretty pass when they ask the shirt-maker to stay.'

In Germany and America the businessman is of a far higher caste, and at the same time more democratic. In America, even though the men on the shop floor call the managing director by his Christian name, no one looks down on him socially. Advertising is also much smarter in America because Ad men get paid such vast sums of money.

'Advertising is still not considered a fit occupation for a gentleman,' said David Ogilvy recently. 'If I were top of another profession, such as law, I would be in the House of Lords today. If I were an actor or even a jockey I would have been knighted. As it is I get the CBE. When the Queen heard what I did her expression was a mixture of amazement and amusement.'

On the other hand, the laid-back, lotus-eating entrepreneurial atmosphere of advertising is very well suited to the upper classes.

'What do you do?'

'Nothing.'

'In which agency?'

*The aristocracy*
> *Lord Finchley tried to mend the Electric Light*
> *Himself. It struck him dead: And serve him right!*
> *It is the business of the wealthy man*
> *To give employment to the artisan.*
>
> HILAIRE BELLOC

Nobility of birth commonly abateth industry, said Bacon, but during the twentieth century the gospel of work has spread to the upper classes. What career, then, is open to Georgie Stow-Crat? He's unlikely to go into any of the professions (Lord Colwyn as a trumpeter and a dentist being a rare exception) because he lacks the application to train for six years and he'd find the people too stuffy and boring. One aristocrat who actually managed to pass his bar finals left the legal profession after a year:

'I couldn't stand the other barristers. They were so pompous and middle-class, and only interested in talking shop.'

Georgie might temporarily become a stockbroker, like the Marquess of Tavistock, or dabble in accountancy, like Lord Greenock. This would help him run his estate later and teach him the rudiments of tax evasion. Others take up 'head-hunting' or go into property where they do very well because they know all the right people and get hot tips about whose land is coming on the market. Georgie might also run a restaurant or add kudos to a smart nightclub, acting as bait to rich upper-class friends, and even richer nouveaus.

Some aristocrats try photography because it gives them the chance to get at pretty girls; others flatten their 'a's and go into the pop music business or produce films. They are very good as front men in PR because they know the right people, but they are better at charming the press and clients than dealing with all the follow-up work.

A lot of them go into Sotheby's or Christie's or smart art galleries, because, being surrounded by beautiful things at home, they're supposed to know something about furniture and pictures. They don't, of course. One Christie's valuer told me that only once, in all the houses he'd visited, was he made to dine in the kitchen with the servants, although in another house there was an old nanny in residence who wouldn't let him watch television after 8:30.

Then there are the Whore Lords, who get their names on to as many firms' writing paper as possible. Kind hearts may mean more than coronets, but a lord on the board means business and impresses customers, particularly Americans.

Georgie is most likely to end up farming his own land. If he were a younger son, he'd probably go into the army. Cirencester Agricultural College prepares heirs for the task of managing their estates, and currently (1979) boasts three sons of earls, three sons of viscounts, two barons' sons, a peer and, much to the joy of the popular press, a bewildered-looking Captain Mark Phillips. Sandhurst takes second and subsequent sons for

*'I don't mind you working at Christies, Georgie, but why on earth do they want to come and look over the place?'*

training in the martial arts. All that shooting is such good practice for the grouse moors later.

There is also a strong correlation between the aristocracy and the arts. Genius, being unbridled, is very upper-class. 'Look in thy heart, and write,' said Sir Philip Sidney, but don't get paid for it. No one worries about that today. Lord Kilbracken and Lord Oaksey are journalists. The

Marquess of Anglesey is writing a four-volume history of the British Cavalry. Dukes and earls burst joyously into print publishing their memoirs, or extolling the merits of their ancient houses. Lord Weymouth paints murals and writes thrillers.

In the same way, there's nothing unsmart about science as long as it's not applied. It is perfectly all right for his lordship to potter around in the west wing letting off stink bombs and making hot air balloons. But it should be pointed out that, in the arts and among academics, social snobbery is invariably suspended in favour of intellectual snobbery.

'When I find myself among scientists,' said Auden, 'I feel like a shabby curate who has strayed by mistake into a drawing-room full of dukes.'

Or as John Betjeman, gently taking the mickey out of donnish attitudes, put it:

> Objectively, our Common Room
>   Is like a small Athenian state
> Except for Lewis; he's all right
>   But do you think he's *quite* first-rate?

That tentative, fusty '*quite* first rate' seems to sum up the whole world of academic snobbery. The egghead is mightier than the strawberry leaf.

'Scientists,' said one sociologist pompously, 'tend to have a classless image, which can be embraced by working-class students without involving a denial of biological self,' which means they have very short hair and are all so common they have to go abroad to achieve any status, or hide themselves in laboratories engaged in what they call '*ree*-search'.

Most academics get on together talking shop, but all hell breaks out when their wives meet and are expected to get on.

'It was dreadful,' said one sociologist's wife after a dinner party. 'All the walls of the lounge were papered in different colours.'

You may be a giant among bio-chemists but a pygmy at the local PTA.

### Compute, compete and commute

'To the middle classes,' wrote Dahrendorf, 'the career is the supreme reality.' Fear of failing is almost as strong as the urge to succeed. The fittest survive and escape to another rung up the ladder, the unsuccessful are ostracised. The historical origins of the middle classes lie in trade. They can be traced back to the bourgeoisie in the chartered towns where they grouped together to demand their rights and govern the towns, terrifying the aristocracy in much the same way that the Trade Unions scare the middle classes today. (Samantha Upward's mother thinks TUC stands for 'Terribly Unkind Communists'.)

The middle classes didn't become really powerful until the Industrial Revolution, when the development of industry brought the need for new types of work: insurance, banking, accounting, engineering and science. Many of the people who entered these professions were successful craftsmen or farmers who had left the land. The penalty of failure was to sink back into the ranks of the working classes, so a gulf grew between them. As the big towns grew, so did the middle classes. They moved out of the towns and built suburbs and dormitory towns, and this seclusion enabled them to copy the way of life of the upper classes. Their children, as has been pointed out in chapter 4, were sent to the new boarding schools and developed refinements of dress and speech and, like all newly risen classes, walked through life gingerly as though they were treading on eggs. Their distinctive characteristic was that their work was not manual. Like the working classes, however, they had numerous rankings within themselves, which included manufacturers above the grade of foreman, most farmers, the majority of civil servants, professional people, businessmen and shopkeepers who owned their own shops, as well as independent craftsmen. It seems ludicrous to lump the small shopkeeper with the great banker, but all were united by their dedication, persistence and desire to get on.

Ever since the Middle Ages the 'professions' have considered themselves superior to bankers and businessmen and regarded themselves as a class on their own. Medicine, law and the church were suitable occupations for a gentleman; they did not dull the brain like manual work, nor corrupt the soul like commerce. They did not advertise. Some sort of qualification was needed, so they formed professional associations and became members of closely knit, protective groups.

The smartness of the various professions is subject to changes. Architects are considered smart today because there is something creative about their work. There was not, until recently, any stigma attached to a young man going into the Church, because the upper classes have to believe in God. Indeed a country parish was traditionally the destiny of younger sons with small private incomes. Medicine, as we have pointed out, is on the way down, except in the private sector. Dentists, on the other hand, are on the way up. They tend to make much more money than doctors, because they've escaped the clutches of the National Health, and because the desire for perfectly capped teeth has spread from America. Vets are also on the way up, aided by a little touch of Heriot in the night.

Schoolmasters could be described as middle-class, but again there is a vast difference between the headmaster of one of the great public schools, or fashionable prep schools, and the junior master in an urban sink school. On the whole the private sector look down on, but feel guilty about not being part of, the public sector. On the other hand they make exceptions. I was talking about the headmaster of an élitist primary school the other day.

'Oh yes,' said the head of my son's prep school. 'He's obviously a coming man. *I've met him at a dinner party.*'

Engineering has always been an unsmart profession, partly because no one knows what it involves. Harry Stow-Crat thinks it is something to do with driving a train. When people asked me what my father did I always used to say he was in the army or that he was a scientist because I thought that sounded more romantic and boffinish than being an engineer. But once again things are changing.

Among the great variety of middle-class occupations there are three main strands which are particularly in evidence: the 'burgesses', the 'spiralists' and the lower-middle class. The terms 'burgess' and 'spiralist' were coined by W. Watson in his article 'Social Mobility and Social Class in Industrial Communities' (1964). The burgess tends to stay put in the neighbourhood where he was brought up or started work, and establish prestige in the community. He is often the country solicitor, accountant or local businessman; he takes an interest in the community and often gets into local government to further his business interests.

In *Middle Class Families* Colin Bell quotes a burgess describing his life. He is a typical Howard Weybridge. The Weybridge expressions are italicised.

'My *people* have always been *comfortably off.* After going into the *forces*, I went into *Dad's* business. We have several *representatives*, who have come up from the shop floor . . . I am a very keen member of *Rotary* [on a par with Teacher and Doctor]. I belong to many clubs and associations because I think it's a good thing other Swansea *folk* see me at the right *functions*, and realise we are not just tradesmen. I also belong to several *social clubs* as a duty, so that I meet the important Swansea people.'

This is typical middle-class behaviour, the careerist socialising, the pomposity of expression, the desire to be a power in the community, a big fish in a small pool, and the joining of clubs, which would all be unthinkable to the working or upper classes.

The second category, the spiralist, moves from job to job and place to place, upping his salary and his status as he goes. Colin Bell quotes a chemist from a working-class background who is far more upper-class and direct in his language than the burgess.

'I went to a grammar school and then to a university, very red brick and provincial. I worked like hell and got a first, then did a PhD in chemistry to avoid going out in the world. Meantime I got married and had several children; after that I moved from firm to firm, upping my salary every time. Then I was promoted to Holland' (where class and accent didn't matter).

He then left the research side, because, if he didn't, he wouldn't get on, and went into the middle-class admin' side, which was far more cut-throat, but which counted for more. Now, as the head of a large industrial plant, he had to decide whether to move to head office in London to up his salary or change jobs. His only friends were people he worked with, his wife's only friends their wives. The only way to get on, he felt, was to move. He hoped it didn't interfere too much with the children's education.

'If I get a couple of notches further up,' he concluded, 'I'll send them to boarding school. Not that I really approve of it, but it will make moving about easier.'

Here you have a man, sometimes working-class, sometimes lower-middle in origin, who is prepared to sacrifice friends, children and principles to his career. In fact he's eager to leave his family and the friends of his childhood because they might be a social embarrassment. Later the spiralists often jettison their wives and trade them in for a Mark II model that goes with a new life-style.

Interesting, too, that this particular spiralist showed working-class shyness by cocooning himself against the world and taking a PhD. He made a typically working-class early marriage to combat the loneliness, but then made a deliberate decision to move over to the middle-class admin' side because it would further his career.

In a survey of managers' wives, it was shown that they all wanted their daughters to marry a 'burgess' in the professions. All believed this would provide more security and status than industry. They did not realise how many young barristers have to tramp the streets for months after qualifying before they get any work. Nor could they appreciate the status props that go with the spiralist's job: the houses, the company cars, trips for wives, gardeners and chauffeurs, the source of which can all be concealed from the neighbours.

The salient characteristic of the spiralist, whether he is from the working classes or the lower-middles, is his adaptability and his total ruthlessness. He is the cog in the wheel, the corporation man who can charm his colleagues while trampling them under foot with his slip-on Guccis. His mecca is the conference.

'I've come a long way,' said one spiralist. 'My parents were working-class in the North-East; my expectations were at best tradesman. When I'm at conferences I feel how far I've come.'

On the other hand his social mecca would be Sunningdale or East Horsley, so he often ends up turning into a Howard Weybridge.

I went to a conference recently where the spiralists were rampant. The 'venue', as they would call it, was the Café Royal, and it was all firm handshakes and announcing of names:

'Vic Taylor. Pleased to meet you Ji-ell' (always two syllables), accompanied by a card pressed into one's hand.

Another favourite gesture on seeing an acquaintance was the thumbs-up sign, or jerking the head to one side and winking simultaneously. (The middle classes, particularly schoolmasters, tend to raise one arm at about 20 degrees.) The smell of *Brut* fought frantically with that of deodorant. Most of the spiralists had goalpost moustaches and brushed-forward thatched-cottage hair, with that flattened lack of sheen which comes from

*'It's great, Angela! I've been promoted to Patagonia!'*

being washed every day under the shower, rather than in the bath. They all wore natty lightweight suits in very light colours.

On their lapels, like the faded square on Harry Stow-Crat's drawing-room wall where the Romney's been flogged, are unfaded circles which have been protected by conference badges. One could hear the rattle of Valium as they took off their lightweight long-vented jackets to reveal belted trousers. Their accent is mid-Atlantic, justified by the fact that they've spent a lot of time in the States (Non-U for America), which usually means a cheap weekend on a Thomson flight.

Their vocabulary is peppered with expressions like 'product attributes', 'growth potential', 'viability' and 'good thinking'. Perhaps it is some unconscious search for roots, but whenever they meet, they start tracing advertising genealogy.

'That's Les Brace, he used to be Saatchi and Saatchi, Garland Compton, before they became . . .', with the same intensity with which Caroline Stow-Crat and her group of jolly nice girl friends are always saying:

'Sukie Stafford-Cross, she was . . .'

Conscious of their seemingly effortless mobility, spiralists always have razors, toothbrushes, Gold Spot, pyjamas and a drip-dry shirt in their briefcases.

Our third strand is the lower-middles, who don't rise and who Orwell described as 'that shivering army of clerks and shopwalkers. You scare them by talking about class war, so they forget their incomes, remember their accents, and fly to the defence of the class that's exploiting them.' They are also the sergeant-majors, the police sergeants, the toastmasters, Prufrockian, neatly dressed, cautious, thrifty. 'In the old days,' as Len Murray pointed out, 'they had an affinity with the boss, who saw them as people who could be confided in and trusted. They haven't the bargaining power, now there's more education about.' The nineteenth-century en-trepreneur has gone, and in his place have come huge management empires, where the smooth pegs thrive in round holes.

If the ex-working-class spiralists' mecca is the conference, the lower-middle's mecca is the 'function', where, in hired dinner jackets (which they call dinner 'suits'), they play at gracious living and the 'Olde Days'. Howard Weybridge goes to lots of such occasions and rather takes them for granted. But Bryan Teale's ambition is to be president of the Stationery Trade Representatives' Association for one year, and stand with a chain round his neck, beside his wife, who has a smaller chain and a maidenhair corsage, graciously welcoming new arrivals, and being stood up for and politely applauded when they come in to dinner. Throughout the five-course dinner which starts at 6.30 they will 'take wane' with each other and various dignitaries and past presidents and their ladies down the table. As this is a Ladies' Night, each lady will get a gift of a manicure set or an evening 'pochette' in uncut moquette by her plate. Later there will be Olde Tyme dancing, interspersed with popular favourites. Bryan will 'partner' Jen in the valeta. They both enjoy 'ballroom dancing'. The conference gang, on the other hand, bop until their thatched hair nearly falls off. The difference between the lower-middle 'function' set and the spiralists is that the former crave the 'dignity' of a bygone age, while the latter, with their natty suits, their bonhomie and their slimline briefcases, are geared towards America and the future.

But the real battleground in the late 1970s was between the 'function' brigade of the clerks and insurance salesmen, and the skilled manual worker one rung below. For a long time the skilled worker has been earning far more money than most clerical workers, and because the former tend to live in rented council flats, rather than paying commercial rents or buying houses on mortgage, and have all the kiddies at state schools, they have far more money to play around with.

One notices, too, that, in the light of extra cash, people tend to think of themselves as being in a far higher class than they really are. In Woodford, which is a predominantly lower-middle-class area, 48 per cent of the skilled workers interviewed said they were middle-class, but in Greenwich, a more down-market area, only 23 per cent said they were middle-class, whereas in Dagenham, which is a working-class and principally socialist stronghold, only 13 per cent claimed middle-class status. The working classes tend to think that class depends not so much on education and income as production and consumption. Large numbers of miners interviewed in a similar survey called themselves upper-middle-class, whereas the Census would have called them upper-working-class.

# SEX AND MARRIAGE

*'My period has come upon me,' cried the Lady of Shallot.*
As was pointed out at the beginning of the last chapter, the chief factors affecting social mobility are career and marriage. If Sharon Definitely-Disgusting blossoms into a beauty and lands Georgie Stow-Crat, her future will be completely different from that of her brother Dive who marries a factory girl. If you marry beneath you, and have plenty of money, it is

possible to yank your partner up to your own level. By the time King Cophetua had given the beggar maid a few elocution lessons and smothered her in diamonds and sables, she was probably indistinguishable, save for a few 'tas' and 'pardons', from the other ladies of the court. But take a plunge both in class *and* financial status, and it's a different matter. If Queen Cophetua had fallen for a beggar, however handsome, and been cut off with 10p and forced to live on his lack of income, they would both have vanished into obscurity.

Although kings have married beggar maids, and peers' daughters eloped with garage mechanics, the fact that gossip columnists get so excited when this happens stresses both the news value and the rarity of such an event. Most of us commit endogamy, which is not a sophisticated form of bestiality, but merely marrying someone of the same class. In fact, Sir Anthony Wagner, the Clarenceux King at Arms, has gone so far as to say that a social class for him means 'an endogamous class, one that is whose members normally marry within it'. The main reason why the classes have tended to pick partners in the same stratum is to exclude the classes below. The upper classes, for example, married each other to keep their land to themselves. The bourgeoisie did the same because they didn't want to share their capital with the working class.

Much has been written about the social mobility triggered off by the sexual revolution of the sixties, with working-class lovers surging up from the East End, public school boys melting down their accents, and upper-class girls, in a glow of egalitarianism, taking on a string of down-market lovers – lorry drivers one year, negroes the next and beards the year after. But as *Harper's* has pointed out, 'Her final choice remains strangely unaffected. Somewhere there is a chartered accountant with her name on him.' Or, in Fiona Stow-Crat's case, it's back to Squire One.

### Courting

The working classes get off the mark very early. Dive Definitely-Disgusting, having gone to school locally, meets the same members of the opposite sex all the year round, like. He goes about in mixed gangs at first; then one day on the way home from school he offers to pay the bus fare of one of the girls and has the mickey taken out of him by all his mates. From then on he and the girl go round entwined like a three-legged race. As neither has a telephone at home they spend hours on the doorstep necking, or gazing into each other's eyes like cats. If they ever do talk on the telephone, the conversation is punctuated by long, long pauses. Embarrassed by tenderness or compliments, they indulge in permanent badinage and back chat. This behaviour in extreme form was ritualised by the punk rockers:

'When you fancy a girl, you spit in each other's glasses. Then the boy punk says, "Do you?" The girl answers, "Yes", and you go to the toilets.'

Jen Teale is very strict with Christine and hangs around at teenage parties, finally falling asleep at two o'clock in the morning under a pile of crisp packets like a babe in the wood. Naturally Christine reacts against Jen and she and her friends escape to London, live in hostels, go in pairs to wine bars and pick up men with eye-meets. They are very keen on what they call 'Chinese Nosh' or a 'meal e-out', and use expressions like 'a curry' or 'a wine'. Having been told since childhood to behave like little ladies, they are the most overtly flirtatious of all the classes, fluttering their eyelashes, pulling faces and rolling their eyes like Esther Rantzen, which they call being 'unimated'. When she goes into a party or a restaurant Christine always looks round to see what effect she is having on men. The upper classes never bother – and they never fidget either.

Zacharias Upward starts courting much the latest. The upper-middles haven't the self-assurance of the upper classes and, locked into a single sex school, Zacharias makes do with Thalia's friends who've been asked to stay in the holidays. Howard Weybridge and his friends are much better off. Too inhibited to pick each other up, and considering it common anyway, they have evolved an elaborate system of legitimate pick-up places: tennis clubs, rugger, golf and hockey clubs, where sporting events take place to heat the blood, followed by drinking to release the inhibitions before anyone can get going. Jim Callaghan, who was working-class, had to join the tennis club in order to court Audrey, who, by his definition, was middle-class because her parents had a car, a char and went on holiday.

Later the upper-middle classes also escape to London where they share flats with other girls and boys of 'roughly the same sort of background' (their euphemism for 'the same class'). They tend to meet the opposite sex through work, nurses going out with doctors, secretaries with bosses.

The upper classes have far more confidence. They all know each other anyway, and their parents, who they call 'wrinklies' or 'jarryatrics', have full enough social lives not to bother themselves too much about their children's morals. They worry far more about drugs and car smashes after drinking than loss of virginity.

Georgie Stow-Crat meets girls at dances in the holidays, at the Fourth of June, in Scotland in August or at the Feathers Ball, once described by the

'We're goin' steady!'

*Observer* in very unsmart terms, as the 'do of the year for those of first-class stock'.

Unlike Thalia Upward, if Fiona Stow-Crat sees a boy she likes:

'I dance over and hope he notices me. If that doesn't work I find someone who knows him and get that person to introduce me. If he still isn't interested I give up.'

When they're older, the upper classes meet skiing, shooting and at various up-market occasions like Ascot and Henley. At parties they go in for lots of horse play and shrieking. Linda in *Love in a Cold Climate* was far more attractive to the opposite sex than the more beautiful Polly because she was a 'romper' – almost a sort of chap. The upper classes are inclined to lean out of windows and pour champagne on tramps and parked cars, or to charge around at dead of night changing road signs. The sexes also meet each other at drinks parties in the girls' flats in Knightsbridge and Belgravia. Even if the party isn't being given in her flat, the hostess sends out 'At Home' cards, and the recipient automatically runs her thumb over the words 'At Home' to see if they're engraved.

### The season

Up to the late fifties most upper-class girls 'came out'. One's mother, who'd been presented herself, presented one to the Queen, and the Nouveau-Richards bribed some impoverished upper-class woman to do the same for Tracey-Diane. In 1958, however, the Queen abolished the whole presentation ceremony, which meant that anyone could become a deb. The season was swamped by social climbers and lost any kind of cachet.

Despite this setback, a few hundred girls still come out every year. The process is to write to Peter Townend, the social editor of *The Tatler*, for a list of 'gairls' doing the season. Then follows a string of luncheons where the mothers get together, see that party dates don't clash and make sure that their daughters get asked to as many things as possible. Clued-up mothers have stickers printed with their own and their daughter's addresses on. The minute the first luncheon reaches the coffee stage out come the diaries and everyone charges round seeing how many stickers they can get into other people's diaries.

Many of the upper classes sell farms or woods to pay for dances. It is also necessary to suck up to Peter Townend in order to get your daughter's picture in *The Tatler*. He can also produce young men out of a hat whose background, education, regiment or sheer cash-flow make them eligible. Most of the young men live in the country or a precious stone's throw from Harrods.

One of the great dangers is that one's daughter may fall in love with one of them at the beginning of the season and wreck her chances with other men. 'Don't you dare go steady,' I heard one mum say recently. 'Just like the lower classes.'

One has the feeling that the mothers enjoy the season almost more than the daughters. Many of them, still youngish and pretty, have the chance to meet up with old gairlfriends and flirt with old flames.

At the end of the season I asked a deb's mum, did she feel all the expense had been worth it?

'Oh yes,' she replied. 'The gairls have all had such fun, and at the worst, they'll have built up a network of jolly nice gairlfriends.'

'And even if they do go astray', boomed her friend, 'one knows they'll go astray with the right sort of chap' (which is back to endogamy again).

### Rough diamonds are a girl's best friend

'When the mind is full of tit and bum,' a friend of mine once said, 'it tends to be a-critical,' meaning that, in the first flush of love, you don't mind what class a person is. The fact that he's not 'the right sort of chap' makes him even more attractive. When they are young, the insecure of both sexes tend to drop class. Older upper-class men love going to bed with working-class girls. It reminds them of nanny. For the same reason, they adore big strapping Australian girls. One Australian journalist went to interview an earl about wealth tax and only moved out six months later.

Equally, going out with a yobbo gives the middle- and upper-class girl a feeling of superiority. She also finds working-class men more respectful but at the same time more dominating than their public school counterparts. (Geoffrey Gorer claims that the skilled worker has the highest sexual energy – so she's on to a good thing.)

It should be pointed out here that the working and upper classes tend to be far more chauvinistic than the upper-middle and middle-middle classes. This is perhaps because they are more reactionary, but also because they tend to have everything done for them by their mothers or nannies; whereas the middle-class mother, struggling for the first generation without servants, is much more likely to have made her son run around fetching and carrying for her. The middle-class man will therefore be far more prepared to reverse roles. This is important because it is crucial to an understanding of the different attitudes to sex, dating and women in general.

The first great love of my life was a miner's son who'd become a millionaire. I was working on a newspaper in Brentford. He passed by in a vast, open, dark green car, and screeched to a halt. I bolted into my office, but when I sidled out two hours later he was still waiting. He was the most handsome man I'd ever seen, and it was all very disgraceful and wildly exciting. He took me straight back to his house, whereupon he told me to go and make him a cup of tea. I was far more shocked than if he'd tried to seduce me. None of my stuffy middle-class boyfriends had ever bossed me round like that.

We went out for nearly three years . . . Whenever he went abroad on business, and, I suspect, pleasure, he never wrote. This broke my heart. I only discovered years later that he was ashamed of being ill-educated. He was shocked if I said 'blast', and would never come to any of my parties, although I was dying to show him off, because he was frightened of not knowing how to behave. He went to see his mother every day.

He was bossy, yet socially tentative, prudish yet unfaithful, and mother-fixated – all working-class qualities; yet we had three marvellous years. He was incredibly generous, showering me with presents which cost a fortune and which were returned (my middle-class background again) whenever we had one of our periodic bust-ups. And he was far more masculine, more reassuring and more fun than any of the uptight barristers, stockbrokers and account executives I'd run about with before. If he had asked me to marry him, I should certainly have said yes, but he had the good sense to realise we were far too different for it ever to work. For when the class war and the sex war are joined, hostilities always break out in the end.

Alan Coren said that, when he was at Oxford, upper-class undergraduates screwed nurses and married upper-class girls, while working-class undergraduates married nurses and screwed upper-class girls, yelling 'One for Jarrow' at the moment of orgasm.

Richard Hoggart, that champion of the lower orders, says that one of the most valuable characteristics of the working classes is the ability to take the mickey and say 'Come off it', which the middle classes usually translate as having a 'bloody great chip on one's shoulder'. This trait frequently comes out in working-class intellectuals when they have affairs with middle-class girls. One remembers Jimmy Porter constantly bitching at his gentle, long-suffering wife.

Another example of working-class chippiness coupled with macho occurred recently with a beautiful girlfriend of mine who was running two men at once, one of them an underwriter and the first man ever to wear full eye make-up to Lloyd's, the other a working-class pop music promoter. One day the Lloyd's underwriter took her for a row in Hyde Park. They were just pulling into shore when the music promoter leapt out of the bushes where he'd been lurking and pushed the underwriter into the lake, where he stood spluttering and threatening to call the police.

'If he'd been working-class,' said the music promoter later, 'he'd have slugged me back. I didn't throw him in the water because I was jealous about you but because he was upper-class.'

If Zacharias Upward goes out with Christine Teale, Gideon and Samantha will talk scathingly about 'Not quite PLU [People like Us] darling' or 'rather Pardonia', and pray that their children will grow out of it. Middle-class parents also become particularly tolerant in the face of eligibility. If you go out with someone much grander than yourself, you tend to take on some of their mannerisms. Friends noticed that when Roddy Llewellyn was going out with Princess Margaret he assumed the patrician poker face, used the pronoun 'one' instead of 'I', and started walking around with his hands behind his back like Prince Philip.

## The date

When Dive Definitely-Disgusting takes a girl out on a date he's likely to be much cleaner than Zacharias Upward who often goes out straight from the office. Dive has a bath and a good scrub before getting dressed for the evening. He'll reek of Brut and over-scented deodorant and wear an open-necked shirt to reveal a hairy, muscular chest clanking with medallions. He'll be extraordinarily generous with drinks, but he won't give the girl dinner (having already had high tea, so as not to drink on an empty stomach) because he's frightened of 'resteronts' as he calls them. He can't understand the menu if it's in French, he doesn't know how to order wine or how to eat asparagus, and is terrified of making a fool of himself asking for steak tartare to be well done or complaining that the Vichyssoise is stone cold. This is why many restaurants qualify food on the menu, like 'chilled' watercress soup, and probably explains the popularity of melon because it's the same in French and English.

Being taken out to dinner is such a treat for Sharon Definitely-Disgusting that she always goes right through the menu, and always has pudding. She won't comment on the food or say 'Thank you' afterwards. One working-class girl I know went out with a lower-middle sales rep who had an expense-account acquaintance with 'resteronts'. 'He was so charming and well spoken,' she said afterwards, 'and such a gentleman. He kept telling me what knife and fork to use and correcting my conninenal accent.'

'Waiter! There's an
eyelash in my friend's soup.'

Georgie Stow-Crat would never correct pronunciation or comment on table manners. If his companion wants an 'avocado' pear, let her have one.

The manager of our local restaurant is a great observer of dating couples. 'You can always tell a girl who's escalated,' he says. 'She talks direct to the waiter, instead of letting the man order for her. Artichokes are a great leveller; I saw one girl trying to eat the whole thing.'

'People who belong,' he went on, 'always hold their coats in mid-air when they take them off. The *nouveau riche* never say "good evening", are curt with waiters, snap their fingers and then over-tip. They also put vinegar on their chips.'

Both Christine Teale and Sharon Definitely-Disgusting prefer sweet drinks to dry: sweet Cinzano, Martini, Baby Cham and orange (a sort of Doe's fizz), Tia Maria, Crème de Menthe. If they drink gin, it's with orange.

Sharon also likes a man to be neatly dressed on a date. 'If he had a holey sweater or holey jeans I wouldn't entertain him,' she says. 'And he must be clean. I couldn't stand all those rockers a few years back with dirty hair. I like a boy with a bit of life in him, but not rough.' She would also say, 'I've got a snapshot of him indoors' (which is working-class for 'at home').

Christine Teale refers to a boyfriend over twenty-one as a 'boy' ('I'm going out with a wonderful boy'). Most people say 'boyfriend' or 'man'. The upper classes, when they're trying to be democratic and trendy, say 'guy' in inverted commas. One should never talk about an 'escort'. According to *U and Non-U Revisited* one should say 'male companion', which seems a bit pedantic. Most people merely say the person's Christian name, and leave you to guess who they're talking about. It is also vulgar to say, 'May I bring my girl?' as opposed to 'a girl' when you mean a girlfriend.

Unlike the working classes who don't bother about the morrow, Wayne Teale tends to be tight with money. To splash it around is both prodigal and cheap. He won't buy a girl dinner, so he'll put on a paisley scarf, which he calls a 'cravat', tucked into a sweater, and take her to a bar where he knows the landlord by his Christian name. This he calls 'social drinking'. If he's over thirty, he might wear a white orlon polo-neck jersey which he'll call a 'rollneck' (to rhyme with doll) sweater, because a touch of white is so flattering after a certain age and the neck hides the wrinkles in his throat. He refers to a girl as an 'attractive young lady'. He would prefer her to wear a skirt than jeans, even though his trouser creases are sharp enough to ladder her tights. He's also read somewhere that it's common to say perfume, but scent sounds too foxy, so he settles for 'fragrance'. Gideon would probably say, 'That's a nice pong'.

Caution is the watchword of the lower-middles. Wayne daren't be romantic in case some unsuitable 'young lady' traps him into matrimony.

He would call it getting 'invōle-ved' with a long 'o'. He doesn't resort to insults and backchat like the working classes, but his conversation is arch, and rather hearty with an air of continual interrogation, rather like Bob Dale or the non-yokels in *The Archers*. He will use expressions like 'Chop Chop, Young Lady', or, even worse, address his girlfriend as 'Woman'. She will say in reply, 'Stir your stumps, Wayne Teale.' It is frightfully lower-middle to address people by both their Christian name and surname. Any money Bryan makes will be spent on what he calls 'home improvements' or on his car, which has a Christian name and is always referred to as 'she'.

Zacharias Upward likes entertaining girlfriends in his flat where he can show off his gourmet cooking. This is cheaper than going to restaurants, saves on petrol, and is much nearer the bedroom. All his friends say Zak is very 'hos*pit*able' (the upper classes emphasise the first syllable).

Howard Weybridge's idea of an exciting date is to ask his girlfriend to freeze on the touchline while he grapples muddily with a lot of other fifteen-stoners on the rugger field. Later she will be expected to talk to rugger wives about deep freezes while he frolics naked in a plunge bath with the rest of the team, and then make one warm gin and tonic last all evening while he downs pints and pints of beer. In summer she might get taken to cricket, which is sometimes warmer but goes on longer.

Georgie Stow-Crat will be very generous to his girlfriends – like Oscar Wilde who, when asked why he gave champagne to a barrow boy, replied, 'What gentleman would starve his guests?' Georgie can't cook and would starve in a well-equipped kitchen. So, as he is too thick to make conversation for very long, he takes girls to dine in a night club or a disco. Romance, according to Tina Browne in *Over 21*, blooms in the twilight gloom of smart places like Wedgies and Annabels. As the upper classes tend to leave London at the weekend, Fridays and Saturdays are very bad nights at Wedgies.

*Who marries whom*
*'Education! I was always led to suppose that no educated person ever spoke of notepaper, and yet I hear poor Fanny asking Sadie for notepaper. What is this education? Fanny talks about mirrors and mantelpieces, handbags and perfume, she takes sugar in her coffee, has a tassel on her umbrella, and I have no doubt if she is ever fortunate enough to catch a husband, she will call his father and mother Father and Mother. Will the wonderful education she is getting make up to*

*the unhappy brute for all these endless pinpricks? Fancy hearing one's*
*wife talk about notepaper – the irritation!'*

Uncle Matthew in
*The Pursuit of Love*
by Nancy Mitford.

As the upper classes all know each other, they get in a panic if their children get engaged to someone they haven't heard of.

Georgie Stow-Crat plays around with girls of other classes before and after his marriage, but he'll try and settle for one of his own kind. For what are a few nights of passion for a lifetime at the wrong end of the table? Lord Lichfield took out a string of models and actresses, but he ended up with Lady Leonora Grosvenor. More recently the Marquess of Douro married the Princess of Prussia, the Duke of Roxburghe married Lady Leonora's sister, Lady Jane, while their brother, the 6th Duke of Westminster, chose Miss Natalie Phillips, granddaughter of Sir Harold and Lady Zia Wernher. As the aristocracy are forced 'to straphang through life like the rest of us', they are closing their ranks and marrying the sort of gairl who will bring some cash or property with her, or as one aristocrat put it, 'can make a decent lunch for a shooting party'. 'The reason why my marriage came unstuck,' said a duke's daughter, 'was because I was upper-class and he was only landed gentry.' The moment Georgie Stow-Crat gets engaged he takes the girl to meet nanny, which is far more of an ordeal than meeting Harry and Caroline.

What the upper classes really dread is their child falling for someone middle-class.

'A thoroughly conventional man in good society,' said Edward Lyttelton, a former headmaster of Eton, 'would rather that his son should consort with prostitutes than that he should marry a respectable girl of distinctly lower station than his own. Indeed it is not going too far to say that he probably would rather his son should seduce such a girl, provided there were no scandal, than marry her.'

In order not to be continually irritated by class differences the aristocracy often marry rich Americans or foreigners, who they can instruct in upper-class English behaviour without being too insulting:

'In England, Ortrud, we have a funny national custom of not saying "horse racing".'

If Georgie Stow-Crat did marry down, he would tend to pick a very beautiful girl, which is why the aristocracy is so good-looking. In general, good-looking people marry up – Tony Armstrong-Jones and Captain Mark Phillips being notable examples – and the insecure and ugly tend to marry down. Just as they dropped class while dating, they tend to pick a partner who'll look up to them and make them feel superior.

When people get married for the first time late in life – in their forties or fifties – parents are inclined to waive class prejudices out of sheer relief that their 'child' is finally off their hands.

It is debatable whether the middle classes have any real desire to land an aristocrat any more. As has been said already, the lord is no longer the favourite hero of romantic fiction (unless he's in costume of course) and has been replaced by the middle-class doctor or surgeon.

Heather Jenner says her marriage bureau clients 'don't give a hoot' what class people are any more. 'Why should they want to marry a lord and cope with a falling-down overgrown house? On the whole blue-collar men are far better at giving a woman a good time. One upper-class woman was so fed up with the sexual and financial ineptitude of the aristocracy she put "Working Class Only" on her form.'

On the other hand, another girl who ran a marriage bureau, discovering she had a baronet among her clients, promptly whipped him off the books and married him herself. Another friend of mine, born on a council estate, can pinpoint the moment she fell in love with her future husband, who is a peer: 'He signed a cheque to pay for our dinner with his surname only.' Finally one has only to read the small ads in *The Tatler* – 'Very attractive blue-blooded academic in his early thirties equally at ease on the hunting field or engaged in economic and political discussion' (sounds hell) – to realise that class does have a pull. The Blue Bloody is still holding his own against the Blue Collar.

The upper-middle-class man, preferring to get his career together before settling down, tends to marry late, between twenty-eight and thirty-two; his bride will be in her mid-twenties. Often they live together first, particularly if one set of parents disapproves. Then gradually, out of sheer force of habit, or desire for grandchildren, the parents come round.

Samantha Upward, who's always taught Zacharias to be unsnobbish, finds the thought of being a mother-in-law awfully trying. First there was Zulunka from the Fiji Islands, who was really wonderfully dark, but who spoilt it all by referring to all those nice Africans as 'no-good blacks'. And now there's Mikki (who's really called Enid) who appears to have no surname. Mikki does something nebulous in the music business, is totally uncultured, but full of pretensions. In referring to herself and Samantha collectively as 'middle-class folk like ourselves' she is obviously totally unaware that Samantha's family is much better than hers is. Even more maddening Gideon obviously thinks that Mikki is quite, quite perfect, particularly as she doesn't wear a stitch in bed. Gideon insists on taking her a cup of tea first thing to admire her early morning teats.

The lower-middle parents, being materialistic, aren't sure whether to oppose early marriage as unsound financially or welcome it as better than pre-marital promiscuity. One lower-middle spiralist said the reason he finally decided to marry his wife was because she'd been brought up in a careful household, and therefore would be a good manager of his money. Believing in deferred satisfaction, Wayne tends to be engaged for several years, rather than live with a girl, so he can put down a deposit on a house. He will 'study for exams' in the evening, his 'fiancay' Shirl will work in a bar, and bank the lot, so they have enough money to move into a perfectly 'decorated home'. Shirl can't stand disorder – she must have everything nice. The upper-middle girl who wanted to get married in a hurry would be perfectly happy to move into a rented box in Fulham and run up an overdraft doing the place up, or expect Daddy to fork out for carpets and things later.

The Nouveau-Richards will be absolutely furious if Tracey-Diane doesn't marry up. In the same way that the middle-class Princess Grace was livid, having hooked a prince herself, that her daughter settled for a middle-class industrialist.

Parents are very seldom cross about upward mobility. Even when engagements are broken off, they can make social capital out of it, like the mother who went round telling her friends:

'It's such a bore having to pick the coronets off all the linen.'

Dive Definitely-Disgusting marries the earliest. This is probably due to frustration. He's likely to have no flat or car to make love in. If he goes home Mrs D-D and the children are watching the telly – and it's too cold outside, except in summer. They also started dating earlier anyway, and if they do screw they don't bother to 'take precautions', get pregnant and can't afford abortions.

'I didn't *have* to get married, I married for love,' a working-class minicab driver told me the other day, as if it were the exception to the rule.

Engaged at seventeen Sharon Definitely-Disgusting gets 'eternised' at eighteen, which means she receives an eternity ring from her betrothed. At Christmas and birthdays she will send him a four-foot-square card padded with red satin, saying 'To my Darling Fiance' (without the accent).

The word 'fiancé', perhaps because so many people live together now, has become distinctly vulgar, particularly when it is pronounced 'fee-on-*cay*' with the weight on the last syllable. Debs get round sometimes by saying 'my fiasco' or 'my intended' in inverted commas.

## The wedding

The wedding is another occasion when the classes meet head on. People who marry up choose tiny churches, or have registry office weddings so they don't have to invite less grand relations. It doesn't matter having common friends; everyone thinks one's frightfully democratic. But common relations are quite a different matter. Wedding presents aren't displayed either, because they might cause derisive mirth at the reception. Embarrassing relations also show up less at a stand-up reception with food you can eat with your fingers (which Jen Teale calls a 'finger buffet'), so people's table manners don't show up – and with any luck working-class relations will push off early because they hate not being able to sit down.

There will invariably be a panic about protocol. One girl said her mother poured over *The Tatler* for months, studying every detail of the weddings, muttering 'we're going to get this right if it kills me'. 'We even put a sleeping pill in Grandad's cocoa the night before, because he refused to wear morning dress.'

When John Betjeman married a very upper-class girl, he drove his future mother-in-law insane at the pre-wedding party by wearing a made-up bow tie on elastic and flicking it all the way through dinner.

But, however critical he or she may be of the behaviour of others, the true aristocrat is a law unto himself. The men had just finished dinner at a stag party in a private room at a London club when the bridegroom's father, an aged Earl, suddenly beckoned to a waiter and said, 'Pot'.

'We're not allowed to supply it, Sir,' said the waiter, nervously.

'Don't be bloody silly,' roared the Earl. 'I mean piss-pot.' Whereupon a huge chamber pot was brought down from one of the bedrooms and the Earl proceeded to use it in full view of the other guests.

The upper classes get married in the country in their own churches. As they are accustomed to giving and going to balls and big parties, the wedding is not such an event as it would be in a middle-class family. Quite often the bride wears her mother's wedding dress, and a 200-year-old veil of Brussels lace held in place by the family tiara. (One upper-class bride was so relaxed she spent her wedding morning washing her horse's tail.) She doesn't usually have a long engagement or any of the hassle of finding a house, because her parents or her in-laws have already given them a 'place' with lots of 'pieces' in it.

The wedding invitations are engraved in black; the service cards have the bride and bridegroom's (pronounced 'gr'm' not 'grume') Christian names printed at the bottom. Flowers in the church are usually something unostentatious like lilies of the valley, with the bride's bouquet (pronounced '*book*-kay' not 'buke-*ay*') of white roses or spring flowers.

The men wear their own morning coats. There are usually hordes of little bridesmaids called Sophie and Henrietta, a page with patent leather hair wearing a replica of a Blues and Royals uniform, and a labrador who wriggles ingratiatingly into the wedding photographs. No one minds about the music – 'Here Comes the Bride' up, Mendelssohn down. The bride agrees to honour and obey. It used to be unsmart to get married at the weekend, particularly in London, as everyone had gone away. But now that most of the upper classes and their show business friends have jobs it is considered perfectly all right. Saturday police have to be deployed from the local football match to deal with the traffic. Several of the guests arrive by helicopter.

After the service the line-up to shake hands with the couple takes hours and hours. We queued interminably at a royal wedding a few years ago – it was rather like mountaineering. You crawled along for ten minutes, then turned into the next room to find another queue, and then another up a staircase and then another. People kept giving up, and doing U-turns to go out to dinner. One felt they ought to provide something to sustain one during the waiting: champagne at the foothills, or brandy at the South Col, or at least lay on buskers.

At another very grand wedding, having been nervously practising my curtsey all the way, I found, when we finally reached the bride and bridegroom, that everyone was shaking hands with them.

'I thought we were supposed to bob,' I muttered to a friend once I was safely inside.

'I was damned if I was going to bob to that jumped-up trollop,' she said, 'and after that everyone followed suit.'

The reception at an upper-class wedding is a very cheerful occasion, once again because everyone knows each other, and it doesn't matter that there's no introducing. None of the women look the least self-conscious in hats. The cake is decorated with white flowers, and often cut with the bridegroom's sword, the nearest it ever gets to active service. Really grand weddings include busloads of tenants from both families. Usually they sit around with red faces, shiny blue suits and tumbrilcreemed hair. But at Earl Grosvenor's wedding recently morning coats were hired for all the tenants, so that they wouldn't feel out of place, and they were all flown down by aeroplane.

Georgie Stow-Crat hates his honeymoon because he misses Snipe. Upper-class girls often take Teddy on honeymoon.

When Georgie marries Tracey Nouveau-Richards no expense is spared. Tracey's tiara is so heavy her head droops like a snowdrop. The 'floral decorations' composed of 'Football Mum' chrysanthemums, nurtured in Mr Nouveau-Richards' conservatory, are described by Mrs N-R's friends as 'tasteful'. Mrs N-R hires a hundred out-of-work actors to pose as relations, and two hundred more as tenants. They rather overdo the Somerset accents and rust-coloured country suits. The wedding takes place in Guildford Cathedral, with a reception at the bridal home in Sunningdale. The marquee extends beyond the garden and covers much of the golf course. Guests keep falling down the holes. Three tons of Joy are squirted into the swimming pool on which float the words 'George' and 'Tracey-Diane', written in salmon-pink carnations.

Mrs Nouveau-Richards has had orchids and maidenhair corsages in little test tubes of preservative liquid made up for herself and Caroline Stow-Crat, who surreptitiously tries to rip off the maidenhair during the service and only succeeds in burning a hole in her new coat and skirt with the preservative. Signing the register takes longer than usual as Mrs N-R's hat gets stuck in the door.

Harry Stow-Crat has a wonderful time. There's plenty of champagne – Tracey-Diane's endowment of worldly goods means he needn't worry about death duties anymore. All Mrs Nouveau-Richards' hired relations turn out to be his show business cronies, which persuades him the N-R's do know some quite amusing people after all.

The Upwards are simply furious they haven't been invited.

'You can't ask everyone,' says Samantha bravely, although Mrs Nouveau-Richards seems to have done just that.

The upper-middle wedding is far more depressing. Samantha, wanting to be different and stress how 'cultured' and musical she is, chooses hymns the congregation don't know. Lists are placed at Peter Jones or the General Trading Company, so everyone knows what they're getting. Waiters keep the napkin over the champagne to hide the lack of vintage. No one wears maidenhair behind their carnations except a few *déclassé* cousins in lounge suits.

As the upper-middle classes don't all know each other, but are too grand for a sit-down meal, their weddings tend to be rather heavy going. The women's heels sink into the lawn so they can't circulate. The merriment is not aided by a long speech from the bride's parents' most upper-class friend. No one can clap properly at the end because they're holding empty glasses. Thalia's husband hates his honeymoon and thinks they're so called because they're so sticky.

Howard and Eileen Weybridge's wedding is held in the function room of the Olde White Hart (circa 1937) with French windows opening on to the patio. The women look very self-conscious in floppy hats, and show too much hair at the front. The bride makes her own wedding dress, or buys it off the peg. According to one manufacturer, royalty influences far more wedding dresses than show business, and the less virginal a girl is the more covered-up she wants to look. Howard Weybridge and his ushers are photographed outside the church in hired morning coats with maidenhair rampant behind every foiled carnation, and their top hats on the sides of their heads. The reception starts off with sweet and dry sherry followed by Asti Spumante ('bubbly' is too expensive). Everyone sits down to lunch of a nice smoked trout, chicken and bombe surprise, after frightful rows over the seating arrangements. The speakers, likely to be local councillors or secretaries of the tennis club, who adore the sound of their own voices, go on for ever, and every dismally unfunny telegram is read out.

The bride's mother finds the 'holl' occasion very 'meuving'. 'It's such a nice opportunity to meet and converse with relatives,' and Eileen's had 'some wonderful wedding gifts'. The father says, 'Look after yerself,' as Eileen goes away in the Austin Princess and a navy costume with beige accessories. The honeymoon is spent in the bridal suite of a hotel in Devonshire.

The lower-middles are the tiredest when they get married, because they've just 'decorated and renovated their new property' themselves. (Georgie Stow-Crat would say 'done up the house') all ready to move in.

Bryan Teale has his stag party two nights before the wedding because Auntie Jean has to be met off the train from Scotland on Friday, and the car has to be put through the car-wash before they go away. No one wears a morning coat; the men are in three-piece waisted suits; the best man goes off to buy shoes with built-up heels on the morning of the wedding so his trousers hang better. The 'bridal gown' is based on the latest royal soap opera with Mrs Fitzherbert sleeves. The photographer snaps away throughout the service at all the most solemn moments. People are shown to their seats by 'groomsmen' rather than 'ushers', and the results are put in a white album with spider tissue paper. The service cards are printed in silver Gothic script and decorated with silver bells and the bride and groom's initials. The bridegroom has to remove his initialled signet ring to his right hand to make way for his wedding ring, and the happy couple, smothered in confetti and rice, leave the church in a white Rolls-Royce.

The reception is held at the Dainty Maiden Tea Rooms, and thirsty cyclists who've ridden over from Godalming are told to go to the Hand in the Bush Tea Rooms down the road, as the place has been taken over for a 'function'. Sherry is followed by *vin rosé* or sparkling hock. Everyone eats ham, chicken and salad. The wedding cake is topped by a papier mâché replica of the bride and groom both wearing lipstick, and decorated with silver shoes, horseshoes and plastic flowers.

The bride, wearing a tangerine 'skirt suit', and the bridegroom, in an even lighter coloured and more waisted suit, go off to Majorca for the honeymoon where the new Mrs Teale loses her virginity on the third night.

The working-class wedding is the jolliest. Mrs Definitely-Disgusting has even forgiven Stan for putting Sharon in the club – at least he's white. The hall is hired at the Goat and Boots; the bar is open all day; everyone sits down or dances – the working classes never stand because of their corns. Dad soon gets down to the piano, and starts playing 'golden oldies' like 'Deep in the Heart of Texas'. Auntie Eileen leads the singing. Even Mrs Definitely-Disgusting is persuaded to do a knees up. Sharon wears an empire-line dress to hide the bulge and feels sick all the time. The honeymoon is spent in Jersey. Having never been away from home before, Stan and Sharon are very homesick.

### Oh come oh come non-Manuel

It is difficult to generalise about sex and class. Hunter Davies, a working-class writer so successful that he has certainly become middle-class in life style, expressed his bewilderment in a recent *Sunday Times* article at his thirteen-year-old daughter going out with boys and demanding parties with drink: 'Brought up on a council estate in the 'sixties, I married the school swot. It took me three weeks even to hold her hand. My dad knew what it was like for me when I was courting, but things have changed so much in the last ten years that I haven't a clue what it's like to be Caitlin. She's a different age, a *different class*, a different society.'

With the advent of the permissive society, one hopes that the young of all classes are getting better at sex and more aware of 'the great discovery of the age', as Hugh MacDiarmid calls it, 'that women like it too.'

But there are still vast pockets of male chauvinism among the upper and lower classes, particularly in the north. It is possible that young Georgie Stow-Crat and Dive Definitely-Disgusting are fairly competent operators, having picked up a few tips from the cinema and Anna Raeburn, but their fathers are probably still floundering around in the dark ages.

Harry Stow-Crat's attitude to sex, for example, is the same as that of our late lamented English setter, who was spoilt, goofy, terrifyingly tenacious and with a totally unbridled sex drive. If he got on the trail of a bitch, he would charge across three main roads, race twenty miles until he caught up with her, and then mount her from the wrong end. His libido was only equalled by his sexual ineptitude – rather like one peer who discovered after three years during which no heir appeared that he'd been buggering his wife all the time.

Another married aristocrat I know was so wild to pull a girl he'd had lunch with that he smuggled her into the Great Western Hotel by a side door, broke into an unoccupied bedroom and was just settling down to work when the management rumbled him. Only a lot of fast talking and a fistful of fivers stopped him being arrested and the most frightful scandal ensuing.

If Harry fancies a girl, particularly a lower-class one, he will pester her until he gets her, and then it's wham, bam, thank you, ma'am. He's far too used to poor Caroline shutting her eyes and thinking of England to believe a woman should derive any pleasure from the act.

The telly-stocrat and the pop singer have the same exalted approach. 'It's so easy,' sighed one rock star. 'You have all these groupies; there's no time to romance (lower-middle for to court) on the road, so you just say, "Get your gear off".' A sort of *droit de Singer*.

My favourite mini-cab driver has a theory that tall people are good in bed because only they can reach the sex books that librarians insist on putting on the top shelves. But this doesn't explain why aristocrats, who are generally tall, tend to be hopeless. Maybe they never go into public libraries, or don't read anything except the *Sporting Life* and Dick Francis. Harry's sole aim is vaginal penetration; he can't even count up to foreplay. When a girl kisses him, she can feel his narrow stoat's head under his straight mousy hair, totally devoid of any Beethoven bumps. As he thinks aftershave and deodorant are vulgar, and he doesn't have any middle-class hangups about being nice to be near, he might even be rather dirty.

Aristocrats often break their toes on stone hot-water bottles climbing into other people's beds at house parties. One wonders what the procedure is. Does the hostess sleep with the man in the right-hand bedroom for the first half of the night, and the man in the left-hand bedroom for the second half? Presumably anything goes as long as you're back in your own room by dawn so as not to upset the servants. Most of the upper classes share beds with their dogs for warmth. When a lover leaps into bed and thinks he has encountered something interesting and furry, he may easily get bitten.

As they have all the freedom and restlessness of inherited wealth, there is a wild decadent fringe of the aristocracy, whose sexual appetites are so jaded that they're into every perversion under the eldest son. Having enjoyed beatings at Eton, both Harry and Georgie Stow-Crat adore being whipped. You can recognise an old school bottom – striped with red, white and blue weals – anywhere.

Most life peers, who have been far too busy making it to the top to get any practice, are absolutely hopeless in bed.

### Once you have found her never let her come

The upper-middles used to be even worse than the aristocracy. Too inhibited even to have Harry's *joie de vivre*, their upper-middle lips were far too stiff for them to be any good at oral sex. Gideon's parents must have had terrible sex lives because of overhead lights in the bedroom. Once they'd switched the lights off by the door, the room was plunged in darkness, so it is a miracle that they even found each other and managed to produce Gideon.

Moving down a generation, Gideon is very enthusiastic, but a bit mainline – *Playboys* in the lavatory and a finger under his next-door neighbour's roll-on at New Year's Eve parties. He knows all about middle-class sophistication and de-furred satisfaction and longs for Samantha to shave her bush off. She did once but it was awfully itchy, and as the whole family have baths together, it might have put Zacharias off his O-levels. But she's frightfully understanding about Gideon's *Playboys* and allows him to do anything he likes to her in bed, shutting her eyes and thinking of Great Britain and the Common Market. She does her yoga every morning to keep herself young and attractive.

The best lover of all is the upper-middle-class intellectual. Having been made to run round by his mother when he was young, he's into role reversal and a woman having as much pleasure as a man. His already vivid imagination has been encouraged by voracious reading. He's just as randy as the aristocrat, but he tempers it with finesse and humility. Lucky the girl that lays the golden egghead.

A male stud who has done extensive field work agrees that middle-class intellectual women are also best in bed. The *Guardian* reader, he says, is the easiest lay of them all, because she feels she ought to be liberated and knows all about rejection and blows to the male ego. She always refers to coming as 'a climax', says 'penis' and 'vagina' and talks about her friends having 'lovely breasts'.

The lower-middles tend to be too cautious. It's all 'nudge nudge', prurience and not much pleasure. Jen Teale is also terribly difficult to get at because she wears such an armour-plating of full-length petticoats, which she calls 'slips', corselettes, five pairs of 'punties', tights with trousers, which she calls 'punts', and 'punty girdles'. Dainty and fastidious, she would never make love while she has the curse (which she calls a 'period') and she is 'revollted' by anything slightly off-centre. Afterwards she says, 'that was very pleasant, Bryan.'

Mandy Rice-Davies, interviewed in a sex book, is a good example of lower-middle refinement: 'Looking sexy is a very low-class turn-on . . . I've had brief affairs with Lord Astor and Douglas Fairbanks Jr. [here she displays parvenu boasting and lack of discretion] but none of those involved anything remotely kinky.'

*Working-class sex*
The working classes have a reputation for potency and being good in bed – a myth probably started by middle-class novelists and by graphologists who claim that anyone with loopy writing must be highly sexed. Randy they certainly seem to be. According to an Odhams Survey, the working-class couple makes love more than any other class, but the woman enjoys it less.

'We don't fight,' said one builder's wife, 'only over money and sex, especially sex. He always wants it. He'd do it now if he came in and you weren't here.'

Geoffrey Gorer maintains that the skilled worker (Class III) would appear to have more sexual energy than the other classes. But he says that there does not seem to be any factual basis for believing that the working classes in general are more sexually potent. He quotes an upholsterer who only had sex three or four times a month, and a welder who only had it once a month (perhaps he got stuck).

Mrs D-D calls sex 'having relations' or 'in-ercourse'. If there were any

*'Oh my Gawd!'*

sexual problems, she would be far too embarrassed to discuss them. Mr D-D is not into foreplay; he uses that finger to read the racing results.

A divorce lawyer told me that the working classes hardly ever see each other naked, probably because they often sleep in one room with the children, and if Mr D-D takes his clothes off Mrs D-D might see 'Rosy', 'Mum', 'Nancy' and 'Doreen' tattooed all over his body and get jealous. As he also imagines all women have *retrousée* tits, sopping wet hair and full make-up like page 3 of *The Sun*, Mrs D-D undressed might be a bit of a disappointment.

### Marrying up

No one understood the nuances of class better than Chekhov. At the beginning of *Three Sisters* Natasha, Andrey's fiancée, is seen as a lower-middle-class social outcast. Everyone laughs at her and the three sisters tell her her clothes are all wrong. Then she marries their brother and gradually she gains ascendancy. She starts bossing the sisters about, henpecking her husband and being beastly to the old servants ('I don't like having useless people about'). Soon she is cutting down trees on the estate and moving the sisters into smaller bedrooms, until by the end they are meekly taking criticism from her about their clothes.

People who marry up are more insistent than most on having their new status recognised. I'm sure that Cophetua's beggar maid, despite her lovesome mien, made a perfect nuisance of herself queening it over everyone, and we have all seen how the middle-class Princess Grace became far more regal than royalty once she landed Prince Rainier.

One woman who married a duke suddenly insisted on having a room to herself at the hairdressers, 'because I'm not just anyone anymore.' Often they can't quite master the new vocabulary.

'We're spending the weekend at Bath's seat,' said a secretary who'd just landed a peer.

Women who marry up also become frightfully strict about their children's manners, because they're terrified that any lapse in behaviour will be attributed to a mother who doesn't know what's what. In the same way, stupid women who marry clever men are pushy about their children's education. Middle-class women who marry into the upper classes say 'se-uper' a lot, and become very good cooks to cope with picky aristocratic appetites.

When men marry up, they usually move away from their home town, buy horses and farms and take up patrician pastimes like hunting and shooting. They also become totally bilingual, putting on very grand voices when they're out hunting, and lapsing into their mother tongue when they're talking to garage mechanics.

If you marry someone who constantly tells you you're pretty, you begin to think you are. In the same way if you marry someone who thinks you're frightfully grand, you begin to believe him. As a result lots of middle-class women married to working-class men get very smug and think they're far more upper-class than they really are. Men who marry up often put their wives on pedestals and then run around with other women. Parvenus, in fact, are invariably unfaithful. It's a back-handed blow for the class war. John Osborne's Jimmy Porter is a classic example, as was the late President Kennedy. Upper-class women, brought up to expect infidelity, can handle this; that's why they build up that network of jolly nice gairlfriends to fall back on; and anyway they're so busy sitting on committees, organising charity balls and wondering what to wear at Ascot that they don't miss sex much.

The middle classes, like Eileen Weybridge and Samantha Upward, can't cope at all.

'Oh Keith,' said one middle-class wife, 'I can't bear to think of your penis in Mrs Peacock.'

Which brings us to. . . .

*Adultery*
*The way to helly is paved with bed intentions.*

Harry Stow-Crat has never been faithful to Caroline, like the earl who made a good start to his marriage by asking all his old girlfriends to sleep with him as a wedding present. Traditionally, as was pointed out in Chapter 1, marriages were arranged to improve one's cash situation and to increase one's land; one got one's fun elsewhere. Not all aristocrats are rich, of course, but it is much easier to play around if you don't have a job, own several places, have a helicopter (helly) to whisk your mistresses round the country, and plenty of cash to take her to smart restaurants and hotels. Upper-class males also tend to lead separate lives from their wives in any case.

'Where's Daphne,' I remember asking one peer. 'Oh, she's stalking in Scotland,' came the reply (the prey wasn't specified).

If ennobled, aristocrats also have a perfect alibi in the House of Lords. One's wife never knows if one's in the House or not. In fact a friend recently discovered a peer screwing a girl on the woolsack, but no one sneaked on them; there is honour among strawberry leaves. Location can also curb the libido. A girlfriend of mine said her lover, who was an Hon, wouldn't even hold her hand if they were walking across the Knightsbridge side of the Park, but would neck ferociously on the non-smart Bayswater side (because he was unlikely to see any of his wife's friends up there). And in the undergrowth of Wimbledon Common he would fornicate freely ('because there's not the slightest possibility of ever bumping into anyone I know in the suburbs').

An aristocrat who came up to London to take me out to lunch booked a table at a restaurant in Holland Park, which he also regarded as suburbia and quite safe. Alas, we couldn't get a taxi afterwards, and to his extreme consternation had to walk all the way to Knightsbridge before we could find one.

Upper-class wives can occasionally be just as unbridled sexually. One even has two telephone numbers, one for business and an ex-directory hot line for lovers. She was livid when one editor (who was an ex-lover) rang her about a feature on the lovers' telephone. When one peer's daughter discovered her MP lover had ditched her and returned to his wife, she stuck a huge placard on his car, which was parked in the street outside his house, saying: 'Do you really want to vote for an adulterer?'

The upper-middle classes used to concentrate on their careers to keep sin at bay. But all that changed with the advent of the country cottage. With

Samantha in the country and Gideon at his little flat in the Barbican, the fun is unconfined, although Gideon's frolics are slightly inhibited when Thalia decides to leave Wycombe Abbey early, take a secretarial course in London and live with Daddy.

The seven-year itch often finds some basis for truth among the middle classes. Samantha marries at twenty-four, has Zacharias at twenty-six and Thalia at twenty-eight. Three years later, when she's been married exactly seven years, Zacharias starts full-time school and Thalia goes to play group. For the first time in years she has the house free; she also has a feeling of nagging inadequacy – that the children are no longer a full-time job, justifying her being just a housewife. Hey Presto, in moves the lover.

The upper-middles, not having living-in servants, often have a sexual renaissance when the children go to boarding school and they have the house to themselves for the first time in years. On the debit side, one friend said it was very difficult to keep lovers at arm's length when one no longer had the excuse after a liquid lunch that one must rush away and pick up the children from school at four o'clock.

All adultery grinds to a halt during the school hols, which is the main reason – not tiredness – why mothers get so bad-tempered. The lower-middles tend to be far too cautious to commit adultery; it might upset the extra bright children. Instead they go to wife-swapping parties and pool all the children with what they call a 'sitter'. Sometimes Bryan Teale, when he's not working out the commission he's made that morning, makes love in the back of his car on the edge of the common in the lunch-hour, which is why he equips his car with cushions, and coat-hangers so that his cheap suit won't crease.

Working-class adultery, however, is much harder to achieve. No telephone to arrange appointments, possibly no car to draw up in lay-bys. Because of shift work and overtime, the lover never knows if the husband will be there or not . . . when the coast is clear the wife puts a packet of OMO in the front window, which stands for 'Old Man Out'.

The upper- and upper-middle classes talk about 'having an affair' with someone. The media and the trendy middle-class call it 'having a relationship'. The working classes say 'going with'; 'I think he's going with another woman.'

## In-laws and parents

Many working-class couples, unable to afford a place of their own, are forced to live with one set of parents after they are married, often with the wife's mother bringing up the children. This is why the mother-in-law problem is more acute among the lower echelons, and is the basis for so many music hall jokes. In the past, when the mortality rate was very high and husbands were likely to desert or be put out of work, the wife had to fend for herself, so she clung to her own family, particularly her mother. As has been pointed out, many working-class men visit their mothers every day and, if their wives are working, go home for lunch. Although the old matriarchies are breaking down now that most couples can afford cars, and move to jobs away from home, working-class mothers tend to be far more possessive. At Christmas and birthdays they have truces and send each other large, spangled 'Dearest Mother-in-Law' or 'Daughter-in-Law' cards.

Among the middle classes the social gradations are so complex that you often get both sets of parents thinking their offspring have married beneath them.

'Oh, Tom has got a nice little wife,' a mother will say. 'We're getting used to her saying "garridge" and "Port-rait".' ('Little', as in 'little shop-girls', is a euphemism for 'common.')

If, however, the 'nice little wife' looks after her husband well and produces a son fairly quickly, she will soon be forgiven her low caste. Heirs are a daughter-in-law's crowning glory. In many ways, too, a slightly common daughter-in-law is preferable as long as she's respectful, because it makes the mother-in-law feel superior. One girlfriend said she didn't speak to her husband for three days after a weekend with her in-laws. In the middle of dinner her mother-in-law asked her to pass the cruet, and her son, half-jokingly said,

'Oh, Angie thinks the word "cruet" is common.'

In the same way, if Thalia Upward were to marry Dive Definitely-Disgusting, she would start making Mrs D-D feel that her anti-black and generally xenophobic attitudes were uncouth. Mrs D-D, in retaliation, would disapprove of the way Thalia made Dive do the housework, get his own supper when she went to maths workshops, and even went out to work when she needn't.

The middle classes, disliking friction, try to keep a superficial peace with their in-laws, even if they disapprove. The upper classes don't bother. A middle-class friend of mine was pointedly told by her very grand old mother-in-law, 'Divorce is considered perfectly respectable now.'

On the middle-class front, one often gets antagonism between two sets of in-laws if the wife is working. Samantha's parents say, 'You must be getting *so* tired. Gideon really ought to be able to support you, darling.' Colonel and Mrs Upward, nettled by such disapproval, retaliate with 'Poor Gideon being hampered in his career by having to help with the housework and cook dinner when he gets home in the evening.'

Parents whose children marry and move away often complain that young people today are selfish and ungrateful. 'He's become like that Greta Thingamy,' grumbles Mrs D-D. 'He wants to be alone.'

One girl who married a man in the RAF said it was a nightmare everytime her working-class parents came to stay.

'Dad sneers every time Don brings out a bottle of wine at meals, and says, "We *are* pushing the boat out, aren't we?" Then he expects Don to take him for a drink at the Officers' Mess. If only they'd behave like the jolly kind of people they normally are.'

'My daughter goes to sherry parties now,' said another working-class mother sadly, 'and has a little car of her own. She asks me to go and stay but I don't go. I might show her up.' Stay in your own world, you're OK. Move up and you're out of step.

As Tracey Nouveau-Richards says, 'If Dad wasn't my dad, I'd laugh at him myself.'

One lower-middle girl I know describes a horribly embarrassing occasion when she got engaged to a peer's son and his father came for a drink to meet her parents.

Her mother's first words were, 'We're all of a flutter. We don't know whether to call you "Your Grace" or "Dad".'

*Divorce*

As you go down the social scale, the more rigid and unforgiving you find the attitude towards infidelity . . . The upper-middle-class couple, according to Geoffrey Gorer, believe in talking over the situation if they discover one of them is having an affair. The lower-middles would try and reconcile their differences, and get over what they hope will be a passing fancy. The skilled worker might advocate separation but not divorce. But Classes IV and V would be all for punitive action: clobber the missus and clobber the bloke, and after that the only answer is divorce.

Of all social classes, in fact, Class V clocks up the most divorces. This is probably because they marry so young, often having to get married, and because they find it impossible to discuss their problems when things go wrong. The husband can't cope with the pressure of so many children, and as he often takes casual labouring jobs in other parts of the country, the temptation to shack up with another woman is very strong. He can also get free legal aid, and doesn't have to pay for a divorce, and, finally, because the parental bond is so strong, it is quite easy for both husband and wife to go home and live with their own parents, whereas the middle-class wife, having achieved a measure of independence, would find this far more difficult.

What else wrecks a marriage? The middle classes mind most about selfishness, conflicting personalities and sexual incompatibility, while the working-class wife objects to drinking, gambling and untidyness, and the husband going out on his own with his mates.

Despite all the country cottages, Class I (engineers and oculists) has the fewest divorces, probably because they can't afford two mortgages and two sets of school fees if they marry again, because no one's going to give them legal aid, and because they think divorce would be bad for their careers.

According to Ivan Reid's *Social Class in Britain*, the lower-middles get divorced more frequently than the skilled workers. Maybe this is because the lower-middles, working together in offices, have more opportunity to meet the opposite sex on a long-term basis, while the skilled worker is stuck on the factory floor assembling tools. Maybe, too, the skilled worker has enough potency to keep both girlfriend and wife happy, and has no particular desire for a divorce.

The aristocracy, statistically negligible though they may be, tot up more divorces even than Class V. Since the turn of the century, thirty-three per cent of all marquesses and earls have been married twice, twenty-four per cent of viscounts and twenty per cent of barons. That's why *Debrett's* is such a fat book, listing all the marriages.

'The reason for this,' explained a peer 'is that few blue-blooded aristocrats have inhibitions about what their neighbours think.' Presumably if you live at the end of a long drive the neighbours don't get a chance to see anything.

Only three per cent of life peers get divorced – too busy getting to the top to have anything on the side, and too hopeless in bed for anyone to want them.

One of the saddest victims of the class war is the wife of the ambitious spiralist. While *he's* been living it up in foreign hotels, eating expense-account lunches and playing golf with the boss, she's been stuck at home with the children. He has a whole new life-style, and he wants a new wife to complement it, someone more glamorous and more socially adept. Husbands justify abandoning the first wife by saying:

'Anita didn't travel with me' or 'I married a local girl [euphemism for 'common'] first time round'.

People who've been married several times tend only to mention the grandest ex they've been married to. Woodrow Wyatt has had several wives, but in *Who's Who* only lists the one who was an earl's daughter.

## HOUSES

*I recall, I recall, the property where I was a happy event.*

It is not possible to determine what class a person is solely from the house he lives in. Some of the upper classes have execrable taste and don't give a fig about their surroundings, while some working-class people – probably homosexual – may have an instinctive sense of what is beautiful. How people do up their house is also considerably affected by fashion. A few years ago flying ducks were only acceptable if they were outside and moving. Now they've become *kitsch* and the young and trendy, raising two fingers to convention, are putting them on their walls. Or take someone who's just moved in to a new house. The haste with which they explain away the ox-blood fleur-de-lys wallpaper in the drawing-room as the taste of a previous owner might be more an indication of social insecurity than the wallpaper itself.

Electric logs have long been considered a Jen Teale indicator. My husband once worked for a man, whose son (an Old Etonian whom I will call Ambrose) asked us to dinner. The other guests were a very smart couple, whom Ambrose was determined to impress. We arrived first to find him switching off some electric logs in the drawing-room. He was worried the smart couple might think them common.

'My mother, being Spanish, has terrible lapses of taste,' he said apologetically.

So the three of us sat frozen to death until the smart couple arrived an hour later. Instantly some devil overtook my husband. He crossed the room and switched on the logs.

'Have you seen Ambrose's mother's splendid fire?' he asked the smart couple.

There was a ghastly pause. Ambrose's face whitened like that of someone close to death. The merry flickering of the electric logs was nothing to the blaze of rage in his eyes. The evening was a disaster and my husband was fired within three months.

And yet I know two peers of the most ancient lineage who have electric log fires. One even has bright blue water in his lavatory – the upper classes do what they want.

Nevertheless, the house that you live in, like the education you receive and the accent you speak with, is one of the determining factors that indicate the class you belong to. A girl I know was terribly keen on a tall, thin, very artistocratic-looking young man until she discovered that he lived with his mother in a bungalow in East Sheen.

In Putney, where I live, the people in the big Victorian houses on the Common look down slightly, albeit unconsciously, on the people in the large semi-detached houses in the next road who in turn look down on people in similar houses in a street with slightly heavier traffic, who in turn look down on the people in the neo-Georgian houses on the edge of the common, who in turn despise the people in the terrace houses behind them who won't have anything to do with the Council estate beside the river.

In *Voices from the Middle Classes* by Jane Deverson and Katherine Lindsay, a journalist is quoted as saying:

'A house is a complex thing; it represents a social position. We found living where we were (a smartish London suburb) without meaning till we had acquired several friends who see themselves as the same sort of people as we were because they live in the same sort of house. Painting and decorating is a middle-class thing,' he went on. 'You say you've been decorating and you get an immediate response.'

Harry Stow-Crat wouldn't dream of painting his own house or putting up shelves and would regard any such activity as distinctly working-class. Equally, Mr Definitely-Disgusting wouldn't bother to do up his house either because he considers it the council's responsibility. The moment he buys his own house, however, he crosses one of the great class divides from Council Tenant to Owner Occupier and starts to become bourgeois. He'll immediately drop the word 'mortgage' in the public bar, and begin building a new porch or slapping paint on the front of the hosue to distinguish it from the houses on either side and to show he's not Council anymore.

The expression 'they live in a bought house' would be a term of admiration among the working classes, but of contempt from the upper classes who have usually lived in their own house for generations, inheriting it as they inherit their furniture and silver. (One of the upper-class definitions of the middle classes is the sort of people who buy their own silver – particularly when they call it 'cutlery'.)

Another crucial point to remember is that the Stow-Crats of today were the Nouveau-Richards of a few hundred years ago. 'How often have I wondered,' wrote Lord David Cecil, 'at the difference between the stately beauty of a great house, so exalting and tranquillising, and the fierce restless unscrupulous character of the men who were so often responsible for its original building. Perhaps a gentler, more contented spirit would not have felt the urge and vitality to create such buildings.'

At the beginning of the eighteenth century the very rich Yorkshire baronet, Sir John Smithson, married Elizabeth, sole heiress of the rich and ancient family of Percy. So great was the extent of their joint estate that Sir John was able to persuade George III to grant him the dukedom of Northumberland. Anxious to establish his new status, the first Duke set about transforming Alnwick, the neglected castle of the Percys. Capability Brown (who'd been such a success at Warwick Castle) was called in to rebuild the towers and add seven turrets and a complete new garrison of stone warriors was stationed on the battlements. At the same time Robert Adam arrived to re-Gothicise the interior. Everything was done to make the castle as luxurious and self-consciously picturesque as possible. And no doubt the old aristocracy, who regarded any peer created after the Middle Ages as an upstart, thought the whole thing both phoney and vulgar.

So it was that generations of new noblemen harnessed the best talents of their time, as today David Mlinaric and David Hicks move around forming the tastes of the uncertain and the newly rich.

In the same way the pop star who makes it big immediately buys a large house in the Thames Valley with high walls and installs burglar alarms and vigilante systems as daunting as any medieval drawbridge to keep out the fans. He will decorate it to the nines to impress other rising pop stars, and in his spare time take up market gardening, breeding race horses and farming. The Rolls is replaced by a Range Rover. The Showaddy Waddy even hunt with the Quorn.

What is regarded as the height of vulgarity today – the huge oval bed humming with dials or the onyx and marble double bath with 22-carat gold-plated mixer taps – will probably be considered exquisitely beautiful when it is unearthed from the rubble in the year 2500. Certainly the furniture and building trades would grind to a halt if it weren't for people erecting monuments to new splendour or ripping out the taste of previous owners because they consider it too grandiose or too vulgar.

Although they may have originally been built, to quote Ivy Compton-Burnett, 'as huge monuments to showing off', few buildings quicken the pulses more than the great English country house, with its 'towers and battlements . . . bosom'd high in tufted trees', its sneering stone lions at the gate, and long avenue of chestnuts leading up to the russet walls rising gently from soft billowing green lawns which eventually melt into the park.

Harry Stow-Crat does not refer to his house as a stately home but as an ''istoric hice'. Perhaps he pronounces 'house' as 'hice', because he usually has more than one, like mouse and mice. The word 'home' except for putting 'At Home' on an invitation or saying 'I'm going home' is very common. It has been taken up by the media, so now you have the awful 'stately home', 'family home', or, even worse, 'they live in a lovely home'. Other horrors include 'homebuying' instead of 'buying a house' or 'home improvements' instead of 'painting one's house'.

Vita Sackville-West once said that the best historic houses grew in a leisurely way over generations, sprouting a wing here a tower there, like the oaks and elms that surrounded them. They grew inside, she says, in the same way as outside. 'There is no question of the period room, so beloved by professional decorators. Everything is muddled up: Jacobean paintings, Chippendale tables, chinoiserie wallpaper, Carolean love seats, Genoese velvets, Georgian brocades, Burgundian tapestries, Queen Anne embroideries, William and Mary tallboys and Victorian sideboards, all in a mixture to make the purist shudder.' But it is this feeling that each succeeding owner acquired beautiful furniture and pictures as the fashion of his generation dictated that makes up the glorious historical hotch-potch of the great house.

Lord Weymouth, who has contributed his own splendidly colourful murals to the walls of Longleat, says that everyone in his family 'has been raised from birth to be an acolyte in the temple'. This sums up the attitude of the aristocrat: good husbandry rather than good husbands or 'old masters and young mistresses', as Peter de Vries put it. 'I don't mind black sheep in the family,' said Lord Carrington. 'What I can't stand is people who don't put back something into the house.' Which explains the fearful chuntering over Lord Brooke flogging his Canalettos and the famous Warwick vase, and why so many aristocrats make very considerable sacrifices to keep their houses going when it would be so much easier to sell up and go abroad.

*'One has one's own piped music.'*

Most upper-class houses, therefore, have a certain shabbiness about them. (There ought to be a shop called 'Shabby-tat' where Mrs Nouveau-Richards could buy aged-up furniture and materials.) The festoons and rosettes on the ceiling show the traces of the years, the pink and white striped silk cushions are falling to pieces; the faded red damask sofa is covered in dog hairs. On the walls, like the circle on the spiralist's lapel, are squares of much lighter paper, where a Lawrence or a Romney has been flogged to pay taxes. When you go to bed you draw the pale blue, watered-silk curtains with care. The aristocracy believe in buying the best – silks especially woven in the colour they want – and then making it last. They'll probably only redecorate their rooms every fifty years. Upper-class colours therefore tend to be faded into softness by antiquity – like a Beatrix Potter picture. The faded rose-reds and golds of the Tailor of Gloucester's coat are particularly popular, and ice blue is very in at the moment. Green is never popular because there's so much of it outside in the park. In upper-class London houses (perhaps because they miss the green of the country) you get a chilly Eaton Square eau-de-nihilism.

The floors are polished, and three-quarters covered with very good, very old, patterned carpet. Caroline Stow-Crat wouldn't dream of buying a modern patterned carpet, but Casa Pupo rugs are somehow considered all right. Until recently she's resisted plain fitted carpets as being an example of the middle classes boasting that they've got enough carpet to cover the entire floor. But convenience is a great leveller and, if you haven't got a servant to polish the floor, you may sink to a fitted carpet. In the same way duvets are being surreptitiously smuggled into four-posters, particularly for the children, and the silver centrepiece in the dining-room, which is made up of forty individual bits and used to take two men three days to clean, has now been lacquered over.

Caroline also resists any man-made fibres, and certainly anything plastic, which Harry and his mother still call 'plarstic'. The upper classes wear leather on their feet and on the elbows of their coats, but not on their sofas or their backs. Their rooms tend to be very leggy, like the bottom half of the paddock, because all the furniture has long, spindly legs. Huge libraries of memoirs and sermons are kept behind grilles. The bedrooms have slots on the door for the guest's names, and interlocking doors, so people can bedhop easily without the servants finding out. The ceilings are particularly beautiful, so Caroline can admire them when she's in the inevitable missionary position, as a change from shutting her eyes and thinking of England. On the whole the upper classes prefer things to be beautiful or functional. They wouldn't hide the television in a repro cabinet, or the Kleenex in a dainty flowered box with a slit in it.

The rooms are lit by crystal chandeliers or candelabra, or by lamps with no tassels. Tassels on anything – umbrellas, lights or chairs – are very vulgar.

The bath and basin are always white; the lavatory is white with a chain that pulls and a wooden seat which is often agonisingly cracked, and gives exquisite pain by nipping the Old School bottom. All upper class loos smell of asparagus pee in June. The kitchens are traditionally hellish because that was where the servants lived.

As the outdoor life has always been more important to the English gentleman than indoors, the field more alluring than the hearth, their houses tend to be terribly cold. (One member of the landed gentry always asked you to bring old telephone directories when you went to stay to feed the insatiable boiler.) On the walls hang huge paintings of battles, hunting scenes and ancestors. There are also portraits of the dogs, the horses and the children. As the last go off to boarding school so early, it's useful to be reminded of what they look like.

The upper-class man always has a dressing room. Even though Harry sleeps in the same room as Caroline, he would refer to it as 'Caroline's bedroom' if he were talking to an equal, 'my wife's bedroom' if he were talking to a higher echelon servant like the woman who shows people over the house, and 'Lady Caroline's bedroom' to a maid.

One very grand old lady said, 'When Willy and I went to stay with some people in Norfolk, they didn't give Willy a dressing room but they provided a screen in the bedroom so we managed very well.' This was when they'd been married forty years – back to the Definitely-Disgustings again!

Because they have had their houses for hundreds of years, the aristocracy take the beautiful things in them for granted, and tend not to comment on them in other people's houses.

'Fellow noticed my chairs,' said a surprised Earl of Derby after a visit from the Duke of Devonshire.

Equally it is not done to show someone over your new house unless they ask specifically or they pay at the gate.

There was an embarrassing moment when an actress we know, who was justifiably proud of her very expensively decorated house, asked an upper-class friend if he'd like to see over it.

'Whatever for?' came the curt reply.

In very grand houses they have an estate carpenter permanently on the premises doing repairs. One friend got locked in the lavatory when she was staying in Yorkshire, and her host fed her Bloody Marys through the keyhole with a straw while they waited for the house carpenter to come and free her.

> *The poor man in his castle*
> *Sells tickets at the gate*
> *While all the rich plebians*
> *Have fun on his estate.*
> Leonard Cooper

'Between the duties expected of one during one's lifetime, and the duties exacted from one after one's death, land has ceased to be either a profit or a pleasure. It gives one position, and prevents one from keeping it up, that's all that can be said about land,' said Lady Bracknell in *The Importance of being Earnest*, admirably summing up the plight of the aristocracy.

In the old days Harry Stow-Crat's ancestor would have looked out of his top window and owned all he surveyed. Now someone else probably owns much of it. Most of the upper classes are feeling the pinch, and the days when they could man a chauffeurs' second eleven against a footmen's third eleven are over. Some peers, like Lord Montagu and the Duke of Bedford, who obviously have a strong streak of showmanship in their make-up, seem to rather enjoy it. Others hate it, like an earlier Lord Bath who was found cowering in a cupboard by one of the visitors, or Vita Sackville-West who hid in the roses. Some peers try to keep up standards and shock visitors to the house by putting up signs saying *lavatories* rather than *toilets*, but most of them descend to the level of public taste by flogging the most appalling souvenirs – key rings, caps, T-shirts, replicas of the house in a snow storm, bottled Welsh or Scottish garden fragrance – in order to keep going.

When we went to spend the weekend at Longleat, as we drove up the drive my children's eyes grew rounder and rounder as they took in first the green mist of flat-bottomed spring trees, the herds of cows and sheep, then the lions, leopards, rhinoceros, monkeys and a giraffe. Finally, as the great golden house came into sight my son turned to my daughter:

'He's got an awful lot of pets,' he said in awe.

When a Mrs Definitely-Disgusting visited an 'istoric house recently there was a frightful squawking match because she refused to pay to go on the little train which ran round the estate, saying,

'We don't have to pay for things like this. We ought to go free. We're the underprivileged.'

### Buying-up and doing-up

The upper-middle classes, not subscribing to the law of primogeniture and tending to move where their jobs take them, seldom live in the same house for generations. They start off in a flat in London or in some other big town when they get married, then move to a terraced three-bedroom house with the first child, then to a five-bedroom house when the second child arrives, because they need room for an *au pair*, or possibly for a lodger to help with the mortgage. Samantha Upward prefers a student, so she can combine altruism, free baby-sitting and help with Zacharias' maths prep, which will soon – despite workshops – be quite beyond her. To live in a house with more rooms than you have family is regarded by the working classes as a middle-class characteristic.

The major change in the upper-middle-class house over the last twenty-five years has been the kitchen, which used to be an airforce-blue barracks where a sucked-up-to maid sourly banged saucepans. In the seventies financial necessity, coupled with the absurd stigma attached to domestic servitude, forced all but those with very young children out to work. The status-conscious upper-middle classes promptly revamped their houses. If Samantha Upward occasionally has to sink to housework or cooking she must do it in congenial surroundings. Kitchens became more and more like drawing-rooms with sofas, low lighting, Welsh dressers covered in ornaments and books, pictures on the walls, and a low pine table for the children to play improving games. As it was essential for the children to play on the ground floor near their parents, the dining-room was also turned into a 'playroom', and in order that Samantha shouldn't miss a word of the intelligent dinner-party conversation, as she was flambéing chicken breasts, or whipping the zabaglione, the kitchen was turned into a dining-room as well. The drawing-room by this time was feeling a bit neglected and was consequently filled up with plants and natural earthy colours until it resembled Kew Gardens. The garden filled up with furniture, reclining chairs with gaudy seed-packet upholstery, stone lions and white wrought-iron chairs and tables. What was once the 'terrace' became the 'patio', or, as Mrs Nouveau-Richards would say, the 'pate-io'.

As stripped pine and William Morris are taken up by the lower-middles, the upper-middles have latched onto rattan and art-deco sofas and chairs, French and English antiques when they can afford them, good Chinese furniture and Laura Ashley itsy-bitsy cottage prints (sort of William Morris Minor). Recently a friend heard a builder showing a plumber over the house they were working on.

'They've got Philip Morris curtains in the lounge,' he said.

A word might be said here about the words 'drawing-room' and 'sitting room'. Both seem to be acceptable except that 'droin' room' is slightly more formal, and 'sitting room' more easy and relaxed. You'd never have a 'droin' room' in a cottage for example. 'Living room', a ghastly modern compromise, is extremely vulgar. So are 'lounge' (except in an hotel), 'front room' and 'parlour'.

In Samantha Upward's house you would find a few antiques and some

*'Zacharias is very creative at the moment.'*

good china and silver. She thinks repro furniture is very common, and whereas she might put prints or reproductions in the lavatory or the children's room, they wouldn't be allowed in the drawing-room. Nor would a Victorian painting from her parents' house of a four-year-old girl in a boat with a grizzled fisherman entitled 'His Mate' get further than the landing. All her curtains would be on brass rails. Her carpets would be plain but fitted, and relieved by a few rugs, and her counterpane would be distributed evenly over the whole bed, not mill-pond smooth and then edged in a fat sausage under and over the pillows. Since the middle classes discovered sex in the seventies, she'd probably have a bidet in the bathroom, next door to Gideon's and her bedroom. The bidet is a constant reproach as Gideon is usually far too tired and too drunk to want sex. Samantha is gradually installing 'continental quilts', as she insists on calling them, in every bedroom; she thinks the word 'duvay' is vulgar. Zacharias's cello is allowed to stay in the drawing-room among the *Spectators* and *New Statesmans* and the clutter of books. Samantha spends a lot of time removing the jackets from books to make them look more read. Dried flowers, or honesty in a pewter mug, gather dust on the window ledge.

In the downstairs lavatory, as a sort of 'bogography', Gideon modestly records his achievements, with photographs of himself in school hockey, rugger and cricket teams. In his dressng room are concealed all the atrocities Zacharias and Thalia have given him and Samantha for Christmas over the years – china poodles, cats wearing bow ties playing the banjo, glazed china flowers and so on. He also has to put up with all rich Aunt Mabel's paintings on the walls which are whipped down to the drawing-room when she comes to stay, and a photograph of Samantha, framed by herself at evening classes, taken 20 years ago when she had a beehive. Samantha waits till the daily woman goes home to loosen up the serried ranks of cushions on the sofa.

Upper-middle-class houses smell of beeswax, drink and sometimes cats. As their owners are always knocking things over when drunk and not being able to afford new ones, they have a lot of Christopher Wray lamps with bites out of them.

On Saturday mornings throughout outer central London – Fulham, Clapham, Islington, parts of Hackney – the streets are alive with the sounds of 'gentrification', as coats of paint are slapped on the front of terraced houses, rooms are knocked through and the net curtains of previous occupants are shoved in the rag bag. The upper-middle classes would far rather spend a bit of money knocking a Victorian workman's cottage into shape than move into a modern house where everything worked, so they quite happily rip plywood off doors to reveal the original mouldings, strip banisters and replace aluminium windows with wooden frames as close to the original as possible. Soon follow the French number plate, the brass letter box, the trellis for the honeysuckle from the garden centre and the bay tree which soon gets nicked. Blue tubs, bought cheap from the brewery round the corner, are fast filled up with bulbs or pink geraniums (Samantha thinks red ones are rather common). Vivaldi pours out of the stereo into the street, and balding architects can be seen drawing lines at their desks and drinking coffee out of Sainsbury's mugs.

Having also cottoned onto the fact that they can get £25,000 tax relief for an extension, and with the price of houses being so prohibitive, my dear, and the traffic being so frightful we never get down to the cottage till midnight, the upper-middles are beginning to sell up their 'shacks' in the Isle of Wight or Gloucestershire and build onto their houses instead. Gideon and Zacharias are working at home so much now, they both need a study. And as Samantha so often wants to watch opera and Gideon late night sport, it avoids so many rows if they have two televisions in different rooms, and now that Thalia's getting a bust it's not quite right for her to entertain boys in her bedroom which calls for a second sitting room where they can all play pop music as loudly as possible. As a result £300 worth of clematis and hydrangeas are crushed under foot as an extension is slapped on to the patio.

Another trick of the middle classes is to buy old houses, then form a pressure group to have their street declared a Conservation Area in order to stop the compulsory purchasers touching it or building flats nearby. They then get absolutely livid when the Council rather understandably drags its heels over planning permission for an extra music room or a new bathroom.

*Don't say 'pardon', say 'Surrey'*

> *Merridale is one of those corners of Surrey where the inhabitants rage a relentless battle against the stigma of suburbia. Trees, cajoled and fertilised into being in every front garden, half obscure the poky 'character dwellings' which crouch behind them. The rusticity of the environment is enhanced by the wooden owls that keep guard over the names of the houses, and by crumbling dwarfs indefatigably poised over goldfish ponds. The inhabitants of Merridale Land do not paint their dwarfs, suspecting it to be a suburban vice, nor for the same reason do they varnish the owls, but wait patiently for the years to endow these treasures with an appearance of weathered antiquity, until one day even the beams in the garage may boast of beetle and woodworm.*

John le Carré, *Call for the Dead*

'Oh look,' said a friend as we drove through a rich part of Surrey, 'all those houses have been Weybridged.' This is a practice of the socially aspiring who've made a bit of money and want to shake off the stigma of suburbia by living in Sunningdale, Virginia Water, or any rich dormitory town.

First you buy a modern house, which you refer to as a 'lovely property', then you age it up to look like a Great West Road pub. Rustic brick with half-timbering and leaded windows are very popular, with a lantern or carriage lamp outside the front door and a name like 'Kenilworth' or 'Decameron' carved on a rustic board. A burglar alarm is discreetly covered by creepers.

An alternative is white pebbledash with a green pantile roof and matching green shutters with cut-out hearts, and the name in wrought-iron treble-clef writing on the front of the house. Wrought iron, in fact, is everywhere.

A few years ago a Weybridged house would have had a chiming doorbell, but, suspecting this to be a bit suburban, the owner has responded to an ad in *Homes and Gardens*:

'No more electric bionic ping pongs . . . every lover of style can now capture the elegance and tranquillity of less hurried days with a real brass doorbell, complete with mechanism and most attractive pull arm to enhance your doorway.'

The hall, as Anthony Powell once said, looks like the inside of a cigar box, with a parquet floor, panelled walls and a very thin strip of carpet running up the polished stairs. At the top is a round window with a stained glass inset. The Weybridged house smells of self-congratulation and Pears soap.

In the living-room (they've heard 'lounge' is suburban but can't quite bring themselves to say drawing-room) you find wall-to-wall glossies and coffee-table books. On the walls are imitation candle brackets, with fake drips and little red hats, bumpy white and gold mirrors and pictures by real artists from Harrods and Selfridges. The carpet is tufted two-tone, the curtains pinch-pleated, the 'settee' and 'easy chairs' are covered in terra-cotta velvet Dralon. Repro furniture is inevitable to give a nice 'Olde Worlde' look: 'period doors', a Queen Anne 'bureau' and Regency Chippendale cabinets to hide the TV (the upper-middles call it 'the box', the upper class 'the television') and the 'stereo'. Every piece of furniture has mahogany or teak veneer. The Weybridged house suffers from veneerial disease. A Magi-Log fire flames in the repro Adam fireplace – 'the ultimate in realism' – with incombustible oak logs knobbly with knotholes and twigs. The alternative might be a 'feature fireplace' in stone. The *Radio Times* is wrapped in a sacking cover with a thatched cottage embroidered on the front. If you came for drinks, you would be offered goblets.

In the dining-room lacquered silver candlesticks sit on the Elizabethan repro table even at lunchtime, and an Ecko hostess trolley keeps the rack of lamb, creamed potatoes and garden peas piping hot. There will be an overhead light, or more bracket lights with fancy lots, and six chairs with oxblood and silver regency stripes.

Howard has a 'den' where he's supposed to work at weekends, but in fact does nothing but read *Penthouse* behind Saturday's *Financial Times* and long to be asked to a wife-swapping party. Poor Howard feels he is not 'olde' enough for the house; if he plays with himself a lot it might age him too.

The kitchen is usually very pretty and quite indistinguishable from the upper-middle, or even modernised upper-class kitchen. Next door a 'utility' room is filled with expensive machinery – the word 'dishwasher' as opposed to 'washing-up machine' is very Weybridge, so is 'freezer' instead of 'deep freeze' and 'tumble' instead of 'spin dryer'.

In the 'master bedroom' tufted carpeted steps lead up to a dais on which a huge brass four-poster bed swathed in white Norfolk lace sits like a wedding cake. The lampshades match the duvet cover and the wallpaper.

Next month Mrs Weybridge will receive her eighth German porcelain coffee cup and saucer from the 'Collector of the Month Club' special offer and be able to hold her first coffee morning.

*Better Nouveau than late-Victorian*
The Weybridged house is very 'olde' and tasteful, as opposed to the Nouveau-Richards' mansion which is very plush, ostentatious, and modern – another great monument to showing off.

Reacting against the working-class over-the-wall familiarity, Mr Nouveau-Richards has high walls built round his house and the whole place is burglar-alarmed to the teeth. Ten-foot-high electric gates protect him from the road. As he arrives in the Rolls he presses a button and the gates open. The drive is lined with toadstools which light up at night. The garage for five cars opens by remote control and, so you don't get wet, a lift takes you up to the hall.

Every room in Mrs Nouveau-Richards' house has a rake for the shag pile. The daily woman's visit is a sort of rake's progress, nor does she much like having to climb into the onyx and sepia marble double bath to clean it, and having to polish up the 22-carat gold mixer taps with headworks of solid onyx. She nearly got her hand chopped off when she was shaking her duster out of one of the electric windows the other day. When she answers the telephone she has to say, 'Mrs Nouveau-Richards' residence'.

In the lounge acrylic pile tiger skins with diamanté collars lie on the ebony shag pile. Mrs Nouveau-Richards reclines on the leather chesterfield in front of the heated coffee table, while Mr N-R revolves in his captain's club chair in deep-buttoned hide. The walls are covered with black and silver flocked wallpaper. When the maid in uniform hacks her way through the 'house plants' to bring in 'afternoon tea' she is sent back because the sugar bowl doesn't match the tea cups. A ship's bell summons people to dinner, and the nautical motif is maintained by a bar in the corner with a straw ceiling covered in lobsters. After a few drinks they crawl by themselves. In the bar every drink known to man hangs upside down with right-way-up labels. Mr Nouveau-Richards doesn't drink very much because it makes his face red and his accent slip. Off the lounge are the solarium, the gym and the swimming pool, kept at a constant temperature of eighty degrees by the pool attendant. The stables are built under the lawn, so the horses can look out of their boxes into the pool like Neptune's mares. In Mr N-R's library, in all the books which were bought by the yard, he has eighteenth-century repro library steps. When he presses a button the entire works of Sir Walter Scott slide back to reveal yet another bar. Even the goldfish tank is double-glazed.

Everywhere there are executive games played with clashing chrome balls, and orbs with revolving coloured oils. Mr N-R is very proud of his dimmer switches; in a mellow mood he'll give his guests a *son et lumière* display. In every room musak pours out of speakers, even in the loos, which have musical lavatory paper, fur carpets and chandeliers. The lavatory has a wooden seat. Mr N-R responded to an ad in *House and Garden*:

'After years of mass-produced plastic, feel the warmth of solid mahogany. Each seat is individually sanded and french-polished. Hinges and fittings are made of brass, and we offer as an option at no extra cost a brass plaque recessed into the lid for your personal inscription.' Mr N-R has 'Piss Off' wittily inscribed on his.

In the guest bedroom, as Mrs N-R calls it, everything is upholstered in peach satin, with a peach fur carpet. The master bedroom, however, has a vast suède oval bed, so humming with dials for quadrophonic stereo, radio, dimmer switches, telephones, razors and vibrator (which Mrs N-R uses for massaging her neck) you don't know whether to lie on the thing or hi-jack it.

Such houses are always blissfully comfortable to stay in: 'Chandeliers in the loo and a bidet on every bed,' as my mother put it.

## A word about nets

The world is divided into 'Haves' and 'Have-Nets'. The upper classes never had net curtains because, if you live at the end of a long drive, there is no likelihood of being overlooked and, not being worried about other people's opinions, you don't give a damn if anyone sees what's going on anyway.

The upper-middles, aping the upper classes, don't have net curtains either. They traditionally had servants to keep their houses tidy, so it didn't matter anyone seeing in and, as they only had sex at night (unlike the shift worker coming home for lunch), they drew the curtains if they wanted privacy. Samantha Upward wouldn't dream of having net curtains; she wants the whole street to look at the gay primary colours and extra bright drawings and posters in Zacharias's playroom.

The middle classes sometimes have net upstairs. If Eileen Weybridge is changing out of her tennis shorts in the middle of the day, she doesn't want the workman mending the road looking in. If they have nets downstairs, they might explain it by saying they've got an American mother.

The rough and friendly element of the working classes never bother with net at all and have an expression for someone putting on airs: 'Net curtains in the window, nothing on the table.'

It is where the more thin-lipped element of the working classes blends into the lower-middles that net reigns supreme. You can see out and chunter over everyone else's behaviour, and twitch the curtains to indicate extreme disapproval, but they can't see you. Suburban privet hedges and Weybridged latticed windows fulfil the same function.

Jen Teale, however, wanting to priss everything up and shake off the stigma of upper-working class – which is a bit too close for comfort – hangs pink jardinière festoon cross-over drapes which leaves three-quarters of the window clear. This allows space for 'floral decorations' on the window ledge, makes the windows look 'so feminine' and enables the neighbours to see how 'spotless' (a favourite lower-middle word) her house is. Other examples of the lower-middles trying to go one better are ruched nets, putting a row of package-tour curios on the window ledge outside one's nets, or hanging one's curtains so the pattern shows on the outside. Mrs

Definitely-Disgusting tried yellow nets once, but they made the whole family look as though they'd got jaundice.

*Behind the mauve front door*

Jen Teale, liking to have everything dainty, wages a constant battle against dust and untidiness. Bryan sits in the lounge with his feet permanently eighteen inches off the ground in case Jen wants to 'vacuum' underneath. In a bedroom, a Dralon button-back headboard joins two single divans with drawers underneath for extra storage, into which Jen might one day tidy Bryan away for ever. Gradually all their furniture – wardrobes, sideboards, cupboards – is replaced by fitted 'units' which slot snugly between ceiling and floor, rather like Lego, and leaves no inch for dust to settle.

As soon as the Teales move into a house the upper-middle process is reversed: all the doors are flattened so the mouldings don't pick up dust any more; the brass fittings are replaced by aluminium, which doesn't need polishing; all the windows and old 'French doors' (as Jen calls French windows) are replaced by doube-glazed aluminium picture windows. Being hot on insulation, because they loathe wasting money, the Teales even have sliding double-glazed doors round the porch. Bryan does all this with his Black-and-Decker.

The mauve front door has a rising sun in the bottom left-hand corner of the glass. The doorbell chimes. The house smells of lavender Pledge and Freshaire. In the lounge the fire has a huge gnome's canopy to concentrate the heat and keep smuts at bay. Beside it stands the inevitable Statue-of-Liberty combination of poker, brush and shovel in a thistle motif. On the walls Bryan and his Black-and-Decker have put up storage grids, like vast cat's climbing frames with compartments for the hi-fi, records, scrabble, the odd spotlit bit of Wedgewood or 'vawse' of plastic flowers. ('Fresh' flowers, as Jen would call them, drop petals and paper ones gather dust.) A few years ago the Teales wouldn't have had any books – too much dusting – but as culture seeps downwards, there might be a few book club choices tastefully arranged at an angle to fill up a compartment.

The lounge suite has easy-fit nylon William Morris stretch covers which have interchangeable arms that can be switched from unit to unit or rotate on the same chair to give that straight-from-the-showroom look which is the antithesis of the shabby splendour – 'majestic though in ruin' – of the upper classes. Jen also rather likes the continental habit of offering lounge furniture as a group, comprising three-seater settee, two-seater settee and one armchair, called 'Caliph'. (Down-market furniture invariably has up-market names like 'Eton' and 'Cavendish'.) There is also a Parker Knoll recliner in case an 'elderly relative comes to visit'.

As well as her books Jen also has her Medici prints and her Tretchikoff (under a picture light, to show there's no dust on the frame), and in the dining-room there's a David Shepherd elephant gazing belligerently at Bryan's vintage car etchings. There is no bar because the Teales are tight with drink; Bryan keeps any bottles in another room with measures on. Just as a guest is putting his glass down, a mat with a hunting scene is thrust underneath to stop rings on a nest of tables called 'Henley'.

The kitchen is like a laboratory. No ornaments alleviate the bleakness. As the lower-middles disapprove of money spent on luxuries, Jen probably wouldn't have a washing-up machine. She doubts it would get things really clean. She calls washing up 'doing the dishes'. She washes, Bryan 'wipes' with a 'tea towel' rather than a 'drying-up cloth'. (Caroline Stow-Crat would call it a 'clawth'.) Jen also does a lot of 'handwashing' and, as she's very conscious of understains, she 'boils' a lot. Friends say her whites are spotless.

In the bedroom a doll in frills, to show Jen's just a little girl at heart, lies on the millpond-smooth candlewick bedspread. (Caroline Stow-Crat has a worn teddy bear.) 'Robe units' with motifs and very shiny lacquered brass handles slot into the walls. Jen tidies her make-up away in a vanity case. The only ornament on her white formica-topped vanity unit is a circular plastic magnifying mirror. When she makes up and brushes her hair, she protects her clothes from 'dandruff' with a pink plastic cape. The matching bathroom suite, in sky blue or avocado, with a basin shaped like a champagne glass, has a matching toilet cover, toilet surround and bathmat in washable sky-blue nylon fur.

A Spanish 'dolly' with Carmen skirts discreetly conceals the toilet tissue (pronounced 'tiss-u' not 'tishu' as Samantha Upward would pronounce it). Jen, being obsessed by unpleasant odours, has Airwick, potpourri and a pomander on top of the cistern, and a deodorant block hanging like a sloth inside. In the toilet there is bright blue water. Bryan and Jen prefer showers to baths; they waste less water and are easier to clean up after. Jen calls a bathcap a 'shower cap'.

Although she keeps her house like a new pin, Jen always does housework in tights and a skirt rather than trousers. Her whole attitude is summed up by her feather duster, which keeps dirt at a distance.

### The chrome squad

There was an advertisement recently in a magazine called *Home Buying* offering 'Modern houses in Wood Green, the ideal site for those who want a convenient rung on the home-ownership ladder'. Among the other attractions was 'garage with space for work bench'.

This was aimed at the spiralist who is continually buying houses, doing them up, selling them at a profit and moving on to a better part, which means a safer suburb, with a nicer class of child, more amusing parents at the PTA and no danger of coloureds (although a black diplomat is OK). Usually the process is to start with a flat, then move to a terraced house, then to a large 'period semi', where you let off the top flat to pay the mortgage. Then, as soon as the house is done up, you buy a cheap flat for the sitting tenant, put it on the market and look for an even bigger house. The process is basically the same as that of the upper-middle-class couple, except that the spiralist moves as soon as he's got the house together, while the upper-middles wait until they've run out of room.

Spiralists like anonymous furniture – chrome, glass, and unit sofas and chairs – because they can be shifted around to fit into any size of house. Just as they often adopt a phoney American accent to hide the Cockney or the Yorkshire, they also embrace American terminology: 'trash cans', 'garbage', 'closets' and 'car ports'. Even in the short time they stay in a place the spiralists are deeply competitive.

The spiralists are likely to buy a three-piece suite in a sale, then put it in a Harrods depository so it can be delivered three weeks later in a Harrods van.

They are the estate agent's nightmare – they never stop arguing and expecting more for a house because of another brick on the night storage heater. Evidently the upper-middles treat the agent like a pro, because they're used to one chap doing one job.

### Home suite home

When Mr Definitely-Disgusting thinks of buying a house other than his own council house, he fills in a coupon and goes off and sees a show house on an estate called some grandiose name like 'Northumbria' and puts his name down for it if he likes it. Attractions include 'teak laminated kitchenette, stainless steel sink, coloured bathroom suite with matching vein tiles, veneered doors in the living room, kitchen dinette and shower room'.

Ads in the 'homebuying' press show neighbours looking friendly and

175

*'Well it's the
Council's job, innit?'*

helpful in wide-bottomed trousers, so as not to intimidate Mr Definitely-Disgusting. In a comic strip guide to 'homebuying' the solicitor has spectacles and brushed-back hair, and wears a suit and a tie, while the buyer has wide trousers again, an open-neck shirt and hair brushes over his ears. His wife has shoulder-length hair swept back from her forehead by a kirby grip, and a skirt on the knees. This is presumably the ideal working-class prototype.

The Definitely-Disgustings hurry now and buy everything from Williams's sale, even the once-famous actor with tired eyes doing the telly commercial. Up to their necks in HP, they get carried away by the ads and buy three-piece suites in deep-pile uncut moquette and wildly expensive domestic appliances, which go back when they can't keep up the payments. The house-to-house upstaging is as subtle as the spiralists.

'You can't hang your washing out anymore, because everyone'll know you haven't got a tumble dryer,' said one wife.

Mrs Definitely-Disgusting, on the other hand, buys a fridge for the first time and stands at the front door saying, 'I'm worried the kiddies will catch their fingers in the door,' just to show she's got one.

(My favourite advertisement of all time appeared in an Indian magazine and showed a woman and child gazing admiringly up at a huge fridge with the caption: 'Just right for our living room'.)

Mrs Definitely-Disgusting's front room, if she's feeling flush, will be dominated by a black cocktail cabinet with interior lighting, containing every drink known to man, just like the Nouveau-Richards, and a glazed tile fireplace with a gas fire (although councils are beginning to put in what is known as a 'fuel alternative'). Most of the ornaments look as though they have been won at a fair, or bought for his mother by Zacharias Upward: china Alsatians, glazed shire horses, china ladies in poke bonnets and crinolines. Here also are the curios from a hundred package tours – green donkeys with hats and panniers, matadors under cellophane, a mass-produced plastic bull with a piece of the next bull's back attached to its cock, ashtrays barnacled with olives and souvenirs of trips to historic houses. There might be a few very small reproductions: Constable's Haywain, Van Gogh's Sunflowers, or the Queen by Annigoni.

The colours are garish, with everything – wallpaper, sofas and chairs – in different patterns. The carpet, a symphony of yellow, nigger brown and orange exploding in circles, doesn't cover the linoleum. On the huge colour television there might be a clock with the works well exposed under a pyrex dome. Mrs D-D's plastic flowers differ from Jen Teale's in that they make no attempt to copy the originals: mauve snapdragons and blue roses, pink primroses and da-glo tulips mass gaudily together in a sharply cut glass vase (to rhyme with praise).

The less respectable element of the working classes would have no ornaments or pictures, having smashed the lot during drunken brawls. The room would be furnished by a huge colour television and biked bean tins.

Working-class houses and flats tend to smell of cabbages and leaky gas, and Jen Teale, wrinkling her retroussé nose, would claim, dirt. One of the ensuing battles in the class war is Samantha Upward, Eileen Weybridge, Jen Teale and Mrs Definitely-Disgusting all accusing each other of being a slut.

The Bronco is hung up with string in the outside lavatory, which is probably shared with several other families. This explains why so many of the working classes suffer from constipation. Only two per cent of the professional classes are overcrowded, compared with over fifty per cent of the working class.

# GARDENS

*Climax into the patio, Maud.*

The Englishman traditionally loves his garden. It needs cherishing and tending, but doesn't answer back. It is hardly surprising, therefore, that class distinction should be almost more rampant outside the house than in it. Once again garden centres – like furniture shops – do a roaring trade because of snobbery. People are constantly ripping up the plants and paving stones of previous owners – 'Too ghastly, my dear'. I remember being mystified once when a friend came to stay. We were having tea outside, enjoying the sunshine and the quiet (for once the aeroplanes were silent) when suddenly she fixed me with a beady eye and said,

'You know, it's frightfully common to have Peace in one's garden.'

It was a few minutes before I realised that she was referring to the beautiful pink and yellow rose next to the magnolia which flowers so gallantly and continually all summer. I can only suppose that she thought it was vulgar because it is so universally popular.

In the same way Caroline Stow-Crat wouldn't touch gladioli, begonias and chrysanthemums, or fuchsias – except in the conservatory. Also on the index would be gaudy bedding plants like petunias, French marigolds, calceolarias, cinerarias, calendulas, salvia, Californian poppies, zinnias, asters and yellow daisies, although Michaelmas daisies and white daisies are all right. Colour is also important: the white and green tobacco plants are much more upper-class than the red or mauve ones and dark red wallflowers better than yellow or mauve. Trails of pale blue lobelia are all right, but Oxford blue is very common, particularly when combined in military rows with white alyssum and scarlet geraniums. Caroline wouldn't be keen on any flower of a different colour to that which nature intended – blue roses, brown irises, pink forget-me-nots or daffodils. Daffodils, she feels, should be planted in long grass, not in flower beds. She hates tulips. If she had rhododendrons she would have not individual ones, but great clumps lining the drive. A friend once asked a West Country peer how he achieved his magnificent multi-coloured display.

'Oh, I move them around,' said the peer. 'When I want to change the colour scheme, I just get twenty men up from the factory.'

'Yellow and green should never be seen', so Caroline would soon rip out anything variegated such as laurels or, even worse, privet and mother-in-law's tongue.

Some trees are more upper-class than others: one thinks of the great flat-bottomed oaks, beeches, limes and chestnuts, that look, as Taine said, as though they'd been tended for hundreds of years like the children of rich parents.

If you discount the cedars planted by Capability Brown, indigenous trees are considered much smarter than foreign ones, which is why the white double cherry scores over the imported pink one, and why the Stow-Crats tend to despise the silver birches and conifers of Surrey. Willow trees are all right growing naturally by a lake or stream, but would be considered the height of vulgarity in the middle of a suburban lawn, particularly if planted in a circle of earth.

The suburbs in spring, with their candy-floss mass of pink and white cherry, dark pink crab-apple, almond, laburnum and lilac, are quite beyond the pale. Pink hawthorn, although considered much more common by the upper classes than white, is for some reason more acceptable in the suburbs.

The names of buildings in the garden are also pronounced differently. Harry Stow-Crat says 'garidge'; Samantha Upward, wanting to show off her French pronunciation, says '*gar*-azh; the Weybridges say 'gar-*arge*' in order to upstage the lower-middles who say 'garidge' like Harry Stow-Crat. Mrs Nouveau-Richards has a carport. Harry has a 'gaz-ee-bo' in his garden. Samantha calls it a 'summerhouse', while Mrs Nouveau-Richards reclines in her 'gayze-bow'. Harry pronounces 'loggia' 'lodger', but the Weybridges call it a 'lowjea', in case there is any confusion about paying guests when someone says Howard is relaxing on the loggia. A friend says that his very grand grandmother used to refer to ants as 'aunts', saying, 'There's an aunt-heap in the garden', which sounds like a great fleshy pyramid of maiden ladies.

The point about the upper-class garden is that it should look as 'natural' as possible – great sweeps of mown grass leading down to the lake, huge trees with new little saplings always being planted and nurtured, trout streams, parks full of deer, and cows swishing their tales knee deep in the buttercups. Away from the house there might be a series of flower gardens, divided by walls, or hedges of box or yew, a conservatory full of nectarines, peaches and the oldest vine in Europe, a herb garden and a huge vegetable garden. Around the house, plants will grow in genuine Versailles pots, which are made of wood, are square and topped with balls. 'Everything to do with balls is very U,' says Harry Stow-Crat.

But everything would be mellowed and weather-beaten, the walls and roof of the house 'stained by time and many-coloured lichens, and overgrown with creeper to a richly variegated greyish red'. The drive would be made of stone chippings or gravel – not black tarmac or concrete like the M1.

The Stow-Crats are very keen on vistas (Mr Nouveau-Richards thinks they're something to do with chicken curries). Through a gap in a wood you might see a temple of Flora, a folly or a bend in the river. But it must look natural.

The great gardens, in fact, show the ideal blending of classic and romantic. At Sissinghurst, Nigel Nicolson attributes the firm perspective of the vistas, the careful siting of an urn or a statue, the division of the garden into a series of small separate gardens to his father's classical influence.

But, in the overflowing clematis (Howard Weybridge would call it clem*a*tis) figs, vines and wisteria, in the rejection of violent colours or anything too tame and orderly, one discovered his mother's romanticism: 'Wild flowers were allowed to invade the garden. If plants strayed over the path they must not be cut back. Rhododendrons must be banished in favour of their tender cousin the azalea, roses must not electrify, they must seduce.'

Once again the secret is sweet disorder and faded Beatrix Potter colours. Weeds in moderation don't matter, because the plants are so closely massed they don't show the earth beneath. A dearth of earth is very upper class.

Sissinghurst, too, is the elder sister of the cottage garden – a law unto itself with all the flowers the Stow-Crats love jockeying for position: rosemary, drifts of lavender, ramparts of honeysuckle, an ancient wisteria, sweet peas, hollyhocks, lupins, delphiniums, pinks and mignonettes, love-in-the-mist and cornflowers, clove carnations, pansies, sweet william, white stocks and phlox, Canterbury bells and lilies; moss and plants instead of cement fill the cracks in the flagstones.

Percy Lubbock, writing about the easy abundance of a particular upper-class garden, realises that it's not the plants themselves but the way they are planted that matters: 'Lobelia stripes, for example, and those marigold patches, which might have looked harsh and hard (one knows how smartly odious they can look in a well-kept garden), all rejoiced together, rambling and crowding in liberal exuberance. The gardener might wreak his worst will, but the free soul of the garden escaped him and bloomed tumultuously.'

A garden like that, however, requires not just money and genius ('Planted 400 bulbs in the orchard this afternoon,' wrote Vita Sackville-West to Harold Nicolson) but also gardeners you can bully.

In the old days gardeners used to wash all the vegetables and take the thorns off the roses before they were sent up to the house. An eighteenth-century handbook advised them to look clean and neat: 'Your employer will not wish to look on a dirty, ragged, uncouth, grinning or conceited biped in his garden.' They were also instructed to 'put the manure on the flower beds early in the morning, so the putrescent vapours may not prove offensive to the owner of the garden and his friends.'

But as costs get higher and gardeners get scarcer, it is becoming increasingly difficult to keep up a large and beautiful garden. In the country, gardens tend to get smaller and smaller, and the orchards bigger and bigger. Donkeys are becoming increasingly popular for keeping the lawn down. That mixture of concern and self-interest which always colours the master-servant relationship was neatly summed up by a woman I met at a party the other day who said:

'Our darling old gardener died last week – isn't it *maddening*!'

In Harry Stow-Crat's London garden you find a few bulbs in window boxes, followed by pink geraniums and ivy, followed by irises and Albertine, a pale pink rose which stops flowering in June. After that the upper classes are always out of London so it doesn't matter what their gardens look like.

In the country the upper-middles tend to have beautiful gardens, with shrubberies and herbaceous borders more related to the house and not set aside in separate gardens, although the vegetable garden will be separate. Plants and flowers grow round the house and on the terrace you might see imitation plaster Versailles pots by Julian Jenkinson, an Old Etonian who copied them very successfully from genuine pots at Lord Harcourt's house. The lawn will be well tended, but there will be more brown patches on the lawn because upper-middle-class dogs are less likely to pee in the house than upper-class dogs. As manure is seldom available all the time, there will also be greater interest in compost. The roses and dahlias will be very fine and the colours slightly brighter than in the upper-class garden. As we go down the social scale gardens tend to become neater and gaudier.

Samantha Upward is very proud of her green fingers, particularly as she lives in London. She reads Wordsworth to her potted plants, rushes out with a shovel every time the police horses go by and, by feeding Zacharias' daffodil with John Innes and Liquinure, she won him first prize in his form's flower-growing competition. But, alas, the herb garden she planted so she could have all the ingredients in Elizabeth David's recipes has been turned into a cats' lavatory by visiting toms. She knows, too, that plastic flower pots and plastic hanging baskets are frightfully common, but such is the greenness of her fingers that she couldn't possibly afford pottery flower pots for all her plants. She's also far too soft-hearted to rip out that variegated horror donated by a neighbour that time she had shingles, or the rose that looked the palest pink in the catalogue, but turned out bright crimson and clashes horribly with the da-glo orange rose beside it. She knows, too, that dear funny Sir John Betjeman said that every time he looked at a rhododendron he thought of a stockbroker, so she moved her two mauve ones under the catalpa, but, alas, they're doing *terribly* well. At least she hasn't descended to crocuses in a wheelbarrow, or a plastic Venus de Milo like the one on the patio next door which melted at their last barbecue party.

Her garden would really be quite lovely if only she could stop the gardener, who comes two hours a week, planting tulip bulbs in serried ranks like the ones outside Buckingham Palace. But if she checks him she's terrified he'll take offence and not turn up next week.

Gideon and Samantha sit in their garden on a Sunday morning, swilling back the chilled wine saying, 'This is the life!' and watching the half-leg of lamb rotating jerkily on the barbecue, wafting intimations of garlic, rosemary and envy into the nearby council estate.

## The suburbs

*'Ewbank'd inside and Atco'd out, the English suburban residence and the garden which is an integral part of it stand trim and lovingly cared for in the mild sunshine. Everything is in its place. The leaves of the virginia creeper which climbs the rough-cast wall just below the best bedroom hardly stir.*

J. M. Richards
*The Castles on the Ground*

Nothing has really changed in the suburbs. When we lived in a working-class part of Fulham no one minded that we never bothered with our garden. A few neighbours grew vegetables and fought a losing battle with visiting tom cats, but the rest of us let the weeds flourish and chucked our beer cans and spare-rib bones over each other's fences when we ran out of dustbin space. Only when we moved to Putney, a Madam Butterfly land of cherry trees and flowering shrubs, and inherited a beautifully kept garden which we promptly let go to rack and ruin, did we discover that gardening here was taken very seriously indeed. Soon the whole street were clicking their tongues over our hayfield of a lawn and making cracks about calling in the Forestry Commission to deal with the weeds. Finally a kindly neighbour could bear it no longer and found a gardener to come in three hours a week and sort us out.

More recently the local Conservation Association, which howls with protest if so much as a harebell is touched on the common, produced stern proposals, which were circularised round the district, for tidying up the garden of the only house along the common that happened to be owned by the council. This, they felt, was letting down the tone of the road by the number of weeds. At any minute one expected the dandelion detector van to be policing the streets bleeping noisily outside offending gardens. My husband suggested it would be far cheaper to declare the garden in question an Area of Outstanding Natural Beauty; then the weeds and wild flowers could riot unimpeded.

Though Putney is more upper-middle than suburban, the idea of not letting down the street is shared by the suburbs further out. Few people there are dedicated gardeners in the winter. Unlike the upper classes, they stay inside in bad weather. But, come the first temperate weekend, suburban man peers out of his window at his colourless plot and thunders off to the garden centre to load up the Volvo with bags of John Innes,

bedding plants, do-it-yourself cucumber kits, and a plaster fig-leafless cherub to upstage the plastic Dolphin regurgitating blue water on the patio next door.

For the suburban gardener is deeply competitive: he doesn't want anyone else to let down the street, so that his own glory may be greater when his garden is the best. Rivalry is particularly fierce over roses. Hybrid teas and floribundas mass in clashing colours above a totally weedless flower bed. You can't get a lie-in at weekends either; it's like the pits at Silverstone with the roar of all the mowers revving up, interspersed by the excruciating, teeth-grating rattle as they drive over the crazy pavement.

The patio is also a focal point, a mosaic of Italian tiles, covered with plastic urns filled with striped petunias, deckchairs with foot-rests, canopies and seed-packet upholstery, and sun umbrellas bought with Green Shield stamps.

The Weybridged house has a circular gravel drive bordered by 'rhodos', 'in' and 'out' entrances with no gates, an up-and-over garage door, a swimming pool which, despite its barrage balloon cover, is filled in winter with dead leaves and sparrows, and a dog yard for the terriers to dry off in. Having gone one step up from the suburban garden with its high laurel hedges, Weybridged houses are often open-plan with no dividing fences at all, although there might be a hedge of conifers to shelter the roses from the wind, or interlaced larch fencing around the vegetable garden. Here Howard and Eileen sit in their summer house admiring the well-tended lawn with its crazy-paving stepping stones, the conifers and golden willow in their little circles of earth, the beautifully kept shrubberies full of pampas grass and bamboo, and the thrushes pecking at the rack-of-lamb bone, which hangs from the dovecote (pronounced dovecoat: Harry Stow-Crat says dovec't). A heavily ferned stream flows under a wooden, willow-pattern bridge and over a waterfall by the heaths in the rock garden. Heather, except on the moors, is considered very vulgar by Harry Stow-Crat. Even its Latin name, *erica*, sounds frightfully common.

On Monday, aping the upper classes, Eileen Weybridge feels it her duty to pick up the litter dropped by trippers in the nearby beechwoods before she goes out to bridge or a Conservative coffee morning.

Believing that upper-class women spend their leisure hours doing the flowers, the Weybridges are heavily into flower arrangement by numbers, ramming salmon-pink 'glads' into green foam blocks, so that they stand up in the plastic 'dole-phin' vase and pick up the apricot décor in the lounge.

Yellow 'chrysanths' and button dahlias have always been a talking point too, when arranged in the white basket held by a naked cupid on the dining-room table when Howard's business associates come to dinner. While the orchids Howard raised in the '*con*serve-a-tory' (the Stow-Crats say 'c'n*serv*'tri') look so well in driftwood in the vestibule. The expression 'fresh flowers', to distinguish them from dried or plastic flowers, is also very Weybridge.

Although Jen Teale lives in a house with a number, she has re-named it 'JenBry' which combines both her and Bryan's names; she puts it in inverted commas on her notepaper. This drives the postman crackers. Her wrought-iron gate also incorporates the name. On either side Bryan has built a bright yellow wall, shaped like a doily. A plastic flowerpot container, filled with purple and shocking pink petunias, hangs by the mauve front door. Jen remembers to remove the dead heads night and morning. There are no creepers up the house. Jen doesn't want earwigs in the bath. Most of the back and front gardens have been crazy-paved by Bryan because it looks so much neater, but there are a few crescent-shaped flower beds which might have been dug out by a pastry cutter. Here in neat rows in the spring stand military lines of blue grape hyacinths, yellow 'daffs' and scarlet tulips. In the summer these are replaced by white alyssum, French marigolds, Oxford blue lobelia and scarlet geraniums, or,

*'For God's sake pull the plug out!'*

by way of a change, calceolarias and salvias. Jen loves bedding plants because, once they've finished flowering, they can be thrown away. There is not a weed in sight. The garden is oblong, regular and compact like a park garden. When Bryan is not in his toolshed, he tends his 'chrysanths' and his 'toms' in the greenhouse. It's better than being hoovered under. Occasionally on summer afternoons Jen and the family sit out on tubular steel picnic chairs that can fold away neatly afterwards. There was a nasty moment once when an 'elderly relative come to visit' got stuck in the couch hammock with aluminium frames. Harry Stow-Crat ties hammocks to trees.

As a first-generation gardener, Mr Nouveau-Richards pulls out all the stops. Apart from lighting up his tarmac drive and technicolour lawn with toadstools, he has all his flowerbeds floodlit and coolie-hat lamps stationed like street lights round the garden.

Weeding, watering and edging is all done by electricity, which also keeps the earth warm under the cloches. In the propagating frames all-night fluorescent lighting forces tulips into bloom in November, and vast strawberries to ripen in time for Christmas. Plastic grass lines the outdoor swimming pool which is constantly kept at 80° like the indoor one.

Mr N-R reclines on the underfloor-heated 'pate-io' and plays with a computerised mowing machine, a new toy just imported from Texas. He has just mixed a mint julep from his portable drinks trolley which glides over tiles and shag-pile and was described in the catalogue as 'the ultimate way to enjoy a cocktail on the patio, an aperitif by the pool, or those after-dinner drinks in the lounge'.

Mr Definitely-Disgusting hasn't got a garden, but he grows tomatoes and geraniums on his balcony, and he also has an allotment, which means a lot to him. It is illegal to sell 'produce' (a very Jen Teale word) from one's allotment, but at least he can grow vegetables for all the family. Here stand neat furrows of potatoes, curtains of runner beans, rows of lettuces and 'collys' and, at the end, a blaze of annuals and bedding plants in primary colours to rival Samantha Upward's playroom. When Mr D-D pulls up a lettuce he calls it 'picking a salad'.

# FOOD

*Let them eat gâteau*

*'When a woman asks for back, I call her "madam",' said a grocer. 'When she asks for streaky I call her "dear". You can always tell the gentry,' he went on, 'by their knowledge of cheese. They don't have trouble saying the foreign names.'*

The food you eat often indicates what class you are. The way you eat it, namely your table manners, does so almost more. The upper classes, for example, don't have any middle-class inhibitions about waiting until everyone else is served: they start eating the moment food is put in front of them. This stems from the days when they all dined at long refectory tables and if you waited for fifty other people to be served, your wild boar would be stone cold. Nor would Harry Stow-Crat comment on the food at a dinner party, because one doesn't congratulate one's hostess on something one expects to be done perfectly in any case.

The ritual of table napkins is interesting. The working-class man tucked a handkerchief under his chin to protect his shirt and waistcoat (he would never eat in a coat). The lower-middles, daintily thinking 'napkin' sounded too much like babies' nappies and wanting to show off their knowledge of French, called it a serviette. The middle classes, wanting to go one up, talked about napkins, but, being frugal, also wanted them to last a few days, so they introduced napkin rings. The upper classes, who had plenty of people to do the laundry (Harry Stow-Crat's mother calls it 'larndry'), had clean napkins at every meal and regarded napkin rings as the height of vulgarity. One peer, when presented with a pair in a velvet box, had to ask the mayor what they were for before embarking on his speech of thanks. Even today Caroline Stow-Crat would rather use paper napkins than napkin rings. Mrs Nouveau-Richards, having read in some etiquette book that the word 'serviette' is common, calls them 's-napkins'. In the same way, she only just remembers in time that dinner in the middle of the day is called lunch, and talks about 'd'lunch', which sounds faintly West Indian. Harry Stow-Crat's mother still calls it luncheon.

Both Harry and Gideon Upward would lunch from one o'clock onwards, have tea around four and dinner at eight to eight-thirty in the evening. The Teales would breakfast very early because they don't like to be rushed, so would the Definitely-Disgustings because Mr D-D has to get to work early. Both Bryan and Mr D-D probably have a cheese roll or a bar of chocolate at nine-thirty, followed by 'dinner' at twelve and 'tea' the moment they get home from work about six to six-thirty.

The worst thing about the lower classes, complains Caroline Stow-Crat, is that they never know when to leave. If she asks them round for a quick pre-dinner drink, they've always had their tea first and are all set to carry on drinking until midnight. Samantha Upward gets round the problem by asking Mrs Nouveau-Richards at seven, then lies and says she's frightfully sorry but she and Gideon have got to go out to dinner at eight-thirty. Unfortunately Mrs N-R spoils everything by asking if she can see the kitchen and discovers three large baked potatoes and a casserole cooking in the oven. Samantha stands on one leg and says:

'The *au pair* has the most enormous appetite.'

Then there's a whole new ball game about what to call the courses. Caroline Stow-Crat never uses expressions like 'starter', except in quotes, or 'the soup'. She would talk about the 'meat' or 'main' course or 'cold cuts', but never 'the entrée' or 'the roast'. (The middle classes say 'joint'.) Nor would she refer to chicken or grouse as 'the bird' or 'poultry', although if Harry were farming he might use the word in that sense. Howard Weybridge says 'polltry' and 'casseroll' with a short 'o'. Everything from lemon water ice to jam roly-poly Caroline would call 'pudding': she would never say 'sweet' or 'dessert'. Cheese would be served after pudding, never before. Then, to muddle everyone, this might be followed by dessert, which is fruit, even bananas, eaten with fruit knives and forks.

A few months ago I went to the annual general meeting of the 'Istoric Houses Association, a gathering bristling with members of the aristocracy and the henchmen who organise the people who see over their houses. Having been gossiping in the bar, I arrived late for lunch and found a fat henchwoman sitting by herself, the rest of the table having gone off to help themselves to pudding.

'Who else is sitting here?' I asked, 'anyone exciting?'

'Well ay don't think they were ducal folk,' she said, 'because they were holdin' their knives like pencils.'

Indeed she was right.

One of the great class divides, along with living in a 'bought house' and saying pardon, is the way you hold your knife. The lower echelons hold them like pencils, the upper and upper-middles to a man putting their first finger (the one Mr D-D uses to read with) on the knife where the handle

*'It would never 'ave bloody well 'appened, Ricardo, if you'd 'eld yer knife proper.'*

joins the blade. Harry would also turn his fork over to eat his peas if he felt like it, and pick a bone – behaviour that would horrify Jen Teale.

Michael Nelson, in *Nobs and Snobs*, tells a story to illustrate what a gentleman his grandfather was. When sitting next to his hostess, he saw a slug on his lettuce. Rather than embarrass her, he shut his eyes and ate it. 'And my grandfather,' the story ends, 'managed not to be sick until after dinner.'

While it is a touching story, I think this was the act of a gentleman, but not necessarily of an aristocrat – the two are not synonymous. Harry Stow-Crat wouldn't swallow a slug, nor eat anything he didn't like. Nor would he ever resort to the lengths of a Jen Teale who dropped in on my brother and his wife and was asked to stay for lunch. To eke out the sausages and mash my sister-in-law fried three kidneys, which this Jen Teale was too polite to say she couldn't eat. In silent glee my brother watched her whip it off her plate, when she thought no one was looking, and hold it in her hand all through lunch. Afterwards she sidled inch by inch towards the fire and, choosing a moment when she thought my sister-in-law was pouring out coffee, flicked the kidney discreetly with a brisk backhand into the flames, whereupon it let out a prolonged and noisy hiss.

If someone else was paying for lunch in a restaurant and the food wasn't up to scratch, Mr Nouveau-Richards would complain noisily to the waiter; Harry, however, would keep his trap shut. If, on the other hand, *he* was paying, he would never be too embarrassed to complain, like Gerald Lascelles lunching at the Ritz, who sent a trout back because it was too small. Or the crusty old baronet who peered into the communion cup at early service and, because it was only a quarter full, bellowed, 'That's not enough'.

If you stayed with the Stow-Crats you would go in to dinner at eight on the dot because it's inconsiderate to keep the servants waiting, and you wouldn't sit around the table swilling brandy until midnight, because the servants want to clear away. But the men would stay behind with the port and grumble about estate duty, while the women would go into the drawing-room and probably grumble about constipation.

Things are changing, however. You now find far more upper-class people telling the hostess her food was lovely, because she's probably cooked it herself – and if you've spent two days slaving over a dinner party you want a bit of praise. In London fewer and fewer men wear dinner jackets, although the upper classes and upper-middles tend to in the country, while many of the women still stick to their horse-blanket long skirts and frilly shirts. With the inroads of women's lib, however, upper-middle women are less and less often shunted off to drink coffee by themselves after dinner, the merrytocracy in particular believing in a port in every girl, and as the husband often cooks the dinner he's the one who needs to go upstairs and tone down his flushed face.

The other great change in the upper-middle-class life-style is the swing back to traditional English food. In the fifties and sixties, on those three-week holidays to various costas, the wives picked up tips for five-course dinners. If you put garlic and green peppers in everything it showed you'd travelled. Samantha Upward even used the same plate for all courses, so you could still taste the squid vinaigrette and the boeuf-provençale when you were eating your *Poire Belle Helène*.

As a reaction to all this, the trend now is for simple cooking designed to bring out the flavour of good food instead of concealing it in a cordon blur of cream and wine sauce with grated cheese and breadcrumbs on top. At dinner parties Samantha now serves fish pie, pink beef and, particularly, English lamb. And for puddings it's treacle tart, jam roly-poly and bread and butter pudding, which in a time of insecurity reminds Samantha of nanny, childhood and security.

Meanwhile other trends move downwards. The patrician habit of not commenting on the food, for example, is reaching the suburban spiralist belt.

'Dinner gets more elaborate,' said a wife on a neo-Georgian estate, 'but people pretend not to notice. It's all passed over to prove we're used to avocado pears and brandy in everything.'

Although the Surrey commuters are still wafting out garlic like dragon's breath – a sort of last gaspachio – the return to traditional food is just reaching the Weybridge set. Determined not to let the Chancellor ruin their 'wholl new fun lifestyle', they are into communal dinner parties with one wife cooking each course, and all keeping a stern watch on anyone getting too elaborate and putting in too much cream.

The foreign food bug has just filtered down to Jen Teale; Colman's Cook 'n Sauce is the best thing that has ever happened to her. She has also started tarting up the Oxo stew with package Hungarian goulash, and finds that Chicken Marengo Mix gingered up with garlic salt makes a nice change from an 'assorted platter of cold meats', and all these mixes do save bothering with messy ingredients. Packaged *Boeuf Trogignon* was a smash hit, too, the time Bryan's boss came to dinner. Bryan's boss's wife also admired Jen's table. Pink paper napkins in the glasses, matching pink doily in the basket under the slices of 'crusty bread', pink flowers in the centre of the table, and pink needle-dick candles casting a lovely light. Jen, who believes that things that look good taste good, has decorated everything with radish flowerets and cucumber hearts. And her new tupperware Jel 'n' Serve bowl set the orange mousse in a rose shape, and Jen garnished it so prettily with piped cream and mandarin segments. The one bottle of table wane looked so attractive in its basket too. In the old days Bryan used to decant it, so people wouldn't see the VP label. And Jen made sure no one got tiddly by serving little glass bowls of crisps and nuts with the Bristol Cream before dinner.

Jen's knives have stainless steel handles and resemble fish knives. The forks look like tridents and have long thin handles to keep you further away from messy food. Jen never 'cooks': she calls it 'preparing a meal'. After she's been to a 'resteront', she expects the waiter to ask, 'Enjoyed your meal?'. The word 'meal' is a convenient cop-out when you don't know whether to call it lunch, dinner or tea. Bryan's Rotarian father says 'repast'.

The Nouveau-Richards still over-do their dinner parties – smoked salmon and caviar soufflé to start with, sole flamed in brandy with a Pernod cream sauce, *boeuf en kraut* and a moated sugar castle for pudding, followed by After Ape mints. 'Chá-o bŏ-elled' wine flows throughout. Afterwards all the guests are sick.

The Definitely-Disgustings don't give dinner parties. Everything is geared towards Sunday dinner. In the old days you were paid on Saturday night, rushed off to the pawn shop, got out your Sunday suit and then hurried down to the late-night market to buy food for 'dinner' the following day. The warmth and friendliness of the pub often proved too seductive for the wage earner, and his wife would try to drag him out before he blued all his earnings. When there wasn't enough money to pay for dinner, Charlie Chaplin remembers his brother and he being told to sit down at a bare table and clash their knives and forks together so that the neighbours wouldn't realise they were going short.

Today the tradition continues. Mr D-D starts Sunday with a good breakfast – fried egg, bacon, beef sausages, because they're cheaper than pork, and fried bread. At twelve he goes to the pub and is dragged home at two-thirty for the 'roast and two veg', followed by apple pie and custard, or, as a treat in the summer, tinned peaches and cream. Having slept off the excesses, he would then have whelks and two slices of 'ovis for tea, this being the only roughage he has during the whole week.

### Growing, shopping and cooking

Like Mr Definitely-Disgusting, Harry Stow-Crat has always liked plain unmessed-about food, the Costa Brava/Elizabeth David revolution having hardly touched him. Harking back to the old days, when mediaeval barons had to take care of themselves, the upper-class estate has always been self-sufficient. The Stow-Crats kept their own cows and sheep, shot their own game, caught their own salmon and trout, picked their own fruit and vegetables, and stalked their own deer (which Harry calls 'ven'son').

Harry also likes food that is tricky to eat and holds pitfalls for the socially uninitiated, such as oysters, asparagus and artichokes. The first week a London girlfriend went to live in the country, someone asked her if she could 'draw a mallard'. No one flickered when she said she'd always been frightful at art.

The upper classes tend to be unimaginative in their tastes. Lord Lucan used to lunch at his gambling club every day off cutlets in winter and cutlets *en gelée* in summer. I have a friend whose father always has Stilton and rice pudding for lunch. Lord Ampthill, who is in charge of the food at the House of Lords, has tried and failed to get tapioca taken off the menu.

As has been pointed out, lack of servants has only recently prompted the upper classes to take an interest in cooking. Lord Montagu may get up early and cook woodcock or snipe for his guests' breakfast on Sunday, but more characteristic is a story told by Nancy Mitford about the evening her maid went out and left her some macaroni cheese to put in the oven for three-quarters of an hour. After the allotted time she took it out and was surprised to find it stone cold. It had not occurred to her to turn on the oven.

In Harry Stow-Crat's house an eternal battle rages between the cook, who keeps asking for tiny young carrots and potatoes because they're more tender, and the gardener who wants them to grow to horticultural-show size.

Conversely in street markets you can't sell tiny potatoes, tomatoes or sprouts to Mrs Definitely-Disgusting because they appear to be a bad bargain. Many working-class eating habits are based on eking things out further. Sandwiches are left with the crusts on, lettuce is served with Heinz salad cream, so you need only use as much as you want, rather than wasting the whole thing by drenching it in French dressing. Mrs D-D's cabbages always seem over-cooked because she uses everything and by the time the stalk and tough outer leaves are tender the inner leaves are overdone. Jen Teale calls them greens. As late as 1973 only 37 per cent of the working classes in Britain had refrigerators, which explains why they ate so much out of tins, and why so many things – beetroot, onions, herrings, cockles and whelks – are stored in vinegar to make them last.

Because Mr Definitely-Disgusting likes frozen and marrow fat peas, Jen Teale would refer even to peas that came out of a field in Norfolk as 'garden peas'. Mr D-D in return would take the mickey out of Jen by saying he wouldn't touch any of 'them petty poys'. Jen would ask for 'green' beans, to distinguish them from the Cockney 'biked' beans, while Samantha Upward would say 'French' or 'runner' beans. Jen would talk about 'creamed potatoes' because it was one up on the working-class 'mash', not realising that the upper-middles and uppers talk about mashed potatoes as well. She'd also call baked potatoes 'jacket' potatoes, which she'd cut in half horizontally, spread out like two halves of an Easter egg on a separate plate, and fill with sour cream. Jen thinks chips are very common. If she had to eat them she'd say 'French fries', but she'd rather have sauté potatoes, which Samantha calls 'fried potatoes'.

And so it goes on, the endless one-upping and upstaging between the classes. Another lower-middle expression, attempting to put down the Definitely-Disgustings, is 'fresh fruit' or 'fresh cream', to distinguish it from tinned fruit or cream. The classes above would just say fruit or cream; nor would they talk about 'real coffee' or 'instant', calling it just 'coffee' or 'Nescaffi' – the Weybridge set say 'Nescaff-*ay*'. Trying to disguise their lack of class by using transatlantic expressions, they would also talk about 'burgers', 'crispbreads' and 'crackers' instead of biscuits.

Fish holds numerous pitfalls for the socially unwary. After John Betjeman's poem 'How to get on in Society' received wide circulation when *Noblesse Oblige* was published in 1956, the antique shops were flooded with fish knives, and the upper-middle and some of the upper classes sat solemnly at breakfast trying to bone kippers with forks.

Mr Definitely-Disgusting thinks fresh salmon is utterly tasteless and prefers it out of a tin. He likes pilchard salad too, and cockles, roll mops, eels either jellied or in a pie which he calls pie and mash, and eats with a viscous green sauce. Other favourites include rock salmon, skate, coley and chips, and 'ollibut and 'addick. But the working-class Northerner wouldn't touch mackerel, regarding it as the scavenger of the seas. 'If my missus gave me mackerel for tea,' said one fishmonger, 'I'd go to a Marriage Guidance Council.'

If Mr Definitely-Disgusting went to a 'resteront' he'd probably start off with prawn cocktail, as an acceptable way to eat neat tomato ketchup mixed with salad cream with a few bits of rubber thrown in. Jen Teale talks about tuna instead of tunny fish; she rhymes the first syllable of scallops with 'pal' (Samantha rhymes it with 'doll') and stresses the second syllable of anchovy, while Caroline Stow-Crat emphasises the first. The Weybridge set are particularly fond of scampi in the basket, which they think is both dainty and olde-fashioned, but which is really a corruption of it being deep-fried like chicken in a wire basket.

Another fashion that has moved downwards is the quiche, which was once called bacon-and-egg pie, until it got tarted up with peppers, onions, mushrooms and corrugated pastry, and was produced every time Caroline Stow-Crat had to provide something for a charity luncheon or Samantha had a buffet party. The merrytocracy also found it much cheaper than china to hurl at each other at the end of drunken evenings: 'And then I shut her wild, wild eyes with quiches four.' The Weybridges produce it for rugger and cricket teas, and the trend has finally filtered down to Mrs Definitely-Disgusting who calls it a 'qwitch'.

I think the popularity of quiche may be explained by the fact that people no longer feel easy about using the word 'tart'. Treacle tart and apple tart sound all right, but expressions like savoury tartlets, or 'My son says I make a good tart,' usually get a snigger. 'Queer' and 'gay' have gone the same way. Only Mrs Definitely-Disgusting could still get away with saying:

'I turned queer in the night. It must have been the prawns.'

Mrs Definitely-Disgusting tends to buy meat from the less attractive part of a pig or a cow because it's cheaper: black pudding, tripe and onions, pigs' trotters, belly of pork and faggots. Then she drenches everything in tomato ketchup and HP sauce to take the taste away. Mrs Definitely-Disgusting's mother, being a widow and an old-age pensioner (or, as Jen Teale would say, a 'senior citizen'), is so poor that when she goes to the butcher she asks for bones for the dog. She has no dog, but at least the bones will make soup. Sometimes she asks the fishmonger for pussies' pieces, even though she has no cat. As some compensation, if she lives in the Borough of Camden on her own she is entitled to a free budgerigar. Mr D-D, who is not very keen on his mother-in-law, says the old cow will probably boil that for soup as well.

As one moves through the day the class indicators come thick and fast. The upper classes have coffee or China tea for breakfast, the lower classes Indian tea, which they drink very strong and very sweet. Jen Teale says she doesn't 'favour' a 'cooked breakfast' or a 'continental breakfast', and instead has 'just a drink in the morning', meaning tea. (When Gideon or Harry use the word drink they mean alcohol.) Jen sometimes has 'segments' instead of 'cereal', which means tinned grapefruit pigs. Caroline Stow-Crat has Oxford marmalade on her toast. So does Samantha; she doesn't like it very much but she read somewhere that Golden Shred was common. Mr Definitely-Disgusting has 'two a drip, a chuck a bubble, and a cup of bug,' which, when translated, means two slices of bread and dripping, a plate of bubble and squeak and a cup of tea (which rhymes with flea, hence bug). Jen thinks the word chuck has a nasty derivation so she says 'portion', Samantha says 'helping'.

On to luncheon, at which no gentleman, according to Harry Stow-Crat, has soup – presumably because the upper classes were always out slaughtering wildlife, and soup is difficult to eat when crawling through bracken or sitting on a horse. Jen Teale, knowing the importance of eating a proper lunch, has frozen cod in cheese sauce boiled in a cellophane bag, which is indistinguishable from the dishcloths and tea towels she is always simmering on the hob. 'On the weekend' she and Bryan sometimes have 'an assorted platter of cold meats followed by the cheese board'. As a first-generation 'restront' goer, Bryan has picked up some of the ghastly terminology – 'bill o' fare', 'sweet n' sour' and 'turkey and all the trimmings' (which means a teaspoon of cardboard stuffing and one burnt chipolata). He's very partial, too, to duck 'allaronge' which is a piece of burnt duck covered with mandarin segments with a spoonful of sugar in the gravy. Jen, being a great reader of women's magazines, is fond of adjectives like tasty, beefy, crusty, crispy, garlicky and chewy. Along with the vast majority of her class, she is slowly poisoning her family with convenience foods, television dinners, Vesta beef birianis, cake mixes and instant whips – a sort of national Chemi-kazi.

On to tea, which for the unwary is also full of pitfalls. It is very common to call it 'afternoon tea' to distinguish it from 'high tea'. Now that people of all classes use tea bags, everyone puts the milk in second, so this is no longer an upper-class indicator. The upper classes drink China tea out of china teacups, 'but it's awfully difficult drinking out of hand-painted cups,' said one spiralist's wife, 'so we have mugs when we're alone, and porc-ell-*aine* when we have guests.' (Caroline Stow-Crat calls it 'porsl'n'.)

Jen Teale's tea is a symphony of doilies under pastries and gâteaux, cake forks and scones (with a long 'o'). She provides paper napkins and a knife even if you're only eating sandwiches, which she pronounces 'sand-witch' like 'spin-itch'. Caroline Stow-Crat says 'samwidge' and 'spin-idge'.

*'Don't! It must be decanted!'*

Mrs Definitely-Disgusting says 'butty' or 'booty' if she lives in the north.

Jen would be shocked by Mrs D-D's milk bottle and bloater paste on the table, by the way she holds the bread in the palm of her left hand and spreads it with the right, and dips her biscuit in her tea because of her sore teeth. Caroline has Earl Grey or China tea the colour of washing-up water (just the colour Mr D-D likes his coffee), home-made cake and cucumber sandwiches. White sliced bread is particularly lower-middle because of its lack of roughage.

A fellow journalist tells a wicked story of the time he interviewed a famous romantic novelist who was also a passionate health food freak. During the interview he was subjected to a long lecture on the merits of wholemeal home-made bread. Just as he was leaving, a little Sunblest van came jauntily up the drive.

'Surely,' said the journalist in mock horror, 'you're not buying sliced bread?'

'That, darling,' said the lady novelist airily, 'is for the servants.'

## DEATH

*O happy release, where is thy sting?*

At last we come to Death the Leveller who lays his icy hand on Stow-Crats and Definitely-Disgustings alike. Poets over the ages have been haunted by the theme. Shakespeare wrote of golden lads and girls mingling in the dust with chimney-sweepers. Hardy described the yokels William Dewy and Tranter Reuben lying in Mellstock churchyard beside the Squire and Lady Susan. But even if we are all equal in the moment of death, the living see that our departure is celebrated in very different ways.

Once upon a time funerals were occasions for great pomp – with a long procession of carriages drawn by horses wearing floor-length black velvet, with everyone including the children in deepest black, men and boys doffing their hats along the route, and close relations going into mourning for several months. An outward and lavish display was regarded as a measure of the family's affection for the dead. But, like most fashions, it filtered down the classes, withering at the top, until today only among the working classes, who are usually much closer to their families and like any excuse for a party, does the tradition of the splendid funeral linger on.

Attitudes have changed too. In Victorian times everyone accepted and talked naturally about death. Given the rate of infant mortality, it would have been impossible even for a child to be shielded from the subject. Sex was the great taboo, with copulation never mentioned, and babies being born under gooseberry bushes. Today everyone talks about sex and birth quite naturally, it is death that has become taboo. Perhaps it is because most people no longer believe in an afterlife that they cannot face up to the horror of death and so sweep everything under the carpet. In the old days a man died surrounded by his family; the Victorian deathbed was one of the great set pieces. Today, according to Geoffrey Gorer's excellent book, *Death, Grief and Mourning*, in the upper-middle and professional classes it is rare for a bereaved person to be present at death (less than one in eight).

The undertaker would pick up the body from the hospital, and none of the family would pay respects to it. In the same way, Samantha Upward or Jen Teale, even if their mother died at three o'clock in the morning, would be on to the undertaker in a flash to get the body out of the house. The Definitely-Disgustings, however, would be much more likely to be present at the death, and to visit the body if they were not. When I worked on a local paper, whenever a working-class person died I was always invited in for a cup of tea to admire the corpse lying in his coffin in the sitting room. As cremation gets more and more popular, too, the ashes tend to be left with the undertaker, and even a grave to mourn at is disappearing. According to our local undertaker, the middle classes often prefer not to watch that poignant final moment when the coffin disappears through the doors. They specify beforehand that they don't want the coffin to move, and troop out while it's still on its platform.

Fear of expressing unhappiness is also a characteristic of the upper middles – the stiff upper-middle lip again. Geoffrey Gorer said his own sister-in-law didn't even go to her husband's funeral, she was so terrified of breaking down in front of all her friends and relations and, wishing to spare the children such a depressing experience, took them for a picnic. Yet as a bereaved person, she found herself shunned like a leper. Only if she acted as though nothing of consequence had happened was she again socially acceptable. Thus, not only death but overt suffering is taboo. Perhaps this explains the plethora of euphemisms surrounding the subject. Howard Weybridge never 'dies', he 'passes away', or 'passes on', or 'passes over', or 'goes to God' or 'to his rest'. Death is even described as 'falling asleep'. 'Flowers' become 'floral tributes'; even the undertaker prefers to call himself a 'funeral director', and describes a burial as an 'interment'.

Harry Stow-Crat's father, Lord Egliston, would have had a nice end to his life. He has made everything over to Harry to avoid estate duty, and all the family have been frantically cosseting him to keep him alive the required five years. 'My father's great dread was going senile,' said one aristocrat, apologising for his father who was happily exposing himself in the orangery. 'But now he has, he's enjoying himself enormously.' Since his father's death would be noticed on the obituary page, Harry might not bother to pay for an insertion in the deaths column. If he did, it would be simple, saying where his father had died, and where and at what time the funeral would be held. Gideon Upward would also put his mother's death in *The Times*, and he might add her age (Samantha certainly would, out of spite) and the fact that she was the widow of Colonel Upward. Howard Weybridge would use the *Telegraph*. Jen Teale would use the local paper and add a sentence about 'passing peacefully away', and being the 'loving mother of Bryan and devoted granny of Wayne and Christine'. The Definitely-Disgustings would probably throw in 'a happy release', and 'a special auntie to Charlene and little Terry', and a 'thank you' to the nurses, doctors and district nurses concerned.

When a peer, a peeress in her own right or a baronet dies it is customary for letters written to members of his or her family to be addressed to them by the titles by which they were previously known until after the funeral. Consequently if a friend wrote to Harry saying how sorry he was about the death of Lord Egliston, he would address the letter to the Hon. Harry Stow-Crat, and if *The Times* reported the funeral they would describe him in the same way. At the memorial service a fortnight later he would be called Lord Egliston.

Old Lord Egliston's funeral would be simple. Harry would wear a dark suit and a black tie, Caroline would dress soberly but not in black. Relations and friends might have to walk across the fields while the coffin was carried to the family church, which means Gucci shoes sinking into the cowpats. Although it is more upper class to be buried than cremated it is frightfully smart to *have* to be cremated because your family tomb is so full of your ancestors going back to the year dot that there is no room for you. Lord Egliston might just squeeze into the family grave. The headstone, when it was up, would bear a simple inscription: 'Henry George De Vere Stow-Crat, 5th Baron Egliston, born 12 April 1905, Died 23 April 1979'. People would send flowers picked from their own gardens with plain cards saying 'With Love' or 'In Loving Memory' in their own handwriting. Being old-fashioned like the working classes, they might also send wreaths. Afterwards, everyone would go back to lunch or tea, where, depending on the stuffiness of the family or on the intensity of the grief, a certain amount of drink would be consumed.

When very important men die, what diplomats describe as a 'working funeral' takes place, which means that heads of state from all over the world meet on neutral ground and, while pretending to admire the wreaths, the Chinese and American foreign secretaries can discuss matters of moment out of the corners of their mouths without appearing to fraternise.

The upper-middles would probably drink themselves silly at the funeral, although a few years ago this would have been frowned on. When my husband, in the early sixties, announced that he intended to leave £200 in his will for a booze-up for his friends, his lawyer talked him out of it, saying it was in bad taste and would upset people. The same year his grandmother died, and after the funeral, recovering from the innate vulgarity of the cremation service when the gramophone record stuck on 'Abi-abi-abi -abi-de with me', the whole family trooped home and discovered some crates of Australian burgundy under the stairs. A rip-roaring party ensued, whereupon a lower-middle busybody who lived next door came bustling over to see if anything was wrong. My father-in-law, seeing her coming up the path, uttered the immortal line:

'Who is this intruding on our grief?'

Today, however, anything goes. Samantha Upward would probably get drunk out of guilt when her mother died. She had taken her mother in when she was widowed and bedridden, but it hadn't been a success. Having lived apart for so long, it was a terrible shock when they had to live together. The upper-middles have little respect for the wisdom of age, and Samantha got very irritated when her mother gave her advice about the children or running the house, and Samantha's mother missed her friends in Bournemouth terribly. Our local undertaker also said that the better educated people are, the more matter-of-fact they are about death. They treat the undertaker like a professional and let him get on with it, not quibbling about the price. Usually only the family send flowers; everyone else is asked to send the money to charity instead. A month later everyone gets smashed out of their minds once again at the memorial service.

When Mr Nouveau-Richards dies of a heart attack, Mrs Nouveau-Richards is worried about how she should arrange things. They don't report smart funerals in *The Tatler* for her to copy. She turns up at the church in deepest black with a huge picture hat and lots of make-up. All Jison's telly-stocracy friends turn up and keep a weather eye out for photographers and television cameras. The men wear light-coloured suits and cry a lot. The girls also wear deepest black and picture hats, but cry less in case their mascara runs. All Mr Nouveau-Richards's business colleagues send wreaths with black-edged funeral cards with 'Deepest Sympathy' printed on them. Mrs Nouveau-Richards insists on the undertakers wearing the full regalia of top hats, pinstripe trousers, and umbrellas.

After he was buried in the cemetery (Caroline Stow-Crat calls it a 'graveyard') Mrs N-R would have a splendid tomb built in strawberry roan marble, and engraved with ornate sentiments about Mr N-R 'crossing the bar to his eternal rest', and being 'the beloved father of Jason and Tracey-Diane'.

The Teales would be very stingy and question the price of everything. Jen thinks death is 'not very naice', and would expect the undertaker to do everything. She wouldn't want the hearse outside the house. She and Bryan would drive the Volkswagen to the funeral. After all there's nothing to get upset about: Bryan's mother was 'very elderly' and had been a 'senior citizen' for a long time. There would be no 'sobbing' at the funeral; that's what the Definitely-Disgustings do. Bryan's mother would probably be cremated as it's cheaper, although if she did have a grave, Jen wouldn't want the bother of tending it, so, instead of grass, the flat bit would be sprinkled with emerald green chips which serve the same function as plastic grass. Floral tributes would be particularly tasteful, and Bryan would probably wear a black armband on his sleeve for a few weeks afterwards.

The Definitely-Disgustings really push the boat out. 'I'm going to Florrie's funeral tomorrow,' I heard one working-class Yorkshire woman saying, 'it should be a good do,' a sentiment that would never be expressed by the middle classes.

Mr Definitely-Disgusting even insured for the purpose of being buried right, but, alas, with the cost of living the policy seldom comes anywhere near covering the cost of the funeral, which means Mrs D-D is likely to be left penniless and in debt. The problem, said our local undertaker, is to stop people overspending in a fit of emotionalism. Often they get quite annoyed.

'Are you trying to tell me my missus doesn't deserve the best?' said one man.

One train driver's widow, who could ill afford it, forked out for six cars and a very expensive panelled coffin. Afterwards she came and thanked the undertaker, adding that it was worth it, 'Even if I have to go out scrubbing for the rest of my life to pay for it.'

In the old days the streets used to be sanded to deaden the sound of the horses' hooves. And even today whole streets in the North and in Wales will show solidarity by drawing every curtain from the moment the hearse leaves the house until the funeral party returns.

The working classes still send funeral cards with poems inside and pictures of lilies and purple prayer-books on the front, which are displayed on the window sill outside drawn curtains. Often the men go out specially to buy a black suit, and often as many as six cars filled with tearful relations follow the hearse. Frightful rows ensue, too, because someone who thinks he's important enough to travel in the second car only gets a seat in the third car. Invariably, according again to our local undertaker, it's the 42nd cousin once removed who screams and cries the loudest because he's been on the booze since dawn.

At the funeral of a cockney gypsy who had married again after his first wife died, the first wife's family were lined up on one side of the grave, the second wife and her family on the other, each glaring across at the other. As the coffin was lowered the first wife's son shook his fist at the second wife, hissing, 'He's gone to lie with a good woman now'. Whereupon the son of the second wife nipped round the back, pushed the first wife's son into the grave and jumped on top of him. A glorious free-for-all resulted, which was only stopped by the arrival of the police.

With the floral tributes the working classes really come into their own. Once again, because of their inability to express themselves verbally, they spell it out with flowers. On the hearse are likely to be cushions and pillows with 'Mum' written across, empty chairs saying 'We'll Never Forget You, Dad', teddy bears or favourite dogs for the death of a child, bleeding hearts, harps with a broken string, all made entirely of flowers. Around the Elephant and Castle people often pay tribute to a man's profession. One East-Ender had a whole market stall full of fruit and vegetables, with all the price tickets, made entirely of different-coloured carnations, which took six men to lift onto the hearse. A landlord is often given a glass of foaming beer made entirely of white and brown chrysanthemums, while a bookie might have a floral winning post. One East-End boxer had his last fight almost to scale, with a ring, a referee and two boxers – all made of daisies. A florist told me the working classes would consider it insulting to give someone a small posy of spring flowers. If an old age pensioner comes into the shop and you steer her towards something that looks within her price range, she still insists on buying long-stemmed chrysanthemums at £1 a flower.

The party afterwards will be a terrific booze-up with crates and crates of beer and masses of stodgy food. One scrap-metal merchant even put up a marquee in his garden. Everyone gets plastered and then does song and dance acts. David Storey told me how he once went to a friend's funeral in Yorkshire. Not knowing the dead man's family, it was only after freezing beside the grave for twenty minutes that he discovered, on asking one of the mourners, that he was at the wrong funeral.

'Never mind, lad,' comforted the mourner, 'they'll all be meeting up at the Black Bull same as us afterwards.'

After the funeral Sharon and Dive would club together to buy Mr D-D a headstone, perhaps inscribed with the words 'Have a Good Sleep, Dad'. They would also put another entry in the local paper thanking everyone for their condolences and floral tributes. A year later, it would be considered very remiss if an *In Memoriam* notice didn't appear in the same paper:

> *God took Dad home,*
> *It was his will,*
> *But why that way*
> *We wonder still.*

> *Always in our thoughts, fondest love,*
> *Doris, Dive, Sharon, Auntie Edna and little Terry.*

Quite often there will be additional notices from several other members of the family. Because the working classes tend not to take part in local affairs, birth, marriage and death, or when they get caught nicking a telly, are the only times they get their names in the paper. Howard Weybridge might put an *In Memoriam* to Eileen in the *Daily Telegraph*, or even one to his elder brother who was killed at Anzio.

Finally our heroes reach the Other Side. How will they fare in the after-life? Harry Stow-Crat is thoroughly enjoying himself. He is just expressing delight at seeing Snipe and Nanny again when suddenly a beautiful angel flaps past and Harry can't decide whether to take a pot at her or ask her out to lunch. Jen Teale is speechless with admiration at the whiteness of the angels' robes and wonders whether they use a bio-wash. Mr Nouveau-Richards, having examined the burglar alarm on the Pearly Gates, is boasting to God how much better his own gates on earth were wired up against intruders, and how none of the pearls are as big as the ones he gave Mrs N-R for their silver wedding. Jison is just about to ask Jesus for an in-depth interview. Howard Weybridge is having a round of golf with the Holy Ghost, and Mr Definitely-Disgusting is having a lovely time playing golden oldies on the harp and filling in his football coupon for the match against Limbo in the afternoon.

Only Samantha Upward looks perturbed. Who would have thought, she keeps murmuring to herself disconsolately, that God would say, 'Pleased to meet you', when we arrived?

# INTERLUDE

---

# These
# You Have Loved

# INTELLIGENT AND LOYAL

From men of breeding, I turned joyfully to dogs of no breeding. During the seventies I acquired a brown mongrel called Fortnum, who was found hanging by wire from a tree – a gang of louts had tried to stage an execution. He was cut down, endured another home where they didn't much like dogs, and then came to live with us. A great admirer of the opposite sex, he soon fathered two daughters, Mabel and Barbara, by different mothers, who also came to live with us. As the proud owner of three mongrels, I searched for literature on the subject and, finding none, decided to write a book myself. I put an advertisement in *The Times* and the *Daily Telegraph*, which went:

'Mongrel's Lib. We have had enough books about breed dogs, anyone with good mongrel stories please send them in.'

I expected few replies, but, in fact, received 1500 letters, containing funny and heart-rending anecdotes, and hilarious snapshots. I was enchanted and spent the next year laughing and crying as I sifted out the material and turned it into a book.

As in *Class*, I tried to categorise the mongrel into 27 different types, including the Borderline Collie and the Vertical Shagpile, and then photograph them. Unfortunately our photographer, Graham Wood, was terrified of dogs and advanced on his subjects in thigh boots clutching caskets of choc drops. Being a professional, however, he stopped his hands trembling and the results were magical.

I think the book works even in this small extract because of the mongrels themselves. They were all very like Hugh Walpole's Jacob:

'I have owned a great many dogs,' wrote Walpole, 'some of them very finely bred, very aristocratic, very intelligent, but none of them ever approached Jacob for wisdom, conceit, self reliance and true affection. He was a ghastly mongrel. I tremble to think of the many different breeds that have gone into his making, but he had Character, he had heart, he had an unconquerable zest for life.'

# Intelligent and Loyal

## HOW TO CLASSIFY YOUR MONGREL

From earliest times the dog has been of service to man, guarding his cave, hunting with him for food, and giving him friendship. Gradually, to suit his own purpose, man started to breed specific types of dog to carry out particular tasks. He produced Mastiffs, for example, who were strong and brave enough to fight fiercely in battle. He bred a wolf-like sheepdog, the Alsatian, to frighten off any wolf that threatened the flock. As a double bluff, he even produced the Old English Sheepdog who looked like a sheep, so that when the wolf descended unsuspecting on the fold, he was routed by a great woolly monster. Man also needed fast dogs like the Greyhound and the Foxhound to hunt the rabbit and the fox, he needed Terriers to dig his prey out from their holes, and Spaniels to retrieve it from the undergrowth. As people had more leisure, Pekes, Pugs and other toy dogs were bred for decoration and companionship.

Because each of these breeds was needed for special duties, their value increased, and, as with all expensive things, snobbery crept in. The breed dog became a status symbol, and greedy breeders with an eye to financial gain produced more and more breeds allegedly for different purposes. In fact they seem often to have been creating mere collectors' items. At the same time, a huge sub-culture of mongrels were still carrying on their doggy life unheeded, attaching themselves to various owners, or surviving by scavenging.

The word mongrel, which is pronounced with a flattened 'o' in the same way as *monkey* and fish*monger*, comes from the Middle English word *Meng* (to mix), and from the Old English word *Gemong* (a mingling). A mongrel is a dog of mixed blood, whose parents were not of the same breed, or of any breed at all. A breed dog, say an Afghan Hound, has parents, grandparents, great grandparents and great-greats going back for at least ten generations, who are all Afghans. The mongrel, on the other hand, is usually the product of many generations of chance matings, and may have as many as sixty breeds in his make-up.

As a large part of this book consists of anecdotes about various mongrels of all shapes and sizes, I have tried in this chapter to categorise them into types to make them more readily identifiable, and to save laboriously describing each dog's appearance when I came to it. If I have identified anyone's mongrel wrongly, I apologise; it is often difficult to tell exactly what a dog looks like from a small photograph. If your mongrel doesn't fit into any of the categories, you should be delighted: you are the privileged owner of a unique dog.

## THE RESCUED MONGREL

*Oh rest ye, brother mongrels, we will not wander more.*

'Lucy Nicholas joined our family in 1964,' wrote a friend when she learnt I was gathering material for a book on mongrels. 'My mother bought her out of sheer embarrassment when she came up for auction at a local Conservative party sale. As the auctioneer pointed her out as lot four, a piglet-like creature in an old cardboard box with a head too big for her body, the room fell silent. As the silence continued, my mother felt herself blushing at the humiliation the small creature must be feeling. When finally the auctioneer failed to raise a single bid, she gallantly offered £2 10s. and found herself the owner of the obvious runt of the litter.'

Lucy's new owner displayed that quixotic streak of compassion which I am proud to think of as peculiarly English. It is that same streak which sends thousands and thousands of people off to dogs' homes every year to rescue mongrels that are about to be put down. It is also that streak of compassion for the underdog among underdogs that often makes them, on reaching the dogs' home, choose the ugliest, most pathetic dog they can find.

Brutus Collis, a black-and-white Shagpile from Dorking was rescued from the local RSPCA home. According to his master, 'It was love at first sight. I saw Brutus trying not to look too eager to be picked out.'

Sometimes a prospective owner needs just a flicker of recognition to take on a particular dog. 'The local RSPCA shelter was full of beautiful breed dogs,' wrote Miss Woodrow of Gwent, 'but in one corner cowered a sandy mongrel bitch who'd obviously been ill treated. She gave my hand a lick and that was it – she cost us ten shillings.'

1. The Vertical Shagpile: Profusely covered in long straight hair; eyes seldom visible; comes in all shapes and colours; very sanguine temperament.

2

3

4

5

2. The General Wolfehound: Gentle giant of noble but slightly tousled appearance; coat shaggy but not woolly; comes in all colours.

4. The Woolly Whitejaw: Wiry astrakhan coat, white moustache and beard, elegant Angela Rippon legs; Poodle ancestry.

3. The Romney Marshall: Medium length astrakhan coat, thick heavily-feathered legs; particularly prevalent in Kent.

5. The Michael Foot: Lustrous long-haired red and white coat, long hairy ears set low on either side of head; qualities of leadership.

6

7

8

9

6.  The Borderline Collie:
Envelope flap ears, silky
luxurious coat, usually black and
white; curly tail optional; herds
anything – people included;
highly intelligent and intuitive.

7.  The Family Circler: Soft
longish coat in all colours,
envelope flap ears; will round up
family on walks and before meals;
supremely intelligent and loyal.

8.  The Twentieth Century Fox
Dog: Pointed ears and nose, long
bushy red fur and luxuriant tail;
bays like a fox at night; smooth-
haired version comes in other
colours and has tail without
feathering.

9.  The Ear Commodore: Comes
in all shapes and sizes;
distinguishing characteristic: one
ear standing to attention, the
other at ease; fearless, merry
nature.

10.  The Hover Cur: Smooth hair; all colours but pale blond preferred; coiled tail when static; intensely agile; long-haired version known as *Cross Channel Furry*.

11.  The Spanish Policeman's Hat Ear Dog: Distinguishing characteristic: obtuse-angled ears shaped like a Spanish policeman's hat; supremely loyal.

12.  The Old Sea Dog: Smooth hair, usually black and tan, semi-erect curling ears; distinguishing characteristic: soulful black-ringed eyes and square or triangular widow's peak on forehead; Alsatian ancestry.

13.  The Miniature Magpie: Smooth close-cut white coat with jet black patches; jaunty nature; larger version known as *Standard Magpie*.

14.  The Pied Wagtail: Slim build; smooth, flecked black and white coat; continuously wagging tail.

15. The Jack Russell: Believed by many people to be a pedigree dog but not recognised by the Kennel Club because of the number of variations in colour, size and form. Small v-shaped drooped ears, smooth but slightly woolly coat; white with black or tan markings; intensely individual, sometimes contentious; doughty hunters; highly intelligent.

16

18

17

16. The Prop Forward: Smooth coat; solid compact body, barrel-chested and heavily muscled; boundless energy (particularly sexual); gladiator of the mongrel world. All colours.

17. The Black and Tan Tightskin: All shapes and sizes but coal black with rich red markings preferred; self-drying, sleek coat worn very tight; extremely friendly.

18. The Lancashire Hot Pet: Smooth coat; curled semi-erect ears which flatten close to the head like a seal's when returning from a night on the tiles; white shirt front; deceptively small, slender frame; intensely brave, fiery nature.

19

19.  The Edith Sitwell: Sm
hair, curly tail; excellent sitt

20. The Bertrand Russell: Rough-coated, slightly shaggier version of Jack Russell; comes in all colours; merry nature; highly intelligent; terrier ancestry.

21. The Rough Diamond: Medium-sized, heavily-built, compact body; copious rough, shaggy coat; sometimes distinguished by white diamond on forehead; all colours, effervescent nature.

22. The Rough-and-Reddish: Rough red coat, slim build, medium sized; gentle nature; possible Red Setter/Irish Terrier ancestry.

23

24

25

26

23. The Fetcher: Medium lengt
silky hair, plumed tail; most
common colours: ebony, gold or
red; loves to retrieve balls or stic
and carry newspapers or shoes;
charming manners; excellent
with children.

24. The Satin Crammer: Broad
chested; highly-polished short-
cropped coat, free from all
feathering; very powerful tail;
most common colours: black,
yellow or red; intensely amiable,
incurably greedy; tendency to go
grey around the muzzle early in
life, worrying where next meal i
coming from; Labrador ancestry

25. The Half Cocker: Solid
compact body, flat silky coat, lo
terry towelling ears; long tail
preferred; comes in all colours;
often identified by white blaze o
forehead, widening over the
muzzle; fifty per cent Spaniel
parentage; jolly nature (but min
of own).

26. The Headless Hound: Ver
economical to feed.

Mrs Lynne of Upminster, however, preferred the grand gesture. 'The dogs were penned in twos and threes when I arrived. They were being given their only meal of the day. Ricky left his food to come and talk to me, that was that. He has grown into the most beautiful dog, and is loving to the point of adoration.'

The rescued mongrel has no birthday. Most owners give him an official one like the Queen. He has no parents, so speculation about his forebears is endless and fascinating, but quite unprofitable. Although his owners probably admit secretly that he is not the most classically beautiful dog in the world, they are fiercely protective, and long for other people to admire him. Over the past six years I have hoarded the few compliments my rescued dog Fortnum has received like a miser. They include:

'Intelligent and loyal.'

'Nice broad 'ead.'

'Looks a strong dog.'

'Oo could 'urt 'im, when they're all so lovely, in't they?'

'All muscle, isn't he?'

'Nice teef' (really scraping the barrel).

'Nice silky ears' (ditto).

'Look at his little frown.'

'Nice size.'

'Nice dog.'

'You can't miss 'im.'

'What breed is he?'

Just as owners of pedigree dogs often keep in touch with the breeder, telling her how her former charges are getting on, owners of strays often forge a link with the past by writing to the dogs' home from which they've acquired their dog, giving a report of its progress. Battersea has some marvellous letters from satisfied customers, usually signed with a muddy print.

'Dear Sirs,' wrote Emma. 'Three years ago, my grandmother, my mother and I came to Battersea Dogs' Home, and came away with Jason a lovely mongerell. He is in cracking form, and as fit as a hunter. He is also the best companion I have ever had. I often see him guarding my seven-week-old sister's pram, and sometimes he knocks my two-year-old sister over, but she doesn't like it much. His hairs are gharstly because he is molting now. Still I am very thankful we came that day.

'PS. Jason sends a great slobery kiss.'

# THE MONGREL AND CHILDREN

A dog also provides wonderful protection for children, and often has a far greater sense of responsibility than many parents. The orphaned Romulus and Remus, for example, were brought up by a wolf. If Nana, the St Bernard, hadn't been thwarted by the idiotic Mr Darling, she would certainly have saved the Darling children from being kidnapped by Peter Pan. There are plenty of Nanas, too, in the mongrel world. Fred Grimes, for example, a beautiful Rough and Reddish from Welwyn Garden City, always used to wait outside the school to accompany his mistress's children home, and on one occasion saved a little boy from falling into a deep pond by racing across the fields and heading him off until his mother reached him.

A few months later the same little boy, with a group of friends, walked past a shop where Fred was tied up, and stopped to pat him. 'Don't touch that dog,' said the other children in horror.

'That's not a dog,' explained the small boy, 'he's our Fred.'

One man who never underestimated the bond between a child and his dog was Fred Winterflood BEM who was associated with Battersea Dogs' Home for forty years, but always retained his sense of humour and compassion. One morning he was manning the reception desk when a little red nose appeared over the counter.

'Please mister,' whispered a very small boy, 'I've lost my dog.'

His father, who followed him, said they'd spent the two previous days and nights searching for the dog, an old mongrel who'd grown up with the boy. The child had insisted on leaving his bedroom light on all night to guide the dog home, and was desperately worried because the animal usually slept on his bed. How would he ever get to sleep at night if he didn't have a bed to lie on?

Although the father took several weeks off work to help in the search, and the child checked in to the dogs' home every day, no old mongrel turned up. But the heart of Battersea (hardened so often only out of necessity) was touched by the small boy's desolation. They offered him any dog in the home (including two magnificent St Bernards resident at the time) free of charge to replace his lost pet. He shook his head – he only wanted his old dog.

So Battersea went even further, and had a photograph of the dog blown up and pinned over the door where all stray dogs are checked in on arrival – just in case any of them matched up. Twelve weeks dragged by, then a

particular keeper, remarkable in his skill at recognising dogs, reported to the general office that he thought he'd found the dog – a pitifully thin brown and black mongrel.

Mr Winterflood looked at the animal in question and scoffed. The creature was a completely different size, he said.

'Look at the markings on the back,' said the keeper. 'Remember he's been missing the boy, and probably on the run, for weeks.'

With little feeling of optimism, Mr Winterflood rang up the boy's mother, warning her not to tell the child in case it wasn't the right dog, but just to pop in on a routine visit.

The little dog was tethered to the bars. It waited unkempt, dead-eyed, unsteady on its legs, the picture of dejection. But as soon as the little boy shuffled slowly down the line, listlessly examining each dog, it pricked up its ears, stared for a second, whimpered unbelievingly, then went absolutely crazy with excitement. The little boy was speechless. He just staggered forward and cuddled the dog incredulously as it frantically licked away the tears of joy which streaked his face. So delighted were the staff of Battersea by the reunion that, as a final gesture, they had a whip round and brought the dog a new collar and lead.

# PART THREE

## Urban Village

# THE COMMON YEARS

*The Common Years* is my favourite book because it was based on diaries I kept during the ten years I lived in Putney with my husband, two children and assorted dogs. I am so grateful I have a record not only of the changing seasons of a beautiful place, but also of my family growing up and the funny, endearing, memorable things that children, dogs and even husbands do.

*The Common Years* covers the period 1972–82, but was, in fact, written in 1983, a year after we'd moved to Gloucestershire. Although very happy there, I still missed Putney and my senior mongrel, Fortnum, who died in 1982, quite dreadfully, but somehow writing the book exorcised their ghosts.

It was difficult to know which bits to extract, so we chose an early year, 1974, when my glorious English setter Maidstone was still alive, and 1982, which was the year we left. To this day I cannot read the entry in March when Fortnum died, nor the one about the day we finally piled everything into the Pickfords van and drove away from Putney, without crying.

My only regret on re-reading this book, was that I drew rather unkind portraits of one or two of my fellow dog walkers, which they must have recognised and been upset by. I was hurt at the time because they continually bitched about Fortnum. But hurting other people is not excusable because you've been hurt yourself.

# The Common Years

## INTRODUCTION

For ten years, sometimes two or three times a day, I walked my dogs on Putney and Barnes Commons. Often my children, Felix and Emily, who were two and a half years and nine months respectively when we moved to Putney in 1972, came with me. Occasionally on Sunday, I was accompanied by my husband, Leo. But normally I set out alone.

Because I spent so much time on the Common, and because when the children were young it was really the only quiet place to think, I started taking a note book and pen out with me, and jotting down random thoughts, impressions of people I met, and any changes in the seasons.

To begin with the entries were sporadic. There were periods when I was writing a book or working on some *Sunday Times* piece, during which I didn't write a word in the diary for weeks. But gradually it became a fascination to see that the same chestnut tree, two down from the slide in the children's playground, was always the first to turn gold in the autumn; or that one year the snowdrops would appear much earlier than others; or that certain muggy kinds of weather brought out flashers and undesirables like a rash.

This book is based on that diary but many of the main characters who appear in it are fictitious, although modelled in part on the people I met on the Common in those years.

Putney and Barnes Commons are situated five miles from Hyde Park. I should also explain that, although merging into one another, they are run by different bodies. Barnes Common is looked after by the London Borough of Richmond and Twickenham.

Putney Common, on the other hand, which consists of some forty acres, belonged to the Earl Spencer, whose ancestors over the centuries repeatedly tried to enclose the land. Happily the local people resisted and, in 1871, a Bill was passed which vested control of the Common in the hands of eight Conservators, who were to be elected every three years by the people who lived within three-quarters of a mile of the Common. It is still the same today. Each year Common rates are paid by people living near the Common and every three years they elect eight Conservators, who meet regularly to decide how the Common should be run. (They also control Wimbledon Common.) Part of the money raised by these Common rates pays the salary of a ranger, who takes care of Putney Common, mowing, picking up litter, supervising the planting of trees, reporting undesirables to the police and refereeing fearful squawking matches between dog walkers.

During the ten years we lived in Putney, I mainly took two routes round the Commons, usually walking anti-clockwise, but sometimes clockwise – so as to avoid and fox those people and dogs I didn't want to meet. Both routes are shown on the endpaper map and described in the following pages.

Ten years is a long time to walk over the same small area. I still miss the friends I made on the Common. They were a merry, gallant bunch, who braved tempests, hail and the bitterest cold rather than let their dogs go unwalked. Some of them, as will be seen from the pages that follow, drove me demented, and I them. But a diary is a convenient dumping ground for one's grievances, and, having once dumped them, I would usually be falling on my temporary foes' necks within twenty-four hours.

I think even now, eighteen months after we've left Putney, I could find my way along those routes with my eyes shut, guided by the raw soapy scent of the hawthorns, or the rank smell of the elder, or the sweet elusive fragrance of the wild roses. I never got bored with the Common – each day there was something new to look at, violets suddenly appearing by the railway line, or the return of the toadflax by the football pitch. Each day, however badly I or my dogs behaved, the Common, given the chance, would restore my sanity. Familiarity never bred contempt. I can only look back on the ten years we were acquainted with love and gratitude.

J.C.

*Gloucesteshire 1984*

# THE TWO WALKS

On my favourite walk, you set out to the north down Egliston Road, passing on the right a group of modern houses, known as 'Alimony Villas' because at one time there were so many divorced women and their children living there. Through an archway formed by two huge plane trees lies the first Common. It is divided into two squares by a little road up the centre. The left-hand western square is occupied by the cricket pitch. On the right-hand square on the south-east corner stands All Saints' Church, a solid Victorian pile consecrated in 1874. It has a little white bell tower rising out of the trees like a Cape Canaveral rocket, and several very beautiful windows designed by William Morris and Edward Burne-Jones. The churchyard has no tombstones and is framed by a square of limes, a straggling privet hedge and, on the outside, an iron spiked fence.

Leaving the church, you pass All Saints' School, the 22 bus shelter, and the Spencer Arms public house (named after Earl Spencer) on your right, and cross the first Common, until you reach the fork where the Lower Richmond Road splits in two and continues under the same name on the right, but becomes Queen's Ride on the left. In the fork between the two roads, lies a stretch of grass known as the 'Fair Triangle', because in May every year the Fair arrives and parks here for a month.

Crossing Queen's Ride and the Lower Richmond Road (both busy main roads) at the tip of the Fair Triangle, you reach the Big Common, a stretch of open land, divided by a line of plane trees, and bordered on the boundary by a sluggish overgrown stream called Beverley Brook.

To reach the Brook you pass, on the right, first the ranger's hut, with its little garden, then Putney Hospital rising from a sea of green grass like a great pink liner, then the nurses' home, the bowling green with its crinkly red-roofed pavilion, and finally a block of council flats known as the Ranelagh Estate, past which, to the north-east, Beverley Brook continues its meandering way down to the River Thames.

Between the Brook and the Thames lie the fenced-in Barn Elms Playing

Fields. At the extreme north-east corner of the Common, just before the Brook reaches the Ranelagh Estate, grows a clump of trees and nettles known as 'Cat Corner'; this clump swarms with stray cats and also cats from the estate, who become the target of every passing dog. In the early days, before the two footbridges across to the playing fields and the two paths were built, you could not walk along the north side of the Brook, which was lined with elms. Instead, you turned left when you reached Cat Corner, away from the council estate, and walked along the south bank of the Brook, which was lined with willows, poplars, hawthorns and lush vegetation.

To the south as you walk lie the 'Hillocks', two undulating swells of grass under which piles of bomb rubble were buried after the Second World War. At the end of the Hillocks, you come to the football pitch, and leaving Beverley Brook you swing left along the side of the pitch. Ahead lies an enchanted square of land known as the 'Flower Garden', because it was once allotments, and today is crammed with wild flowers, brambles, dog roses and oak and sycamore saplings. But, instead of entering the Flower Garden, you turn right again, with the football pitch on your right, and a splendid colonnade of plane trees, which border the Flower Garden, on your left, and walk down the grassy path until you reach 'Oedipus Corner' – so named because it is marked by three tall Lombardy poplars, where three paths meet. To the left here, on the north-west corner of the Flower Garden, lies a dense sycamore copse, known as 'Flashers' Point', because so many flashers lurk there in high summer waiting to startle unsuspecting lady dog-walkers.

Leaving Flashers' Point, you can take a right path through low hanging oak trees, or the left path known as the 'Nettle Tunnel', because it is flanked by treacherous beds of nettles, which close over the top in summer.

At the end of both the oak path and the Nettle Tunnel, you come to the grassy boundary of Putney and Barnes Commons. As you carry on westward onto Barnes Common, on the right lie the tennis courts, the putting green, with its little thatched pavilion, and the children's playground. To the left is Barnes Graveyard, which is unfenced and open to the public and every passing vandal. Many gravestones have been broken, stone angels lie battered and armless in the long grass. Most of the more august female statues have black eyes or broken noses. Untended, except (rarely) by morose Richmond council workers, it remains a place of haunting, if desolate, beauty, a forsaken garden beloved of film crews.

On the far west end of the Graveyard, you come to a triangle of parking space, flanked by chestnut trees, known locally as the 'Eternal Triangle', because so many lovers – usually adulterers who can only meet during the day – park their cars there during the lunch hour.

Beyond the Eternal Triangle lies a stretch of rough grass, leading to Rocks Lane, another main road, which crosses the Lower Richmond Road, and later Queen's Ride; but our walk turns left past a stretch of marshy ground, known unromantically as Barnes Bog, and curving back round the other side of the graveyard into the 'Squirrel Wood'. Filled with oaks, thorns, sycamores, and one very beautiful poplar, the wood is inhabited by dozens of grey squirrels and usually rings with the excited barks of dogs chasing them.

Emerging from the Squirrel Wood, you reach the Barnes–Putney boundary again. On the right lies a magnificent avenue of chestnuts. We, however, go straight on, crossing the blackthorn copse on the boundary into the Flower Garden. On the right, beyond the Chestnut Avenue, lies Putney Cemetery, which is framed by an ancient russet wall, and which (in contrast to the lush wilderness of Barnes Graveyard) is beautifully kept.

At the end of the Cemetery wall, the Flower Garden merges into the Big Common down a gentle slope known as 'Dogger Bank', because it is pitted with holes made by all the dogs frenziedly burrowing after voles and shrews.

By Dogger Bank, you can either cross the Big Common diagonally which will bring you back to the ranger's hut again, or turn right along the Cemetery wall, until you reach another wooden hut on the edge of Lower Richmond Road.

Known locally as 'the 'Ut', it is the place where Putney Cricket Club have their tea and booze-ups with opposition teams after cricket matches. The 'Ut is always a good place to catch recalcitrant dogs, because, while they investigate the dustbins for the remains of last Saturday's cricket tea, you can often sneak up on them and catch them by the tail.

From the 'Ut, you cross the Upper Richmond Road and Queen's Ride at the base of the Fair Triangle, which brings you back onto the first Common but on the cricket pitch side. On the right of the pitch lies Chester Close, a row of modern houses. Ahead, to the south, stretching the length of the first Common stands a row of solid, handsome red-brick Victorian houses, called Lower Common South. Each one has its own individual character, because they (like the houses in Egliston Road) were all designed completely differently by the same imaginative architect. They are splendid family houses, with big gardens filled in the spring with apple blossom and bluebells.

Turning left along Lower Common South, you reach Alimony Villas once more, and turn right back into Egliston Road. This walk, depending on whom I met or on the caprices of the dogs, or whether the muse struck, would take between thirty minutes and an hour and a half.

A variation on this route, but one I took less often, was to cross the first Common and turn left along the Fair Triangle, across the Putney–Barnes boundary, which is marked here by an oblong copse of grey poplars and silver birches.

From the boundary, you enter the 'Yarrow Meadow', which like most of Barnes Common – as opposed to Putney Common – is made up of sandy heath, covered with bracken, gorse bushes, oak trees, silver birches and beautiful grasses. In late summer, this stretch is dotted with white yarrow, hence its name.

From the Yarrow Meadow, you cross Common Road to 'Peter's Meadow', so named because, when I first explored it on a glorious summer morning, it reminded me of the meadow Peter goes out into, to the accompaniment of that haunting theme tune at the beginning of *Peter and the Wolf*. Once again this area is dotted with gorse, bracken, oak trees and long lush grass, which is mowed in summer for the local children's school sports. Since we left Putney it has been used in winter as a football pitch.

Along the south side of Peter's Meadow runs the railway line, and on the south-west corner, through a hawthorn copse, you enter a red-brick tunnel, known as 'Mugger's Tunnel', because it contains a blind corner, where bag snatchers lurk and jump out on unwary passers-by.

Through the tunnel, on the left, stands Barnes Station: a Gothic folly with its four mulberry red chimneys. Turning right, you plunge into a chestnut wood, which gives way to more open heathland. Ahead lies a group of splendid houses in the middle of the Common, called Mill Hill.

Turning left towards home, you can either cross Rocks Lane, then bear left over the Lower Richmond Road and follow the route of the first walk home past the Eternal Triangle and Barnes Graveyard, or turn right across the bottom of Peter's Meadow, back into the Yarrow Meadow and home across the grey poplar boundary and the Fair Triangle.

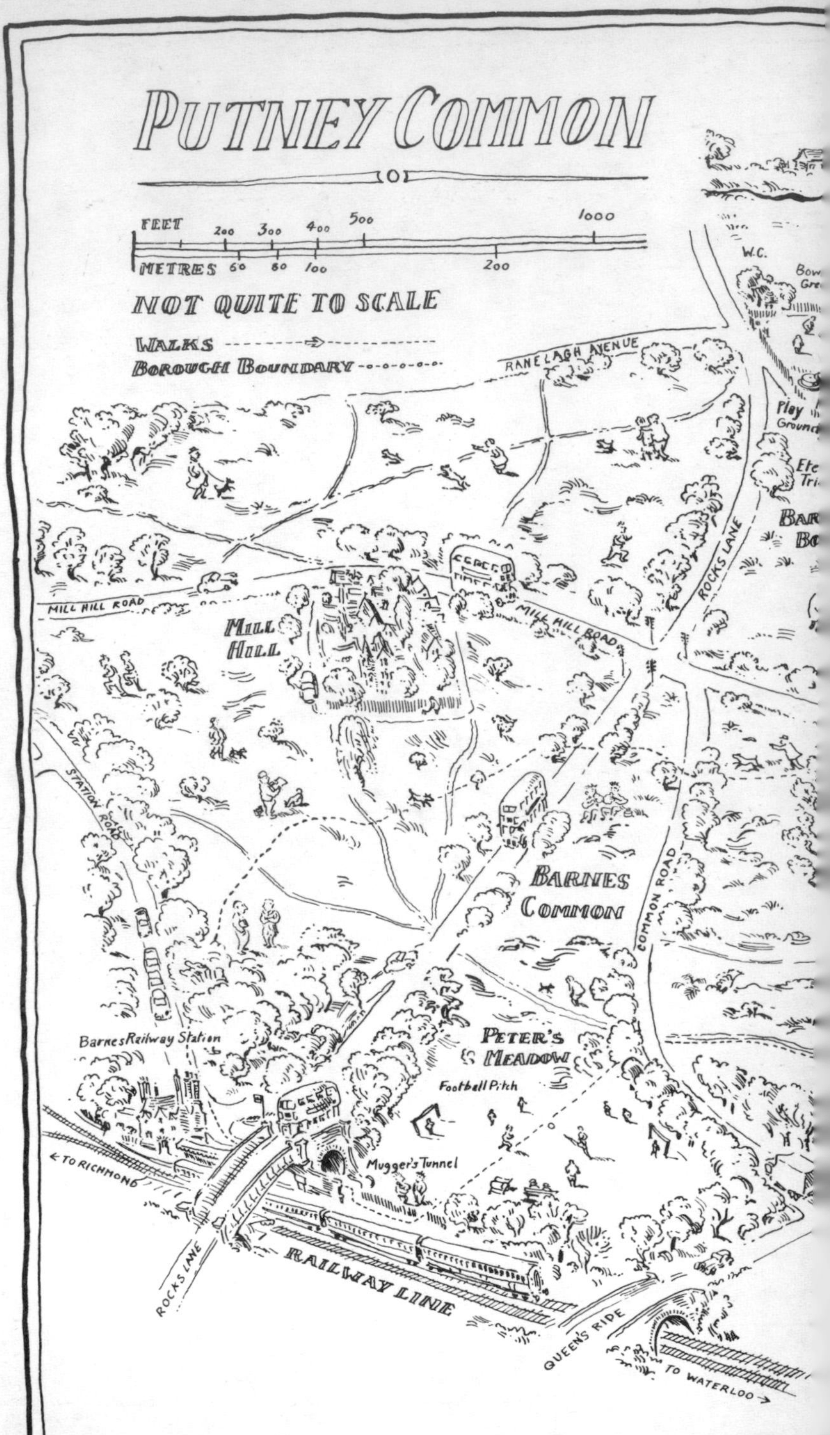

# PUTNEY COMMON

FEET  200  300  400  500       1000

METRES  50  80  100       200

## NOT QUITE TO SCALE

WALKS - - - - - - - →

BOROUGH BOUNDARY - o - o - o - o -

RANELAGH AVENUE

MILL HILL ROAD

MILL HILL

MILL HILL ROAD

ROCKS LANE

STATION ROAD

BARNES COMMON

COMMON ROAD

Barnes Railway Station

PETER'S MEADOW

Football Pitch

Mugger's Tunnel

← TO RICHMOND

ROCKS LANE

RAILWAY LINE

QUEEN'S RIDE

TO WATERLOO →

W.C.

Bow...
Gre...

Play...
Ground...

Ele...
Tri...

BAR...
Bo...

# DRAMATIS PERSONAE

Apart from my husband, Leo, who was thirty-eight, and my children Felix and Emily who were three and a half and eight months when we moved to Putney, the Cast of Leading Characters includes:

MRS BOND, Henrietta's daily

CEDRIC, a glamorous television star

CLARISSA, a retired headmistress

CRISPIN, a budding artist

DAVID, a sculptor, enamoured of Rosie

FRANCES, a feminist harpy

HENRIETTA, a local bossy-boots who regarded herself as lady of the manor

PATTY, our kind, long-suffering nextdoor neighbour

RACHEL, a disgruntled local dog walker, best friend of Clarissa

ROSIE, a beauty and an intellectual

SCOTTISH MOLLY, a ritzy aristocrat from Aberdeen and a former buddy of Rachel and Clarissa

SYD, a right wing carpenter

TOMMY, a charming gay dog walker

# 1974

*Tuesday, February 12th*

Two years ago, just before we moved to Putney, I left 50,000 words of a novel about show jumping behind on a bus after a drunken lunch. I hadn't taken a carbon and I never got the 50,000 words back. So great was the trauma that only now do I feel able to start re-writing it. As all the main characters in the novel live in the country, I need to get the rural details right. I will look an idiot if I have my hero chasing through a field of cow parsley in the middle of winter. Since I have so much time on my hands when I go out, waiting for Maidstone to come back, in future I am going to take a notebook and a pen onto the Common every day, so that I can jot down the changes in the seasons.

Today I notice once again the rosy blur on the five tallest elms along Beverley Brook which I noticed last year. Thank God it means spring is on the way. Also coltsfoot is out, a sudden explosion of sulphur yellow, on the second hillock by the football pitch.

*Thursday, March 21st*

Take Maidstone out at dusk. In the copse near Barnes Graveyard a hawthorn is putting out leaves like tiny green flames. Down by the Brook, I find the first yellow celandine on the bank. Above, the starlings are gathering in my five beloved elms, blackening them against a soft lilac sky. In and out and round about the starlings wheel, with a high-pitched buzz that can be heard for miles around. Maidstone runs down to the Brook, and gazes up at them with his mouth open and his speckled head on one side.

## Thursday, March 28th

Creeping cold and damp. Yellow crocuses, like blackbirds' bills, and mud-splattered daffodils are out in Barnes Graveyard. The blackthorn is also out, and looks as though its sooty branches have been dipped in flour. Coke tins litter the ground after the mild weekend. Maidstone charges about, guzzling chip paper.

'Don't you ever feed him?' asks Rachel as she passes me. When she is not biting my head off, she assumes an arch, slightly hectoring manner, like someone out of *The Archers*.

I have discovered her dog is called Bridie, and that she is the highly efficient part-time secretary of a local solicitor. She is about forty, with a blonde curly perm, blue eyes and flicked-up spectacles. She has the permanently discontented, beady look of a baby bird whose mother is late with the worm.

## Monday, April 1st

Very warm – out without a jersey for the first time. Notice the poplars by the bowling green are thickening with scarlet catkins and bronze leaves. All the young greens are so beautiful: the saffron of the oaks, the buff of the planes, the pale jade of the willows, the acid green of the limes, and the darker inky green of my five lovely elms. But most beautiful of all is a pear tree in one of the back gardens of Lower Common South, which I can see from my study, moonlit green just before dawn, or dancing in the noon sunshine, its white garlanded arms rising and falling.

The blackthorn is already over and the colour of old lace. Progress round the Common is very slow, as Maidstone keeps getting plugged into vole holes.

## Saturday, April 6th

Dandelions and coltsfoot already have clock heads. And cow parsley is swathing Beverley Brook with white. The pink flowers on the elms have been supplanted by new acid-green papery flowers with crimson hearts. On studying my tree book, however, I discover that these paper flowers are actually the fruits of the elm – and the equivalent of acorns on an oak tree, or sycamore keys.

*Friday, April 12th*

Very cold. Along the banks of Beverley Brook, the east wind is scattering the papery green elm fruits like confetti. Notice they are heart-shaped with tiny rose-pink centres. The hawthorn is about to flower, white buds rise from each branch like tiny clusters of balloons.

Today the Common is deserted except for a girl with a Peke. She seems to wander aimlessly. Approaching closer, I find she is dark and extraordinarily beautiful, with huge haunted, violet-ringed eyes. She starts, seems about to speak, then runs away.

I am reminded of Ezra Pound:

> She would like someone to speak to her,
> And is almost afraid that I will commit that indiscretion.

*Friday, April 24th*

Birds are nesting – each tree is a noisy green musical box. Today I bump into the beauty with the Peke a second time. I admire the Peke. She says he is called Michelin, because of his rolls of loose skin. Walking on the Common with another person is rather like having one's hair washed, or sitting behind a taxi driver: there is no eye contact, so people tend to talk about themselves more than they would normally.

The beauty, whose name is Rosie, tells me she split up from her solid reliable husband a year ago, to run off with a handsome lover, who was starting up a garden centre. The garden centre was a flop, all the plants died and so did their passion for one another. Now she lives in a pretty flat off the Upper Richmond Road, with no one pretty to put in it.

She says she is working for a degree in physics at London University. Find this hard to believe, like one of those claims made by prospective Miss Worlds, or nudes in *Playboy*, that their chief interests are archaeology and Japanese court poetry. But there is a vulnerability about her that is very appealing.

On the way home, Maidstone and I pass a single blue suede glove hanging forlornly from the wire fence surrounding the Common ranger's hut. It reminds me of Rosie – no good without a partner.

### Tuesday, April 30th

Exquisite day. Every chestnut candle blazing. The hawthorn blossom is out at last, exploding like white-hot stars from a rocket. Charmed by the piping of birds in every tree, mare's-tails are pushing up their snaky heads all over the Flower Garden. The newly mown Hillocks are a dazzling white-green in the sun, with the tracks of the mower disappearing into the inky-blue shadows cast by my five elms. A very late game of football is being played on the football pitch. A starling keeps imitating the referee's whistle. Maidstone is running everywhere after it. Wish he reacted to my summons with such alacrity.

### Wednesday, May 1st

The Fair has arrived, and is set up as usual on the triangle of grass lying in the fork of Queen's Ride and Lower Richmond Road. The scarlet and yellow merry-go-rounds, and the pink and hyacinth-blue turret of the helter-skelter rise out of the angelic spring-green trees like a fairy city.

### Thursday, May 2nd

Torrential rain. Hellish, hellish morning, searching for Maidstone. In the end, Patty, my kind nextdoor-neighbour drives me round Putney looking for him. We finally track him down at the Fair. He is not buying a bunch of blue ribbons, but has been laboriously losing his virginity to a plump geriatric ginger bitch. He evidently took forty-seven minutes to do so. All the stallholders had bets on how long he would keep going. Appropriately the youth who mans the Big Dipper came closest. Maidstone is nearly black with rain and exhaustion. When he gets home, he sleeps for the rest of the day. Perhaps sex is the answer.

*Saturday, May 11th*
Sex is not the answer. Yesterday, Maidstone bashed another hole in Patty's fence, dug up some carefully tended regalia lilies, then chased Patty's cat back into the house through the cat door, and got stuck. Extracting himself, he brought the entire cat door with him, and charged around the garden, cat flap flying, like a galvanised sandwich-board man.

*Sunday, May 12th*
With the warm weather, the season of sleeping out has begun on the Common. Every night visiting tramps stretch out on the vaults in Barnes Graveyard. Pursuing Maidstone, I discover Rachel clicking her tongue over a splendid orgy that must have occurred last night. A copy of *The Sunday Times* is spread as bedding under a great holm oak, and on a nearby grave lie two chewed raw onions, a ball of yellow wool, an empty bottle of VP wine and a suspender belt.

'Disgusting,' snorts Rachel, then adds that she can't understand why I cannot catch Maidstone, when she finds it so easy.

Refrain from replying that in his new Lothario role, Maidstone is determined to seduce Bridie, who never leaves Rachel's heels – so now he doesn't either.

*Monday, May 13th*
A splendid row has broken out over the Common. In the middle of this perfect spring, the gas board has suddenly decided to lay a huge pipe, under Barnes Common, the Flower Garden, the two Hillocks, Beverley Brook, and down to the Thames. A big red crane already hangs like a malignant stork over my five tall elms. Today the workmen moved their bulldozers in, crashing through speedwell, buttercups and cow parsley, knocking down little hawthorns and oak trees in their green prime.

Even though I've only been walking on this Common for eighteen months, I feel all the outrage of a mother whose child has been raped. The workmen – who are Irish – come in for a lot of flak from the dog walkers, particularly Rachel, who seems to regard them as additionally responsible for all the troubles in Northern Ireland. Every time she passes them a flurry of 'Disgusting's or 'Trust the IRA's' fall from her pursed lips.

*Tuesday, May 14th*

Walk with Rosie, who says she has been mugging up on the quantum theory, the meaning of which she tries but fails to explain to me. Say that I'm too cross about the bulldozers to concentrate. Rosie says gas boards don't even have to get planning permission. It's like *Alice in Wonderland*. Action first, permission afterwards.

*Wednesday, May 15th*

Out on the Common, I find all the Irish work-force in a high state of dudgeon. All their bulldozers have been wrecked by an overnight saboteur. Work will be held up at least a week.

*Sunday, May 19th*

Bulldozers still inoperative. Meet Rosie. She asks me with a smirk if I've noticed anything odd about the bulldozers. Then confesses she was the saboteur. On Friday, she crept out at twilight with wire cutters. Jolly brave of her, considering the bulldozers are parked on the edge of Barnes Graveyard, which is not only reputed to be haunted but always swarming at night with undesirables.

Suddenly, she says, she fell in with a posse of thugs, full of beer and bad intent, who were shambling towards the Graveyard, hell-bent on bashing up the stone angels. Catching the eye of the leader, Rosie asked him if he had any idea how to immobilise a bulldozer.

After several 'Yer wot's', the penny dropped, and, seizing the wire cutters, the youth led his troops onto the three bulldozers. A good time ripping out wires was had by all – no one bothered to bash up the stone angels that night and everyone, including Michelin the Peke, ended up in the pub.

I am so impressed by Rosie's daring, that I ask her to dinner next week, rashly promising that I will find a delicious man for her.

*Monday, May 20th*

Out on the Common, an Irish workman tells me that, on account of the vandalisation of bulldozers, the pipeline will be diverted round rest of the hawthorn copse. Highly delighted, but wish I could think of a delicious man for Rosie.

*Sunday, May 26th*

Spare man proving most elusive. Perhaps it's the weather, and the lush bosky greenness outside, but all the spare men I know seem suddenly to have got hitched up. They'd all love to come to dinner but can they bring Caroline/Fiona/Georgina/Rowena? The result is a colossal dinner party, but, alas, no one for Rosie.

In despair, I telephone an impossibly good-looking, jet-setting art dealer, who has such an exquisite house in the Boltons that I'm convinced he must be queer. By some miracle, he happens to be in London and is delighted to come. Perhaps Rosie can detach one of the single men from Caroline, Fiona, Georgina or Rowena.

*Tuesday, May 28th*

Disastrous dinner party. Jet-setting art dealer takes no interest in Rosie, who is looking stunning. He leaves early. Everyone else stays until three o'clock in the morning until we run out of drink. Feel I have utterly failed as Cupid.

Out on the Common holding my aching head together. Notice the trees are changing, the acid-green variations of spring are giving way to the uniform dark green of high summer. Next minute Rosie bounces up saying thank you for a super evening and a frightful hangover. I say I'm sorry about the art dealer.

'He was perfect,' says Rosie in surprise. 'He took my telephone number in the first five minutes, so we didn't have to bother to talk to each other for the rest of the evening, and he's taking me out on Thursday night.'

Add cautiously that I still suspect he may be queer.

*Friday, May 31st*

Dying to find out how Rosie got on with the art dealer. Walk out on the Common, slap into Rachel in her most belligerent mood. Maidstone, she says, broke into her neighbour's garden yesterday and leapt on her cocker spaniel bitch who is 'in season'. Rachel's lecture is fortunately cut short by Rosie, who has black rings under her eyes.

'How was last night?' I ask.

'I went to a lecture on Rutherford,' says Rosie firmly.

'But I thought . . . .' I blurt out.

'It was excellent,' Rosie goes on, and proceeds to describe a lecture in such abstruse detail, that eventually Rachel stalks off to examine the progress of the wild roses on the Flower Garden.

'I'm not going to let that cow know what I'm up to,' says Rosie. 'Now about last night. Your art dealer friend is definitely not gay.'

Evidently he took her back to dine at his exquisite house, and her suspicions about his masculinity were aroused not only by the perfectly arranged flowers, but also because he cooked new potatoes dripping in mint and butter, but never touched one. Nor did he touch her – all evening – until, positively beady with desire, she started picking on him. Where-upon he told her not to be a bloody bitch. She was about to flounce out of his exquisite house (without the taxi money home) when he gathered up all eight stone of her, carried her upstairs without panting, threw her on his Jacobean four-poster, and took her, added Rosie with a shiver of delight, most gloriously.

As bonus points, Rosie goes on, he didn't even bat an eyelid when he had to drive her home afterwards, because she doesn't like leaving Michelin alone all night. Feel I have played Cupid with consummate skill.

Ahead we see Rachel, making Bridie sit for five seconds, before they cross the Lower Richmond Road. I ask Rosie if she knows anything about Rachel's home life.

'Three children and a husband called Alastair who thinks he married down because he went to a minor public school,' says Rosie. 'Alastair has great charm but doesn't believe a gentleman should work, so he spends his time walking round his estate, which in his case is a three-bedroomed house off the Upper Richmond Road, which leaves him unoccupied and under Rachel's feet for most of the day. Rachel was once very pretty, but is now soured with life's vicissitudes. They are evidently very poor.

Feel I must be nicer to Rachel in future.

### Saturday, June 1st

Dull, gentle, sweaty day. Young bracken is uncurling under the trees in the squirrel wood. Wild roses are out on the Flower Garden. Dotted pale pink over the bushes, they hang like faded rosettes in a tackroom. Also find knapweed, and clover, and bird's-foot trefoil, known as 'bacon and eggs', because of its orange and yellow flowers. Just trying to describe a bank of fat white cumulus clouds gathered above Rocks Lane, when Henrietta sails into view.

Henrietta lives in one of the big houses in Egliston Road. A Virginia Wolverine with a long, pale predatory face and light brown hair drawn back in a bun, she has great organising ability, and considers herself very well bred. Her husband, Ned, who is a stockbroker, always insists on telling everybody that Henrietta was a Wilson-Twickenham before he married her. Henrietta insists on telling everybody that Ned never stops talking in bed. She is very clever, with a second in English, but chooses to stay at home discontentedly, and bring up her five pale, tremendously clever children. If she hadn't made such sacrifices for Ned and the children, she is fond of implying, she would by now be editing *The Times Literary Supplement* or writing definitive biographies. I suspect that, if put to the test, she wouldn't have come up with the goods. People who can write a book usually do.

As with Rachel, I think her bitchiness stems from deep unhappiness. One is reminded of Browning – a 'bitter heart that bides its time and bites' – but this doesn't make her jibes any less painful. Because she has read somewhere that it is good for children to be brought up with animals, she owns a depressed field spaniel called Lady Glencora, after the Trollope heroine, who is walked on the Common about once a fortnight. Today Henrietta is trailing Lady Glencora, and two of her pale children (who always bury their faces in her crutch when one speaks to them).

'What are you writing down in that notebook?' she demands.

I reply brightly that I am studying cloud formations.

'Isn't there going to be too much weather in your novel?' asks Henrietta.

She then goes on to say that she is thinking of buying a horse and stabling it near Ham Common. Why don't I buy a half-share in it, then I can have first-hand experience of horses, which would be far more useful to my novel than rabbiting on about cloud formations?

Mutter that I'll think about it, but that with producing *Sunday Times* pieces every other week, as well as the novel, I don't think I'll have time for a horse.

'What are you working on for *The Sunday Times?*' she asks.

'A piece on housework,' I reply.

'But you never do any,' says Henrietta with a snort of derision.

Gritting my teeth, I break off a plantain.

'Oh look,' I add, admiring its domed brown head with the Saturn ring of white seeds, 'it looks like Lord Longford.'

Henrietta snorts with more derisive laughter, and, putting on a broad West Country accent, says: 'Aaaaaaah, this way they be known as Lard Larngfords.'

Resist temptation to push her into a wild rose bush.

*Sunday, June 2nd*

White valerian flowering by Dogger Bank. Despite its rather boring exterior it has a beautiful smell – mignonette crossed with wild roses. Along Beverley Brook, I notice young emerald green dock leaves growing by a bed of nettles. Reflect that people can be divided into nettles and docks. Nettles sting and provoke you, like Rachel and Henrietta. Patty, my dear nextdoor-neighbour, and Rosie, on the other hand, are both docks, because they're soothing, kind, and always leave you feeling happier after five minutes in their company.

*Monday, June 10th*

Patty once more proves that she is definitely a dock. This morning Maidstone took a running jump at her patched-up fence, landing sideways on all fours. Next minute thirty feet of fence collapsed, flattening my gentle neighbour's newly planted herbaceous plants. Having made our gardens open plan, Maidstone proceeded to disinter several guinea pigs and rabbits which were buried at the bottom of the garden. I wish the gas board would give him a job digging trenches for the pipeline; I'm sure he would be infinitely quicker than the bulldozers.

Over several drinks in the evening, Leo and I promise Patty we will instal new fence to contain Maidstone.

*Thursday, June 13th*

Lovely walk with Emily. It is her third birthday today, and her pace round the Common is about as slow as Maidstone's. We blow dandelion clocks, and look for the two pairs of fairies' shoes, which lie neatly together under the lid of the white dead-nettle flower.

Emily's favourite games, however, are to wash 'the Lady', and put flowers in the Fairies' Swimming Pool. 'The Lady' is the lovely bronze of a woman's profile set in a broken-off tombstone, lying in the long grass on the edge of Barnes Graveyard. The lady's name is Maria Kathleen Ayoub. According to the tombstone, the bronze was cast by her husband, an artist who outlived her by twenty-five years. She has a fine, long-suffering face, not unlike a kind Henrietta. I always have the fantasy that she was one of those high-principled Edwardian ladies, married on impulse to this talented but feckless Middle-Eastern gentleman, who gave her a hard time when she was alive, but missed her when she died.

Rain-water often gathers in the hollows of the bronze. Emily likes to wash Maria Kathleen's face with it, then give her a muffler of grass or leaves to keep her warm – although she hardly needs keeping warm in this weather.

Our other ritual is to float flowers in the Fairies' Swimming Pool, which is a six-inch hollow in the fork of the huge holm oak on the south of the Graveyard. In wet weather it fills up and overflows like a rain gauge. Today we float two white dog daisies in the pool.

*Thursday, June 20th*

Rosie is still madly in love with her art dealer. He appears to have given up jet-setting in favour of staying in London and sleeping with Rosie. It's so sweet, she says, the way he folds up both his clothes and her clothes before getting into bed.

*Monday, July 1st*

The Common has reached the tatty stage when it needs sun. All the long grasses are turning yellow. Lime tree wings litter the churchyard. Emily and I collect some today and float them in the Fairies' Swimming Pool, in case the Fairies need spare pairs.

*Thursday, July 4th*

Oh dear, oh dear. Leo went off to the country to play cricket today. I went to a local party, and drank too much wine on no breakfast, then Henrietta asked me back to lunch. She always makes me feel such a lousy and superficial writer, and after three hours in her company, she really convinced me that part-owning a horse would be the only way of bringing authenticity to my show-jumping novel.

In the afternoon we went to see a charming chestnut gelding and I was horrified to hear myself saying what fun it would be to buy him.

Now back home I am feeling depressed and deeply apprehensive. When will I have time to exercise and look after a horse every day? I can't afford it, and he's bound to bash the stable door down like Maidstone with the fence and cavort all over Ham Common. Darling Leo returns from cricket. I confess that I have given Henrietta the impression I will buy a half-share in the horse.

'Well, you'll get the back half,' says Leo. 'Ring her at once and say you can't.'

Telephone Henrietta. Can tell she's absolutely livid.

Five minutes later she is on the doorstep trailing five pale children and Lady Glencora. Leo answers the door and blocks Henrietta's entrance. She insists on having it out with me.

'Well you can't,' says Leo.

'Well fuck you,' says Henrietta, all in front of the pale children, Lady Glencora and Maidstone, and storms off.


*Sunday, July 7th*

After sleepless night, I spend the day not answering the telephone. Alas, the perfidious Maidstone keeps escaping through the hole in Patty's fence, always along Egliston Road, so I have to crawl after him on my hands and knees in front of Henrietta's house, so that she won't see me over her wall.


*Monday, July 8th*

Crawling on my hands and knees after Maidstone, I go slap into Rachel's stockinged kneecaps. If she's so broke, I think irritably, why doesn't she wear trousers and save on the expense of tights?

'What *are* you doing?' she demands.

'Going to Canossa,' I mutter.


*Wednesday, July 10th*

Beautiful warm day. My five elms arch in the sunlight like dark green paperweights. Sorrel, rusted the colour of dried blood, stabs the cool green, newly mown Hillocks like murderers' daggers. Why do poplars always shiver – even in high summer? Meet Rosie who tells me that Henrietta has bought the horse with another Putney housewife. They have found livery stables near Richmond Park, and the horse is to be called Phineas, after the Trollope hero.

*Monday, July 15th*

Solid new fence is installed between our garden and Patty's. It is both hideous and hideously expensive. Take Maidstone out to admire it. Within minutes, he has bounded onto the rubbish heap, and is tightroping gaily along the wall at the bottom of our garden. Now he looks into neighbouring gardens, with the triumphant air of some mountaineer who has scaled a peak, can see into five counties and is making up his mind which to drop into. He chooses a garden on the far left and lands on a lot of rhubarb, to the outraged shrieks of the garden's sunbathing owner.

*Monday, August 5th*

Very depressed. The moment we finish impregnably barricading off Maidstone's access to the rubbish heap and the back wall he starts examining the fence on the left-hand side of the garden, trampling down clematis and plants at 50p a throw. We go out on the Common not speaking. Maidstone chases butterflies and gets covered in burrs.

It is extraordinary how our attitude has changed towards the Irish workmen on the Common. Over the past months, we have become firm friends, they always talk to the children, and help me catch Maidstone. One of them who drives a gas board van has even become my admirer. He has a squint, brushed-forward black hair and a fund of stories about previous conquests. As he sweats round the Common after me, reeking of Brut, he keeps saying: 'Why are you so scruffy, Jill? I cannot understand why you're so scruffy.'

He might be echoing Rachel.

Today he tells me that last night he scored with a barmaid who had nipples which stuck out like acorns. Feel he may have taken the simile from the acorns which are already crunching underfoot at the entrance to the Flower Garden.

On the way home, I meet Henrietta's husband coming home from the City. To my relief, he is very matey.

'You're well out of it,' he says gloomily. 'Phineas has already tossed Henrietta off fifteen times,' which sounds most dubious.

*Saturday, August 10th*

Go out early on the Common. I am accosted by Old Dick, a local stalwart, who winter and summer wears a black beret like an onion man, and who lovingly tends the garden round the ranger's hut. Today he gives me a bunch of yellow roses, and asks me if I'm coming to the meeting tomorrow.

When I look blank, he says the Putney Improvement Society, backed up by the local cricket club, are planning to build a second cricket pitch on the Big Common. Tomorrow at the local Methodist hall, the Improvement Society will reveal the findings of their working party. Dick is dead against another cricket pitch, and says he needs my support.

*Sunday, August 11th*

Leo and I attend meeting in the Methodist hall, together with assorted dog walkers, including Rosie, Rachel, and Henrietta, who has brought along her daily woman, Mrs Bond. Henrietta nods frostily at me and Leo. Sitting beyond Henrietta are Old Dick in his black beret breathing fire, and Ken, the ranger of Putney Common, a charming, gentle, blond young man, who dropped out of advertising, and who now spends his time watching out for flashers, picking up litter on the Common and mediating between the dog walkers. Presumably he will now be expected to look after a second cricket pitch as well.

Also present, but sitting on the other side of the hall, are a depressed-looking curate, representatives from the Scouts, a militant lobby from the local cricket club, and a posse of vigorous lady botanists. Leo and I are not speaking to one another because he is supporting the local cricket club, and is in favour of a second pitch.

Feelings run high, as a handsome grey-haired man with a commanding manner, looking not unlike Gary Cooper, gets up onto the platform. 'That's Judge Hamilton – high Tory,' snorts Henrietta, disapprovingly.

Judge Hamilton then outlines the proposals of the Putney Improvement Society's working party.

After a preamble on how the working party was set up, which sends Mrs Bond, Henrietta's daily woman, fast asleep, the Judge produces a map of Putney Common.

Pointing with a stick to the two Hillocks south of Beverley Brook, he says: 'We feel there is much room for improvement here, for more interesting trees and shrubs to give the area an appearance of natural beauty as on Barnes Common.'

This is a red rag to a bulldozer. There is colossal rivalry between the two

Commons, and although Putney Common may lack the rather stylised lushness of Barnes Common, no one who has seen the sun slanting on the newly mown Hillocks or my beloved five elms rising out of the Brook could call the area deficient in natural beauty.

Judge Hamilton's stick then passes over the lovely green stretch of the Big Common, rumoured to be the site of the second pitch.

'Now this area,' he says with deep cunning, 'could never become an area of natural beauty.' He then becomes as lyrical as Edmund Blunden: 'But what better sight here than lots of people in white flannels playing cricket?'

'And losing matches,' chorus the dog walkers.

He then points to the section of the first Common next to the church.

'Nor is there any facility for young people to play football. A properly laid out football pitch for boys – and if necessary for girls,' he adds hastily, 'is a reasonable thing.'

He then proceeds to stun the meeting by saying the working party intend to turn the Common into a sports arena, with not merely a new cricket pitch, but two football pitches, a putting green, and two kiddies' adventure playgrounds.

'There'll be balls everywhere,' says Henrietta in a ringing voice.

'Bloody Wembley,' shouts Rosie.

A coffee break follows. Cabals gather in every corner muttering furiously. For once Rachel, Henrietta, Rosie and I are on the same side. After the interval the fun becomes fast and furious.

Now it is the turn of the residents of the adjacent flats to kick up a fuss about the noise from the proposed Kiddies' Adventure Playgrounds. A bright spark suggests putting the Adventure Playground near Beverley Brook so it won't disturb anyone.

'Won't the kiddies drown in the Brook?' asks an anxious mother.

'Not the sort of children we have in mind,' says Judge Hamilton blandly.

'Inflatable ones,' mutters Leo.

With feelings running high, we move on to the cricket pitch.

'Why do the cricket club need a second cricket pitch?' asks Rosie.

Because, she is told, the clubhouse (which everyone else in Putney calls the 'Ut) is too far away from the present pitch, and it means that the little colts have to cross dangerous roads to get to it.

'They'll be allowing horses on the Common soon,' snaps Rachel, earning a filthy look from Henrietta, who is obviously hoping to be tossed off by Phineas nearer home.

'Why not move the 'Ut then?' suggests Rosie.

'The reason they want a pitch near the 'Ut,' says Old Dick, 'is because they drink so much Red Barrel beforehand, they don't like to have to run across two main roads every time they go to the toilet.'

Rousing cheers all round, counterpointed by loud snores from Mrs Bond. Someone then asks Judge Hamilton to show how far the proposed playgrounds and pitch will reach. To howls of derision, he draws two minute football pitches, and a tiny cricket pitch.

'A mouse could hit a six on that,' says Leo, who appears to be changing sides.

'And there's plenty of room for a hockey pitch in the middle,' adds the Judge with a placating laugh.

The audience gaze at him stonily.

Mrs Bond, having been nudged sharply in the ribs by Henrietta, wakes up suddenly, and says: 'Let's get up a partition.'

'Let's have a vote,' yells Old Dick.

Judge Hamilton then says quickly that it isn't the aim of the meeting to have a vote, and that the working party's proposals will be put to the Conservators, who run Putney and Wimbledon Commons, in the autumn.

'But how will the Conservators know the strength of the opposition unless we vote?' protests Henrietta.

Judge Hamilton shrugs.

'Then what was the point of our coming here?' demands Rachel indignantly.

'I don't really know,' says the Judge.

The meeting breaks up in disarray. Walk home with Rosie who says her art dealer has given her a Picasso drawing.

*Tuesday, August 20th*

Having written a piece for *The Sunday Times*, describing the protest meeting, I have become the temporary heroine of the dog walkers, and particularly Old Dick, who talks to me over the netting every time I pass, and offers me bunches of roses, or whatever is blooming in the ranger's garden. Today he offers me a huge marrow. Ask if I can collect it on the way back.

I am just admiring a clump of toadflax by the football pitch, with its lovely orange and yellow snapdragon flowers, when I see Judge Hamilton striding across the Common, no doubt to re-examine Putney's lack of natural beauties. I should have kept the marrow for protection. Bolt to safety into the Flower Garden, where the pipeline has been laid and covered over with earth. Notice dandelions are already growing over it. Nothing is indestructible. Pondering on mortality, I encounter an old lady in a pork pie hat and an orange wig, with a face as wrinkled as a dried-up river bed.

She tells me she was once a newspaper columnist: admired, controversial and widely read. Now in old age, she is bored, friendless and alone. Wonder, with a shiver, if this will be my fate.

*Saturday, October 5th*
So busy finishing a book that I haven't kept my diary for weeks. Out on the Common, the bracken ranges from hot red setter red to pale gold to labrador yellow. Chestnut leaves are much more systematic. They go brown round the outside first, then gradually the rust creeps inwards.

Everything looks glorious. I am delighted to hear from Old Dick that Judge Hamilton's plans to turn the Common into a sports arena have been scrapped.

In the afternoon, I walk with Emily. We cover the Lady with little gold oval-shaped acacia leaves. The Fairies' Swimming Pool is overflowing. Fill it with sycamore keys.

*Friday, October 25th*
Go out in vile temper. The children's Nanny, who replaced my Irish housekeeper a year ago, announced yesterday that today she was going for an interview for another job – in Leicester of all places. Today, to add injury to injury, she commandeered the services of the gardener (who only comes for two hours a week anyway) to drive her to Paddington, leaving me with a *Sunday Times* piece to finish, and two children to amuse. Find myself shouting a great deal.

Take the children out on the Common and shout some more. We take the path between the tennis courts and Barnes Graveyard, and I feel very ashamed when I read a tombstone, engraved with the words:

'Jane Selwyn, died 1889 – her children shall rise up
and call her blessed. Her husband, also he praiseth her.'

Very much doubt if the stone masons will chisel such a flattering epitaph on my tombstone, and make a big effort to be nice.

Eventually cheered up, first by the beauty of the day. A soft west wind is turning all the leaves inside out. Leaves, on the ground, curl up like brandy snaps. Rain has stripped away the down from the thistles. Conkers litter the ground like Paynes Poppets.

Then Felix picks up a very spiky conker husk, and says: 'You're going to find a big prick in your bed, tonight, Mummy.'

Returning home, however, I work up new rage against incumbent Nanny for leaving me in the lurch. I'll give her several pieces of my mind for annexing the gardener.

Later she returns with a bunch of freesias, saying it was a bloody job and she doesn't want it at all. Feel so relieved, I decide not to mention annexing of gardener.

### Monday, October 28th

Notice poplars keep their top leaves longest – as though their nails were painted with gold – but limes lose their top leaves first. A bare lime is an unruly ugly tree, spiky like Fuzzypeg or Struwwelpeter. The poplar, on the other hand, stripped, dancing and pale silver in the half light, is a thing of frenzied, naked, decadent beauty. Pondering on beauty, I bump into Rosie, who looks a bit sheepish. I ask after her art dealer. She says he's fine, but she does wish he wouldn't fold up their clothes every time he climbs into bed. It's getting on her nerves.

### Thursday, October 31st

Deeply irritated to get telephone call from Rosie's art dealer. Poor Rosie has 'flu, and can't have lunch with him, could I possibly pop down to the shops and take her some roses and some grapes, and give her his love? Wonder crossly why he can't ring Interflora, and why everyone thinks writers don't work. Discover grapes are £2 a pound, and roses a good deal more. Wonder even more unworthily if I'll ever get my money back.

Go round to Rosie's and bang on the door. She answers it, reeking of scent, obviously just about to go out, and flushed not with 'flu but embarrassment. Sourly I give her grapes, roses and the art dealer's love. She looks sheepish, but also bursting with the desire to impart information. Then she admits she has gone off the art dealer – it's *so* boring and predictable to have someone who always rings and arrives on time. She has fallen madly in love with a doctor. Married? I ask. Yes, sighs Rosie, but utter bliss.

I suppose now the Picasso drawing will become the victim of a broken home.

*Sunday, December 1st*

Have just finished a great jag of writing. Endless rain for a fortnight has turned the Common into the Great Lakes. It is very beautiful. Misty grey skies reflected in sheets of water. Raindrops gleam on the flat clover leaves. Halfway down the path by the tennis courts, one of my favourite trees, a huge muscular chestnut, soars bronze and drenched as though it has been hewn by Michelangelo.

On the other side of the Graveyard, I meet an old lady called Mrs Woodward. She is eighty but still most attractive. She has a charming cairn bitch, who is being hotly pursued by a wonderfully vulgar mongrel with a smooth brindle coat, greyhound ears, and a curly tail. He has a jaunty battle-scarred face, and the outwardly relaxed air of the competent sexual operator.

Mrs Woodward says in her youth, those kind of mongrels were called 'butcher's dogs' because they always followed the butcher's van. I said at home we'd always called them tight-skinned-curly-tails.

Her one terror in life, Mrs Woodward says, is that her little cairn will outlive her and be alone.

*Tuesday, December 10th*

Maidstone escapes yet again. Discover him fornicating joyfully on the Big Common with the brindle butcher's dog. Rachel, as disapproving as ever, tells me the butcher's dog lives in one of the council flats on the Ranelagh Estate beyond the bowling green. He is called Rex, known locally as 'Sexy Rexy', and always out making a nuisance of himself.

*Thursday, December 12th*

I don't know who is more in love: Rosie with her married doctor, or Maidstone with Sexy Rexy. Have the feeling that both liaisons will end in tears.

Today I go on *Desert Island Discs* with Roy Plomley. He is an enchanting man, like a little elf, and an inspired listener. We have lunch first, and discover we both live in Putney. I drink wine, he doesn't. Afterwards the programme goes splendidly, and we get fearful giggles, mentioning Putney as often as we possibly can, in the hope that we can push the value of our houses up.

*Wednesday, December 25th*

Our Happy Christmas is not helped by Maidstone escaping through the left-hand fence, because Leo and I are cooking Christmas lunch, and have not yet had time to take him for a walk. He stays out for four hours – longer than ever before. We are all desperate. At two in the afternoon, we decide to go ahead and open our presents, but it is all hopeless. Every present opened – a doll for Emily, a space ship for Felix, a silk scarf for me – has a card with 'Love from Maidstone' inside it. Emily, Felix and I are all crying when the telephone rings. I pounce on it. It is from a call box, and misfires twice. Finally a voice asks:

'Have you lost a 'uge grey spaniel?'

'Oh yes,' I squawk, making frantic thumbs up signs to Leo and the children.

'Where is he?'

'In Roehampton,' says the voice.

'That's three miles away,' I think in horror.

''E don't seem to want to come home,' the voice goes on. ''E's 'ad a turkey dinner, and he ate everything except the sprouts.'

Leo sets off grimly to collect Maidstone, and says we shall have to put up a new fence on the left side.

# 1982

*By this time, the children, Felix and Emily, were thirteen and ten respectively, with Felix at a weekly boarding school. Maidstone, our beloved English setter, had been put down for killing cats and we now owned Fortnum, a brown mongrel who tended to pounce on every bitch he met and fight with every dog. We also acquired, by different bitches, Fortnum's daughters; the saintly, lovely-natured, retiring Mabel and the lippy, unrepentant, adorably naughty Barbara.*

### Friday, January 1st
Change over to new diary. Riddled with guilt at all the telephone numbers I wrote down on the back pages of the old diary and never did anything about. Who could I possibly have been going to ring up at the Kensington Hilton? I thought only airline pilots stayed there.

The nutty temporary has gone; Maxine is back. Never so pleased to see anyone.

### Monday, January 4th
Felix goes back to school today. We have a last walk together. I am always reminded on these occasions of Meredith's *Modern Love*:

> Love that had robbed us of immortal things,
> This little moment mercifully gave.

Alas, today we didn't even have 'this little moment', because Clarissa bears down on us. I love her but I wish that like all dog walkers she realised that I get precious little time with my children, and when I walk on the Common with them we want to be left alone.

Today Clarissa is very worried that in a flippant moment, she quoted:

> Adultery do not commit,
> Advantage rarely comes of it,

to Frances the feminist, then remembered one of Frances' frightful children was the result of a bunk-up with a married man. Did I think Frances
would be terribly hurt? Before I have time to answer, she tries to engage
Felix in conversation. He was so enraged at having our tête-à-tête interrupted, he answered only in monosyllables. In a pathetic attempt to keep
the conversation going, I find myself answering for him – which I know
Clarissa, as an ex-headmistress, regards as a heinous crime.

Walk the dogs late at night after taking Felix back to school. Orion is
brilliant above Cedric's house. It is difficult to pick out the fainter
constellations because they are overshadowed by a dazzling, diamond-
hard, five-eighths moon. Think of the same moon shining on Felix at
school; oh, I hope they take care of him.

*Tuesday, January 5th*
The dustmen still haven't been. We'll be asked to bring out our dead soon.

Out at lunchtime – very mild, midges everywhere, and a marvellous
bilberry-blue blur on the wet trees. Blackbirds, thrushes, sparrows,
chaffinches and robins all carolling, like a lunchtime concert at All Souls',
Langham Place.

*Wednesday, January 6th*
Walk with Rosie, who is looking ravishing – thin and 'sheeny' as Leo calls it
from desire and being desired. She is still besotted with David the sculptor.
He drops in every day. Her mother approves and thinks David has a very
sexy voice. Rosie also had breakfast yesterday with an old lover, lunch
with a glamorous man in advertising and dinner with an actor.

The man in advertising evidently said they must lunch once a fortnight
for the rest of their lives. He's just paid off all his debts, his business is going
brilliantly, his marriage is wonderful, in fact he was all poised for the big
dive – falling in love with Rosie.

She returned from lunch to find the telephone ringing, it was David the
sculptor, 'How can you possibly lunch with anyone in advertising, they're
so superficial!' Then to get his own back he raved about some ex-girlfriend
in the BBC.

'So we had our first quarrel,' sighed Rosie. 'But we made it up half an hour later. He calls me his sylph.'

'Ha, ha,' I say. 'Then when he doesn't see you, he can say I'm not feeling my sylph today.'

As we walk home, the safety-pin holding my trousers together slips and plunges into my stomach. Make mental note to lose weight and look less repulsive. Coming across the first Common on a bicycle, cloak and long skirt flying, rather like a very pretty version of the witch in *The Wizard of Oz*, comes Pandora, our local biographer, who, unlike Frances the feminist, gets her books published. I introduce her to Rosie, who says she's also writing a book.

Pandora says she has been asked to write for some travel magazine, and the editor keeps pouncing on her, but she's not going to give even a fraction of her all, until he's written her a letter officially commissioning the piece.

'Piece now,' I say, 'or forever withhold your pounce.'

Pandora then informs us she hasn't had sex for four years which makes all the men she meets absolutely insane with desire, and they rush round with champagne and intentions. This must all be part of the New Celibacy that is being so bandied about in London.

I get home to be greeted by an ecstatic Maxine. Her boyfriend has rung, he's taking her out tonight, and she's already got butterflies in her stomach.

'You are lucky,' I say, unable once again to suppress a stab of jealousy for all these wildly desirable ladies. 'I haven't had butterflies over a man for years.'

Maxine looks amazed: 'I always think how lucky you are,' she says, 'having Leo coming home every night to you, knowing he'll always be there.'

This pulls me up with a start. I shouldn't presume he will always be there, but it makes me realise how immeasurably fortunate I am.


*Thursday, January 7th*

Very cold suddenly, with a bitter north-east wind, which makes the unsheltered walk down to the first bridge extremely unpleasant. The birds appalled by the change in the weather have suspended their matings and are totally silent. Hope the same thing doesn't happen to Rosie, Pandora and Maxine. The crimson mugwort stalks are brown now, the knotweed has lost its orange fire, all the undergrowth along the Brook is drained to a pale donkey brown.

Meet Mrs Willis with her darling plump, piebald mongrel, Spot, who says she had a nice Christmas but quiet, and Spot enjoyed his turkey dinner. She then wishes me "appy new year' twice, in case I hadn't heard the first time. Otherwise the Common is deserted, which is lucky because the low winter sun at twenty-five degrees shines blindingly into the eyes, so I can't see any enemy dog coming.

The dustmen come at last: they are so anxious to ingratiate themselves with the public after their strike, that they don't even kick up when they have to carry a thousand and one empty bottles out of our house – the result of Christmas excess. Several bottles are dropped in the road, covering it with green glass. Horsey Miriam comes out with her BMW, sees the glass, and rushes inside for a broom. She is joined by the Car-Respondent also with a broom. They click their tongues and sweep the street talking loudly to draw attention to their act of philanthropy. Deliberately don't let them see me looking out of the window.

### Friday, January 8th

Mornings are so dark – I find it impossible to get up early. Walk with Emily – it is her first day back at school but she doesn't have to clock in until eleven o'clock. It is bitterly cold. Emily wants to discuss rape, which seems to be dominating all the papers, particularly since a Judge ticked off a Devon girl who got raped, for hitching a lift at night after a party.

Emily wants to know *all* about it. I tell her about rapists being let off, which is wrong, but also add how stupid any girl is who hitch-hikes at any time of the day. We are joined by John B the television director who says I am quite wrong. How can I be *so* sexist as to think of men as creatures who cannot control their appetites? I stammer that I don't really, but I still think girls who hitch-hike after parties are daft.

John B says he *always* gives lifts to hitch-hikers. He hitch-hiked so much in his youth and feels he is paying people back. His car can carry four people and it is a sin for it to be empty, when people sometimes have to wait for hours for buses in the most terrible weather.

Warming to his subject, he goes on that the transport is so awful in Yeovil, that there's often only one bus a day, and if you miss that you've had it.

He makes me feel middle-aged, and horribly unphilanthropic, particularly when Emily keeps pausing to bounce on puddles, and break up the ice so that the 'poor birds' can get a drink, and I, getting frozen with waiting, tartly tell her to buck up. John B then shoots me a shocked look, and goes back and jumps on puddles with Emily, telling her what a 'good, caring little girl' she is to think about the birds. Emily, scenting conquest, goes and swings on a dead bough of the nearby acacia.

'Don't do that, it's dangerous,' I snap.

Whereupon John B goes back and very carefully explains to Emily the branch is dead, and she might fall and hurt herself. Emily beams up at him, and he gives me a reproachful 'they'll do anything, if you treat them properly' look.

Get my own back by saying that by an extraordinary coincidence Maxine lives in Yeovil, and as John B is so keen on giving people lifts, why doesn't he give her a free ride every time he goes home. Immediately he looks at his watch, says he must rush and vanishes like smoke.

*Midday:* even colder than this morning. All the runnels and ridges in the quagmire forged by dog walkers, dogs and bicycles over the last week are now frozen razor sharp, and cut through the soles of my gumboots. Push leaves aside by the Bryants' grave on the edge of the Eternal Triangle, and find first snowdrop shoots.

*Monday, January 11th*
Go out early. A huge aggrieved full moon looks down the white gardens of Lower Common South, like a gardener complaining that the frost has got his roses. The birds are all shouting and congratulating each other on surviving the rigours of the night.

*Tuesday, January 12th*
Prettiest morning yet: even colder and icier with a brilliant gentian-blue sky above soft grey-blue clouds and a saffron sun, warming all the trees and putting a gold rinse on the grey and yellow boles of the plane trees. The traffic is so bad that a coloured necklace of cars, still shining with melting ice, is strung motionless along Lower Richmond Road and Queen's Ride. No one smiles or waves you through – bad temper is rampant. A new layer of ice has formed like windows over the patches of grass showing through the snow.

Meet Clarissa and Rachel, who point out that some strange mediaeval monster appears to have come up the Brook, and bashed up all the ice to let the water through. Is it the friends of Barnes Common on a trip of altruism? It looks more like a sinister lava path, or a bomb site with broken window panes. It is such a lovely day, and we are all progressing happily, when a jaunty grizzled red setter bounces round the corner and starts chatting up Barbara. Fortnum rushes up, and despite Clarissa's bellows and my shouts goes straight for the setter's throat, but, thank God, catches hold of only his collar and red fur.

Remembering how effective the driver of the van had been when he threw his coat over Fortnum, Clarissa, Rachel and I all whip off our coats and throw them over Fortnum. Despite looking like the hostess's bed at a party, Fortnum takes no notice. Only when the owner comes up and kicks his ribs in does he finally drop the setter. The setter owner, who is very handsome, with red hair slightly grizzled like the setter, is understandably very cross. He says Fortnum ought to be put down, and what will happen if he attacks a child?

Later we pass him again in the Squirrel Wood, and I go up and apologise profusely. Would I have bothered if he hadn't been so good-looking? He is very nice, and says the setter had started a few scraps himself in his youth. Rachel and Clarissa mutter about muzzling.

Go out in the afternoon. See man who owns two beautiful grey deer hounds having a shouting match with a man with a stroppy Alsatian. Evidently the two deer hounds chased the Alsatian across two main roads, and he nearly got run over.

A kind old man, who caught the stroppy Alsatian and took it back to its owner, tells me he thinks those 'two German dachshunds', are very dangerous and should be kept on a lead.

Try to identify pine tree in Barnes Graveyard: it has long needles in bunches of five, and long curved cones. Could be Mexican white pine, Japanese pine, Bhutan pine, or a Weymouth pine. Give up – it's just a pine.

On the Eternal Triangle, I appropriately pass two women discussing kitchens: 'I don't know how to describe it really,' says the first, 'but it's one up from pine.'

*Wednesday, January 13th*
Heavy, heavy frost makes snow more magical than ever. Underfoot it is absolute murder; the Common paths are as treacherous as the pavements. Fortnum is very helpful, and pulls me up hills whenever I have him on a lead.

Out in the afternoon, the frost has gone leaving the trees the softest taupe above the white sparkling snow, with a grey-blue haze above gradually blending into an almost hyacinth-blue sky overhead. Winging overhead comes a seagull, its snowy undercarriage almost incandescent. Feel my heart expanding with love for its beauty. As a result almost fall over a sweet man with a mobile, lined, character actor face and two Alsatians. He agrees that the snow is beautiful, but adds that it puts some people like him out of work. He explains he is a roofer, but at least 'wevver' like this makes people realise their roofs need mending. Remember two-foot icicles hanging from our gutters and say he'd better come and have a look at ours.

*Thursday, January 14th*
Beverley Brook is completely frozen over.

Bump into Rachel and Clarissa, who are getting terribly thick, and make me edgy because they have lots of private jokes. We discuss Mrs Thatcher's son who has disappeared on some safari rally.

Rachel says very beadily: 'There are other people lost on the rally – why all this fuss about Mark Thatcher?'

I say I hold no particular brief for him, but I just feel very sorry for Mrs T.

We progress towards the Flower Garden, where Clarissa claims that she has seen some poor model being photographed in tennis clothes in the snow. We round the corner, and sure enough rearing out of the bracken is a huge amazon with oiled brown legs and arms, wearing nothing but a skimpy tennis dress. A male photographer and his assistant, both in fur coats, are leaping about taking pictures.

We all mutter loudly about sexist photographers exploiting women *and* on the coldest day of the year.

'Oughtn't we to remonstrate with them?' says Clarissa.

But on getting closer, we discover our sympathy is wasted: the model turns out to be a dummy. We tramp off towards the Flower Garden feeling foolish.

Clarissa goes on to say that she once worked on a magazine and had to organise models. If they were tiresome, she made them wear awful clothes. She then broaches the subject of Fortnum's muzzle yet again, and what a good idea it would be. She's been discussing the problem with several dog trainers, she says. Her sister also had a fighter, and muzzling worked on him, so why don't I try one on Fortnum?

She leaves us. I walk miserably home with Rachel and make a crack about the Dog in the Iron Mask.

Rachel puts on her Mrs Thatcher voice (if she dislikes our Prime Minister so much, she shouldn't try to sound like her) and says this is a serious matter. Clarissa is only trying to help, and sooner or later someone will make an official complaint.

Find it impossible to explain that if they didn't lecture me so much, I wouldn't be so uptight and Fortnum would fight less. Think about Fortnum in a muzzle, never being able to bark or vole or fascinate, and feel horribly depressed.

Back home, Emily is reading about rape. She explains that her form mistress has told her to read the papers, as in the forthcoming exams for their secondary schools they may well get asked general knowledge questions. 'What,' she goes on, 'does "semi-naked" mean?' Do not feel this will really help her get into St Paul's.

### Saturday, January 16th

Hooray it's thawing. Like an army defeated, the snow has retreated. Everything is dripping. Rape has been suspended as the chief subject of conversation by grumbling about dustbins not being emptied. On the one hand the local *Borough News* congratulates the council workers for putting in a twenty-four-hour day to grit the road and pavements (which is rubbish – they've never come anywhere near our road), but on the other hand there has been no dustbin collection for ten days, because the pavements are supposed to be too dangerous for anyone carrying heavy loads. Discuss this with Crispin the artist and Rosie.

'What,' says Crispin, 'about old-age pensioners coming home weighed down by two carrier bags?'

'Old age pensioners,' points out Rosie, 'rarely have enough spare cash to fill two carrier bags.'

We pass Mrs Bond. We are all horrified when she tells us that the temperature in her front bedroom the other night was thirty-two degrees.

After she walks on, we all ponder gloomily on the fate of the aged and hypothermia, until Crispin tells us about an old lady who fainted by the cheese counter in Sainsbury's last week. A doctor was called, who examined her and went into a long rant about hypothermia and how badly the English treated their old people. Finally, however, he removed her hat and found she was harbouring a frozen chicken underneath.

### Sunday, January 17th

Woken by terrible wails and groans. Think it's one of the children being murdered, rush upstairs and find Felix, who's home for the weekend, singing to Adam Ant with headphones on. As a result get out early on the Common, overtaken by Clarissa, Rachel and Crispin. We are all watching the sparrow hawk, which I think is a kestrel, being mobbed up by a troop of magpies, when we suddenly realise Scottish Molly has crept up on us.

Rachel and Clarissa, who are still not speaking to her, turn away in disgust. To their intense irritation, Crispin and I say 'hullo'. Molly winks and passes on. Barbara takes advantage of my inattention to roll in goose's crap, and later has to have a bath.

*Monday, January 18th*

It is lovely to see green grass again. The snow has thawed in patches, leaving fantastic shapes – a sea horse there, a camel here. Across on the Barn Elms playing fields, the snow stretches in sheets like flooding.

Go out in the afternoon. By Beverley Brook, we see one of Fortnum's rivals, a little black mongrel, mounting a terrier bitch. They are having a lovely time. Fortunately Fortnum is on a lead, but Barbara, enraged by evidence of sexual enjoyment in which she is not participating, charges the happy couple so fiercely, that they both fall into the icy Brook. It obviously has the effect of a cold shower. They emerge two minutes later, chastened, and trot off home in separate directions.

*Friday, January 22nd*

The latest hideous development is joggers who have earphones plugged into transistors attached to their waists. How can they enjoy the rustle of poplars, or the song thrush on the sycamore or the merry barking of dogs, if they're listening to pop music all the time?

'It's not their fault they do not know/The bird song from the radio,' claims John Betjeman.

It bloody well is.

Green lichen on the trees is beautiful – particularly on the sycamores where it is a violent Dayglo green. There seems to be more lichen on parts of the tree that are facing north.

Meet sweet old man who admires the dogs. He says he once had a bull terrier like Fortnum who was terribly aggressive and fought on until he was seventeen. One night he started a fight with another dog, just as the crowds were coming out of the cinema. The old man was so frightened his dog was going to bite someone that he hoisted both dogs on top of a car, where they carried on fighting on the roof rack.

I ask him if his bull terrier ever attacked cats.

'Attack them!' he says. ''E once swallered an old lady's cat whole.'

I don't know why but these stories made me feel better. Tell Rachel who's not amused, and says fighting is a serious business.

*Saturday, January 23rd*
Cheered up walking with dear Rosie. Things are going wonderfully well with David the sculptor. Gradually she seems to be shedding her other admirers. The other day, she said, she and David were walking down the street and bumped into Graham (the hairdresser, who was having a walk-out with the architect who liked having balloons popped at the moment of orgasm).

Afterwards, Rosie asked Graham the hairdresser, what he thought of David.

'Well dear,' said Graham, 'he's all right if you like that sort of thing. But for my money, the sexiest man in Putney is that butch Leo Cooper.'

When I get home I ring up Leo to tell him.

'Ask him round for a drink,' says Leo. I can detect his smirk down the telephone wires.

Barbara has been spayed. She's so brave, bless her. She came out of the vet's very tucked up, with flattened ears and tail, and rushed upstairs the moment she got home, and jumped up over the brass rail onto our bed. Mabel as usual seems much more upset than Barbara, and stood over her whimpering, and nudging her with her nose. I'm so relieved it's done – I couldn't have borne sending her to kennels again.

*Sunday, January 24th*
Happy because Barbara is much more cheerful; she's eating well, if pickily (rump steak and chocolate biscuits), but not going out yet. I love the way

she preserves her energy, and won't romp because it hurts so much. Mabel is blissful, going out without Barbara.

Meet Clarissa and Rachel. Clarissa looks pointedly at Fortnum and then says she's been looking at long leads in the pet shop. At that moment, dear Hugo lets her down by attacking a passing shaggy dog. Resist the temptation to say Hugo should be muzzled and put on a long lead. Clarissa, by way of exoneration, says Hugo always mistrusts dogs with shaggy faces whose eyes he can't see. What is so unfair is that Hugo often attacks other dogs, but because he's castrated they feel it is below the belt (or the collar) to fight back.

*Monday, January 25th*

Walk with dear Tommy. We discuss Rosie. He says people are like their dogs. Michelin is very secure and serene like Rosie. Wonder where that puts me? Am I a belligerent sex maniac like Fortnum, or a shy, lovely-natured darling like Mabel, or a lippy clown like Barbara?

*Tuesday, January 26th*

Walk over to the Yarrow Meadow at lunchtime, it is a lovely mild afternoon. On the apple tree with its grey sooty buds, a robin is singing, its little orange throat vibrating, its black eyes so shiny. I throw it some biscuit crumbs, which Fortnum immediately snaps up.

Go to seek out the aspen on the corner of Rocks Lane. According to Kenneth Allsop in his book, *In the Country*, it should have pink and purple shoots in the spring, but when I get there these are too high for me to see.

Talk to darling elderly lady who used to have a black spaniel. She says she still misses him particularly on spring-like days like this, but she still goes on the same walk, even without him, and wasn't the snow lovely? It came over her gumboots one day, but she didn't mind because everything looked so beautiful, and she saw the television reporter, Jon Snow, skiing on Barnes Common.

'In the bleak mid-winter,' I say.

She looks blank.

'Snow on snow,' I say.

'He's just as nice in the flesh as he is on television,' she goes on. 'Very natural.'

Meet woman coming out of Putney Hospital, who admires Fortnum and Mabel, saying they're beautiful dogs. She had a setter, she says, who lived until he was thirteen; she misses having a dog, but it's difficult at her age.

At this juncture, Fortnum starts straining after a passing hospital cat, so I say, 'It's difficult at any age.'

*Wednesday, February 3rd*
Notice alder catkins by Beverley Brook; they are made up of tiny yellow checks edged with red like Harrods golf stockings. Meet Clarissa by the second bridge.

'Enjoy your dogs while you may,' she cries, advancing towards me over the bridge.

'Oh God,' I say, 'is there a writ out for them? Is a dog catcher going the rounds?'

'Crackers,' she says. 'Went to the vet yesterday, who diagnosed cancer – evidently his lungs are quite eaten away. He's on steroids and will have to be put down at the end of the week.'

Oh poor Crackers. He was the most beautiful, gentle, liver and white pointer, and only seven.

'How dreadful,' I say. 'How did he get it?' (Resist temptation to ask if he smoked heavily.)

'It's the level dogs are,' says Clarissa. 'They just breathe in all the exhaust and fumes from cars.'

'Does his owner go to our vet Mrs Fraser?' I ask.

'No, one in White Hart Lane,' says Clarissa. 'He's a very caring vet, and is always sending dogs to dog training classes.'

At this utterance, Fortnum gives Clarissa a very old-fashioned look, and even Mabel starts walking to heel.

*The next weeks were gruelling. Emily took exams to get into four different schools. This also involved interviews with all the headmistresses, so Emily and I were racketing around London like the proverbial foxes with burning tails in the Bible. Towards the end of the exam stint, Fortnum, Mabel and Barbara were invited to go to Cruft's to appear on the Russell Harty Show, and take part in an obedience test.*

*Thursday, February 11th*
Evidently Rachel and Clarissa are apoplectic at the news that Fortnum is doing an obedience test at Cruft's, and think that I'm going to make a complete fool of myself. Happily I don't. We have a lovely day. All the dogs went to a photo-call outside Cruft's in the morning and posed with Judy Geeson, Bill Pertwee, Bob Wilson, and Faith Brown and their dogs.

Fortnum's photograph appeared in the *Daily Mail* under a Smirnoff Vodka poster saying: 'It bites.' He looked absolutely sweet, except that the *Mail* caption called him Barbara, which is a slight affront to his doghood.

In the evening, all three dogs went on the Russell Harty Show; and, because Leo was there (whom Fortnum regards as his pack leader), Fortnum, relieved of his responsibilities, behaved impeccably. Through-out the proceedings, despite growling from Vince Hill's English sheepdog, barking from Faith Brown's Labrador, and snarling through chair legs from John Noakes' sheepdog, he maintained a quiet dognity. Just before the transmission, when I wasn't looking, Leo gave all three dogs massive doses of tranquillisers. As a result, although the programme was live, Mabel and Barbara jolly nearly weren't. Both kept collapsing cross-eyed onto the floor, and falling asleep – although Barbara did manage to struggle to her feet when Russell Harty came up to speak to us.

He asked me why I like dogs so much. I stammered because I was basically shy, and found dogs easier to communicate with than people. At that exact moment, Barbara stepped forward and goosed Russell Harty vigorously.

I said: 'You see I'd love to be brave enough to do things like that.'

The audience were in stitches. Fortnum appeared totally unaffected by the tranquillisers, and did a brilliant obedience test; the judge said if it had been an official test, he would have won. So boo sucks to all the ladies on the Common.

The loveliest moment was after the programme, when I let the three dogs loose and they ran round the huge Cruft's exercise ring, which tomorrow will be full of breed dogs and champions.

*Friday, February 12th*
Bump into Rosie and Tommy who say Fortnum and the others were smashing on telly. Rachel and Clarissa join us – they make no comment.

Tommy says: 'I've given up smoking, so I'm going to jump all over that bunch of snowdrops.'

*Monday, February 15th*
Emily goes off to school to take her last exam for a boarding school in Berkshire. She is very tired and depressed – so am I. I go for very cold walk feeling miserable. As I am shambling towards second bridge with Rachel, a bird comes whirring towards us.

'The kingfisher!' I cry. 'Look, look!' And there it was, flashing past the most ravishing streak of turquoise and pinky coral, like the colours of some Derby winner, dazzling against the beiges and greys of winter – then it is gone.

### Tuesday, February 16th

Out about nine in the evening. Meet the Brigadier returning from the pub in merry wood. We admire the Pleiades. The Brigadier quotes a line from Tennyson, about a shoal of silver fishes in a net. Then he says that three of his old aunts have recently died, so now he and his wife don't have to worry so much about money, and can even take taxis.

I say the nice thing about money is that it gives you the freedom to do everything you want.

'Not everything,' says the Brigadier, giving me a foxy squeeze round the waist.

### Friday, February 26th

Find beautiful dead fox with blood seeping out of its mouth, lying in the middle of the Fair Triangle. It is about three feet long; it must have been hit by a car. The foxes are barking a lot along the back gardens at night – I suppose it's the mating season.

### Saturday, February 27th

In the first minutes during the past few weeks when I haven't been worrying myself sick about Emily getting into a school, we receive a letter telling us she's got into the boarding school in Berkshire. I burst into tears of joy and hug her until I nearly crack her ribs.

Go floating on air out on the Common. Find the first coltsfoot, or coltsfeet I suppose, below the osiers on the second Hillock.

### Monday, March 1st

Very proud of darling Emily. She ploughed St Paul's, but got into three other schools. The Common is swarming with bitches and amorous male dogs. But perhaps because I'm so relaxed and happy about Emily, Fortnum picks up the vibes and hasn't had a fight for ages. Rachel and Clarissa, however, are still stepping up their campaign to get him muzzled and put on a long lead.

### Thursday, March 4th

Clarissa and Rachel are getting thicker and thicker. Meet Clarissa who is pacing up and down saying, 'Rachel's late today,' then she remembers: 'Oh it's Thursday, she'll be doing her double wash.'

Find speedwell and celandine out along the Brook. Once again the green woodpecker is laughing his head off. The green flames of the hawthorn are out, and there is a lovely red haze of lime twigs round the churchyard.

### Wednesday, March 10th

Meet Clarissa and Rachel in a state of chunter. They were walking quietly along with Crispin, they tell me, when Molly suddenly emerged like a jack-in-a-box from the bushes in Lurker's Paradise, and called out: 'I don't want to drag you away from your harem, Crispin.'

'We ignored her,' says Clarissa.

'Disgusting,' says Rachel.

Poor Crispin evidently rang Molly afterwards and said despairingly, 'But I like you all!'

Fortnum loses a fight with huge blond dog, who pursues us across the Common. The dog is so tall, Fortnum can't reach his throat. Instead the huge dog gets Fortnum's head in his teeth. The owner sensibly keeps his distance, and eventually the big dog drops Fortnum who trots back to me very bloody but unbowed.

### Tuesday, March 16th

Find heartsease and red dead-nettle in Barnes Graveyard; the ground is littered with red poplar catkins, and last year's black alder hops. So busy supervising Fortnum, I miss a glorious row on the Common. Tommy and Rosie rush up gleefully and tell me about it.

Evidently Tommy was walking along the Pineapple Walk with Clarissa and Rachel, when suddenly Molly reared out of the knotweed on the opposite bank crying out: 'Haven't you two ladies had your pound of flesh?'

'What?' shouted back Clarissa.

'Haven't you two ladies had enough revenge?' yelled Molly.

'Don't be childish, Molly,' bellows Clarissa.

'What?' echoed Molly.

'Clarissa said "don't be childish",' snaps Rachel.

'What?' said Molly, and passed on. And all ringing across the sluggish mud of Beverley Brook.

Tommy evidently got the giggles and lurked behind to walk with Molly.

Next day, Rachel, all of a chunter, sidled up to Tommy saying, 'I'm so sorry we left you in the lurch with Molly, yesterday.' Whereupon darling Tommy snubbed her very politely saying he was devoted to Molly and hadn't seen her for ages.

*Thursday, March 25th*

Meet nice deputy headmistress with red-gold dachshund. She says when
she had some friends over to tea at the weekend, the dachshund sneaked in
and devoured all the cake, doughnuts and buttered buns beforehand.
When she scolded him, he waved his brown plumed tail and looked quite
unrepentant.

*Friday, March 26th*

Hear tragic news that Mrs James, a local schoolmistress, has finally died of
cancer – she was so young, and so brave, and hung onto life so tenaciously.
It must be terrible to leave a dear husband and three such beautiful
children, and never to see them grow up. The youngest child, Sybilla, is
only seven. I feel eaten up with sadness for the whole family.

*Sunday, March 28th*

I think this is the worst day of my life and it started so beautifully. I had a
lovely walk with Emily. We looked at the closed-up celandines rising like
crowns of lamb by the Brook. Fortnum had a long flirt with his girlfriend

Blossom, who gets so excited when she sees him that she bounces around lifting all four legs off the ground. Then Maxine, who'd gone out the night before looking smashing in white tie and tails, slightly startled the Sunday morning car washers by returning in broad daylight in the same kit at 11.30 am. She'd had a riotous night with two young bloods which involved playing bears round the furniture in some flat in Sloane Square and getting whacked on the bum with a copy of *The Sunday Times*.

Then Mr James came for a drink. He was *so* brave about his wife's death. He looked shattered, but still thank God retained his sense of humour.

His seven-year-old daughter, Sybilla, had evidently said:

'Now Mummy's dead, Daddy, why don't you make some money selling your double bed, and buy a single one?'

Then we went to have a drink with Rosie and drank a lot of Bloody Marys, and came back home and had roast pork for lunch. In the afternoon Felix took Mabel for a walk, and later Emily and I followed him with Fortnum and Barbara. Floating along in an alcoholic haze, I insanely let Fortnum off his lead. The next moment he'd shot round the corner and was swinging what I thought was a squirrel – shaking it like a rat. I rushed forward yelling to stop him, together with the conductor and the driver from a parked 22 bus, then realised, to our horror, that it was not a squirrel but a tiny Yorkshire terrier. By the time we reached it, it was dead. The men from the 22 bus found me a cardboard box, and I carried it home. It had no collar or identity disk. Poor little Emily fled crying to one of her friends down the road.

Back home, I telephoned the police, and told them Fortnum had killed the Yorkshire terrier. A sweet policeman came straight round. He was a 'dog 'andler' himself, he said, stroking Fortnum, and Fortnum was obviously a nice calm dog, who didn't bite people. I then said numbly that I'd have to have Fortnum put down. The policeman didn't agree.

'It's 'uman nature,' he kept saying somewhat illogically, and I would be being very hard on Fortnum to put him down. Then he rang the RSPCA who arrived with a van and took the little dog away, they were terribly kind too.

Then Emily returned very tearstained from down the road. She'd told poor little Sybilla James about Fortnum. And Sybilla said: 'Poor Emily, poor Jilly, but a much worse thing's happened to me this week.'

Then the children and I mindlessly watched a James Bond film on television, and the nice policeman turned up in the middle. He said he'd found the owner of the Yorkshire terrier; it was a policeman, but actually the dog belonged to his thirteen-year-old daughter. And I wasn't to ring now, as the child was so upset, but could I telephone tomorrow afternoon? Oh poor, poor little girl – I know what she must be going through.

Oh God, what am I to do? Everyone says don't put him down. But if he lives, chaos will come again. The witch hunt will start. Dog wardens will come to Putney, and pick Fortnum up every day, when he's off on his outings around the streets. And if we ever move to the country, sheep certainly won't graze safely. And what about all the dog owners who are terrified by Fortnum, and terrified for the safety of their dogs? Once blooded, he may kill others. And, worst of all, what about the poor little policeman's daughter and wretched little Yorkshire terrier?

But I love him so so much – with his fat paws, and his lovely solid body and grey scarred face, and his merry canter and his blazing neurotic loyalty. Can I possibly bear to take him round to the vet's tomorrow?

### Monday, March 29th

*Midnight:* Fortnum is dead. Christ, I wish I hadn't done it. I took all three dogs out very early. It was very cold and grey. Fortnum never left my heels the entire walk. He knew something was up. Then I saw two magpies for joy rising out of Barnes Common boundary; their credibility is gone for ever.

Coming home, I met Rachel on the edge of the Lower Richmond Road, and started to cry, as I explained I was taking Fortnum to the vet to have him put down.

'Don't do it,' she said. 'Have him "carstrated", put him on a long lead for the rest of his life, and never let him out in the street.'

But I couldn't do this to him. Life would be unendurable. No outings, no kingdom, Fortnum's occupation gone.

Then Fortnum and I walked up to the vet's. All the blossom was out and shivering in the icy wind. We didn't have to sit in the waiting room, thank God, but went straight in. Mrs Fraser was angelic. She was the one person who agreed with me. She said Fortnum would reduce me to a complete nervous collapse soon, and there was no guarantee that castration would work; and it would not take effect anyway for six months or so, by which time he could easily have killed another dog.

She told me not to stay, but I wanted to. I felt I'd let Fortnum down in life, without leaving him at the end. I warned her he'd need a massive shot because he was such a powerful dog, so she had two injections ready.

I held him in my arms, and as the first shot went in, he turned round and gave my face a last lick and then collapsed, but it wasn't enough, because he went into the most frightful convulsions, and she had to give him the second injection to finish him off. She said it wouldn't have hurt him, that the convulsions were just anginal spasms, but I think she was being kind. I don't remember going home. But I took a minicab back later in the day to collect him, while the gardener came over and dug a grave.

I wrapped him in the blue and orange knitted blanket he'd arrived with seven years ago, and buried him at the bottom of the garden beside the gooseberry bushes that he'd spent his life proving puppies weren't found under. He looked so sweet and at peace. I made a wonky cross out of bamboos and stuck it on the grave.

About 1.30 there was a terrific thunderstorm. I felt crucified, because I wondered if Fortnum was aware of it, and would be panic-stricken if there was no one up there to comfort him.

Maxine, who was in floods all day, said the thunderstorms must have been Fortnum arriving in heaven and showing everyone who was boss. I hope he is with Maidstone. What a disastrous dog owner I've been. What a squandering, through my soppy indulgence and inability to discipline a flea, of two marvellous dogs.

Emily was at school, but Felix was absolutely angelic, he kept saying: 'Put your head on my shoulder, Mummy, and have a good cry.' The next hurdle was ringing up the policeman whose daughter owned the little Yorkshire terrier. He was incredibly kind and understanding, and refused my offer to buy the little girl a puppy. Then later I had to tell Leo who is heartbroken, too, but won't talk about it.

*Saturday, April 3rd*
Life goes on. Thank God, I am desperately busy finishing a piece on men and how wet – or wimpish – they've become for *The Sunday Times*. I took the dogs out today and poor Mabel who's been searching for Fortnum everywhere, suddenly barked in delight and took off after a brown dog. Then slunk back to me despondently when she realised it wasn't Fortnum.

Shambling through Barnes Graveyard, I find an urn lying among the pine needles with 'Dear Dad' engraved on it, and am tempted to pinch it for Fortnum's grave. Adding her usual note of bathos, Barbara bounces out from behind a tombstone with a rotting fairy cake in a plastic bag attached rakishly to a pointed bottom tooth.

*Wednesday, April 7th*

Walk with Molly, who wrote me a lovely letter about Fortnum. Young goosegrass is rampaging everywhere, cow parsley and speedwell are out on the Hillocks. Molly immediately gets onto the subject of Rachel and Clarissa. Do I think they'll ever bury the hatchet? I sigh, and say I don't know. (Feel privately that I will never forgive either of them for being right about Fortnum.) Molly says Rachel refused to look her in the face – 'like a sacked housemaid,' she adds. But the other day she could have sworn that Clarissa's husband, Ronald, gave her a ghost of a wink as he passed.

Today Barbara riots so joyously with Molly's Dalmatian Ophelia, that she hurts the leg that was run over, and can only just hobble home.

*Thursday, April 8th*

It's like the ten little nigger boys. Fortnum gone, Barbara confined to barracks with a bad leg – just Mabel and me, desolate on a cold grey morning.

The leaves that come before the acid-yellow flowers are out fizzing like sherbet on the two Norway maples on the Fair Triangle and on the south of the first Common.

Deeply saddened that the Spencer Arms by the 22 bus shelter has been gentrified. It has been painted bottle green with gold lettering, festooned with carriage lamps, and surrounded by tables with blue and white striped umbrellas. Saddest of all, the words 'Function Room', which used to make Leo and me giggle so much, have been painted out. I suppose this tarting up is all to compete with the old French Revolution pub, across the road, which has been mock-Tudored and gentrified up to the eyeballs and renamed the Beefeater.

*Saturday, April 10th*

O God – I miss Fortnum. But I feel relieved: I have finally dispatched the piece on wimpish men to *The Sunday Times*. I pray that they like it – it's awfully contentious.

*Sunday, April 11th*

Work and Fortnum dying have distracted me from the Falklands Crisis – it's all very alarming. The euphemism 'task force' is being bandied about. It sounds like a posse of debs from an agency converging on one's filthy house to blitz it at £2.50 an hour.

Today I talk to the man who instead of walking always sits under the trees in a deck chair reading *The Sunday Telegraph*, while his dog barks after the squirrels. He works at Peter Jones, he says, and is on his feet all day, so he comes out on the Common for a rest and to read the paper. What a refreshing change from all those joggers! We discuss the Falklands Crisis, and admit a sneaking admiration for Mrs Thatcher, and agree What Else Could She Have Done?

I have been reading about gorse in a flower book. Evidently when gorse is in flower, England will never be beaten. But alas on the Common no gorse is out.

Return home to find Felix, who is home for the weekend, and who should be mugging up the Old Testament for his Common Entrance exam next month, reading a comic and watching television. I tick him off for not working. He replies airily that he has given up scripture for Lent.

*Monday, April 12th*

Barbara better and back on the Common. Liberated from Fortnum's belligerent chaperonage, she is busy acquiring admirers. Chief among them is Rufus, a very handsome golden retriever. Today Barbara meets Rufus in the Squirrel Wood. She behaves exactly like a socialite at a drinks party, chatting animatedly to him, but glancing over his shoulder all the time, searching the trees for squirrels.

I was worried that, with Fortnum dead, Barbara and Mabel wouldn't defend me; but comfortingly if I go out with them at night, they bark their heads off if anyone comes within twenty yards of us. Last night walking home up Egliston Road, I nearly died when what appeared to be two huge figures, leapt over a flowering currant bush, and landed at my feet. Both dogs went berserk and opened curtains all the way up the street with their barking. I screamed my head off, but felt a bit silly. The 'huge figures' turned out to be two local twelve-year-olds returning from Scouts.

*Saturday, April 17th*
Not a word from *The Sunday Times*; I do hope the Wimp piece is all right. Paranoia is not helped by Emily who comes for a walk with me, and gets wild with rage when anyone else tries to join us. Seeing Rachel and Clarissa bearing down on us, Emily looks bootfaced: 'I'm going to be like Daddy from now on,' she announces loudly, 'and be rude to people.'

*Tuesday, April 20th*
Out on the Common. Beautiful radiant blue day. Just crossing Flower Garden boundary when I see my roofer friend, with the two Alsatians and the character-actor face, running towards me shaking with rage and horror.

Some bastards, he says, attempting a vile black magic ritual, have killed a puppy and hung it on the stone cross in Barnes Graveyard. It is about Barbara's size – a little brown and black very thin bitch, still with its woolly puppy coat. Blood is dripping from its mouth, and oozing all over the white steps of the grave. One can imagine the terror the little creature must have felt. The murderers had trailed bramble strands in parallel lines from the steps of the grave and put a large broken branch of cypress across the bottom to form a ritualistic square.

My roofer friend says he can't get the puppy down, because his dogs will grab it. I go and find Ken the Common ranger. Crying all the while, I find I have no paper handkerchief, and have to resort to my sleeve. Ken, mercifully, probably, is very matter of fact about the whole thing. When we get back to the Graveyard, the roofer man has lifted the puppy down. Lying dead on the gravel, she reminds me so poignantly of Fortnum. Go home utterly sickened and miserable. I can't stand living in Putney much longer.

*Wednesday, April 21st*
Walk early in the morning – no one about. It is very spooky; death seems to lurk everywhere. Still haunted by the little brown and black bitch.

On the way home Mabel meets a ginger mongrel and, as Barbara is on the lead, immediately goes into her sweet flirting act, flattening, ears back, followed by a lightning pirouette, then flattening again. Perhaps she is going to have a Roman Spring.

Next minute, however, we bump into Buster, the collie, one of Fortnum's great enemies. Barbara, who has no filial loyalty, immediately charges up to Buster, and starts chatting him up. Mabel, however, the dear principled creature, snarls, wrinkles her nose and refuses to be friendly. Buster's mistress, who can now afford to be magnanimous, says that Fortnum was a fine-looking dog, and that Buster still barks at Fortnum's ghost in the churchyard.

### Thursday, April 22nd
I do miss Rosie. Most of her time is taken up with David the sculptor, and as Michelin, her Peke, had a heart attack last week, she no longer takes him out on the Common.

### Friday, April 23rd
Leo and I have a long, long discussion and decide we're definitely going to move to the country soon. As it may be our last Boat Race in Putney we decide to go and watch it for the first time in ten years. On the way, Barbara rolls liberally in goose droppings, and then plunges into the muddiest part of Beverley Brook, emerging with thick shiny black leg warmers. I suppose it's one way of dispersing the crowds along the towpath. Actually the race is boring. Just two crews flashing by, followed by a lot of red-faced men in launches yelling into speaking trumpets. Until we get home we don't even know that Oxford have won.

### Saturday, April 24th
Still no word from *The Sunday Times*, but bolstered by nice talks yesterday to the *Mail on Sunday*, who would like me to go and work for them. Their first issue is due on May 2nd, but after thirteen and a half years it would be a terrible wrench to leave *The Sunday Times*. Also cheered up by exquisite day and warm weather bringing out the lilacs, the double cherries and the wisteria in all the gardens.

Bump into Mrs Bond, who is exploding with indignation. One of her daughters (deserted by her hubby, and left with five kiddies) is living with a lorry driver, and evidently drawing social security. A German woman who lives in the council flat next door has, says Mrs Bond, tipped off Social Security that her daughter was living with the lorry driver.

Her daughter, she added, 'When she 'eard about it, followed the German woman down the street with language and other fings. And what are

Germans doing in our council houses anyway, after what they did to us in the war?'

Having regaled me with this tale for at least fifteen minutes, Mrs Bond says she can't waste time chatting all day, and scuttles off to char for Henrietta.

On the way home I pass the lurcher man and his three lurchers, who gambol most charmingly with Mabel and Barbara. Also very ashamed to notice that the lurcher man himself is not black-eyed, black-haired and gypsy-faced, as I've always claimed him to be, but blond, brilliantly blue-eyed and very good-looking with his arms full of bluebells. I've heard of *names* being blackened by prejudice, but never eyes and hair. I hope I never have to be a witness in a murder case. And talking of murder, I really think we're right to think of leaving Putney. On the way home I bump into Rachel, who tells me an old tramp has been battered to death near Barnes Graveyard. Everyone is very jumpy.

*Wednesday, April 28th*
Still no word from *The Sunday Times*. The woman's page editor rings me up about my next piece and I ask her if she knows anything about the

Wimp piece: 'Ah,' she says, 'none of the top floor like it, they're all going round saying: "Jilly's got men wrong, my wife says I'm not like that."'

Whether this is true or not, it makes me feel deeply irritated. Ring up *The Mail on Sunday*, and say would they like me and the Wimp piece? They answer yes to both questions. Go out to lunch with the editor of the *Sunday Express* colour magazine, who left *The Sunday Times* about three months ago. He very kindly offers me a job, too. We proceed to drink far too much champagne.

Walk from Barnes Station through Mugger's Tunnel and along the path by the railway line. Find clumps of palest purple violets in the copse opposite the last platform. Above them on a lime tree, two fat squirrels are guzzling nuts – little hands working, black eyes sparkling, cheeks bulging like Timmy Tiptoes. Their coats are half-rust, half-grey. They are totally unafraid.

Get home at 5.30, to find the woman's page editor of *The Mail on Sunday* has sent me armfuls and armfuls of white freesias and bluebells, like the lurcher man, plus a note saying the Wimp piece is marvellous. Feel gratified and quite sick all at the same time. After thirteen and a half years on *The Sunday Times*, it is rather like walking out on a husband.

Maxine tells me that Barbara, in anticipation of new riches, has chewed up a five pound note.

*Friday, April 30th*
Walk with Syd the carpenter, who tells me that on the morning the old tramp was murdered, he (Syd) was out very early about 7.30, when a strange figure lurched towards him then lurched away. Syd then rounded the corner, bumping into a pretty girl with a Munsterlander bitch, who was in a frightful state because she'd just found the tramp's bashed-up body by the tennis courts. The poor girl, understandably, hasn't been seen on the Common since. Syd is convinced the first man was the murderer. He's been interviewed by the police. Having exhausted that subject, we then talk about El Alamein. Syd says he was a sergeant fitter. He thought Monty was a twerp and a butcher.

*Saturday, May 1st*
Very cold and blustery. Walk with Rachel who has had her blonde perm cut very short. She is fuming because she is going to a wedding today, and the cotton suit that she's spent a fortune on is going to be too cold. Still

utterly shell-shocked from leaving *The Sunday Times*, I suddenly feel faint crossing the Lower Richmond Road, and nearly black out.

'Perhaps it's the Change,' says the ever-tactful Rachel.

Change of newspapers more likely, I mutter under my breath.

### Sunday, May 2nd

Leo and I take the dogs for a walk at dusk. The Fair is here. There is a new roundabout composed of coloured umbrellas flying round, lovely against the soft lit-up massed spring greens and bronzes, topped by pink and white chestnut candles.

Go home and watch a programme showing clips from the last Russell Harty series. And suddenly there is Fortnum, taking his Obedience Test at Cruft's, looking so alert, well behaved and sweet. He was such a beautiful dog. It is nice to remember him during his finest hour.

### Wednesday, May 5th

Rosie rings very early to say Michelin was put down late last night. He had throat cancer. She is incredibly brave; she says she is going to have him cremated rather than buried at the bottom of our garden beside Fortnum, because, if we're thinking of moving, the new owners might dig him up. Feel desperately sorry for her.

Go out on Common – it is bitterly cold. As a result of making a commercial for *The Mail on Sunday* yesterday, I have bright scarlet nails, which clash horribly with my butcher-red and purple hands. As there was no time to cook last night, we had take-away curry. The dogs who wolfed all the leftovers are now desperately eating grass.

Meet Tommy who admires my nails then says he's very worried about Rosie, and is going to ring up Peke Rescue and see if he can get her another dog.

We are then joined by Crispin, the artist, who also admires my nails. He said that in America women come up to the counter after a manicure, hands with still-wet nails turned out, and say to the girl behind the till: 'My credit card's in my blue jeans pocket.'

Walking along by the tennis courts, I am horrified to find that the council have been at work again with the weedkiller, destroying all the wild flowers growing on the west end of the Graveyard, burning the blossom and leaves off the nearby chestnuts, as well as the needles off two pine trees. They have also left a disgusting smell of chemicals.

Rachel joins us also in a high state of chunter. I say I will write to the

*Richmond and Twickenham Times* and complain – I bet I never get round to it.

On way home we meet Mrs Willis and her lovely mongrel Spot. She says her neighbours on the Ranelagh Estate have complained because 'sometimes Spot has a bark of a night,' and aren't dogs 'better than 'oomans?'

After she's gone, Rachel puts on her Mrs Thatcher voice and says, 'Isn't it tragic?'

'What?' ask Tommy and I.

'That dog,' says Rachel, 'is younger than Bridie, and look how fat it is.'

### Thursday, May 6th

Photographed for *The Mail on Sunday* by Norman Parkinson. He is divine. Like a kindly Great Agrippa in *Struwwelpeter*. He says he was born in Putney, and used to go to Westminster School every day in a top hat, and all the louts of Putney threw all sorts of *dee*-tritus at him. His mother had an allotment on the Common with lots of roses. As usual Barbara insisted on getting in every photo.

### Saturday, May 8th

Just walking down to the Common, when a silver-grey BMW screams to a halt; it is Horsey Miriam who says ecstatically, 'She had a little girl, all by herself in the night.'

Totally bemused by this piece of information – surely Miriam can't be referring to her daughter, who is unmarried and only eighteen. Then suddenly twig she's talking about her mare who's just had a foal. She is utterly enchanting, says Miriam, and striped like a humbug. Such is her euphoria she doesn't even mind Barbara standing on her hind legs scrabbling at the silver flanks of the BMW.

Out on the Common, meet Bea, a very pretty girl with a splendid rotund sleek black mongrel called Otis, who dotes on me because I always give him dog biscuits. The Fair, says Bea, has been all too much for Otis. He discovered two chips dropped by the 22 bus stop, and was dragged past them on his long green fishing rod lead (the kind Clarissa wanted me to have for Fortnum) like a great black whale. Let loose by the Brook, he ran the quarter of a mile back to the bus stop, across the two main roads, to collect the two chips.

Rosie comes round for a drink in the evening. She is so brave about Michelin, and not a bit self-pitying. She was immensely cheered because the vet wrote her a lovely letter afterwards, saying, 'We see a lot of dogs, but even we could see Michelin was special.' (I suppress ignoble thought that vet probably fancied Rosie rotten.) As the vet said, Michelin *was* special. Rosie says she misses him terribly. She got him just after she split up from her husband eleven years ago. It's been the longest relationship she's ever had with anyone.

David the sculptor, says Rosie, has been quite marvellous about the whole thing.

'What about his wife?' I ask cautiously.

Rosie shrugs and says the marriage is in injury time anyway. Hope to God it is.

*Sunday, May 9th*

Leo and I return at midday from a dance in Oxfordshire to find Felix with a huge black eye. He got beaten up by a gang of thugs at the Fair, after winning the jackpot on the fruit machine. Fortunately, he fended the thugs off, until the man who owned the fruit machines came to his aid. Leo bawls Felix out for going late to the Fair, but adds privately to me that this is one more reason for leaving Putney. Details of country houses are flooding in from house agents all over the place. The ones in Berkshire and Oxfordshire are ridiculously expensive. I am having slight cold feet about country life, but Leo is hell-bent on moving.

Felix and I walk on the Common. He has his French oral Common Entrance exam next week. So I attempt to question him in French round the Common. When I ask him his favourite food, he answers, '*Amburger et Cheeps*'. Suggest it would be better if he replied '*Harry Co Vert, et Pommes Freets*'. Felix says he can't cope with that. Then I ask:

'*Combien de chiens avez-vous dans vôtre maison?*'

'*Un chien, Monsieur,*' replies Felix.

'But we've got *two*,' I protest.

'I know,' said Felix, 'but I can't remember the French for two, and anyway the examiner doesn't know we haven't got only one dog.'

Gloomily feel that his chances of passing are rather *mince*.

*Friday, May 14th*

To my incredulous delight, Felix rings up from school and says the examiner has told him that he has just scraped through his French oral. Wonder all the same if French is actually still taught in schools.

*Sunday, May 16th*

Leo and I leave for a week's holiday in France. God I hate going away; I know I'll love it when I get there but the garden is looking so exquisite, full of lilies of the valley, wallflowers, bluebells, lilac and Solomon's seal, which was given me last year by Rachel. On the Common the hawthorn is just coming out, and the chestnuts are in their full glory.

As we leave, the dogs look at me with huge reproachful eyes. The children get up at six in the morning to say goodbye, both fighting back resentment. How can I ever move to the country, if I can't bear to leave Putney for a week?

We take the car on the ferry from Portsmouth and watch all the ships sailing out of the harbour waved off by cheering crowds as they set off for the Falklands. It gives me a sick feeling inside to see all those spruce young sailors lined up on deck. Will they ever return?

*Tuesday, May 25th*

Back from France, having spent a week renting a house in the heart of Normandy. It was so beautiful and so quiet. I manage to read fifteen books on how animals have been used in war, for my next book. Decide I will be happy in the country after all, but are holidays different from real life? Will I get bored without Putney bustle and gossip?

*Friday, May 28th*

Very late walking the dogs because we watch the Pope arriving at Gatwick on television. Cedric does the commentary quite admirably.

Leo, who violently disapproves of the Pope's visit, puts on a black shirt and tie this morning. His disapproval turns to horror when he sees the papal helicopter landing on a cricket pitch. Will the wicket ever recover? Having just come back fat as *beurre* from France I can only admire the nimble way the Pope bends down to kiss the earth and think how fit he must be.

*Sunday, May 30th*

Leo and I spend the weekend at Longleat, where Mabel and Barbara take part in a sponsored dog walk called the Great Paw Trek. Leo and I sleep in the Kama Sutra room in a huge four poster with a mirror in the ceiling. After a heavy evening, we fall into bed too exhausted to realise that Barbara is slumped between us. Waking at dawn, Barbara sees her reflection stretched out in the mirror above, thinks it's another dog, barks her head off, and rouses the entire household.

At lunch the next day, Leo gets tipped off about a ravishing house in Gloucestershire which is just coming on the market.

### Tuesday, June 1st

Gorgeous weather. Lovely row over official opening of Putney Hospital. Two hundred people from NUPE (and very un-COHSE) chant rude slogans throughout the ceremony, in an attempt to drown all the speeches. According to the *Wandsworth Borough News*, the canteen staff were on strike, 'and the Friends of the hospital had to provide refreshments in the form of tea and biscuits for the visiting dignitaries'. After that din, all they probably longed for was a stiff drink.

### Wednesday, June 2nd

Meet my director friend Peter Duffle, who says he is soon to start work on a film of *The Far Pavilions* in India. I haven't seen him for ages because he's been living in the country for several years. He says he is terribly glad to be living in London again. One of the things that put him off the country was his beautiful bearded collie getting kidnapped, and then being found a few days later run over on the motorway.

He now has an adorable new bearded collie puppy called Pompeii, who gallivants wildly with Barbara.

'Beardies,' the breeder told him, 'are very anxious to please.'

This beardie has eyes covered in hair, cannot see his master, hares enthusiastically up to everyone else in an attempt to find him, and sends Clarissa and Rachel flying.

### Thursday, June 3rd

Emily and I stop to talk to Rachel, who has been gathering stones on the Common for her rock garden. She is resting on the much graffitied bench backing onto Putney Cemetery. Emily insists on reading out the latest graffiti in her piercing voice:

'Virginity is like a balloon: one prick and it's gone.'

She then asks: 'What does virginity actually mean, Mummy?'

Hastily point out new post-Pope graffiti.

'JPR has made more conversions that JPii.'

*Friday, June 4th*

Heavy thunderstorms just before dawn. So strange not to have Fortnum's terrified trembling body in my arms. Pray for the thousandth time for him to be all right in heaven.

Common is rough mown for the first time – grass lies like shorn locks on the hairdresser's floor.

Meet Clarissa who gives me a four-leaf clover, and says: 'Last night I'd just put on my housecoat, and taken a sleeping pill, when one of my battered wives rang in hysterics from the police station. She had two black eyes, and the police insisted on sending her home.'

Clarissa then nobly got dressed and drove down to the police station to take the battered wife back home at 1.30 in the morning.

'What does your husband look like?' asked Clarissa.

''E's short,' said the battered wife.

So Clarissa and the battered wife crept back dodging short men.

I think Clarissa must have read somewhere of the importance of getting bereaved people off the subject of those they have lost. Every time I mention Fortnum's name, she cuts through the sentence and starts talking about her mother-in-law or some book she's been reading. I wish I could explain. It helps if I can talk about him occasionally.

*Saturday, June 5th*

Still very hot and thundery; smell of elder and white valerian particularly strong. Meet Molly with heavenly friend Mrs Tomkin who has a big black mongrel called Max.

Max is a great barker, explains Mrs Tomkin, and the police called to complain, so she now keeps him in a play pen in the garden during the day.

'At night,' she says, 'Max likes to use Father's artificial leg as a pillow.'

'Isn't it rather small?' I said, mishearing, and thinking she said 'egg'.

'No,' she says, 'it's the same size as his other one.'

She then says Mabel and Barbara (who are charging about romping with Ophelia) ought to join the IRA, they're so good at bashing knee-caps.

While I am pondering why I don't in the least resent Mrs Tomkin making cracks about my dogs, when I mind them so passionately from Rachel and Clarissa, the latter two come over the brow of Dogger Bank, and catch me giggling with Molly. Why do I find myself going scarlet with guilt, as though they've caught me stealing sweets? Vow to try and mind less what people think.

Go home and write a stern letter to the *Richmond and Twickenham*

*Times* complaining about the wantonly haphazard use of weedkiller which has destroyed the wild flowers, shrivelled the chestnut candles, and finished off two perfectly good pine trees in Barnes Graveyard.

### Sunday, June 6th

Everyone revving up for Putney Arts Festival. Drop into the church and find people hard at work arranging pews front to front, and pinning orange felt over them, so objets d'art can be displayed.

The butcher's daughter has produced the most ghastly mirrors decorated with coloured tiles. Would it be worth buying one for the sake of perfect steak for years to come?

Frances the feminist, in a caftan, is handing round cucumber sandwiches made with wholemeal bread. Perhaps she should put her spurned book on sisterhood on display. She hopes I'm going to be 'supportive' and buy a lot of pottery. A girl with bright crimson hair tied up in a ponytail going blonde at the roots is going mad trying to catalogue brooches.

The south-east corner (where dreadful paintings of celebrities are being hung) is known as the Top of the Flops. Michael Foot, Ted Heath, and George Melly are only too glaringly recognisable.

'I'll give you £100 if you take one away,' says a jolly lady in a folk weave skirt.

### Monday, June 7th

The poplar fluff is drifting, but not covering all the adjacent trees in a total grey snowstorm as it did last year.

Attend the opening of the Putney Arts Festival. Talk to Cedric's wife. Cedric is standing beside her trapped by a ring of admiring bores.

Notice him pressing her collar bone with his thumb, harder and harder, like a duchess imperiously ringing for a butler. Suddenly she winces, starts, and says:

'Oh gosh, we must go or we'll be late for dinner.'

Ten minutes later I see them deep in conversation with Our Member. Perhaps it was *me* she wanted to escape from.

### Tuesday, June 8th

Very hot but less muggy. Meet great friend called Bruce who used to be a stockbroker, but whose firm went to the wall in the great crash of 1974. He now works as a chauffeur, and has just acquired an adorable Jack Russell puppy.

Barbara, Mabel and the Jack Russell suddenly see a tramp with a bicycle standing deep in the nettles on the north side of Beverley Brook, and all go into a frenzy of barking.

My suspicions expressed to Bruce that the tramp may be a flasher or a glue-sniffer are quite unfounded. He turns out to be a middle-class man with a beard and a paint-stained smock, who is clipping elder flowers to make wine. He gives Bruce and me the recipe. When he reaches the words 'Yeast Extract', I start glazing.

He says if he puts a carafe of elder flower wine on the table it always goes before the red or the white. Bruce asks him to make him some whisky.

We overtake Clarissa and Rachel who are in high indignation because a two-feet-wide edge of long grass has been mown along Beverley Brook, cutting down the salsify in its prime.

'Sappho,' I say wistfully, thinking of the poem about the plough share slicing through the poppy.

'No, no,' says Clarissa impatiently, 'salsify.'

I give up. The charming clump of yellow irises, that always get nicked within twenty-four hours, has come out on the edge of the football pitch.

Out in the afternoon. Alas, the wild roses are nearly over in the Flower Garden, but delighted to find a new bush has seeded itself. The flowers are whiter and more anaemic than the pink roses on the other bushes, but the smell is heavenly.

Wander through Barnes Graveyard and put a bunch of dog daisies on the grave of Francis Turner Palgrave, sometime professor of poetry at Oxford, born September 28th, 1824. He also produced *Palgrave's Golden Treasury*, an excellent poetry anthology, much used in schools in my day. I suppose he'd need to be born in Libra to be diplomatic enough to cope with all the poets who were livid with him for leaving them out, or not putting in the poems they like best.

Finally identify the pine in the graveyard as a Weymouth pine; it is already putting out pale green cones beside the old brown ones.

*Friday, June 11th*

Meet nice man with tiny moustache and tight-skinned mongrel called Edgy. Edgy's master, he says, is in the Falklands in the Welsh Guards. All the family sat down and cried when the Welsh Guards copped it, but he thinks Edgy's master is OK. He says it won't be easy to capture Port Stanley, because of all the Falklanders living there. Feel depressed by this piece of news. Wish I wasn't always influenced by the last person I've talked to. Wish the war was over.

Meet Emily and Maxine back from the shops. Emily has had an appallingly short haircut. I know it's fashionable, but it's dreadful. Try to pretend I like it.

Leo comes back from seeing the house in Gloucestershire about which he was tipped off at Longleat. He is very pale. He says it's the loveliest house he's ever seen but he doesn't want to pressure me; will I go and see it very soon?

*Sunday, June 13th*

The Putney Common show has grown so large it is spread over two weekends. The first weekend includes a horse show – and, for the first time terrier races. They are terribly funny. The competitors are all Jack Russells who bark and bark at each other, and break off to have tremendous fights in the middle of each race. They rush down the straight after a fluffy rabbit on a piece of string. The finish is piled bales of hay, with a hole big enough for one winning terrier to race through after the rabbit. The rest nearly concuss themselves on the bales, or surge over the top, and are grabbed by the scruff of the neck by their owners, before they lay into one another again. The din can be heard from Egliston Road.

In the middle a kind local policeman comes up and says I'd better tell my son to pick up his bicycle from the grass, as this lot are likely to nick it.

Emily, deeply affronted at being thought a boy, decides maybe her hair is too short.

At the show I judge the Fancy Dress. It is the usual rat race of trying to distinguish between the professionals who clean up at all the shows, and the amateurs whose mothers have toiled all night over their costumes. Nor do I have the support of Anthony Andrews, who is too busy to judge this year. According to his wife, he's 'up to his neck in the Pimpernel.'

I've just reached Beauty and the Beast in the line up, when a horsey female steward cries out, 'Look out, she's staling,' whereupon Beauty's horse lets out a stream of pee, and a succession of very loud farts. I, after several gins in Miriam's caravan, get dreadful schoolgirl giggles, and have to bury my face in the shoulder of a nearby Arab Chieftain's horse.

In the end I give the prize to three adorable children carrying candles and their pony, who was covered in white net. They are supposed to portray a nightmare. Everyone afterwards tells me who else should have won. Judge not that ye be not judged.

*Monday, June 14th*

After watching terrier races very carefully yesterday while she was on the lead, Mabel rushes back to the track this morning to find the fluffy rabbit. Both she and Barbara examine the hole where it went through, and not finding it, wee on the bales in disgust.

Felix starts Common Entrance today. Pray so much that he passes.

*Tuesday, June 15th*

Everything revving up for the second big Show on Saturday. Attractions include steam-rollers, mowing machine races, the Marines (wildly popular since the Falklands Crisis), and the King's Troop. The Common is now overrun with roaring Rotweillers, caravans, washing and jolly whistling soldiers, saying, 'Nicest thing I've seen today,' to every girl who passes.

Council workers, racking their brains as to where all the tents should go, mark their territory with lengths of string, which trip up unsuspecting old ladies. Yet another Fair has also arrived with a roundabout, reducing Rachel to apoplexy. She is very cross there is not an arts and crafts tent at the show.

Meet old lady with adorable little dog. She says it is an Australian breed called a healer, and what absolutely delightful habits healers have. Fortunately she cannot at this moment see little healer and Barbara who are busily guzzling manure behind a hay bale.

*Wednesday, June 16th*

Walk with Clarissa and Rachel round the football pitch, from which we're really forbidden. Excited by fresh territory, the dogs snort a lot. We find cranesbill, speedwell, and a beautiful white and purple vetch like a lupin that none of us can identify.

I am about to tell Clarissa that I haven't slept for a week worrying about the results of Felix's Common Entrance exam, but decide not to because I know any reference to public schools will enrage Rachel.

In the afternoon after a jolly bibulous lunch with two senior boys from Radley, who'd come up to interview me for the school magazine, I am photographed in Barnes Graveyard by the *Richmond and Twickenham Times* who are actually going to publish my letter. In vino I find it very hard to look suitably outraged and upset by the devastation caused by the weedkiller. Rachel and Clarissa are pleased with me.

*Thursday, June 17th*

There is nothing as beautiful as the whitening grass on a warm June day, the weather is perfect. The Falklands War is now over. Lefties and Liberals are finding it very difficult to curb both elation and emergent jingoism. Nor do the media make any attempt at impartiality. I heard a man on Capital Radio today saying: 'I'm sure we're all absolutely – I mean I'm sure *Mrs Thatcher's* absolutely delighted that we've taken Port Stanley.' I think it's wonderful. Hurray for Maggie, she should call an election now. How disgustingly right wing I've become.

Yesterday, I fell in love with the house in Gloucestershire. I drove down with Leo, who is right: it is utterly magical. We make an offer, even though we haven't looked at any other houses. All the same I wish Putney wasn't looking quite so enchanting. Warmed by endless lovely days, then fierce rain refreshing everything at night.

*Friday, June 18th*

Muggy, still day – grey sky lovely against the deep summer greens. The King's Troop are rehearsing on the Big Common for Saturday's display. Goodness, some of the officers are glamorous. I know I'm a sexual snob, but they do look so much more attractive than the men, principally I think because they're allowed to have longer hair, growing at least an inch under their caps, which is far more becoming than the troopers' crew cuts. Also their charges have long manes, while the troopers' horses have hogged manes. To emphasise further that there is one law for the rich, the six officers' chargers are stabled in separate loose boxes – three in a row, and back to back – while the troopers' horses are tethered in the horse lines, tied by their off fore and near hind legs.

I talk to Paddy, the King's Troop vet, who owns an enchanting lame Labrador who spends his time slavering outside the cookhouse. Paddy tells me about some of the individual horses: Wincanton, known as Cyril, who bites and kicks but is a brilliant ride, and Rebel who is forever kissing you if you've got nuts and sugar, and Yum Yum ridden by trumpeter Mason – who one year at the Royal Tournament was enjoying the applause so much that he refused to leave the ring and Trumpeter Mason was reduced to setting about the horse with his trumpet.

Paddy, the vet, also said the men were devoted to their horses: 'They'd kill a comrade, screw a girl, beat up their wives, rifle their mother's handbag, rather than let a hair of their horses' heads be hurt.'

Out in the ring, the Troop were practising pulling their gun carriages in figures of eight with a tremendous jangling. Some of the turns looked terribly hazardous. Paddy said the ground was very bumpy, and a gun carriage might easily overturn.

The Troop, he tells me, are due to do a display in Aldershot early next week, but may have to rush back to London to fire the salute in Hyde Park if Princess Diana's baby is born.

Any further chat was drowned by the deafening crash of the thirteen pounders, now firing blanks, but all used for real in the First World War. If Fortnum had been alive, he would have bolted halfway to Hyde Park by now.

### Saturday, June 19th

Putney Show. Out early. Barbara and Mabel suddenly see a Peke beside the first bridge, and charge over, thinking it's Michelin. When they get there and realise it isn't, they start snarling in rage and disappointment. Find that more of the lovely lupin vetch that we discovered on the football pitch is growing in white and blue on the north side of the Flower Garden. Finally identify it as goat's rue. It is strange that when you discover a new flower (like learning a new word) it suddenly seems to crop up everywhere, and you can't imagine how you've missed it all these years.

Barbara, who's thoroughly over-excited by the Show (so much to roll in), follows a man in braces into a wooden privy. He swears at her, she shoots out again, like a jack-in-a-box, straight into the jaws of a huge Rotweiller.

The King's Troop display in the afternoon was truly splendid; all dressed up in their scarlet and blue, they are a magnificent sight. I notice the officers' quarters are strategically placed under the nurses' home, with a large sign saying Orderly Officer. I wonder if they'll scale the wall in the middle of the night and catch some matron unawares.

### Monday, June 21st

Out on the Common, find the King's Troop packing up and in considerable disarray. Princess Diana, says Paddy the vet, has gone into labour. Half the troop are on their way in horse boxes down to Aldershot, and will have to do U-turns on the motorway and come back to London again.

I bid them a fond farewell and walk on, passing an earnest woman in rubber gloves with a bawling child busily trowelling manure into a black dustbin bag.

'I am getting it for the garden,' she says with a defensive laugh.

Borne down on by Rachel and Clarissa.

On the north side of Beverley Brook, Rachel suddenly asks if Rosie is having a walk-out with David the sculptor. Cornered I hum and haw, and say yes she is, but it's all right because they're terribly in love. And David the sculptor's been miserable for ages because his wife's had lovers dripping out of her ears (not sure she has at all) and Rosie has picked up the pieces wonderfully.

Hope I haven't landed Rosie in it. But all worry about Rosie or Clarissa or Rachel is driven out of my head by Leo ringing up and saying we've got the house in Gloucestershire.

### Tuesday, June 22nd

On the common meet Otis, the greedy black mongrel on his green fishing rod. Bea, his pretty mistress, says he is still disgracing himself by charging across main roads after rubbish, and eating one of the Show Rotweiller's dinner while it was barking impotently inside a caravan. Worst of all, yesterday, he rushed into the tent, where all the soldiers were having their breakfast.

So she called in a high voice: 'Come here at once, Otis.'

And all the soldiers shouted back. 'No, no, you come *here*, sweetheart.'

On the way home, I bumped into a nice minicab driver in his sixties walking five dogs: two Bedlingtons and three mongrels. He says he has just got married to a rich wife also in her sixties. Both were widowed before. Now they have five tellies, three video machines, three mowing machines, five children and five dogs between them.

Tonight Leo is going to an Old Boys' dinner and committee meeting. He says he may get an intimation whether Felix has passed Common Entrance and got into the school or not, but he won't be back from the dinner much before midnight, so I'll have to bite my nails until then.

I can't work for worrying about Felix. The only answer seems to be to get tight, which I do with an elegant young estate agent, from Knight, Frank and Rutley, who's come to talk about selling our house. He admires the sign saying 'Lost Children', which I pinched from the Putney Show, but says the best sign he ever saw was at the Game Fair, and said, 'Shooting Dogs' Lavatory.'

At five to twelve Leo comes through the back door, and falls over the doorstep. He looks like a thundercloud, so I realise there's no hope and Felix hasn't made it. Then he grins and puts his arms round me, and says:

'It's all right, darling, he's in.'

I burst into floods of tears, and rush round the house waking Mabel, Barbara, Emily and Maxine, who are all thoroughly over-excited. Then I ring my mother. Evidently when Leo arrived, the headmaster said, 'Can I have a word with you after dinner?' so Leo had to bite his nails throughout the committee meeting and dinner before he knew. This means Felix is the fourth generation Cooper to go to the school, and it means so much both to him and Leo. Keep waking up all night in a daze of happiness – all this and Gloucestershire too.

## Wednesday, June 23rd

Walk very late to avoid the regulars, as I'm terrified of telling them we're moving. I don't know why the hell I should be, but having never dropped any hint that we might be leaving London, it seems rather a bombshell to suddenly say we've found a house and we're off. Everyone will probably be thrilled.

Meet Molly and Mrs Tomkin, Max's wonderful owner, who is wearing lots of face powder, and in a high state of excitement.

''Ave you heard,' Mrs Tomkin asks, 'about the Activities? The police 've raided the brothel in Rocks Lane. Absolutely disgusting, the owner was using his own son – and he's only thirteen.

'And there's a house full of "those men" four doors down the road from the brothel,' Mrs Tomkin goes on, 'and they said to me this morning, "'Ave you heard about the Activities, Mrs Tomkin? It gives us such a bad name – we're not like that with kiddies you know; we thought the police was after us, when we saw all the flashing lights and all," and they're all such nice quiet fellows and very artistic.'

We then have lots more lovely lurid details about vicars and MPs caught *in flagrante* running out of the brothel into the night in their underpants.

Molly and I try very hard not to giggle.

The 'Activities' takes us three-quarters round the Common, and then Mrs Tomkin confides she thought the police and the flashing lights were after Max her dog.

''E used to bark at passers-by, and they complained to the police, and they came round and told us to keep Max under control. I mean it's not very nice to have a big black face looking over the fence at you, is it?'

I pat Max and says it depends very much on the face.

*Friday, June 25th*

Everyone is excelling themselves over our move to the country. It's as though we've committed some frightful crime like going over to the Russians.

'But we thought you loved Putney,' they chorus accusingly.

I still haven't had the guts to tell Clarissa and Rachel. This morning they descended on me, and Clarissa said: 'I saw your letter in the *Richmond and Twickenham Times*.'

'I haven't,' I said.

'Oh well, I'll cut it out for you,' said Clarissa, and makes no other comment.

*Saturday, June 26th*

Come back from a night in Yorkshire. Maxine says she walked the dogs, and was joined by Rachel.

'Isn't it exciting?' said Maxine.

'What?' said Rachel.

'About Jilly and Leo moving to Gloucestershire?'

'When?' snapped Rachel.

'In the autumn,' said Maxine, 'they've bought a house.'

Next moment they were joined by Clarissa, and Maxine said Rachel couldn't wait to shake Maxine off, so she could impart this piece of news to Clarissa.

*Sunday, June 27th*

Out with a hangover. Bump into Henrietta, who is at her most bossy and unlovely.

'I hear you're moving to Gloucestershire,' she says. 'Why Gloucestershire – it's so unfriendly? Why not Wiltshire? But I suppose you want to be near the Royal family. What about your contracts?' she goes on.

So I wearily point out that there are telephones and letter boxes in the country, and the cheap day return fare from Gloucestershire is less than a minicab to Fleet Street.

'Won't you miss all those brilliant witty remarks you always claim to hear at London dinner parties?' says Henrietta sarcastically.

'What's the point,' I say, 'if I'm too plastered to remember them next morning?'

*Wednesday, June 30th*

Our house goes up for sale. Two men from Knight, Frank and Rutley put up the 'For Sale' sign. Between hammer blows, like the end of *The Cherry Orchard*, they ask me why I want to leave a lovely house like this.

Feel slightly sick, and take the dogs out on the Common, trying to work out really why we're leaving. Because I'm sick of living in the Gold-fish Bowl; because I can't get any peace; and because people pour through the house all the time drinking our drink, and I never have any time to see Leo or the children. And because I hate seeing Leo come home white with exhaustion every night having spent two hours in traffic jams on the 22 bus. And because I never get a moment really to think about work – particularly on the Common because of all the people that come up and talk to me; and because if they don't and if I have to walk alone I'm frightened of rapists and murderers and flashers.

Above all I miss Fortnum. Every time I return to Putney I half expect to see him on the look-out, rootling round the churchyard, waiting to throw his portly body on me in ecstasy. Every blade of the Common is etched with his memory. I know it sounds melodramatic, but until I get away from Putney, I don't think I'll really get over his death.

*Saturday, July 3rd*

Now that we are selling our house the locals divide into two camps: those who say gleefully that the bottom has fallen out of the market, and those who try and make us push up the price of our house as high as possible, so that when it sells they can bask in the knowledge that their house round the corner will go for twice as much.

*Sunday, July 4th*

The Common is nearly back to normal after Putney Show, except for a bare brown stretch, where the King's Troop had their horse lines, and the six brown hopscotch squares, where the six officers' chargers lived in their loose boxes.

*Monday, July 5th*

As a result of a piece in the *Standard* mentioning that we are selling our house, prospective buyers are pouring in. I don't think I'm very good at selling. I keep pointing out loose floor boards here and saying the cellar's a tip. The only stipulation I make is that anyone who buys the house shouldn't dig up Fortnum's grave. Two couples, both very nice, seem extremely keen. I don't mind who buys the house, as long as they really love it.

*Tuesday, July 6th*
The house is sold to a family I really like, so that's that.

*Wednesday, July 7th*
Find first toadflax on the Flower Garden, but no pink soapwort yet. Red admirals are guzzling themselves silly in the knapweed. Find Rachel

picking elderflower heads. She says they're delicious with gooseberries. She makes no comment about our move, so I don't.

Out at lunchtime, the tennis courts by Barnes Graveyard are absolutely packed with people playing with post-Wimbledon vigour. In a week or two they'll revert to their usual pat-ball. On the way home I bump into Ken the Common ranger. Suddenly see black smoke belching out of the hospital chimney.

'How do they get away with it in a smokeless zone?' I ask.

'They've got a new incinerator,' says Ken. 'All the sawn-off limbs from Queen Mary's, Roehampton come down here in a van to be burnt. Now that they've installed the incinerator they've got to use it.'

On such a macabre note, I am quite pleased to see Frances the feminist, and her vegetarian dog.

'I hear you're moving,' she says. 'I suppose you'll keep a place in London?'

'No,' I say.

'What about Leo?'

'Leo's got a bed in his office,' I say. 'He'll go up to London on Tuesday, and come back on Thursday night.'

Whereupon an almost lascivious look comes over Frances' face.

'Do you trust him,' she says, 'with all those predatory separated women on the loose in London?'

Snap back that soon, no doubt, I'll have MFHs falling out of my ears.

On the way home, I meet a local who works on the *Financial Times*. He says he can't decide whether us leaving the area will make house prices in Putney go up or down.

*Friday, July 9th*

Notice fleets of goldfinches swooping in and out of the thistles. I never realised before what a heady delicate Buddleia smell thistles give off after rain. After a very hot day yesterday, it is a sweet sight to see all the butterflies swimming through the light drizzle and enjoying the green cool after the baking heat. Melted butterflies, I suppose.

In fact, three days of heat wave have triggered off the great autumn caravanserai. The balsam has suddenly popped out and the east end of Barnes Graveyard is lovely: lavender, foxgloves, evening primroses, swathes of cranesbill and veronica in white flower, all held together by the long arms of the brambles.

Meet Clarissa who is singing the praises of Jennifer Bailey, a new Richmond councillor: 'Jennifer and her husband are very fine citizens, and have a strong sense of public duty. Jennifer Bailey has never not done anything she said she would, [how unlike me] and what's more,' continues Clarissa, 'the Baileys have never produced an ugly kitten.'

*Saturday, July 10th*

My mother rang today to say that my father is dying in the nursing home in Haslemere. I must get down to see him. Oh God, that I weren't so hellishly busy – and I keep putting it off on the excuse that he probably wouldn't recognise me anyway.

His must be the cruellest of all deaths: the slow torturing erosion of a brilliant brain. I remember how he used to do *The Times* crossword in a few minutes, then gradually it took him longer and longer until he couldn't complete a single word in the book of children's crosswords that my mother had bought for him; and the endless heartbreaking lists he made of things not to forget in a desperate attempt to keep some control of life. And he was so brave, never a word of complaint or a grumble at the frightful pain that slowly curved his spine over like the handle of a walking-stick. No one could have a better father; I wish I were worthy of him.

Musing on the king my father's death, I go out on the Common and meet a pretty foreign lady in her sixties with a plump and genial dachshund, who she says belongs to a friend who is bedridden. It is seven years, she tells me, since she fell in love with Putney Common, and there has been no sign of an itch.

Then she says she's sad I'm going to live in the country.

'The whole of Putney will mourn when you go, Miss Cooper,' she adds. 'Every tree on the Common will hang its head down and cry.'

I almost cry too. I am so touched. It's not true. There are loads of people who'll be only too happy to see the back of me, but it's lovely of her to say that.

*Sunday, July 11th*

Today I was woken by Emily saying, 'Granny's on the telephone.' I saw it was only 8.15, and said 'Oh God.' 'Granny sounds quite cheerful,' said Emily. For a second I thought egotistically that she might have got up early and liked the piece I'd written on Henley for *The Mail on Sunday*. But she just said that Daddy had just died. Evidently he sat up, shook hands with the nurse, then lay back and died. How typical: courteous, kind and formal to the last. He was such a dear, brave man, totally without vanity or duplicity. I shall never look upon his like again.

Feel bitterly ashamed of myself for not getting down to Haslemere to say goodbye to him.

Arrange to go straight to Brighton to be with Mummy, but take the dogs for a quick cold walk first. Wish I could take them too to comfort me.

Notice, despite weedkiller, the heartsease is blooming again in the stricken Graveyard – but not for me. Two magpies for joy rise out of the blackthorn copse – the same as they did the day Fortnum died. Their credibility has really gone for ever now.

Crossing the Fair Triangle, I see the woodspurge is out, with its acid-green flowers, with their three cups. I am reminded of Rossetti:

> From perfect grief there need not be
> Wisdom or even memory;

One thing then learnt remains to me–
The woodspurge has a cup of three.

I am also bitterly ashamed that I feel a stab of disappointment at having to go to Brighton and missing my last Putney street party this evening. Is grief ever perfect?

*Thursday, July 15th*
Daddy's funeral. He was buried on his birthday, St Swithin's Day, and it rained and thundered as it did the day Fortnum died. Mummy was wonderfully brave, and the service was lovely. The priest read out a fragment which seemed to sum him up so well:

He nothing knew of envy or of hate,
His soul was full of worth and honesty
And of one thing, quite out of date, called modesty.

which was evidently written by the Duke of Buckingham of his father-in-law General Fairfax.

He was such a shy man; I keep worrying he'll be lonely in heaven.

In the late afternoon I came back to Putney, went out on the Common in my black dress and gumboots, got absolutely soaked, and felt a little better.

Notice horseradish leaves have been eaten to tatters by caterpillars this year. Is this because there are more butterflies about this year laying eggs?

*Friday, July 16th*
There are already a lot of green sloes on the blackthorn. I am going crackers trying to identify plants. Cannot decide whether tall ugly purple nettle growing along the Brook is downy woundwort or black horehound. It is probably the former, as the leaves are pointed and the trumpets that hold the flowers are clustered together, but it doesn't look pale or downy enough.

Nor can I identify a yellow clover-like flower growing in a huge clump on the north-east corner of Barnes Graveyard; nor a hideous shocking-pink flower, near Flasher's Point, which I think is possibly pink toadflax.

Feel I should produce *An Inconcise British Flora* by Feeble Martin.

*Saturday, July 17th*

Some men with swords have reaped the horseradish, gouging out the roots and discarding the leaves, which are already turning yellow at the bottom of the Flower Garden.

Meet jolly barman from local pub with new Jack Russell called Henry. Henry, he tells me, was acquired for two bottles of Scotch. I said Henry was worth at least half a dozen bottles.

Meet Clarissa at Lurker's Paradise. She is in fits of laughter because yesterday the retired Barnes district nurse, Miss O'Brien, was flashed at on the Common and didn't bat an eyelid.

'I've seen enough of those things in my time,' she told the flasher scathingly. He retreated abashed.

Rachel joins us, and we pass Horsey Miriam, and Sampson her red setter. After they've gone, Rachel makes some disparaging remark about how callous it is of Horsey Miriam to keep Sampson alive, when he's so old and frail.

I snap that Sampson is fine, and the best-looked-after dog in Putney, and they're a lovely family. Clarissa tactfully changes the subject, and says that she nearly walked slap into Scottish Molly at the Barnes Fair, and had to pretend to be endlessly counting the number of balloons in a taxi to avoid talking to her.

We then try to identify tall shocking-pink flower by Flasher's Point. Rachel thinks it's sticky catchfly, which sounds rather dubious, bearing in mind its location.

Then Clarissa and Rachel say they saw Rosie and David the sculptor, wandering hand in hand across the Common yesterday.

'He has a neurotic face,' says Clarissa bleakly.

'So he should have,' I say, 'after all the hassle he's had with his wife.'

Rachel says, 'He looks like a fallen angel.'

I say, 'He's certainly fallen for Rosie.'

Suddenly realise Barbara has vanished. Return to Squirrel Wood, and spend five minutes trying to catch her as she whisks round and round, eyes sliding. Finally she collapses at my feet.

'That dog,' says Rachel acidly, 'is just like her mother.'

For a second, I think she means me; then realise she is referring to Barbara's mother, Skip.

Can feel great waves of disapproval breaking over me.

Rachel then raises the subject of chasing sheep.

I say I really must find a farmer when I get to the country to lend me a ram, to butt Barbara about to put her off sheep.

'You must,' says Rachel bullyingly, 'or she'll get shot.'

I say that farmers are bloody trigger happy.

'It's a farmer's right,' goes on Rachel, sanctimoniously. 'I don't blame them. I hope,' she adds heavily, 'that your fences in the country are secure.'

Go home in vile temper – why can't she leave me alone?

In the afternoon, Rosie rings up and says that she and David the sculptor bumped into Clarissa and Rachel yesterday. 'They couldn't even bear to smile at us,' she says.

I tell her about Rachel asking if my fences were secure.

'Quite secure enough,' says Rosie, 'to keep out bitches like her.'

She then tells me what Molly actually said about me last year, which Rachel and Clarissa flatly refused to pass on to me because it was so dreadful, and which triggered off the great row, and which I'd always assumed was that I was an adulteress or had maladjusted children or something. Apparently she remarked that even if I walked round the Common with three crocodiles on a lead, Rachel and Clarissa would still rush up and walk with me. Not entirely sure that I believe this.

*Friday, July 23rd*

Identify disgusting shocking-pink flower near Flasher's Point as purple loosestrife. Strife seems the operative word on the Common at the moment but no one seems to be losing it.

*Saturday, July 24th*

The slain horseradish leaves litter the Common like chamois leather.

Meet my dear friend Mrs Murdoch, with the straight back, and the two golden retrievers. Today she looks very furtive. When I ask her what's up, she says she's just graffitied a bench. Someone had carved the words: 'Gays loved here' on it, so she crossed out the 'Gays' and wrote: 'Don't you mean perverts?'

*Sunday, July 25th*

Walk across the Yarrow Meadow; fronds of the wavy hair grass voluptuously caress my bare legs. The catkins are turning brown on the silver birches. Lots of meadow-brown and chalk-blue butterflies are fluttering around. So thrilled they're coming back; a few years ago one never saw a butterfly all summer on the Common.

Enchanted, too, to find the harebells again, a little way up on the East side of Common Road near a little sycamore. They are such an exquisite drained purple with their delicate taffeta petals. In folklore they are known as witch's thimbles.

Make dramatic discovery – no doubt obvious to everyone else – that each cherry-red finger of the willowherb eventually splits open, rolls back into four curls, out of which sprouts the feathering. On the way home I find two wrens, with their little tails up, in an oak tree. As I approach they send out that strange burglar alarm rattle.

### Tuesday, July 27th

Autumn is here, but has been kept at bay by the rain. See painted lady in the long grass by the bog. It is absolutely beautiful, but notice it has a very boring brown underside. Perhaps it closes up its wings, when it meets another butterfly it doesn't fancy.

Walking late I meet Mrs Willis and her jolly mongrel Spot, who Rachel thinks is too fat.

Spot, she says, won't touch tinned food, but always enjoys a Sainsbury's steak and kidney pie, potatoes and peas of a Saturday night.

### Saturday, August 1st

Deeply gloomy – people keep telling me how wrong we are to move the children to the country, just at the beginning of their teens, when all they'll crave from now on is parties, bright lights and the King's Road.

Cheered up in the afternoon because Emily returns from staying with cousins who live in the depths of the country. She had a glorious time, she says, rode a pony called Robin, and dyed her hair purple, but it came out in the swimming pool.

Out on the Common there is no sun. Despite the punishing heat, the trees have a flat matt heavy look. Walk with sweet girl who works for Capital Radio; she says her husband runs a radio station in Cardiff, which employs a token gay, a token black and a token feminist. He found one secretary in floods the other day, and said, 'What's the matter?' She said all the typing pool were being bloody to her because they said she was sexist, for wearing lipstick.

On the way home I pass Frances the feminist, who is picking blackberries – presumably for her vegetarian dog's supper. 'What are you going to do about schools in the country?' she asks beadily.

I stand on one leg, then say boldly that both children are going to boarding schools. Frances the feminist instantly becomes the personification of outrage and disapproval.

'Because you're too selfish to look after them yourself,' she says.

I then get a twenty-minute lecture about my deeply 'uncaring behaviour'.

I mutter that I went to boarding school myself, and I survived.

'Hardly,' says Frances dismissively.

I feel so cross with her that I finally resort to below-the-belt tactics of asking what has happened to her book on sisterhood.

'No publisher is brave enough to publish it,' she replies. 'It's too far ahead of its time, so I've decided to shelve it for five years.'

Instead, she says, she's decided to start a feminist workshop in Putney. Thank God we're leaving. There is something infinitely dingy about the word workshop. Pray that England doesn't become a nation of workshop-keepers.

### Monday, August 9th

Rosie and David the sculptor come to lunch. It's the first time I've seen them together; they are at the white-heat stage of sexual attraction when they cannot keep their hands off one another. He strokes her forehead in wonderment and reverence, as though he were an archaeologist who'd just unearthed the skull of Helen of Troy.

He asks me about the new house. I say that it's lovely but getting horribly overgrown, and we've had to spray to keep back all the nettles and thistles.

David looks appalled: 'You can't do that,' he says. 'You'll kill all the butterflies, and anyway nettles and thistles are so beautiful.'

Reply that they lose their charm when you can't see out of your windows. But secretly feel cruel and life denying, and spend sleepless night worrying about the dogs dying from poisoned grass, and wonder if there is any difference between me and the Zombies who sprayed all the wild flowers in Barnes Graveyard.

### Tuesday, August 10th

Rachel points out linum, an enchanting blue flower, which she has found growing on the spot where the King's Troop chargers were stabled.

In the afternoon, I meet Tony Phillips jogging. He says Effie, his big blonde mongrel, had to be put down this week. She was drinking two bowls of water an hour and the vet diagnosed cancer. She was fifteen.

'Every time the doorbell goes,' he says dolefully, 'I can't get used to no bark.'

I say truthfully that a bit of Old Putney has gone.

Effie was a great blonde survivalist, a mafia momma, wise, crafty, tyrannical, and always out on the streets. She and Fortnum ran Egliston Road between them and had total monopoly of all the dustbins. Fortnum was devoted to her, and always popped in to visit her every morning, after he'd paid his respects to Rachel's Bridie. He'll be awfully pleased to welcome her in heaven.

*Wednesday, August 11th*

The situation is becoming ridiculous. Although I walk with Rachel and Clarissa every day, apart from Rachel's crack about my fences being secure they haven't mentioned our move to the country at all.

Today I take out a few photographs of the house to show them. Clarissa makes absolutely no comment at all; Rachel says that it looks nice, and she'd love to get her hands on that water garden.

I give up and hastily change the subject, saying isn't it sad about Effie, and how much I loved her. 'The family,' I go on, 'are utterly devastated.'

'They couldn't be,' says Rachel dismissively. 'They used to let her out in the morning. I've seen her roaming along the Upper Richmond Road. No one who lets his dog out can possibly love it.'

So I say through gritted teeth: 'I let Fortnum out. Are you implying therefore that I didn't love him? You're talking rubbish. Effie came from Battersea and she was already a street dog, like Fortnum, before they got her.'

There is a long pause. Feel tempted to quote Hamlet. The bit about,

> I loved Ophelia: forty thousand brothers
> Could not, with all their quantity of love,
> Make up my sum.

Then realise it goes on: 'Woo't eat a crocodile;' remember Molly's remark about me with three crocodiles on the lead and stop just in time.

There is another long pause, and I stalk off.

'I do like your house,' Rachel calls after me.

*Friday, August 13th*

Clarissa corners me. She is in a confiding mood. She passed Molly in the street in Barnes yesterday, and as she was in a good temper and it was such a lovely day she smiled and said 'Hullo' before she realised who she was talking to. She is worried Rachel will be furious with her for letting the side down, and hopes Molly will not try and walk with them again.

*Sunday, August 15th*

Say to Maxine I am going to avoid trouble by walking to Barnes Station today. Maxine says isn't that where everyone gets raped? Say that I'd rather be raped than bullied. Maxine thought for a few minutes, and said that she thought she'd rather be bullied.

Walking across the Yarrow Meadow, it is a Resolution and Independence Day; everything is sparkling in the sunshine after the heavy rain. Hairbells, crushed by the downpour and by lovers, are strewn like amethysts in the long blond grass. Chestnuts are turning in the wood by Barnes Station. All the oaks look very poorly; their leaves are diseased, and so many of them have that strange lime-green sealing wax formation instead of acorns. Notice sticky buds already forming in the chestnuts. Suddenly feel desolate that I won't be here next year to see them burst open.

*Friday, August 20th*

Admire a huge clump of white soapwort on the north-east corner of the Flower Garden. Usually soapwort is pink, but notice some of these white flowers are tinged with pink.

'You're going to find it awfully quiet in the country,' screeches a voice, making me jump out of my skin.

It is Frances the feminist. She tells me that her sister lives in Gloucestershire, and was so badly snowed up last year that all her pipes froze and the village was cut off for ten days.

'How will Leo get home if that happens?' she says happily. 'Imagine him spending ten days on his own in London.'

Tempted to reply that the one spare woman with whom Leo will not dally is Frances.

But go home depressed. I'm beginning to feel Otis the portly black mongrel is my only fan. Let off his long lead, he pursues me all over the Common for handfuls of dog biscuits – a sort of Follow-my-Larder.

*Wednesday, August 25th*

I am starting to ring up people who've been friends over the last ten years, and asking them to go for last walks on the Common with me. Today I bid farewell to Doreen who was once my secretary, who used to have two perfectly trained Alsatians, one of whom has died. We have a lovely walk together, then Clarissa joins us.

'I've got a perfect leaving present for you,' she booms, 'a tabby kitten.'

'No,' I reply on a note of rising hysteria. 'NO NO NO NO.'

Then I point out more politely that we've already got four cats coming to the country, and that's enough. I then introduce Doreen.

'OH,' says Clarissa jovially, 'you must be Doreen the Alsatian.'

'I am not an Alsatian,' replies Doreen tartly.

Atmosphere becomes very tense. I feel like a piece of beetroot slapped between two very scratchy pieces of wholemeal bread.

*Thursday, August 26th*

Bump into Vic, the printer. As well as his two Dobermans, he has acquired a lovely bulldog puppy called Enid, who is totally unafraid, waddles up to every dog she passes, and tries to kiss it. Barbara does not approve of Enid, whom she thinks is very plain. When she approaches, Barbara turns her head away in horror, rather like the peeress who allegedly put her hands over her face whenever Cyril Connolly approached because she thought him so ugly.

*Friday, August 27th*

I can already smell the poplar scent on the boundaries and on the north-east top of Putney Cemetery. I love the way Barbara flattens her ears against the stings as she runs through the nettle tunnel.

I bump into Henrietta in the local off-licence.

'What are you actually going to do in the country?' she says. 'You won't have any of your friends to gossip to.'

I reply frostily that I intend to take up polo and gliding and to join the Women's Institute. Henrietta's derisive mirth follows me down the street.

*Saturday, August 28th*

Bump into Mrs Bond. She says that she's got to go and tidy up after Henrietta and the pale children who've gone to Cornwall for a month. You can't help being fond of Henrietta, she goes on, despite her funny ways. Find that I can help it all too easily.

*Monday, August 30th*

Toadflax and soapwort are still out in the Flower Garden. And there is a terrific crop of berries, sloes, haws, hips and blackberries.

Coming home, I notice that the silver willow in front of the hospital has lost yet another huge branch; only a quarter of it is left now. I suppose it will last my time. So busy examining it that I do not see Rachel coming and go slap into her. Would like to have preserved an icy silence and moved on. But instead, pusillanimous, placating, terrified drip that I am, I stammer out an apology, and say I've been offish recently because I'm having all the strain of moving. Why the hell do I always say things like this, instead of telling her the truth – that I'm utterly fed up with her, and will never forgive her for implying that I didn't love Fortnum? Rachel is very gracious, and nods understandingly.

*Tuesday, August 31st*

Matthew, a friend, comes for a drink in the evening, and is terribly funny about the tarts in Wandsworth ministering to the needs of the commercial travellers in their cars parked along the Common. Suddenly you see a shuddering *Daily Telegraph*, then a large bum emerges from the car, and the bum moves onto the next one. Nothing like this happens on the Eternal Triangle.

*Sunday, September 5th*

Mayweed has flowered in lush squares and in a long oval on the space where the King's Troop stabled their horses.

Go out in the afternoon to take a farewell signed book to Mrs Willis and her mongrel Spot.

Her sister has just died, she says, from cancer. 'It was very sad, but she felt no pain – she just slipped away.'

Mrs Willis adds that she's so pleased to see me, because she thought I'd also slipped away without saying goodbye.

Oh dear. Is that what going to the country will be like – a kind of death?

### Monday, September 6th

Autumn is here. Michaelmas daisies are out. Jays, blue wings flashing, are screeching in the trees; the grass is strewn with gold leaves. The chestnut, two down from the slide, is turning first as usual. Yellow sedum that crawls over the gravestones is just a cluster of grey stars.

Thank God I am terribly busy writing a book which has to be handed in the first week of December, which at least stops me brooding on leaving Putney. I find my moods are terribly up and down, but today I was cheered up by a friend of Leo's who tells me that the tobogganing is terrific in Gloucestershire.

### Tuesday, September 7th

Walk with Emily. Want to spend as much time with her as possible, as she's off to boarding school in a week.

She says in a disgruntled voice: 'I have a lovely life, but I don't like anything on me.'

She is referring to two spots on her forehead, and her hair which won't stay brushed upwards.

### Wednesday, September 8th

Because I want to savour my last few walks on my own on the Common, I've been getting up very early to avoid other dog walkers. Instead I seem to spend most mornings doing a four-minute mile round the Common keeping up with Syd the carpenter, who walks terribly fast. As we whizz round I have no time to appreciate turning leaves or cobwebbed gorse. All the same he is a sweet man. He says he's been lonely since his wife died, and feels particularly sad because his daughter is about to have a baby, and his wife would have so loved being a grandmother. He is very right wing, and loves to talk about politics, so we have dreadfully fascist conversations.

In the afternoon, Leo and I take Felix back to his new school. He is nearly as tall as me now, and I have annexed all his prep school uniform – and can see myself striding round Gloucestershire in grey flannels, a green peaked cap and a hockey shirt.

*Thursday, September 9th*

Less than three weeks left. I walk early with Rosie, because we never seem to have time to see each other. She is thinking of getting another dog, and moving in with David the sculptor – evidently his wife has pushed off. I say I think both are splendid ideas.

To avoid the Heavy Brigade we walk across the Yarrow Meadow, and find delicate cobwebs all silvered with dew spread over the grass like table mats.

'And you're really happy?' I ask.

'Oh yes,' sighs Rosie, 'I never want to get out of bed.'

Returning via the Flower Garden, we find yellow tormentil, with its four heart-shaped petals. Its Latin name, says Rosie, is *potentilla erecta*, which brings us back to David the sculptor, again.

*Friday, September 10th*

Beautiful morning. Why does this particular September have to be so lovely just to torment me, with its soft low sunlight, and the amazing opaque bands of mist rising above the golden grass? At night it is heartbreaking. Pegasus gallops above the church, and Andromeda stretches over the hospital, but it's been too misty to see the Pleiades.

*Saturday, September 11th*

Go out with Emily and see three magpies for a girl rising out of the blasted oaks on the edge of the Flower Garden. Syd the carpenter comes rushing up, red-eyed from lack of sleep, and says that he's got a granddaughter: he's so excited.

'It's a little girl,' he keeps saying.

As soon as we are out of earshot, Emily says in shocked tones: 'Isn't he rather old to have a baby?'

*Tuesday, September 14th*

Out on the Common, breathe in heady autumn smell of mouldering leaves. I am joined by Rachel and Clarissa. We proceed along in a solemn pace. Suddenly tempted to sing that Joyce Grenfell song about 'Stately as a galleon I sail along the floor'.

'I caught you on television the other night,' says Clarissa heavily.

I brace myself and say: 'Oh yes?'

'I caught you too,' says Rachel.

Clarissa said: 'You should sit in the middle.'

I protest that I couldn't have, unless I'd sat on Lord Norwich's knee.

'You didn't get into the camera at all,' said Clarissa, 'and you ought to get another chairman.'

I protest that the chairman is lovely and a new friend.

'I don't care if he *is* a new friend,' says Clarissa. 'He's so patronising.'

By second post I get a lovely letter from Felix. He is OK. 'As Daddy predicted,' he writes, 'I am very occupied.'

*Wednesday, September 15th*

Emily's last day. We walk clockwise round the Common together, in the hope that people will leave us alone. Walking towards Beverley Brook, we meet Rachel and Clarissa. Rictus grins all round.

'Is this the day of execution?' says Clarissa.

They both wish her good luck and have the sensitivity not to turn round and walk with us.

Before Emily goes off there are the usual photographs in the garden. She looks very glamorous with a new punk hairstyle, wearing new jeans with red braces and a dark blue shirt. How different from the hideous navy blue coat and skirt, and red tie which I wore when I first went away to school.

It was a lovely day for a journey down. I held Emily's hand – those lovely smooth hands of childhood; her trunk in the back was like a coffin in a hearse. Her housemistress gave us a lovely welcome.

'I'm not going to look when you drive off,' said Emily. 'It's unlucky.'

My last glimpse of her was standing very tall, slim and smiling and looking speculatively round rather like Barbara, and deciding which of the other little girls she was going to bounce up to.

Now it is night time. I went into Emily's room at midnight, and found the needle had stuck on the record of *Fame* and was still playing. The room looked so bare because all her ornaments are now in packing chests. The bed was stripped and a moth was bashing against the window pane. Even worse, there is no one anymore to leave a light on on the landing for, to ward off the nightmares and the hobgoblins.

Oh please God make her safe, and don't spoil her lovely merry nature. Slightly relieved that I feel far far worse than I did when Barbara went to kennels.

*Thursday, September 16th*

We are having an Indian summer. Wonder if Indians have English winters? The little alders below the rowans on the second Hillock are wilting from the heatwave. I don't think they've been planted near enough to the Brook. The clover is shrivelling; the everlasting pea is still in gaudy bright pink flower.

Walking through Barnes Graveyard, I find a man gathering up the fragments of Maria Ayoub's tombstone which was smashed by the vandals. Although no one has found the bronze of her face, which must have been stolen, I am delighted to hear that her tombstone is to be stuck together again.

Rachel and Clarissa bear down on me

'What about Grace Kelly?' asks Clarissa.

'What about her?' I say.

'Dead,' intones Clarissa.

'How dreadful!' I say, very shocked.

'I don't see it's dreadful,' snaps Rachel, 'just because she's famous.'


*Friday, September 17th*

We have a very nice new nextdoor-neighbour: a widower with an ancient springer spaniel. The only problem is that he is between jobs, spends a lot of time walking his dog on the Common, and always seems to combine his lunchtime walk with mine. What with Syd in the morning and the widower at lunchtime, I have absolutely no precious time on my own to take leave of the Common.


*Sunday, September 19th*

Have lunch at Langan's with an eighty-eight-year-old Dutchman, who's been writing to me about my books and pieces since I joined *The Sunday Times* thirteen years ago. The place is dripping with chums, and a lot of inter-table gassing goes on. Wonder for the millionth time whether we're making a lunatic mistake leaving London?

On the way home I go to the loo in Green Park Tube Station. See fat blonde with red face, dressed in black trousers and a shirt; turn sideways, she's still fat, and realise to my horror it's me. I look like a provincial lady before I've even got to the country.

We have to change buses at Parson's Green. Sitting down on the new bus, I drop and smash the bottle of hock given to me by the eighty-year-old Dutchman. Consequently, the bus absolutely reeks of drink. Suddenly, sitting opposite, see Matthew Roberts who used to be at All Saints' with Felix, and who, according to Felix, couldn't climb ropes because his willy was too big. He now goes to Wandsworth Comprehensive and is rather sexy looking. Feel that this is where I came in.

### Friday, September 24th

Pickfords turn up to talk about the move, which is going to be hell. With two massive fish tanks, two dogs, two cats, 8000 books, and more than 100 plants to transport to the country, it's going to be like conveying the Pacific Ocean, the zoo, and the Bodleian Library, as well as Birnam Wood to Dunsinane.

Pickfords scratch their heads, and say 'We'll need three pantechnicons, plus an extra van for the plants, but we won't take the goldfish; and the actual move will take four days.'

Leo, who has dazzling powers of organisation, runs the whole thing like a military operation, and draws up a movement order.

*Thursday,* 10.00 hours: LC leaves for the country with two fish tanks.

*Friday,* 06.00 hours: Cats to be caught, drugged and boxed by JC.

06.45 hours: LC to convey cats to Gloucestershire.

His able adjutant in this undertaking is Maxine. I spend my time getting in the way and court-martialled.

### Saturday, September 25th

Last walk with Crispin. I shall miss him very much. I'm sure one day he'll be very famous and a budded artist, and earnest young reporters will come and interview me in my dotage about having known him.

We discuss moving to the country. I say at his age, when one has no ties (which always sounds like an incomplete wardrobe), one is better in London where the action is.

On the way back, we meet Buster, the collie, and his mistress. She says that Buster still barks at Fortnum's ghost in the churchyard. Feel stab of anguish that he may still haunt the Common, desperately searching for me after I'm gone.

### Sunday, September 26th

Everyone keeps telling me that after bereavement and losing one's job the experience likely to cause most stress is moving house. Having lost my father, Fortnum, *The Sunday Times* and Putney in six months, I suppose I can be excused for being slightly uptight.

Certainly moving has many of the trappings of death: the flowers and good luck cards (today I got one from Otis the rotund black mongrel), the farewells, the feeling of total unreality and being endlessly chilled to the marrow, the agonising sorting out and throwing away.

Then there are the ridiculous tears which keep sweeping over me – when Putney Garden Centre gave me a farewell plant this morning; and when Ossie, who runs the local delicatessen, and who shares Leo's passion for highly-spiced food, announced that he had created a special Leo and Chile salad in our memory.

### Monday, September 27th

What I hate most most of all is seeing our darling house stripped of its riches. Go out on the Common to escape pictureless walls, tables without ornaments, bookless shelves. The mirrors were packed up this morning. Unable to see myself, I shed even more of my identity.

At home in a jelly of indecision, I try to sort out my bedroom and study, failing to throw away any clothes, in case the children need them for dressing up; or toys, because the way I feel I may be a grandmother any minute; or make-up, because Emily, or worse still Felix, might want to use it one day. After hours of sorting, I only manage to jettison fifteen Biro tops, and page one of Mozart's *Rondo in A Minor*.

### Tuesday, September 28th

Ludicrous day. Full of spats. I go out on the Common having arranged with Molly to meet her by the Eternal Triangle so we can have a last walk together. As I leave by the Yarrow Meadow, the heavens open. I get absolutely drenched. I hover for about twenty minutes by the Eternal Triangle, looking at the revolting triffid burr marigold and watching the sun rush in and out, and all the grass dancing and sparkling. I have a nice farewell chat with the man who read the *Sunday Telegraph* in a deck chair in the Squirrel Wood; then suddenly to my horror I see Rachel striding towards me.

I am too frightened of her to say that I am waiting for Molly; instead I move off, praying that she will go in the other direction – but she follows and walks with me round the Common.

Suddenly as I reach the ranger's hut, I see Molly waving in the distance, and say to Rachel that I think that as it's my last Sunday, and I really want to take a last proper look at the Common, I'll walk round again.

'I'll come with you,' says Rachel.

To my eternal shame I am too chicken to say that I'm off to see Molly, so I say, 'Oh well, I've changed my mind, I'm going home after all.'

So Rachel says: 'Well I will too.'

And poor Molly goes unmet.

As soon as I get home I telephone Biffo, to ask him to explain to Molly what's happened. He says he's never heard anything so ridiculous in his life, and I can't be *that* scared of Rachel.

'I am Biffo,' I said sadly, 'I am.'

Leo, meanwhile, is cooking lunch.

He says will I pack up all my underwear into a big plastic bag, as I don't want the removal men rifling through it?

'Oh they won't mind,' I say. 'That's why it's called a Pant-technicon – ho, ho! Anyway, they've seen worse things than my underwear.'

'I doubt it,' says Leo heavily.

Brisking about and trying to be efficient, I throw away what I think is vegetable water in the sink. It turns out to be the marinade, in which Leo is intending to braise the beef. He hits the roof. I burst into tears.

'A brawling husband in a wide house,' I sob. 'I don't want to live all by myself in Gloucestershire with you shouting at me.'

So we make it up. Then I laugh because he'd told Maxine to pack all the kitchen equipment and there's nothing to carve the beef with; so we start rowing again.

In the afternoon there is yet another row, because we do the change-of-address cards, with Leo roaring round the kitchen, saying, 'If you send one to that bore, or that bore, I'm leaving home.' When I point out that he's leaving home anyway on October 1st, it improves his temper even less.

Out on the Common in the afternoon, I bid farewell to everyone I meet, just in case I don't see them again before we go.

*Wednesday, September 29th*

The move proper begins. I rise early, find empty dustbins and burst into tears because I haven't said goodbye to the dustmen. Go out on the Common, and meet all the people I bade fond farewells to yesterday. Returning home my heart sinks to see two huge pantechnicons outside the house. Next moment the Pickfords foreman comes out staggering under a packing chest full of books:

'You ought to see the bleedin' lot we've got to shift here,' he grumbles, then realising it is my house, straightens up hastily, saying: 'Good morning, Madam.'

Evidently he'd asked Maxine earlier what kind of dogs we'd got, and when she said mongrels and not very big, he said: 'Thank Gawd for that – from the size of them baskets, I thought they was bleeding polar bears.'

In fact all the removal men are marvellous, very giggly, and after being primed with Party Fours by Leo, incredibly accommodating.

There is Ralph, the foreman, who has the soul of a poet. Danny, the handsome clown from Fulham, and Derak from New Zealand who tells me that his father, also a removal man, had once dropped a piano into Sydney Harbour, which was never found again.

All day it pours with rain. Maxine and David, our cleaner, clean and clean. The cats have a ball jumping in and out of packing chests. Mabel and Barbara shiver miserably, trailing me, their only constant, from room to room, as each familiar object disappears and their world seems to crumble round them.

By 4.30 I am so bombed producing endless cups of tea that I decide to have my first drink of the day, pouring out gin, then tonic, putting in ice and lemon then solemnly taking a bottle from the fridge and topping up the whole thing with milk.

*Thursday, September 30th*

Brilliant sunshine – a two-edged blessing. Everything sparkles after the rain. The Common has never looked more seductive. Keep re-meeting all the people I bade farewell to on Monday, Tuesday and Wednesday. Feel rather like Tosca, hurling herself to her death over the battlements onto a trampoline and bouncing back into view again and again.

Jump out of my skin as I see Rachel and Clarissa coming striding across the Flower Garden. They turn round and walk back with me to the ranger's hut. I bombard them with questions about their respective families, anything to keep off the subject of our move, as Leo has told me not to give them our new address – not that I expect that they'd want it. As we get to the hut, Clarissa says she won't see me tomorrow as she's going to the country, but am I coming out today at my usual time at lunchtime? I say not today because I'm knee deep in packing chests. There is a long pause.

'Well goodbye then,' I stammer, and turning on my heel, cross the Lower Richmond Road, so quickly that I'm nearly run over.

Go home feeling bitterly miserable; what a shabby way to take leave of them after so many years of walking together.

I'm very fond of Clarissa. If she hadn't become so thick with Rachel, I'm sure we'd still be friends. Even Rachel could be very nice on occasions; I just don't want to be a whipping girl any more.

Back home I find Maxine and David still cleaning and cleaning. I drift about dispiritedly peeling off glow stars, and getting on everyone's nerves like a spare Pickford at a wedding. The drawing-room sofa is removed to reveal a disk of ancient cat sick dating back to the seventies.

At 10.00 hours Leo departs for Gloucestershire with two half-full fish tanks. David, our cleaner, looks at the slopping water with concern and suggests the fish would travel better packed in ice. Have grisly visions of the tanks leaking on the motorway, and the water rising over Leo's chin like *Morning Departure*.

The removal men are very skittish. Danny, the handsome cockney from Fulham, unearths a huge naked four-foot-high doll of Emily's from the attic. He christens her Erica, after the stripper at Twickenham, and sits her on a little sofa outside our house with her legs apart. From the upstairs window I watch the reactions of the passers-by. Rachel comes past with Bridie, I can see the word 'disgusting' forming on her tight lips.

Danny, getting thoroughly carried away, puts a beer can in one of Erica's hands, and a lighted cigarette in the other.

All day a stream of people pour in for farewell drinks: Tommy and his boyfriend; Rosie and David; Scottish Molly; Horsey Miriam; and Mrs Bond, who gives me a card wishing me Good Luck in my New Home. Various other Putney friends turn up. Some haven't met before and get on very well, arranging to meet next week. Feel wildly jealous. Why the hell am I leaving Putney?

Next minute Frances the feminist waltzes in uninvited. I give her a drink, and she takes me aside, and says is it really necessary to have that naked doll sitting outside, and don't I realise how it degrades women?

By the time she leaves, Danny has dressed the doll in a Pickfords' jacket, which flops open like a flasher's mac. Frances, who doesn't seem to feel this is any kind of improvement, goes off also with pursed lips.

Just before she leaves, Rosie takes me aside, and says that she's moving in with David the sculptor next week. She looks radiant; I'm so pleased for her.

The tank corps then rings from the country to say that the goldfish are ensconced near the Aga simmering nicely and Gloucestershire is looking magical.

By nightfall, Leo is back again and the house is nearly stripped, so we take the dogs out to a touching farewell dinner arranged by six best friends in Lower Common South. Teeter home at three in the morning, and express mawkish satisfaction that all the winter stars, Orion, Castor and Pollux, and the Dog Star have come out to say goodbye.

'There'll be perfectly good stars in Gloucestershire,' says Leo acidly.

Make pilgrimage to the bottom of the garden. Moonlight floods Fortnum's grave.

'Rest, rest, perturbed spirit,' I whisper.

According to Leo's itinerary, LC and JC are supposed to spend the remaining hours sleeping rough with cats and dogs in drawing-room. It turns out to be very rough indeed. The next three hours are spent shivering on a mattress shared with two equally shivering dogs, worrying about the future, and despairingly watching the sun rise for the last time over the mulberry tree.

### Friday, October 1st

07.00 hours: woken from punishing hangover by Leo saying he is late, as he's got to let the first Pickfords van into the Gloucestershire house at 09.00 hours, and the cats have been drugged, boxed and loaded.

As his car disappears, senior cat can be seen furiously wriggling out of his Pak-a-Pet box, and peering drunkenly cross-eyed back at the house.

I have more grisly visions of the first Pickfords van with its 8000 books stalling on the steepest hill in Gloucestershire and Leo looking at his watch like Michael Caine in *A Bridge Too Far* saying:

'This is actually the wide bit.'

The whole day, in fact, becomes a farce. I set out with the dogs, feeling very ropey and hungover indeed. Am just wondering whether to be sick behind an acacia tree, then Syd the carpenter hovers into view, very full of his new granddaughter.

Belting round the Common beside him makes me feel slightly better. He says he'll drop in and see us, if he's ever doing a house in the area. Would like to have taken leave of the Common, but not in a fit state for aesthetic appreciation.

We are scheduled to lock up and leave by nine o'clock. But as Ralph, the foreman, has disappeared to Gloucestershire with the first van, and the expected reinforcements haven't turned up, poor Danny and Derak are left to load the last two vans single-handed.

By 11.00, out of sheer despair, Maxine and I join the work force. Maxine lugs up boxes and chairs from the cellar. I help Beau Derak load the plants. Steadying the necks of huge rubber plants, I feel like Alice playing croquet with the flamingos.

Next minute Rosie rolls up to have a quiet weep over the Cooperless house, and is rather irritated to find me still *in situ*. From the downstairs loo comes a scream that we've run out of loo paper. I knew I should have hung onto page one of Mozart's *Rondo in A Minor*.

Finally, at one o'clock reinforcements arrive, furious at being taken off another job. Through gritted teeth I ask when we'll be away.

'Well, the men have to have lunch. About three, I should think.'

At two o'clock I take the dogs out for yet another 'last walk'.

At least my hangover has receded and I now have a chance to say goodbye to my darling Common at my leisure.

I am just crossing Peter's Meadow, looking at the little oaks for the last time, and quoting Housman to the empty air:

> For nature, heartless, witless nature,
> Will neither care nor know
> What stranger's feet may find the meadow
> And trespass there and go,
> Nor ask amid the dews of morning
> If they are mine or no?

when a voice says: 'Haven't you gone yet?'

It is my nice new nextdoor-neighbour, the widower with the ancien springer spaniel. As we walk through Mugger's Tunnel, he tells me he i thinking of buying a new car. All the way back to Barnes Graveyard, w have the relative merits of the Ford Sierra and the Metro. I have hardly time to pick a sprig of heartsease to press between the pages of my diary before he progresses onto the Leyland Princess. This carries us through my precious Flower Garden, whereupon we move onto the advantages of a second-hand Cortina, which last until we reach the ranger's hut.

'Then, of course, there's the Toyota,' he adds as we cross the first Common.

As we reach Egliston Road, David the sculptor drives past radiant, no doubt from Rosie.

'I thought you'd gone,' he yells slowing down.

'That's a nice car,' says my companion. 'Italian I suspect.'

'How are you?' asks David.

'Fed up with Bloody Putney,' I shout, whisking into the house.

'That's the spirit,' says David driving off.

But inevitably, as I check through Pickfords' list of last-minute instructions, there is the lightning change of mood. 'Have you remembered to turn off the main cock? Have you left anything behind?' Only my heart, oh Putney, Putney.

Overwhelmed by contrition, I rush out and post change-of-address cards to Clarissa and Rachel. On the way back, I look into the removal van.

There's my wedding dress in its polythene bag, and the doll's house Daddy made for me with such loving care for my fourth birthday, and Felix's hobby-horse, with the nose chewed off by Maidstone, propped against Fortnum's old basket. Suddenly all my past seems to be unrolling before me.

But finally the last room is empty, the last van with its forest of plants has rolled away. Maxine and I lock up, place a last milk bottle of Michaelmas daisies on Fortnum's grave, bid farewell to the dear gallant house which had sheltered us so bravely and pile into the car.

As we drive off, the Brigadier saunters back from his lunchtime visit to the pub, blows us a last kiss, and I lose sight of him in a mist of tears.

What was that poem we learnt at school?

> Crack goes the whip and off we go.
> The trees and houses smaller grow.
> Last round the woody turn we swing.
> Goodbye, goodbye to everything.

But as the dogs fall into their first sound sleep in days, and the car clocks up the miles, we begin to perk up. Slowly the country gets lusher, the dogs wake up and start sniffing frantically at the crack of open window, and suddenly there's the church spire, and the valley, 'deep-meadowed, fair with orchard lawns and bowery hollows,' and our house, lying back, golden against its dark wood with its arms out to welcome us.

Leo, who's been supervising operations all day, and humping furniture around like Atlas, has already got the 8000 books up in their shelves, and all the furniture from the first van in place.

It is nice, too, to see familiar faces. The senior cat is purring in a kitchen drawer near the Aga. The junior cat miaows piteously behind a block of furniture in the cellar – in danger of getting boarded up like the Canterville Ghost.

At that moment, two beaming Gloucester removal men stumble in with Felix's fruit machine.

'Upstairs in the nursery,' I say.

They've just staggered up two flights of stairs when Leo appears, and says tartly that the fruit machine is supposed to go in the downstairs loo and will the men please take it down again, and that things will get unloaded much quicker if I make myself scarce.

In the hall, I meet a third beaming removal man carrying my feather boas.

This is the loveliest move I've ever had, he says dreamily, cannoning off the wall, 'I've never tasted whisky before – hic – and I've really taken to it.'

Gloucestershire – it seems – is going to be exactly like Putney.

# PART FOUR

# Rustics and Nouveau-Rustics

# HOW TO SURVIVE CHRISTMAS

One advantage of being a writer is that even the most harrowing occasion can later be turned into copy. One of my abiding nightmares every year is Christmas, which is a particularly frustrating time for the freelance writer. For while the rest of the world is enjoying nine days' paid holiday, the freelance gets nothing and every additional day of basting turkey or putting crosses in the back of sprouts makes him feel guilty he's not working.

To get round this guilt I decided one year to keep a diary cataloguing Christmas hour by hour, so in the spring I could write a short book on the subject. This I did, the only problem being that first having undergone Christmas, and then having to spend a further two months writing about it, I felt I had experienced two Christmases in five months and nearly boiled over like an old car on a hot motorway with venom and bile.

In fact on finishing the book, I was so convinced of its awfulness that I was amazed my publishers didn't turn it down. Fortunately, my dear Methuen editor, Geoffrey Strachan, hates Christmas too, so I found a sympathetic ear, and as they'd already publicised the fact that the book was coming in their autumn catalogue they were stuck with it.

I think, too, writers are the worst judges of their work. Some of the passages I've thought worthy of Dickens at the time have turned out to be the most shaming junk, whilst others written very quickly in the heat of rage and passion, take on a life of their own, and work all right.

*The O'Aga Family*

# How to Survive Christmas

## INTRODUCTION

In the pages of this book you will meet a Christmas family. They consist of a housewife, Scarlett O'Aga, so called because she is always bustling about not very efficiently, saying she's 'got to get on', and has a shiny red face all Christmas from toiling over the Aga. Like many women, Scarlett is an Xmasochist, who only feels she is doing the festive season properly if she worries herself into the ground. Scarlett is married to Noël, so called because he is absolutely no-elp-at-all. Noël has a Scroogian attitude towards Christmas, a mistress called Ms Stress, and an undemanding job in the City, which he feels justifies his spending most of the festive season slumped in front of the telly, or boozing with his cronies in the Dog and Trumpet. Noël and Scarlett have two teenage children, Holly and Robin, two little ones, Carol and Nicholas, and a dog called Difficult Patch.

Finally, if this book appears a little jaundiced, I must apologise. It is simply that, having lived through Christmas 1985 from October to December, I then had to relive it all over again from January to March, as I wrote the book; and two Christmases in six months is rather too much.

*Countdown*
>  *I can call spirits from the vasty deep freeze.*

My most depressing and abiding Christmas memory is of Bentalls of Kingston on Christmas Eve 1978, when a fat woman charged the men's toiletries counter and having bought ten bottles of Brut Aftershave, which were reduced because of battered packaging, announced in satisfied tones that that was all her menfolk's presents sewn up for Christmas 1979. Almost as frightful is the behaviour of eager beavers who rush off to sales on 27 December to buy Christmas cards and wrapping paper at half price for next year; or of the *Observer* Woman's Page who in December 1985 was telling its readers the best place to order their 'corn-fed gobblers' for Christmas 1986.

There is no doubt, on the other hand, that being prepared is the secret of a more harmonious Christmas. If Joseph had booked a room in advance, Jesus would not have been born in a stable, and as most of us, like Mary and Joseph, are taxed out of existence and very short of funds, it's better to spread the cost of Christmas over a few months.

From September onwards experts in the media will provide you with countdowns on Christmas activities:

> *Six weeks before Christmas:* make 550 tartlet cases and freeze (in our house you freeze anyway).
> *Five weeks before Christmas:* make 550 kiwi-fruit possets and freeze.
> *Four weeks before Christmas:* construct festive dinner-table centre-piece from gilded fir cones and milk-bottle tops and freeze.

Our hero, Noël, is so fed up with reading about Christmas preparations and listening to his wife Scarlett's endless recitation of tasks ahead that he fantasises wildly about a countdown à la Crippen:

> *Twenty days before Christmas:* mother-in-law pops in with Xmas gifts, batter her to death and freeze.
> *Ten days before Christmas:* father-in-law arrives in search of mother-in-law, batter him to death and freeze.
> *Seven days before Christmas:* Holly and Robin return from school and receive ditto treatment.
> *Two days before Christmas:* batter Scarlett, Nicholas, little Carol and Difficult Patch and freeze.
> *Christmas Eve:* buy one-way ticket to Rio.

### Christmas Eve

Christmas Eve - and the excitement starts to bite. Little Nicholas and Carol, already in a frenzy of excitement, are opening the penultimate door of their Advent calendars. The wireless is playing a jazzed-up version of 'God Rest Ye Merry Gentlemen'. For Scarlett, there's not much rest ahead, but she hopes everyone will be merry.

Granny and Grandpapa arrived yesterday. Having been woken twice in the night, firstly by the departed neighbours' burglar alarm, and secondly by the lodger coming in tight at three o'clock in the morning, they are downstairs by 8.30 a.m., shivering, their breath rising like incense. Scarlett can't light a fire because the log man still hasn't arrived.

Leaving the children with their grandparents, she escapes after breakfast to do some last minute shopping, and wishes she hadn't. Using holly as knuckledusters and Xmas trees as battering rams, shoppers are fighting their way ten deep along the pavement. Bad will is rampant.

At the supermarket there are no trolleys, because everyone's wheeled them five miles back to where they parked their cars and abandoned them. Scarlett wonders whether to start a home for Lost Trolleys.

'Mary was that mother mild', sings the loudspeaker, as inside the supermarket, mothers laden with loot bash and scream at older kiddies, and crash double prams of bawling twins into other prams. Terrible rows break out as last-minute presents are snatched from emptying shelves.

'I knew that carrier bag wouldn't 'old,' says a husband smugly, as a 100-ton oven-to-table lasagne dish, destined for Auntie Hilda who's been learning Italian at evening classes, crashes to the ground on a toddler's foot, and the queue is held up for another ten minutes as some distraught cashier brandishes a red net of nuts which has lost its price tag.

*'Shall I put on another Chippendale?'*

In department stores, men are sweating at ladies' underwear counters muttering, 'I'm sure Sharon said a 25-inch hip'; and girls are fighting their way to the men's jerseys counter, wondering whether Trevor would look more macho in burgundy or pine green.

In every pub a rugger scrum of husbands, waiting to meet brothers-in-law, so that they can swap over carrier bags of presents for their respective families, is drowning its sorrows. At the prospect of going home to their visiting in-laws, their sorrows come up for the third time.

Outside it is raining. Other husbands, drenched and weighed down by carrier bags, like First World War pack horses on the way to the trenches, wait miserably for their wives who have disappeared and do not know where the car is parked.

At home, early on Christmas Eve morning, families committed to away fixtures gloomily listen to news of fearful traffic build-ups on every motorway. The children are fighting over who is to sit in the front. Ten miles down the motorway, the baby throws up all over Mummy.

Hours later at tea-time they reach Granny.

'Here you are at last,' she cries in fluting reproach, rushing out in her medium-heeled court shoes and wool dress, embracing gingerly as she inhales a waft of dried sick, trying not to wince, as older children tread mud all over the carpet.

Soon they're all into the obstacle race of family tea and Granny asking if anyone wants sugar, milk, a knife, jam, butter or a piece of Christmas cake. Her son-in-law, who's got sugar when he doesn't take it, is wondering how soon he can decently ask Grandpapa for a drink; the older children sit round in silence, already jittery because they can't monopolise the television and the telephone. There is a scream as the baby attacks the Christmas tree and the floor is soon covered with broken glass.

Over to mid-afternoon at the home fixture. Noël returns in a vile temper, hung over from several office parties, and aware that because of guilt and lack of time he has spent far too much on not very exciting Christmas presents. Seeing the tasteful holly wreath, trimmed with red ribbon and gold-painted kiwi fruits, hanging like a life-buoy on the front door, he wishes he could float away on it to oblivion leaving Christmas behind.

Depressed that he's not going to see Ms Stress for ten days, the sight of scurrying set-faced Scarlett doesn't make him any happier. He won't get any sex this side of New Year. Perhaps he too ought to buy a green plastic container from Woolworth's to prevent needle drop.

Now, as a final straw, he finds that Nicholas and little Carol are seriously in need of tranquillisers, and that Scarlett has barricaded herself into the kitchen stuffing the turkey, listening to the Festival of the Nine Lessons and Carols from King's College, which seems to come from a different planet of serenity and light. What can those angelic choristers know of the fever and fret of Christmas?

Noël's mother-in-law, after her night interrupted by drunken lodgers etc., is having a rest, and his father-in-law wants to know which is the best route back to Petersfield on the day after Boxing Day, and what has happened to the cake tin with Battle Abbey on the lid in which they brought the home-made flapjacks. If only there were a test match to keep him quiet.

The old bugger is now looking at his watch, and saying he'd better go and rouse Mother, as it's Nearly Time for Tea. Some hope, mutters Noël, thinking of Scarlett, still stuffing in the kitchen.

Noël is dying to get drunk again, particularly as Scarlett's sister, her fascist husband and their out-of-control children, who are coming to stay for four days, are due any minute – which means that Noël won't have any pillows on his bed tonight. If only the older generation could get plastered as well, they wouldn't mind meals always being late.

Hearing screaming, Noël goes upstairs, where his children are killing each other, because Nicholas has eaten the sugar mouse Carol's teacher gave her for Christmas. Scarlett, having stuffed the turkey, has sneakily bolted upstairs and locked herself into the bedroom to wrap up her remaining presents. She had to grab the opportunity before the Sellotape, which is as elusive as Sir Percy Blakeney, went missing again.

Unfortunately, the Sellotape itself has already been extracted by some child from that contraption with a serrated edge that breaks the tape off where you need it. As a result, it is Scarlett's teeth which nearly break as the bloody Sellotape ridges, divides and crinkles, and finally emerges into the pack, as she cocoons and papooses her presents.

One needs two people to pack presents, reflects Scarlett, as one does to stuff the turkey – or anything really. She has to re-open several of the presents to see what she put in them. She forgot to get any tags, and maddeningly Biro doesn't show up on that ludicrously expensive dark shiny wrapping-paper. She's been gift-ripped off again. If only she'd bought cheap paper, then at least she'd have a white Santa's beard, or a snowman's belly to write on.

Now she's even run out of paper; but she is not going to risk tin foil after last year when that scatter cushion for Aunt Margery got rammed in the oven by mistake. So she's reduced to pulling out lining paper from her chest of drawers. At least it's better than the year she got plastered and wrapped up her own boots by mistake, and nearly had to go to midnight mass in bedroom slippers.

More screams outside; Granny, unable to find the landing light on an urgent trip to the loo, has fallen down the stairs.

Next moment, the door bell rings and Scarlett's sister and fascist husband and the three monsters arrive at the same time as the log man.

*Christmas dinner*
  *In for a pinny, in for a pounding.*

The kiddies, sleeping peacefully beside their unopened stockings, are woken up by Scarlett O'Aga staggering downstairs, holding her hangover on with one hand, at five o'clock in the morning to put the turkey in the oven. As it's the size of an ostrich, getting it out of the Aga to baste it is like parking a pink car in a garage with millimetres to spare.

Midday and Scarlett O'Aga, who is not very efficient, is beginning to feel overworked and flustered. Yesterday she made the brandy butter, the gravy and the potato croquettes, which only need heating up, and are so much less of a hassle than roast or mashed. But she still hasn't made the bread sauce, or done the sprouts.

But it's advisable not to be too prepared. Added to the feeling of martyrdom that behind every turkey there's a knackered housewife, Scarlett does have the perfect excuse not to go into the drawing-room, where the rest of the family, having exhausted all the conversations about Gordon's marriage, or the possibility of Gwen's pregnancy, are beginning to get seriously on each other's nerves. Now that the invited lame ducks have arrived, conversation gets even stickier.

Little Carol and Nicholas, already bored with their Transformer toys, are clamouring to assemble that toy from Hamleys, which requires both batteries and glue, neither of which can be bought until the shops open. Noël wishes that he could transform his mother-in-law into Ms Stress. She has finished her one glass of sherry – the turkey won't be ready for at least two hours – and his father-in-law is asking directions to Petersfield yet again. Noël has read that at Christmas dinner at Queen's College they bring in a boar's head with an orange in its mouth. He wishes he could ram an orange into his fascist brother-in-law's mouth, to stop him pontificating on about the evils of being taxed at source.

In the kitchen, Scarlett is being taxed at bread sauce. Ignoring the

*'Oh Scarlett, do go upstairs, have a bath and relax!'*

recipe, she has added extra breadcrumbs because it seems too thin, and now the whole thing's setting like cement. The turkey seems to be going backwards.

Noël shoves off to the pub on the excuse of getting brandy for the Christmas pudding, but really to ring Ms Stress. Getting her husband, Gordon, he loses his nerve and is reduced to asking him, Ms Stress and their entire family to their Christmas party next week, which he will somehow have to square with Scarlett. It's hardly the right moment now she is carrying a swimming pool of spitting turkey fat from the oven to the sink, and spitting even more because her sister, having done nothing to help, has just emerged, ravishing in a new pale blue cashmere Christmas cardigan. Scarlett hasn't even had time to change, and the Crème puff kept in the kitchen cupboard, on *Woman's Own*'s advice, to tone down a flushed face is proving utterly useless.

As a final straw, the cat has got into the dining-room and eaten the smoked salmon off two plates. Spreading it around again, hoping that no one will notice, Scarlett longs to leave home. Then they'd be sorry. But

*'Can we have it in front of the box?'*

alas, mini cabs are double fare over Christmas, and she'd never get one anyway.

In the drawing-room, Granny has a completely wet sleeve from putting her hand over her glass to stop her fascist son-in-law filling it up with Noël's champagne. At least there are sounds off of Noël carving.

In hospitals, surgeons, presumably the best carvers in the world, put on fancy dress to do the honours. Never offer to carve in someone else's house. One stockbroker, not famed for his tact, was spending Christmas with his mother-in-law and her new husband, Algy, who was in his seventies.

'Just as we were going in to dinner,' said the stockbroker, 'Algy made some crack about a friend of mine. I shut him up and said I wasn't going to have my friends insulted. Seeing Algy looking a bit bleak, and because being brought up in the war he carves jolly thin slices, I offered to carve for him and took over.

'Twenty minutes after we'd sat down to dinner we realised that Algy wasn't there. He'd gone to bed in a sulk and refused to come down again.'

Soon Noël has served everyone and, despite the fact that most of the children and at least three of the adults are drunk, and that short-sighted Grandpapa has mistaken a holly leaf for a sprout, and is desperately trying to spit it out, Scarlett feels almost happy when everyone drinks the cook's health.

Everyone also oohs and aahs at the blue flame round the Christmas pudding, except little Carol who, thinking the house is on fire, dives under the table.

*Boxing Day*

According to a doctor, the best day to be on call over the festive season is Christmas Day. Hardly anyone is ill: they all manage to postpone their heart attacks, bouts of flu, and appendicitis until Boxing Day, when the surgery is like the first day of the sales.

Boxing Day is also the time when anarchy breaks out in families, because there are no formal Christmas activities to distract people. My beautiful Polish crony, for example, reports that in 1984 the husband and father of a friend of hers mysteriously went missing for the whole of Boxing Day, and were finally run to ground locked in a heated greenhouse with a bottle of whisky and a week's newspapers.

'My new mother-in-law,' admitted a male friend, 'just managed to behave herself until Boxing Day, when she spent the whole time picking on the children from my first marriage, and pointing out how pathetically

'*Would it do for next Christmas, darling?*'

slow they were at Scrabble compared with my stepchildren, at whom she smiled with deep, understanding sympathy every time I raised my voice.'

The upper classes, of course, work off their Boxing Day aggression by murdering wildlife: many of them go shooting. Others attend the Boxing Day meet, with everyone capping everyone else's hangover stories, and grannies, after an indigestion-interrupted night, telling their friends with rather less conviction what fun it is to have a houseful. Often the Master's leftie daughter joins the Antis and knots everything up.

It's a pity that the middle classes can't exhaust their Boxing Day spleen in organised boxing matches, with Grandpapa in the dark blue corner, still asking the best route to Petersfield, doing ten rounds against Rich Great Aunt Phyllis, the south paw in the red corner.

*Post coitum, omnia animalia triste sunt.* After the orgasm of cooking Christmas dinner, poor Scarlett, wearily sweeping up a rubble of cracker mottoes, streamers and spat-out over-rummed truffles, is filled with despair at the prospect of turkey left-overs. Perhaps her fascist brother-in-law will demand right-overs.

*Noël's Fascist Brother-in-law*

Noël, thinking of leg-overs, and deciding to ring Ms Stress, slopes off to the Dog and Trumpet, which is crammed with people, so euphoric at having got rid of their in-laws or their grandchildren that they are buying gallons of whisky for everyone. He returns plastered at 2.30 p.m. and, passing the village shop, misreads the date for Christmas week dustbin collection, and insists that Scarlett puts out all the dustbins that night.

Boxing Day is appropriately named because hopelessly overtired, whining children keep asking their parents what they can do, and on being told sternly that they've got a Whole New Nurseryful of Toys, answer, 'So what?', and get their ears boxed.

In the afternoon, good fathers lock themselves into the nursery to play with the train sets they've given their children, or try to assemble toys, which turn out absolutely nothing like the picture on the box. Others try to assemble kites, but alas there is no wind, except in them; or, if there is, the kites get lodged high up in the trees, and the fathers break their ankles trying to get them down, and join the last day of the sales at the doctor's surgery.

Noël, by now trying to sleep off his hangover in front of the telly, is constantly interrupted by the shrill piercing voices of his children, and wonders why on earth Herod held off until 28 December to slaughter the innocents. Outside the sky is suddenly heavy with impending snow, but not as heavy as Noël's heart at the terrifying possibility that his in-laws may be snowed in, and not able to take any route home to Petersfield tomorrow.

Just as he's dropped off, the door bell goes. It's droppers-in – the enemy of droppers-off; usually a separated father who's got his children for Boxing Day and would rather they broke up Noël's place than his.

On Boxing Day, according to the *Sunday Telegraph*, Victoria Gillick and her husband bundle their ten children into a van and drive round the country dropping in on friends – like a sort of do-it-yourself Arnhem. Imagine the horror of having racing at Kempton interrupted by an implosion of Gillicks playing recorders and inveighing against the pill. Perhaps future generations will amend the last verse of 'The Twelve Days of Christmas' to 'Twelve Gillicks Descending'.

Next morning the badgers, or a passing stray dog, will have upended Scarlett's dustbins and scattered Christmas left-overs all over the lawn.

### Drinks parties

Christmas generally results in a spate of drinks with the locals, in which you stand about, easing your chilblained feet out of high heels, asphyxiated by everyone's toiletries, agreeing with grannies that you can't think how their daughters do it, as little satsumaholics charge out of control through your legs.

No one ever gets off with anyone at Boxing Day drinks, because everyone's wearing their new Christmas jerseys – in wildly unbecoming colours – so that Rich Great Aunt Phyllis who gave it them can see how thrilled they are with it. Instantly when they get home, the jersey is thrust back into its polythene bag because they 'want to keep it for best' but actually because they want to rush into Cheltenham tomorrow and change it.

Misanthropists always hold mulled wine or hot punch parties, because it gives them the perfect opportunity to stay in the kitchen stirring some vile brew and never circulate among the guests. Today you can even buy Glühwein ready made, and heat it up, which must be even more disgusting. The only time it's justified is as a first drink to warm people up on very cold days. When the roads are icy in the country, you get wives arriving at parties not only purple with cold but also with rage, because their husbands have insisted on driving the safer old Land Rover which has neither heating nor windows any more.

Sometimes you are invited round for drinks to meet people's parents. Noël seldom gets asked because he's inclined to get drunk and tell blue jokes to the mothers, and to irritate the fathers by accepting a third drink when there are unmistakable sounds from the kitchen of potatoes being noisily mashed.

Scarlett gets very embarrassed because Noël refuses to go to drinks with bores five miles away on the excuse that he might get breathalysed and lose his licence (he never minds if it's likely to be a good party). She then has to ring and say that Noël has flu, and invariably the hostess's sister on her way to the party apprehends him driving cheerfully up to the Dog and Trumpet.

# I'VE BEEN TO A MARVELLOUS PARTY

'We give parties,' wrote Frank Muir, 'because we are parting ourselves from feelings of guilt that people have had us round to their place, and we haven't had them back; and having them in one fell swoop is easier than two by two.'

Or, as a neighbour said delightfully last Christmas, 'Do come to drinks before lunch on 28 December – I'm asking all the people I can't face having to dinner.'

Here is a typical Christmas party. Noël, determined to keep things simple, has ordered curry from the local Indian takeaway, and told Scarlett not to fuss around with any salads. There is mutiny without any bounty over the guest list.

'You haven't asked *Tristram Piggott*!' storm Holly and Robin. 'He's a wimp – none of our friends will speak to him.'

As more and more people accept, Scarlett smuggles in extra supplies – to no avail. With hordes of visiting teenagers, the red apples for the Waldorf salad go in a morning, and several pounds of grapes, intended for a pudding, are reduced to hedgehogs of stalks overnight.

There's a tricky moment when Noël catches Scarlett in the pantry about to make mayonnaise for some closet coleslaw.

'Bottled will do,' he says firmly.

Meekly Scarlett concurs; the road to Hellmann's is paved with good intentions.

Party day dawns; the rooms are cleared. On Noël's instructions, the daily removes the ornaments from all the surfaces, but the house looks so awful that Scarlett puts them all back again. In a desperate attempt to force them out, she has put the indoor hyacinths in the hot cupboard.

Holly's sole contribution to the party is to drift in to the kitchen at midday in her nightie, say it's naff to have spoons with curry and everyone will expect pudding, and drift out again. All Scarlett's hints about Holly looking so nice 'in your Laura Ashley, darling' fall on deaf, if newly pierced, ears. Holly is hell bent on wearing Scarlett's new backless black.

Despite Noël's claim that even numbers don't matter, Scarlett is fretting about the shortage of spare men. Some girl rings up to cancel.

'Oh goodee, I mean oh gosh, how sad,' says Scarlett. 'We MUST get together in the New Year.'

Zero hour. The house is radiant with candles; the carpets stretch out, virginal. Fortunately, between parties, memory blots out the sheer terror that always grips her before everyone arrives, when all Scarlett craves is a quadruple vodka laced with Valium which would lay her out for ever. Outside, Robin and his mates, already blue with cold, wait stamping their feet, to help park the cars.

Then everyone starts arriving in a rush, eager for drinks and introductions, which Scarlett knows one must do properly, giving people a slight lead: 'This is Fiona: she's a tower of strength at the local Distressed Gentlefolk', or 'This is Charlie, who's just bought Badger Hall.'

It's obvious, too, that even numbers do matter. In one room is a surplus of beautiful women in the 30–40 age-group, who find being squeezed by Noël not *quite* enough. In another, a surplus of ravishing teenage boys with rooster hair stand about having 'When d'you go back,/next week/lucky sod, I go back on Monday and I've got mocks' conversations with one another.

Matters are not helped when a mother expected to bring three exquisite teenage daughters turns up saying that they've all gone skiing with their father; nor when Holly and all her teenage friends take fright and bolt themselves into her bedroom.

'Don't be anti-social,' screams Scarlett, like Wee Willy Wrinkly, through the lock.

She is also very tight-lipped because Ms Stress, having been asked by Noël, who never got round to telling Scarlett, has just rolled up with her ghastly gay husband, Gordon, and two boot-faced children, followed by a whole busload of Noël's cronies from the Dog and Trumpet. There's no way the food's going to last out.

Success at last! One of Scarlett's forty-year-old girlfriends is nose to nose with a beautiful youth with an earring in his left ear. Despite the children telling her hundreds of times, Scarlett can't remember whether left or right means that you're gay. She does hope her friend isn't squandering her wiles on a wrong-sided earring.

Scarlett knows that you're not expected to enjoy your own parties – just act as an unpaid waitress and rescue people whose eyes are beginning to glaze out of drink or boredom – but this one is quite out of control, and Noël says that they can't eat for at least ten minutes. The place seems so much more crowded with all those padded shoulders and there's a yelling bottleneck in the hall, where people are fighting their way into the next room to see if it's more exciting, and, finding it isn't, fighting their way back again. Scarlett's introduced everyone to everyone, and people are beginning to put their hands over their glasses, and say 'I'll fall over if I don't eat.' Difficult Patch is in the hot cupboard with the hyacinths.

Upstairs are scenes of Petronian debauchery, with necking teenagers, their braces locking, occupying every bed and sofa. At least they're too busy devouring each other to want any dinner.

Thank God, it's ready at last. Everyone else swarms into the kitchen and tucks into the curry. Most of the salads go too, but not the cheese which Scarlett panic-bought in Cirencester that morning. She must remember in future that no one eats Stilton at parties unless you provide Gold Spot or Polos for pudding.

The most frequent request now is for glasses of water because the curry is so hot, and for kitchen roll as another glass of red wine is kicked over on the carpet.

Music is now pounding out of Noël's study. The next hurdle is getting people to dance. After food, they tend to sit around for an hour – like no swimming after lunch.

Teenage boys keep coming up to Scarlett and saying, 'Holly has asked me to stay the night.' 'No no no,' screams Scarlett hysterically.

*'Oh, sorry!'*

At least they're dancing now. But still the generations inhibit each other.

'Don't watch us,' grumbles Holly as Scarlett peers into the darkened room to see if she or Robin are getting off with anyone.

Later, however, circling dreamily in the muscular arms of the local cricket captain, Scarlett opens her eyes, and through the fireflies of illicit teenage cigarettes sees Holly and her best friends giggling at her in mock disapproval.

Explaining afterwards that the cricket captain was 'just something to hang on to when one is tired, like the strap in the tube', doesn't wash either.

Noël and Ms Stress have been missing for hours; perhaps they've joined Difficult Patch in the hot cupboard. One of Ms Stress's boot-faced children is trying to murder the other with one of the hired knives. And ghastly gay Gordon has been chatting up Robin for much too long.

By 2.00 a.m. the party is fragmenting. Scarlett doesn't even mind that the only thing she's run out of is salt, which now lies like patches of snow over the wine stains on the carpet.

At 5.00 a.m., Noël, a hard core of teenagers, and sundry drunks from the Dog and Trumpet are playing Twenty-one Aces. Scarlett collapses into bed. Did she dream it, or did she really hear Holly joyfully screaming that Daddy's just eaten two Bonios?

Surfacing four hours later, she finds several pale teenage boys who seem to have stayed the night after all.

'Sorry, there weren't enough girls for you,' says Scarlett.

'Oh, it was a great party,' they chorus. 'Alastair was sick, Henry was sick, so was Marcus, and Anthony and the Jones boys.'

Scarlett thanks God that Robin's going back to school next week to dry out.

Some of the silver seems to be missing, too.

'The night of the short knives,' says Noël.

Scarlett faints when she peers round the door of Holly's room and finds the floor littered with broken glass, fag ends, 20 empty bottles, 15 cups, Scarlett's backless dress, and Difficult Patch finishing up the half eaten plates of curry.

At least the mess is confined to one room. Shutting the door firmly, Scarlett concentrates on the wonderful selection of scarves, gloves and coats that have been left behind by departing drunks; and there are still all the party thank-you letters to look forward to.

*New Year's Eve*

A ghastly hype. For some extraordinary reason, people, particularly those who are unmarried, believe that they have utterly failed socially if they aren't asked anywhere on New Year's Eve. In fact, they would be far more sensible to go to bed early with a good book. If you go out, mini cabs are double fare; you're liable to get your house burgled and yourself mugged or raped; and the entire police force is lurking in bushes waiting to catch home-going motorists.

If you feel compelled to give a New Year's Eve party, don't invite people to arrive too early or they'll go off the boil before midnight. Nine o'clock to nine thirty is about right, which will give them time to have a few drinks and dinner before you gather them all into one room to celebrate the passing of the old year. Do put on the radio at midnight with all speakers blaring, so that everyone can hear the chimes of Big Ben, and start kissing everyone else's wives and husbands and generally behaving badly.

A girlfriend summed up the whole thing. Just as midnight finished striking, and we were all happily knocking back champagne, from a dark corner she could be heard muttering, 'Bloody January again.'

*Twelfth Night*

At home poor Scarlett is slowly ploughing through a vast mountain of ironing, because the children all go back to school next week. She has put the Christmas decorations back in their box, and the tree outside the back door (it seemed such a shame to burn it when it had given them such pleasure) and swept up the pine needles.

She dreads taking down the Christmas cards, because it makes the sitting-room look so drab and colourless. If only she hadn't spent so much on Christmas they could afford to brighten it up with new curtains or at least new cushions. Later she's got to pack up and post back to Petersfield the gloves, boots and quilted hot-water bottle that Granny left behind, omitting to point out that Difficult Patch has punctured the hot-water bottle.

Upstairs, above the pounding surf beat of Robin's record player, she can hear Nicholas and little Carol screaming at each other. Nor can she expect any help in packing the trunk from Holly, who is locked in her room, reduced to the depths of misanthropy by mugging up St Luke for mock O-levels.

Scarlett feels depressed. Sadly she no longer has the excuse that it's still Christmas to justify the midday nip (a treble vodka and tonic) to keep her going; all the parties are over, and she's already broken her New Year's resolution to lose weight. Christmas, with all its faults, was a break in the monotony of life. But at least she's her own boss, unlike poor Noël, who today went back to the relentless treadmill of the office; and who now, unknown to Scarlett, is roughing it at the Ritz over a three-hour lunch with Ms Stress, trying to piece together who it was that he mauled or insulted at the office party before Christmas.

If only, muses Scarlett, one could have Christmas every five years, then it would really be something to look forward to, like a royal wedding, and she and Noël wouldn't be almost bankrupted every January. If they could give up both drink *and* Christmas they'd be quite well off.

Her reverie is interrupted by little Carol howling down the stairs that Nicholas has decapitated her new Christmas doll, because she'd managed to wipe all his computer games.

'Never mind,' says Scarlett comfortingly, 'it's only 353 days until next Christmas.'

# TURN RIGHT AT THE SPOTTED DOG

In 1982, the same year we left Putney, I left *The Sunday Times* for the *Mail on Sunday*. In 1987 we published a collection of pieces from the latter newspaper called *Turn Right at the Spotted Dog*. Included are a couple of pieces on our rural adventures as we adjusted to country life. But on the whole I have found it easier to concentrate on books rather than journalism since I've lived down here, and the bulk of the material about Gloucestershire will I hope appear in a sequel to *The Common Years* to be written in the early nineties.

Writers continually worry that they are 'going off' and I sometimes feel my *Mail on Sunday* pieces lack the bite and freshness of the early *Sunday Times* pieces. On the other hand, *Excuse Me, Your Slips are Showing*, about girls watching cricket, and the *Teen Commandments*, about teenage behaviour, are as acid and beady as I hope anything I wrote at the beginning of my career. Finally, this book would not be complete without a tribute to the lovely Cotswold village into which we moved and which has made us so happy and welcome. This piece ends the book.

# Turn Right at the Spotted Dog

## RAT RACE

I am very much looking forward to my first Christmas in Gloucestershire, but wish it would stop raining. An even worse dampener has been put on the proceedings by the prolonged disappearance of the pub cat, which Leo my husband brought down from London on the excuse that it was an early Christmas present. Fazed, no doubt, by the thought of spending Christmas with four neutered toms, she bolted through the cat-door her second morning and went AWOL.

*Wednesday*

Endlessly comb the surrounding woods and fields looking for cat.

'A fox will have her head off,' says the gardener knowingly, then, seeing my face, hastily adds, 'But don't worry, she'll come back.'

Just hunting desperately for Christmas decorations, which also have gone AWOL in the move, when Stan (the male half of the couple who have come to live with us) gives a shout that the cat's back. Foolishly shrieking with joy, we converge on the hall. Terrified by the din, the cat bolts out into the night. Determined to lure her back, we open the cat-door, and leave large plate of chicken beside it.

*Thursday*

Gratified that the chicken has been eaten – but suspect junior dog is responsible.

*Friday*

Pub cat, now known as the Lochness Mouser, is sighted near the shed. Rain continues to sweep in great curtains across the valley – I'm dreaming of a wet Christmas.

*Saturday*

Junior dog rushes in, crackling. Outside we find badgers have raided our dustbins and scattered tins and chicken bones all over the lawn. Clearing it up, Leo sees large rat strolling past. It gives him an old-fashioned look and trips over a Guinness can.

*Sunday*

Mouse appears on terrace. Leo is so enchanted he fetches it a piece of Brie. I point senior dog's head mousewards, but she looks everywhere except at the offending rodent.

*Tuesday*

Return from Christmas shopping in London to be greeted by Viv, who says that last night all the water went off, including loos; that the pump is on its last legs; that the washing machine blew her across the room; that the small mouse Leo gave Brie to on the terrace is actually a baby rat and growing fat; and that a hundred rats have moved in under the terrace.

*Wednesday*

Deeply disappointed by performance of indoor hyacinth bulbs. Their nasty white beaks sticking a quarter inch above the bulb fibre show signs of being nibbled. Try not to contemplate by whom.

*Thursday*

Gloomily listening to ever-continuing downpour when I hear commotion outside. Find Viv and our two dogs standing on kitchen table, our four cats calmly eating turkey-flavoured Whiskas, as a huge rat saunters across the floor. Join Viv and dogs on table, and give stern pep talk to cats. At this moment two carol singers appear and sheepishly sing 'Silent Night'. Tell them this is singularly inappropriate carol for this house, and overtip.

*Following Wednesday*

Rats still in evidence. Our gardener tells me the place is infested because all the rats have been flooded out of their holes by the rain. Perhaps they should build a gnawer's ark.

Stay up very late doing Christmas cards. Jump out of my skin at sound of squeaking, but realise it is junior dog having a nightmare.

Go downstairs to lock up, wearing thigh boots, to find our two black tom cats in the hall, saying 'After you, Claude, no, after you, Cecil'. Lying between them is a gigantic twitching rat. Cling on to banisters for support but feel I must put it out of its misery. Box file too light, eventually finish it off with *Collins English Dictionary*, which defines rat as a long-tailed murine rodent.

To think we left London to get away from the rat-race.

### Thursday

Council of war at breakfast: no more food to be put out, cat-door to be boarded up. I ring the Council who refer me grandiosely to the Rodent Operative, who promises to come tomorrow. Ring Leo in London, who refuses to take the whole thing seriously, and suggests we put an ad in the village shop for a pied piper.

Sleepless night, listening to rats scurrying, foxes barking, presumably after pub cat, and worrying about the forty-six presents I have yet to buy and whether the turkey will fit into the Aga.

### Friday

Temperature dropping fast. Return from village to find Rodent Operative has arrived. A good-looking, winning young man, he refuses all offers of a Christmas drink – perhaps he doesn't want to be pie-eyed piper – but systematically goes round putting down poison, while Stan boards up all the holes. The Rodent Operative also says we may later need rat de-odorant. As it's Christmas why not after-shave as well?

### Saturday

Hear foxes barking again all night. Milkman says it is going to snow. Feel I must decorate house and ask gardener why our holly tree doesn't have any berries. As he is explaining it is a male tree which doesn't produce any, we both suddenly see several berries on a top branch and look away hastily.

Just having grisly vision of grinning foxes sitting in the wood warming their ginger paws in front of the fire, while the corpse of the little cat rotates on a spit, when suddenly I hear a blood-curdling scream. Rush downstairs to find Viv in the kitchen, with mascara running down her face.

'What's happened?' I whisper.

'She's come home,' she sobs.

And there was the little cat, terribly thin, raging with temperature but still managing to purr like a jumbo jet in Stan's arms. So it was fatted calves all round. The prodigal cat had returned and for her there was to be no more abiding in the fields. For the first time in ages we all slept like logs.

'Twas the week before Christmas and all through the house not a creature was stirring, not even a rat. And a very merry Christmas from me and the pub cat.

## TURN RIGHT AT THE SPOTTED DOG

We have now spent eight long months in this wonderfully hospitable county, but as Nouveau-Rustics, we are still trying to come to terms with the social complications of rural life.

Dining out, for example, is great fun – if you get there. There's no *A-Z* in Gloucestershire. Most people are too grand to put names outside their houses, and my rusty shorthand is quite incapable of getting down those rattled-off instructions: 'You turn right at the Spotted Dog, then you come to a *hideous* modern bungalow – well that's not us . . .'

The result is blazing rows on the way to every party, with Leo careering round the same perilous country lanes saying he's bloody going home, and me, tearfully envisaging no dinner and social ostracisation, saying: 'I'm sure they said left at the Spotted Dog.'

In the end we always have to ask. It must be hell being a yokel in Gloucestershire. Every Saturday your evening viewing is interrupted by twerps in dinner jackets saying: 'Can you possibly tell me the way to the Smith-Binghams?'

The chief problem, however, for the Nouveau-Rustic is sartorial. In London it never mattered what I wore. Here I get it wrong every time. The first dinner party we went to was very grand. I rolled up in high heels, a knee-length velvet skirt and a pleated satin shirt (which had pleats going both ways after twenty miles under a seat belt) to find my hostess in pink cords and a Guernsey sweater.

On my second jaunt, Leo was away. I was invited this time for supper in the kitchen. Natch, I put on cords and a jersey, to be greeted by a vast dinner party, the men in dark suits, the women in silk shirts and velvet skirts, all the silver on the dining room table, and – most un-London of all – a spare man for me who wasn't queer.

The next invitation said 'black tie'. So I deduced we should dress up this time. Alas, the week before, Leo split his dinner jacket trousers at some binge in London, and borrowed a pair from a friend of six foot six. Consequently his cummerbund had to be tied under his armpits like the top half of a strapless bikini. He also found a large wine mark on the lapel of his white dinner jacket, and covered it with an *Animals in War* badge. I wore a long black dress, which plunged to the navel.

We arrived to find all the women covered up, mostly in short wool dresses, several of the men without ties, and our host wearing green cords, an old green coat, a blue striped shirt, a green bow tie and brown suede shoes.

As the evening sun slanted cruelly on Leo's white dinner jacket and my over-exposed, middle-aged bosom, we felt like two Crufts poodles with pompom tails and *diamanté* collars let loose at a rough shoot. Happily it turned out a marvellous evening, with poodles and gundogs frisking merrily together – and, unlike London, no one talked about house prices or education. And that's another thing, never ask men in the country what they do for a living. Very few of them seem to do anything.

I also notice that it's the drawing room tables who seem to wear the long skirts down here, and everyone covers up not only their bosoms but also their plant pots – with flowered vases called cache-pots. Perhaps I should wear a cache-pot to the next party.

But having received all this lovely hospitality, we now have to pay it back. In London we never gave dinner parties. During the week we were knackered, and at the weekend everyone pushed off to the country, and anyway we'd got nothing to give them with.

Consequently, when we had our first dinner party in Gloucestershire, we had to go out and buy three sets of plates, three sets of glasses, knives, table mats, even napkins. Kitchen roll – like patriotism – is not enough.

The party was a moderate success. The pâté tasted of blendered thermal underwear, the pudding of uncooked marmalade. But the venison produced by Leo and my housekeeper Viv was brilliant. The guests included two local landowners and their wives, a couple who weekend down here and their house guests, who turned out to be a boilermaker from Stockport and his wife.

There was a sticky moment when the boilermaker announced to the straighter of the landowners that he always kissed his son on the mouth when they met.

'How old is your boy?' asked the landowner.

'Twenty-seven,' said the boilermaker.

And a riotous moment when the boilermaker's wife asked Leo how he'd cooked the venison, whereupon Stan, my housekeeper's husband – who was serving the pudding – proceeded to tell her. Five minutes later, despite vicious kicks on the ankle from Viv and nine people unserved, the venison hadn't even reached the oven but was still being larded with green bacon and garlic pellets.

No one appeared to drink too much. But after saying goodbye to everyone, I found Leo crawling round the kitchen pretending to be an outside labrador, and Stan sleeping peacefully on the landing.

And now summer is here I am getting nervous about the garden. When people come to dinner, it's still light and they can gaze out of the window on the crimes, as Nouveau-Rustics, we've already committed: planting poplars, which obscure a view, or, even more heinous, putting in strident colours.

'Never have red in a Cotswold garden,' my neighbour told me the other night. 'Pink, blue, yellow, silver and, best of all, white, and do plant your clumps in odd numbers.' And I prayed that my two newly installed red-hot pokers wouldn't suddenly let me down by flashing at her over the terrace wall. But to prove her point, the local nursery told me that recently Princess Michael completely denuded them of plants – but only white ones. It's better to be dead than red in a Gloucestershire garden.

But we're getting on very well. Last week we gave our second dinner party. Among the guests were the new Lord and his wife, who moved into the village even more recently than we did. Viv got so carried away she took the afternoon off to have her hair put up, and wore her wedding dress. The new Lord, perhaps feeling that this was what an aristocrat should wear to dine with the literati, rolled up very handsome in a Fair Isle jersey and one of those hairy tweed coats heroines bury their faces in at the end of romantic novels.

In fact local interest has been slightly diverted away from this New Lord on to an even newer Lord, who's just moved into the next door village and who dropped in on Monday to warn us that his new sheep had jumped out of their field and been chasing dogs all over the valley all the weekend.

He was another surprise. I always thought people who kept sheep wore dung-coloured clothes to blend into the countryside, but he turned up in a pink polo-necked jersey and tartan trousers. Not unlike my very good friend and social adviser, the milkman, who raised two fingers to massive Tory bias on polling day, going on his rounds in a scarlet sweater and a red check shirt. I nearly asked him to stand in the garden beside my two red-hot pokers and form an odd-numbered clump.

The answer, of course, is not to care what anyone thinks and be yourself. But I'm not sure who myself is. I went to a party recently in the London house immortalised last month when Anna Ford chucked a glass of wine in the face of her ex-boss Jonathan Aitken. As I entered the room, my hostess advanced towards me smiling: 'Hullo Polly,' she said.

# THE TEEN COMMANDMENTS

I was thirteen when I wrote my first book. It was called *The Teen Commandments*, and consisted of advice to parents on how to behave and not irritate their children to death. Sadly, before I could ram the book into a safe, and profit from its sage counsel in later life, I lost it.

To jog my memory, and in a faint hope of reducing the guerrilla warfare at home, I asked my own children for their list of Dos and Donts for parents.

Top of the list was unanimously: Parents should not pry.

This involved asking questions such as: 'Where are you going?' 'Who with? Will you be back for supper?' 'Who was that on the telephone?' 'Why were you so long on the telephone?' 'Was it a good party?' And (worst of all), 'Did you meet anyone nice?'

Parents should not then resort to MI5 tactics, ringing up best friend Louise's mother, asking if Louise had a nice time at the party, then casually asking if Louise mentioned Emily getting off with anyone – and then saying, 'Oh, his parents are supposed to be rather nice, aren't they?'

Parents should not force their children to go to frightful parties where they won't know anybody, on the premise that they might meet Master Right.

Parents should cook and foot the drinks bill for their children's parties, but not attend them. Nor should they invite any guest without consultation – just because a boy washes and goes to Winchester, it doesn't stop him being a wimp.

Parents should never make comparisons, saying: 'When I was your age, I had hordes of boys from Eton, Marlborough and Radley after me, but we never did anything, of course – we were so innocent in those days.'

Parents should not regurgitate the past to the accompaniment of violins, recounting how during the war they had nothing to eat, only water at meal times, and had to wash up, dry and put away because there were no dishwashers.

Parents should not automatically turn the volume knob 45 degrees to the left whenever they enter the room. They must appreciate that homework is only possible if stereo, radio and television are blaring. They must never storm into the sitting room, howling: 'I'm not having you glued to television on a lovely day,' then spend the rest of the afternoon themselves watching the rugger international.

Parents should share everything with their children: hair-driers, belts, make-up, and that utterly gross, yucky black polo-neck jersey, which was rejected with screams of mirth in the summer holidays but which has suddenly come back into fashion.

Parents should never make personal remarks. If their children wish to appear with their hair like an upside down lavatory brush, dipped in plum jam, that's their problem.

Parents should provide a twenty-four-hour taxi service and always lend their children the car to practise driving. After all, Volvos are built to withstand a few gateposts and stone walls.

Parents should not be inconsistent, howling with laughter over Adrian Mole and videos of *Animal House*, drooling over Madonna, then going berserk if their children behave in a remotely similar fashion. They should not hold forth on the perils of teenage drinking while clutching a second triple whisky. Nor is a half-empty packet of Rothmans in a trouser pocket proof of heroin addiction.

Parents should never dictate their children's diet. Four Mars bars, seventeen packets of crisps, two pounds of Granny Smiths, a litre of Coke and four mugs of hot chocolate – leaving the relevant milk-coated pans in the sink – are the ideal substitute for three meals a day.

Parents should never answer 'Yes' to the question: 'Is there anything I can do?' Nor make the most biddable child do the most housework.

Parents must appreciate that there's no time like the future. Bedrooms can be tidied next year, washing brought down next week, as long as it's then done immediately, as the child needs it before lunch.

Parents should not throw tantrums over inessentials, such as every towel in the house wet under the bed, topless ketchup bottles, encrusted forks in ancient half-filled baked bean tins behind the sofa, and twelve newly ironed shirts hopelessly creased because someone's rummaged through the hot cupboard after a pair of tights.

Children should not lose too much sleep – their mothers and fathers may just be going through a difficult, rebellious age.

But sadly, as Anthony Powell once pointed out: 'Parents are often a great disappointment to their children. They seldom fulfil the promise of their early years.'

# EXCUSE ME, YOUR SLIPS ARE SHOWING

Two ravishing young girls came to cricket last Sunday. It was their first visit, they said. As their carefully ironed cotton dresses flapped frantically against their blue frozen legs, and through the blizzard the white distant figures of the boyfriends might easily have been mistaken for polar bears, they looked utterly bewildered.

Now that spring finally appears to have arrived, many more girls all over the country will be experiencing their first cricket match. As a grizzled campaigner of twenty-four summers, I feel I should give them a few tips.

For a start, as a cricket groupie, you abandon all lie-ins. Most cricket matches are at least fifty miles from home and go on all day, so it's up earlier than the lark.

Secondly, one's clothes are always wrong. If it's tropical when you leave home, it's bound to be arctic or pouring when you arrive. The only answer is layers: a Barbour, over a Puffa, over a Guernsey, over a shirt, over thermal underwear, so you can peel off. Don't forget the shirt. Zero temperatures at home, by the law of sod, mean heatwaves at the ground, and you'll be microwaved in a cashmere jersey.

Not that it matters what you look like, since you abandon all sex appeal the moment you reach the ground. There is something about donning virgin white and playing cricket that temporarily de-sexes the male. Cricket, remember, is the only sport – like a strip in reverse – where the crowd clap a player for putting his jersey *on*.

Rather like prep school boys who insist that their mother comes to speech day and then ignore her, a cricketer feels it's wet to be seen talking to his girl friend, and it's not cricket to chat up anyone else's.

Thus an average day will go rather like this. You arrive at the ground to find that the opposition, which is probably called something daft like the Fleet Street Fairies or the Bisley Buffaloes, is as usual five men short. Joyfully your beloved will scuttle on to the field to make up the numbers. When the rest of the Fairies eventually show up, he'll promptly put on a white coat.

This, alas, is not the cue for you to indulge your handsome-vet-and-comely-pet-owner fantasies, he is merely off to umpire. Umpiring will be followed by a stint in the scorebox, only interrupted when he has to bat at number eleven. Whereupon he takes a spirited swipe and is clean bowled. He then spends the rest of the match fielding.

If a very good looking player gives you a hot, come-hither smile, run like hell. He is not after your body. He is a weekend father, or a father who's only been allowed out if he takes the children. He will have three little monsters in the boot and will want you to look after them all day. Ditto if he wants you to look after his dogs – unless they're large and furry, and can double up as a rug.

Take loads to eat. Some clubs only provide lunch and tea for players, and there is a feeling anyway that because the chaps have been indulging in manly exercise, women ought to hold back. Being outside all day, albeit doing nothing, makes you wildly hungry. Cricket in fact is the antithesis of those fasting, resting Sundays so beloved by women's magazines, when you lie in bed sipping lemon juice with sliced turnip on your face. Last week, I ate six ham sandwiches, three egg sandwiches, half a Battenburg cake and four scotch eggs, to mop up the alcohol which was keeping out the cold – which leads me on to:

Take loads of drink. Many pavilions don't admit women, and most only provide beer. Last Sunday I got through one bottle of vodka, one of whisky, four bottles of Muscadet and six cans of lager, admittedly aided by two dozen other spectators similarly suffering from hypothermia.

Your survival kit should also include a Jeffrey Archer, or at least two Dick Francis (you have twelve hours to kill), all the Sunday papers (at least players wanting to read them will be forced to come and talk to you) and green foundation to tone down your purple wind-fretted face.

When your boyfriend is batting, you *must* watch the game. If you find it confusing, remember batsmen tend to run after they've hit the ball. If they hit it a long way, for some reason they don't. If it strikes you on the ankle it's a four, on the head it's a six.

Do not clap and jump up and down noisily when someone drops a catch, even if it's clouted by your beloved: it's considered unsporting. Do not flash. It's tempting to keep looking in the mirror to check how ghastly you look, but it may flash sun in the batsman's eyes.

Do not talk as the bowler is coming up to bowl. If you get really lonely, get up and walk in front of one of those big white screens, just as the bowler is running away from you. Everyone in the ground will then shout and wave at you.

Never go to the loo: something exciting like a wicket falling or your boyfriend hitting a six always happens. However he gets out, say: 'That was an *absolutely* brilliant ball. Even Botham wouldn't have got near it.'

When he's bowling or fielding, put on dark glasses, so he won't know you're watching, and get stuck into J. Archer. Then just before close of play, nip round to the scorer, and find out who your beloved has caught and bowled and congratulate accordingly.

Keep a fiver for after the game. He'll be provided with beer from a bottomless, endlessly circulating jug, and will be so engrossed in his own innings, he'll forget about your drink. If you find yourself stuck for conversation with one of the players, merely ask: 'What do you think about Boycott?' The ensuing eulogy/apoplexy will last at least fifteen minutes.

Never offer to do the teas. It's very hard work, and you always get the quantities wrong and are forced to divide a Bakewell tart between thousands, or to eat fish paste for the rest of your life.

Never offer to wash cricket sweaters, they always shrink or run. Never marry the club secretary. Your spare time will be spent typing out fixtures or team lists. One girlfriend said it was only after four years, she realised A. N. Other wasn't a player.

Never marry the captain either, or your night's sleep will be punctuated by players crying off tomorrow's game on the excuse that they've 'suddenly been laid low – retch – by the most awful – retch – shellfish'. After they've finished retching they put down the telephone and say cheerfully to their wives: 'That's OK, darling, we can lunch with Fiona after all.'

Unless you are truly hooked avoid Test Matches; they go on too long. I've never forgotten hearing a young man at Lords saying heartily to his shell-shocked fiancée, 'Don't worry, Lavinia, you'll get the hang of it by the fifth day.'

Having said all that, I must concede that cricketers away from the ground are the nicest men in the world. For cricket as a game requires unselfishness, imagination, patience, honour, perseverance, the ability to withstand boredom and to smile at misfortune, never letting it throw you off balance. All crucial qualities in a husband.

And there are blissful moments – in 1961 at Headingley when two mongrels ran on to the field with a banana skin and held up play for two minutes. In 1964, when my husband made a hundred against the Bank of England after a morning wedding reception. In 1976, when there were endless heat waves, and finally in 1982, at a charity match in Somerset, when an inebriated middle-aged streaker rushed on to the field, and Lesley Crowther who was fielding was heard to remark: 'I couldn't see what she was wearing, but it certainly needed ironing.'

# PLEASE KEEP TO THE FOOTPATH

From the top road, the village of Bisley, with its church spire and ancient blond houses, nestles in a cleavage of green hills like an insurance poster promising a serene and happy retirement.

The promise is not an illusion. After twenty-five years in London, we moved here four years ago. There have been no regrets, probably because we were incredibly lucky. Some villages are unfriendly and soulless, others hopelessly intrusive. But we have stumbled on a magic one, where the old are cherished, the widowed or divorced comforted, and the newcomer welcomed. When we arrived, a local hostess even gave a big party to introduce us to everyone.

There is such a strong community spirit, however, that they do prefer new arrivals to settle here, and contribute something to the life of the village. During our first year, I had frightful flak which totally mystified me. Every time I walked up the High Street, someone would come up to me and sourly accuse us of planning to move on.

This, I eventually discovered, was because everyone in the doctor's waiting room was flicking through the tattered copy of last year's *Country Life* which had originally offered our house for sale. Not checking the date, they automatically assumed it was on the market again.

The acid test, however, was whether we were going to live here, or just use the house as a weekend retreat. Weekenders who strut around in ginger tweeds, force up the prices of cottages beyond the purse of young local couples, and don't use the local shops, are not popular. There was great glee last winter in a nearby village, because some arriving weekenders turned their car over a few miles outside. No one was hurt but their Jaguar was irredeemably impregnated with imported curry destined for Saturday's dinner party.

Not that anyone needs to import anything here. Besides a marvellous hairdresser, an excellent garden centre and a superb restaurant in the High Street, there is an amazingly sophisticated village shop which sells everything from videos to vine leaves, and attracts custom from miles around.

And there's so much to read in their windows: 'My pet chicken is missing,' says a current notice. 'He is four, and has vanished from my garden. He is very frenndly and is cawled Mary.' [sic] And you only have to pop inside the shop to find out anything – whether your daily or your secretary or even your husband is about to leave you. The gossip is so good, in fact, that a local peer implored the owners to install a chaise-longue so he could lie listening all day.

Most villages thrive on gossip, but are outwardly unfazed by it. No one betrayed any excitement four years ago, when a handsome Marquess and his beautiful wife moved into the big house, but when the leaves came off the trees, it was noticed how many of the locals had taken up bird-watching.

Equally in my brother's village in Northamptonshire, there was wild excitement when a member of Shawaddywaddy moved in and, even better, decided to get married in the village church. On the day, the police put yellow cones along the High Street and gathered in force to hold back the crowds. My brother, intent on weeding the herbaceous border, got very tightlipped when my sister-in-law, my two nieces and my mother, aged eighty, all clambered up a ladder on to the flat roof of the garage and settled down with deck-chairs and several bottles for an afternoon's viewing. To their disappointment, only six guests and no rock stars showed up.

Back here in our village, they've recently introduced a Neighbourhood Watch Scheme, which gives everyone a splendid excuse to snoop legitimately. Jeff, our Saturday gardener, who, in between bursts of frenzied weeding, sleeps in his car in the drive, was outraged recently to be roused from deep post-elevenses kip by the police who'd been alerted that a suspicious-looking character was parked near the Coopers' house casing the joint.

But if you're not into snooping, there's still masses to do here: skittle evenings, pony club discos, clay shoots, men-only chocolate cake competitions at the local fête, lectures on glass blowing at the WI and wonderful tobogganing and skiing in the winter.

Indeed it's a good idea to wait a few months before joining anything when you arrive at a village. A bookseller friend who retired to nearby Oxfordshire, and was worried he might be bored, got himself on to every village committee in the first six months, and spent the next ten years extricting himself.

Although my husband has joined the British Legion and the Cricket Club, which slightly makes up for my non-participation, I still feel guilty that I don't have time to run up a sponge for the Distressed Gentlefolk. Recently I went along to their Nearly New Sale, and found the usual lack of charity which surrounds charity events prevailing:

'Look, look at that lovely bargain I got for 50p,' said a fat woman brandishing a tweed skirt.

'You'll never get into that,' said her friend, crushingly. 'That was mine.'

Living here in Bisley in fact is rather like being in an overseas posting in the army. Not only do most of us wear the khaki uniform of Barbours and green gum boots, but just as you can't afford to have a screaming match with the Major's wife over the bridge table, as you'll meet her at the Colonel's drinks party that evening, in a village you can't sack or fight with someone, as you'll find yourself stuck beside them in the hairdresser's next morning.

Nor can you bellow at some dog walker for trespassing on your land, because ten to one, you'll have to eat humble pie because your *own* dog has used their guinea pig as a cocktail snack. A friend nearby, whose Jack Russell ambitiously seduced a prize winning Airedale, tried to placate the enraged owner by offering to whizz the Airedale down to the vet and pay for an injection to abort the puppies, only to be told that the Airedale's owner was Roman Catholic and passionately disapproved of abortion. The row continues.

People in the country have a slightly different attitude to animals. If a pheasant waddles across the road, they are not above urging you to accelerate; and their dogs tend to sleep outside, and, bored and cold, start wandering round the village. One, howling recently in the High Street at midnight, was pelted with pickled onions by the woman living opposite. Unfortunately, the following day, an old lady slipped on one and broke her leg.

Village life is happier too if, again like the army, you stick to a few rules. Keep to the footpaths; look after the badgers; don't cut down trees unless they're dead and you intend to plant some more; pay all local bills on the nail; say 'please' and 'thank you' in the village shop or you won't get bread saved for you when the village gets snowed up. Don't hide your notice applying for planning permission under the honeysuckle, so no one sees it, then put up some hideous modern house in the middle of the village.

Attempts to preserve the unspoilt quality of any village, however, can land one in trouble. Recently, an absentee landowner applied for planning permission to build a house and two garages on his field next to us. Egged on by some locals, I wrote a powerful letter to the council, larded with purple phrases about the rape of the Cotswolds, and how the hearts of generations of wayfarers had been gladdened by an unimpeded view of the village, which roughly translated meant I didn't want a lot of yobboes throwing crisp packets on to our land.

Planning permission was duly refused. Imagine my horror, at a dinner party a week later, when I discovered the handsome, but rather bootfaced man on my right was the returned and very present landowner.

Most villages are resistant to change. Our village idiot, much beloved, remains the village idiot and not a seriously disadvantaged rural person. Gays of both sexes are regarded with suspicion.

'I wouldn't go near 'er, Jilly, she's basstard quee-eer with another woman.'

And because the Cotswold lanes tend to be full of black labradors rather then black people, when a policeman from a nearby village took up with a glorious coloured girl, there was much huffing and puffing. Finally a local worthy headed the protest saying he had nothing against those kind of people, but why couldn't she go back to where she'd come from.

'Come off it,' said the policeman in amusement. 'She was born in Stroud.'

Similarly when our revered landlord retired after twenty-five years from the Stirrup Cup (known locally as the Stomach Pump) the new landlord got the job principally because he was the one applicant who said he didn't intend to change anything until he sussed out what people really wanted.

The Stirrup in fact is a mini Citizens' Advice Bureau. Here you can learn how to increase your marrows, decrease your docks, and dispatch your wasp plague. My husband endeared himself to the clientèle early on by trying to grow the first U-turn carrots in a seed box.

Here you will meet the great local legends, the doctor, so loved that a road was named after him when he retired, a farmer who was so good at imitating the cuckoo that he had local Colonels writing to *The Times* every January, and Leo Davies, a huge bear of a sheepdog, known as the Dogfather, who has sired most of the puppies in Bisley, and always howls at the church bells.

Here too the Cotswold Hunt meet, once a year. Four stalwarts have to block the doorway to stop the gaunt, greedy hounds charging the bar counter and wolfing all the plum cake and sausage rolls, and everyone catches up on hunt scandal: how a handsome husband has changed packs from the Beaufort to the Cotswold to ride beside his new, much married mistress; how the village lecher has been banned from the Hunt cocktail party for lurking in some comely lady rider's garden at dusk.

But if gossip circulates at Bisley so do presents. Open your front door on a Saturday morning, and often, covered in dead leaves, blown in by the bitter winds, you'll find pots of chutney, half a dozen Japanese anemones, or a newly shot pheasant or even a hare. A copse of poplar saplings given us by our nextdoor neighbour when we first arrived is now over twelve feet tall.

Soon after the trees arrived a local builder rolled up with a dustbin in which swam a huge golden fish, poached from a nearby Abbey for our pond.

'It's an orfe,' he said. 'We called it Eff.'

Some villagers are most reluctant to receive. An old lady refused some sticks of rhubarb recently because she hadn't got a dish long enough to cook them in.

But there's always something to laugh at here. Currently the great excitement is that Philip Howard (of Graduate Gardeners), the local landscape gardener, has moved into a new house, where he's building a splendid U-turn drive with an underground car port, flanked by a huge wall, known locally as Howard's Way.

'How high is the wall going to go?' I asked my very good friend, the milkman.

'High as possible,' he grinned. 'His mother-in-law's moving in opposite.'

But the laughter is always gentle. Pretension is chiefly what makes people chunter in a village, like the male half of a couple (who work for a weekending video millionaire) referring to himself as an estate manager, when there's less than two acres to manage; or like a local snob (nicknamed Tugboat because he chugs from peer to peer) who, on being asked the other day if he had any ducks, replied: 'Only on the upper lake.'

In other villages people take fearful revenge. One Wiltshire landowner hated his neighbour so much that on learning his neighbour's daughter was getting married and holding the reception in the garden, he deliberately moved three hundred pigs into the next field on the wedding day. Another villager in Hampshire, who'd been ordered not to take a short cut across her neighbour's field, organised a sponsored walk along his footpath of two hundred dogs who hadn't been let out all day.

In Bisley, to warn neighbour not to fall out with neighbour, there is a tiny lock-up, built in 1824. Here, too, Nemesis proceeds at a more leisurely pace. The ex-landlord of the Stirrup, who was also the village undertaker for some time, was ruminating the other evening about a local schoolmistress who'd bullied them all unmercifully when they were little boys.

'I got my revenge in the end,' he added with quiet satisfaction. 'It was me that laid her out and buried her.'

. . .